The Victorian City
1820–1914

Readers in Urban History
General Editors:
Peter Clark and David Reeder
The Centre for Urban History, Leicester University

THE MEDIEVAL TOWN
A Reader in English Urban History, 1200–1540
Edited by Richard Holt and Gervase Rosser

THE TUDOR AND STUART TOWN
A Reader in English Urban History, 1530–1688
Edited by Jonathan Barry

THE EIGHTEENTH-CENTURY TOWN
A Reader in English Urban History, 1688–1820
Edited by Peter Borsay

THE VICTORIAN CITY
A Reader in British Urban History, 1820–1914
Edited by R.J. Morris and Richard Rodger

The Victorian City
A Reader in British Urban History
1820–1914

Edited by
R.J. Morris and Richard Rodger

LONGMAN
London and New York

Longman Group UK Limited,
Longman House, Burnt Mill,
Harlow, Essex CM20 2JE, England
and Associated Companies throughout the world.

Published in the United States of America
by Longman Publishing, New York

First published 1993

ISBN 0 582 05133 9 CSD
ISBN 0 582 05132 0 PPR

British Library Cataloguing-in-Publication Data

A catalogue record for this book is
available from the British Library

Library of Congress Cataloging in Publication Data
The Victorian City: a reader in British urban history,
    1820–1914 / edited by R.J. Morris and Richard Rodger.
    p. cm. – (Readers in urban history)
    Includes bibliographical references and index.
    ISBN 0–582–05133–9 (csd). – ISBN 0–582–05132–0 (ppr)
    1. Cities and towns – Great Britain – History – 19th century.
    2. Urbanization – Great Britain – History – 19th century. 3. Social classes –
Great Britain – History – 19th century. I. Morris, R.J. (Robert John) II. Rodger,
Richard. III. Series.
HT133.V5 1993
307.76'0941'09034 – dc20   92–28232
                                                                          CIP

Set by 5 in Times
Produced by Longman Singapore Publishers (Pte) Ltd.
Printed in Singapore

CONTENTS

PART THREE: THE SOCIAL FABRIC OF THE CITY

PREFACE

Urban historians face formidable permutations in choosing a dozen items to reflect some of the most stimulating writing on the nineteenth century in recent years. We doubt if any of our colleagues would share exactly our selection, but we have sought to include material which makes both a distinctive contribution to urban history, and reveals something of the fundamental urban processes which applied, if not to all nineteenth century towns and cities, then to a great many.

The nature of urban history publishing is such that articles have been scattered throughout many journals and edited collections. As a result of this, and because of financial constraints on university and college libraries, some of the original publications are difficult to obtain. The decision to include some of these less accessible, but nonetheless stimulating items reflects our conviction that to reprint yet again material available in other collections of social or labour history served little purpose.

We have also tried to provide a shell or teaching framework for courses in which the historical development of towns and cities forms a component. In other words, each chapter provides a set of themes upon which discussion and further reading can be structured. More specialized reading suggestions are provided in the bibliographical selections organized around broad themes at the end of the reader. The introduction synthesises some of the principal strands in the secondary literature, and identifies the historiographical threads which have proved to have had a mould-breaking importance in the emergence of social and urban history.

ACKNOWLEDGEMENTS

We are grateful to the following for permission to reproduce copyright material: Aberdeen University Press for extracts from the article 'Employment, wages and poverty . . .' by H. Rodger in *Perspectives of the Scottish City* ed. G. Gordon (Aberdeen UP 1985); the author, Sally Alexander for her chapter 'St Giles Fair, 1830–1914. Popular culture and the Industrial Revolution in 19th century Oxford' from the *History Workshop Pamphlet*, no 2 (Oxford 1970); Blackwell Publishers for the chapter 'The butcher, the baker, the candlestickmaker: the shop and family in the industrial revolution' by Catherine Hall from Liz Whitelegge et al. *The Changing Experience of Women* (London 1982 – Martin Robertson); Cambridge University Press and the author, Dr D.S. Gadian for his chapter 'Class consciousness in Oldham and other north-west industrial towns, 1830–50' from *The Historical Journal, ***21** (1978); the author, Dr W. Hamish Fraser for his paper 'Municipal socialism and social policy'; Leicester University Press for the article 'The rise of suburbia . . .' by F.M.L. Thompson from *The Rise of Suburbia* by F.M.L. Thompson (Leicester University Press 1982); Routledge for the article Victorian cities . . .' by David Cannadine in *Social History* **2** (1977), the extract 'The railway as an agent . . .' by J.R. Kellett from *The Impact of Railways on Victorian Cities* (1969 – Routledge & Kegan Paul), the chapter 'Urbanization' by R.J. Morris from J. Langton & R.J. Morris *Atlas of Industrializing Britain 1780–1914* (London 1986 – Methuen & Co.); Royal Historical Society for the chapter 'The role of religion in the cultural structure of the later Victorian city' by J.H.S. Kent from *Transactions of the Royal Historical Society*, Fifth Series, **23** (1973); the Editors of the *Journal of Social History* & Carnegie-Mellon University Press for the article 'The policeman as domestic missionary: urban and popular culture in Northern England 1850–1880' by Robert D. Storch from the *Journal of Social History,* **9** (1975/6); The Wellcome Institute for the History of Medicine for the chapter 'Urban famine or urban crisis: typhus in the Victorian city' by Anne Hardy in *Medical History,* **32** (1988).

Chapter 1

AN INTRODUCTION TO BRITISH URBAN HISTORY 1820–1914

R.J. Morris and Richard Rodger

Between 1820 and 1914 the economy and society of Britain became more extensively and intensively urbanized than ever before. Not only was the rate at which people became concentrated in relatively large, dense and complex settlements greater than it has been before or since, but fundamental changes also took place within and between towns and in the relationships of urban places to British society as a whole. These were years in which the scale and complexity of British towns and cities increased many times. The urban history of the period requires an account of why and how this happened and of the opportunities and problems created. Strategies of response to this increase in scale and complexity evolved at the level of institutions, groups and individuals. Although the towns and cities of 1914 were very different from those of 1820, there remained important continuities. Spatial continuity was powerful. It was rare that locations and distributions could be explained without reference to previous generations. Central business districts expanded but were closely related to old city centres. Streets and houses were deeply influenced by former field boundaries, earlier property structures and previous spatial patterns of social status. Most decisions were still made by individuals living within family and household units. A market structure driven by the search for profit within a system of private ownership of property still dominated the allocation of work and of goods and services. Changes were perhaps greatest in the nature of local government and politics, but even here, the notion of a local representative body with revenue raising powers and the ability to make local laws and administrative decisions remained central.

The nineteenth century was the first period for which reasonably consistent measures of urbanization can be made by using the decennial census begun in 1801. Historians must still select from a variety of operational definitions of 'urban'. In theoretical terms, there are two groups of definitions of urban. The first derives

1

from Wirth's claims that the basic characteristics of urban places were size, density and heterogeneity or complexity. This usually translates itself into a simple size definition. Modern United Nations figures are based on settlements of over 20,000, although many historians believe that a lower figure makes more sense in earlier periods. Other definitions are based upon Max Weber's concept of the city as having a fort and a market, and taking place in a system of domination.[1] These ideas usually lie behind data which takes contemporary definitions of 'a town', often based upon some distinctive form of local government. An examination of the census for England and Wales, by C.M. Law, used a threefold criteria. An urban settlement contained over 2,500 people, had a density of more than one person per acre and was nucleated, in other words the buildings clustered together in some recognizable centre. Work on Scotland using the criteria of settlements over 5,000 showed much the same order and magnitude of change.[2] Urbanization was rapid in both countries. The years between 1811–31 were years of particular stress. The last thirty years of the period saw a considerable slowing down of urban growth, due in part to the absorption of neighbouring towns and the redefinition of administrative boundaries. Law's methods, which were designed to standardize the basis of comparison, show that the slow down was mostly due to the fact that the process of rapid urbanization was almost at an end in 1911 with nearly 80 per cent – the highest proportion in Europe – of the population living in urban places.

Urbanization involved more than these rising population totals. There were important changes of balance in the British urban hierarchy. In 1801 only London contained more than one million people – still well over eleven times the size of its nearest rival, Liverpool. By 1861 there were sixteen places already in the 100,000-plus category, and by 1911, there were forty-two. London still dominated but was now only six and a half times the size of Liverpool. Not only was the scale unprecedented but individual growth rates were spectacular. Between 1811 and 1861, Liverpool and Preston multiplied five times, the resort town of Brighton seven times and the worsted textile centre of Bradford eight times. Between 1861

1.   L. Wirth, *On Cities and Social Life,* selected papers with an introduction by A.J. Reiss, (Chicago 1964), pp. 60–83; M. Weber, *The City,* translated and edited by D. Martindale and G. Neuwirth (New York 1958). See also the influential chapter in F. Braudel, *Capitalism and Material Life, 1400–1800* (London 1973), pp. 373–442

2.   C. M. Law, 'The growth of urban population in England and Wales, 1801–1911', *Trans. Institute of British Geographers,* **41** (1967): 125–143; M.W. Flinn, et al., *Scottish Population History from the Seventeenth Century to the 1930s* (Cambridge 1977), p. 313; R.J. Morris, 'Urbanization and Scotland', in W.H. Fraser and R.J. Morris (ed.), *People and Society in Scotland, 1830–1914* vol. 2, (Edinburgh 1990), 73–102.

TABLE 1   Urbanization in England and Wales, 1801–1911

	Urban population as a *% total*	*% growth (per decade)*
1801	33.8	
1811	36.6	23.7
1821	40.0	29.1
1831	44.3	28.1
1841	48.3	25.0
1851	54.0	25.9
1861	58.7	21.6
1871	65.2	25.6
1881	70.0	22.8
1891	74.5	18.8
1900	78.0	17.5
1911	78.9	12.2

Source See footnote 2.

and 1911, Middlesbrough, one of Britain's few new towns in the nineteenth century, grew six times while the resort of Blackpool expanded seventeen times. Colliery settlements, half town and half mining camp, like Mountain Ash and Pontypridd, and resorts like Bournemouth and Southport were new arrivals on the urban list. Specialization grew, both within and between towns. Towns also became more closely integrated, not only through improved transport, but also through improved financial and information networks. This tended to increase the specialization between the producer cities, the ports, resorts and country market towns and the dominant metropolis of London.

Urban population growth may take place through one or both of two processes, either by net in-migration, or, through an excess of births over deaths in towns and cities. Although the evidence is fragmentary, the available figures suggest that, as a result of an urban demographic transition which took place sometime in the eighteenth century,[3] there was by the early nineteenth century a modest level of natural increase in British towns despite the high death rates. There was little overall change in death rates between 1780 and the 1860s, but there is evidence of considerable variations between towns, within towns, and between town and country. In 1861, Liverpool was one of a group of large towns where life expectancy at birth was less than thirty-five years compared to the rural areas of southern and western England where it was over fifty

3. E.E. Lampard, 'The urbanizing world', in H.J. Dyos and M. Wolff (eds), *The Victorian City: Images and Realities*, vol. 1 (London 1973) pp. 3–58.

years. After the 1860s urban mortality rates declined substantially. Reasons for this included better sanitation, the isolation of infectious diseases like tuberculosis and typhoid in hospitals, and improved nutrition, although there was no simple cause-effect relationship. Major causes of death such as typhus declined before most sanitary improvements became operational, and infant mortality remained stubbornly high until the end of the century.[4] The reduction in urban death rates made nothing like the overwhelming contribution it does in the cities of contemporary Africa where expansion is substantially generated through natural increase. In nineteenth century Britain the dominant influence was migration. For example, in the Lancashire cotton town of Preston in 1851, 52 per cent of the population had been born outside the town; and of those aged above twenty more than 60 per cent were born outside the town. The significance of this was modified to some extent since 70 per cent of the migrants had been born within thirty miles of the town.[5] In Preston 14 per cent of the migrants came from Ireland, indeed by 1851, between 5 per cent and 10 per cent of the population of most industrial towns had been born in Ireland. In Liverpool, the proportion reached 22 per cent.[6] Overall, migration was a rural to urban movement, but there is some dispute as to the extent of 'stepwise' migration in this process. Glasgow Poor Law Records show that around 30 per cent of migrants from the Scottish Highlands made two steps before arriving in Glasgow, using a smaller urban centre as a transition point.[7] Migrants tended to be young unmarried people, and women had a greater tendency to take part in this rural – urban movement than men. Women were attracted by jobs as domestic servants and in certain parts of the country by jobs in textiles.[8]

All this was closely linked with a parallel process – industrialization. Current understanding has identified industrialization in Britain as a long-drawn-out process which involved an increased intensity and subdivision of labour, as well as both cumulative and incremental gains

4. R. Woods and J. Woodward (eds), *Urban Disease and Mortality in Nineteenth-century England* (London 1984).
5. M. Anderson, *Family Structure in Nineteenth Century Lancashire* (Cambridge 1971), p. 37; R. Lawton, 'The population of Liverpool in the mid nineteenth century', *Trans. Historical Society of Lancashire and Cheshire*, **107** (1955): 89–120; A. Redford, *Labour Migration in England, 1800–1850* (Manchester 1964); E.G. Ravenstein, 'The laws of migration', *Journal of the Royal Statistical Society*, **48** (1885), 167–99.
6. C. Richardson, 'Irish settlement in mid-nineteenth-century Bradford', *Yorkshire Bulletin,* **20** (1968); R.J. Dennis, *English Industrial Cities of the Nineteenth Century: a Social Geography* (Cambridge 1984), pp. 35–41.
7. C.W.J. Withers and A. Watson, 'Stepwise migration and highland migration to Glasgow, 1852–1898', *Journal of Historical Geography,* **17** (1991): 35–55.
8. T. McBride, *The Domestic Revolution. The Modernization of Household Service in England and France, 1820–1920* (London 1976), pp. 34–48.

in productivity involving a variety of types of technological change. These included improved hand technologies, a gradual move from water- to steam-powered sources of energy and an increasing complexity of chemical and metallurgical processes.[9] In this technological environment, the rational use of knowledge assumed greater significance. Profits depended upon pricing, accounting skills, and an understanding of chemistry, mechanics and medicine. Towns and cities as the initial focus of information had an advantage in this respect.[10] During the first half of the eighteenth century, substantial and expanding sectors of British industry were located in the countryside: nail-makers in the West Midlands, stocking-weavers in Leicestershire, woollen-weavers in West Yorkshire, toolmakers in the south of that county, and fustian-weavers in Lancashire. Towns like Sheffield, Leeds, Walsall and Wolverhampton were centres for marketing, the production of quality goods and finishing. The countryside had the initial advantage of comparatively low rents and labour costs, but in the second half of the eighteenth century, new technologies both of production and labour organization put mounting pressure on this division of labour between town and country. Power was applied to a broader range of textile processes, and the slow application of coal- to iron-based products provided another technological force for larger units of production. Even in these cases the initial location was still rural. Coalbrookdale and New Lanark were typical early locations for these new modes of organizing production. Cheap land, cheap streamside power, and often easy access to improved river and canal transport were decisive influences on early industrial locations.

But slowly and surely industry began to come in from the countryside. In 1793 Springfield Mill was built in the east end of Glasgow. It was steam-powered and employed over a hundred people. It was the first of many. Benjamin Gott built a large woollen factory on the outskirts of Leeds. The Welsh town of Merthyr acquired three major industrial suburbs based upon giant ironworks. Large units of production did not monopolize this growth. Typically, the urban economy which had emerged by the 1850s was spearheaded by a business community dominated by a few large firms but including an increasingly numerous array of small firms.[11] Since firms had to overcome the higher cost of urban land, there had to be compelling

---

9. E.A. Wrigley, *Continuity and Change: the Character of the Industrial Revolution in England* (Cambridge 1988); N.F.R. Crafts, *British Economic Growth during the Industrial Revolution* (Oxford 1985).
10. This process is described in a United States context by A.R. Pred, *City Systems in Advanced Economies* (London 1977).
11. V.A.C. Gattrell, 'Labour, power and the size of firms in Lancashire cotton in the second quarter of the nineteenth century', *Economic History Review*, **30** (1977): 95–139; C. Behagg, *Politics and Production in the Early Nineteenth Century*, (London 1990).

reasons for their decisions to locate in towns. As the intensity of labour increased, many controllers of capital came to favour the better supervision of labour offered in towns by proximity to the point of production. Merchants had always favoured urban locations for the high value finishing end of production for just this reason. As the intensity of competition increased, especially in distant markets, a variety of external economies provided by towns proved increasingly attractive. Thus many machine-builders emerged from the rear of new factories to set up businesses of their own. The clustering of customer firms in the towns offered them encouragement and profitable local markets, for example in Edinburgh, the concentration of printing firms fostered specialist type-founding and printing machine-making firms.[12] Large firms were attracted by the cluster of small businesses which enabled them to respond flexibly to trade cycles, expanding rapidly through sub-contracting during a boom, and forcing output adjustments and overheads on to contractors during an economic recession. Small firms were attracted by the variety of services they could buy in, when their own capital resources were inadequate. The new mode of transport, the railway, which appeared in most towns by the 1840s, favoured point delivery at freight depots and passenger stations, thus further encouraging concentration. Other changes simply saved land costs.

The implications of economic change for urbanization were far-reaching. Regional specialization intensified the demand for transport services. To feed the towns required improved agricultural productivity which in turn required increasingly sophisticated agricultural machinery which contributed in turn to industrial growth in places like Ipswich and Lincoln.[13] Urban food requirements also stimulated cereal and other food imports, thus developing economic activity in many ports. Nor was the relationship of industrialization and urbanization just a matter for towns and cities like Bradford, Preston and Sheffield where industrial production and attendant services were concentrated. It was also a relationship between a system of production and a system of cities. Bath and Brighton, Lincoln and London were all fundamentally affected by industrialization. Industry itself changed the technology of the cities. Gas lighting came to most cities by the 1820s, extending the working day as well as easing the problems of law and order. Glazed pipes were introduced by the 1840s easing problems of water supply and sewage disposal.[14] The railways accelerated the specialization and

---

12. D. Bremner, *The Industries of Scotland* (Edinburgh 1869).
13. N. R. Wright, *Lincolnshire Towns and Industry, 1700–1914, History of Lincolnshire*, vol. XI (Lincoln 1982).
14. M.W. Flinn (ed.), *The Sanitary Condition of the Labouring Population of Great Britain*, by Edwin Chadwick, 1842 (Edinburgh 1965), p. 61.

size of towns and initially intensified the competition for space,[15] but once the iron rail was adapted to the horse-drawn tram the problems of density were dramatically eased as the middle- and white-collar classes bought their commuting tickets.[16] By the 1880s, iron-framed buildings, lifts, the telegraph and telephones combined with trams to create a modern-style central business district with major advances in area specialization and the intensity of interaction.[17] These new industrial technologies could affect the urban system in many different ways. The steel girder appeared in a brutal utilitarian form in the transporter bridge at Middlesbrough, as an elegant prop to cultural advancement in the new industrial museum in Edinburgh, or as the brash centre piece to the hedonistic leisure town as in Blackpool Tower.[18]

Historians have sought to understand the impact of urbanization and the nature of urbanism in this period in a variety of ways. Their work must be placed critically in a wider cultural, political and intellectual context. The British are often considered to be anti-urban in their culture. Indeed a recent account placed anti-urbanism at the heart of a cultural analysis of the relative economic decline of Britain.[19] Suburbanization may itself embody such an interpretation. The period covered by this collection was heralded by poets like William Blake and William Cowper in a fairly uncompromising way:

> In proud and gay
> And gain devoted cities; thither flow
> As to a common and most noisesome sewer
> The dregs and faeculence of every land.

(The Task, 1785)

The nineteenth century was marked by a vast literature on the 'problems' of the great towns. Thomas Chalmers, the Scottish evangelical minister, wrote on the failure of religion and the decline of morality in the great towns. James Kay, as a young doctor, described the disease and breakdown of social order in industrial Manchester in the 1830s. By the 1850s and 1860s attention had switched back again to London and in the final decades of the century, social commentators were ascribing the degeneration of

---

15. J.R. Kellett, *The Impact of Railways on Victorian Cities* (London 1969).
16. A.D. Ochojna, 'The influence of local and national politics on the development of urban passenger transport in Britain 1850–1900', *Journal of Transport History*, **4** (1978).
17. J.W.R. Whitehand, *The Changing Face of Cities* (Oxford 1987); B. Robson, *Urban Growth: an Approach* (London 1973).
18. J.K. Walton, *The English Seaside Resort: a Social History 1750–1914* (Leicester 1983).
19. M.J. Wiener, *English Culture and the Decline of the Industrial Spirit, 1850–1980* (Cambridge 1981), pp. 6–66

the English Saxon race to the influence of town life.[20] Yet a second look shows that the situation was more complicated than this. William Wordsworth, the poet who made his name extolling the moral benefits of 'nature', wrote: 'Earth has not anything to show more fair' when he was describing the same London that had been the target of Blake and Cowper.

At a more mundane level, the culture of urbanism proliferated in many spheres during the nineteenth century. In 1750 there were very few towns and cities which had a regular newspaper, an adequate trade directory, or an accurately surveyed map.[21] By 1850, there were very few without all three. Paintings and engravings celebrated and explored the towns. Guide books, industrial surveys and histories celebrated their identity and achievements. *The Industries of Sheffield, Historical, Statistical and Biographical* which appeared sometime in the 1880s had no time for talk of degeneration: 'In no other feature of Sheffield perhaps is the wealth, the enterprise and progressive spirit of its citizens seen to greater advantage than in the numerous handsome buildings devoted to charitable, religious and educational purposes' (p. 9). The words 'progress', 'growth' and 'improvement' were central to many of these publications. Since the 1820s and 1830s, these ideas were often expressed through large-scale topographical paintings or a series of closely drawn engravings of prestigious buildings, such as those produced by Thomas Shepherd for London and Edinburgh.[22] From the 1850s onwards, urban pride and identity were celebrated in an increasingly assertive series of public buildings, squares and statues as well as in a widening variety of cultural expressions. Leeds knew little about anti-urbanism and acquired a massive town hall in 1853–58,[23] a society devoted to the study of Leeds history in 1889[24] and laid out City Square ready for a statue of the Black Prince in 1896.[25] So successful were these town halls that their images are still used by the modern visual

20. G. Stedman Jones, *Outcast London. A Study in the Relationship between Classes in Victorian Society* (Oxford 1971), pp. 11–16, 127–151; B.I. Coleman (ed.), *The Idea of the City in Nineteenth-century Britain* (London 1973).

21. See P.J. Atkins, G. Shaw and A. Tipper, *British Directories, A Bibliography and Guide to Directories Published in England and Wales 1850–1950 and Scotland (1773–1950),* (Leicester 1989).

22. C. Arscott and G. Pollock with J. Wolff, 'The partial view: the visual representation of the early nineteenth century city', in J. Wolff and J. Seed (eds), *The Culture of Capital: Art, Power and the Nineteenth-century Middle Class* (Manchester 1990); T.H. Shepherd, *Metropolitan Improvement of London in the Nineteenth Century,* (London 1827), and his *Modern Athens or Edinburgh in the Nineteenth Century* (London 1831).

23. A. Briggs, *Victorian Cities* (London 1963), pp. 139–83.

24. R.J. Morris, *Middle-Class Culture, 1700–1914* in D. Fraser (ed.), *A History of Modern Leeds* (Manchester 1980).

25. B. Reed, *Victorian Sculpture* (Yale 1982).

media to introduce items on local government and urban activity. George Square in Glasgow and the Municipal Buildings created in 1883 became a symbol of that city, so much so that by the end of the century every labour and trades union leader knew that to hold a demonstration in George Square was to lay symbolic claim to power within the city. In 1919 it was rumoured that the tanks in the nearby tram depot were there to prevent this process going too far.[26]

The 'Victorian City' was the initial focus of the modern wave of urban history writing which played an important part in changing perceptions of those cities in the last thirty years. For Geddes and Mumford, the Victorian city was a place of chaos and barbarity which broke the long tradition of cities as carriers of civilization and the development of human culture. Lewis Mumford was an American follower of Geddes who was closely associated with planning, and wrote an encyclopedic work, *The City in History*. Significantly the chapter on the industrial city was called 'Palaeotechnic Paradise: Coketown'. His paradigm industrial town was drawn from the fictional example of Charles Dickens's novel, *Hard Times*, a bitterly hostile account of factory industrialism based upon Preston in Lancashire. Mumford was uncompromising: 'Between 1820 and 1900 the destruction and disorder within great cities is like that of a battlefield. . . . In a greater or lesser degree, every city in the Western World was stamped with the archetypal characteristics of Coketown. Industrialism . . . produced the most degraded urban environment the world had yet seen.'[27] His evidence was drawn from the worst aspects of Manchester and Birmingham, whilst the previous centuries had been illustrated by Bath and Amsterdam. This view of urban history was influential in the 1950s and 1960s. Total area plans were prepared by many urban planning authorities in the late 1940s and early 1950s, under the guidance of men like Sir Patrick Abercrombie and other leaders of the town planning movement. The historical sections of these plans reflected this perception. It provided an historical underpinning to the ideology of modernization which guided the wholesale destruction of parts of many cities. In the early plans for London, Abercrombie often juxtaposed photographs of old and new, evil and good, crowded and spacious, insanitary and healthy to prepare readers and policy-makers for the rebuilding and reorganization of London. Dozens of drawings provided enthusiastic omens of the brutal modernistic engineer's architecture which was

26. I. McLean, *The Legend of Red Clydeside* (Edinburgh 1983), pp. 125–6; *Description of Ceremonial on the Occasion of Laying the Foundation Stone of the Municipal Buildings in George Square Glasgow* (Glasgow 1885).
27. L. Mumford, *The City in History* (London 1961), p. 509; P. Geddes, *The Civic Survey of Edinburgh* (Edinburgh 1911); H. Meller, *Patrick Geddes Social Evolutionist and City Planner* (London 1990).

9

to follow.[28] In Edinburgh, Abercrombie was acutely aware of the historical legacy to the city. Princes Street was condemned as a result of 'laisser faire . . . with the resulting lack of any cohesion of design'. He envisaged the eventual rebuilding of the street with planners setting basic standards for the architects. Only three buildings were worthy of preservation.[29] This planning paradigm over the next thirty years saw destruction and rebuilding in British cities on a massive scale; it involved significant redistributions of population and a major remodelling for many city centres. An increase in historical understanding was one of the many influences which brought this modernistic rebuilding and redesign of the urban environment to an end. Asa Briggs's collection of essays, *Victorian Cities*, epitomized this. They were a balanced account of achievements and limitations, in which urban problems were matched against 'municipal pride'. The account of the 'shock city' of Manchester was balanced against the reforming vision of Joseph Chamberlain's Birmingham and the building of Leeds Town Hall. Briggs admired the energy and variety of those who created the Victorian urban fabric but could still regret that this was a period when 'assured standards of taste had lapsed'.[30] He was not quite ready to revel in the glorious eclectic jigsaw which made up the Victorian city but laid the ground for its later appreciation. Patrick Geddes was still influential in the footnotes competing with the mood of the poet John Betjeman:

> Toiling and doomed from Moorgate Street puffs the train
> For us the steam and gas-light, the lost generation,
> The new white cliffs of the City are built in vain.[31]

Within twenty years, admiration of the Victorian and its use as a weapon against modernism was no longer engaging quaintness but had become a central feature of British taste and policy. The turning point came with the argument over the redevelopment of Covent Garden Market, long a by-word for all the evils of traffic congestion. When the fruit and vegetable wholesale market moved out to Nine Elms in 1971–72, the GLC (Greater London Council) was ready with well-researched plans for comprehensive redevelopment. A formidable opposition – New Left activists, historic buildings enthusiasts, local residents and business interests – awaited them. These included a number of well-informed building historians, some attached to bodies like the Victorian Society, and others working within the GLC itself.

---

28. P. Abercrombie, *Greater London Plan 1944* (London, HMSO 1945).
29. P. Abercrombie and D. Plumstead, *A Civic Plan for the City of Edinburgh*, (Edinburgh 1949), plate 31 following p. 60.
30. A. Briggs, op. cit., p. 44
31. J. Betjeman, from 'Monody on the Death of Aldersgate Street Station'.

The eventual planning approval was granted only on condition that a wide variety of buildings from the seventeenth to the nineteeth century were retained. The notion that improvement meant the destruction of old urban landscapes, especially Victorian ones, was on its way out.[32] Instead, Covent Garden was to become a stage set for a post-modern society of variety, consumer experience and multiple use. The understanding of Victorian urban history has had a real impact on late twentieth-century landscape and policy. Indeed by the mid-1980s, the Victorianism of a building had become recognized as a commercial asset. Here began a process which continues in the 'heritage industry', a development which has delighted and discomforted the intellectuals who long ago lost control.[33]

By the early 1970s there was an assertive and prolific confidence in the validity of the city as a focus of historical study. The outcome of this period was an extensive literature which was strong in its accounts of political and social structures, strong in its accounts of the built environment, even stronger in terms of individual urban biographies and case studies but which had little theoretical content.[34] The confidence of this approach began to fade as a result of a series of intellectual and contemporary developments which students need to understand if they are to place urban history in the context of historical and social science studies as a whole. Intellectual doubts were sown by a series of essays from Ray Pahl and a key essay by Philip Abrams. Both suggested that the focus on urbanism concealed a variety of more important explanatory mechanisms. If historians and other social scientists wanted to study capitalist economic growth, regionalism, central–local relationships, class, poverty, collective consumption and service provision, they should do just that and not confuse the issues with questions about 'the urban way of life' or debates about 'parasitic and generative' cities.[35] Abrams warned against the 're-ification of the city', by which he meant that historians and social scientists should not represent the city as if it was an 'actor' in any specific situation, nor should they suggest that the 'urban' was a variable which could be used in any consistent way as part of an explanation. In a paragraph which should be pondered upon by all who seek to understand the impact of urban growth upon British nineteenth century or indeed, any

---

32. L. Esher, *A Broken Wave. The Rebuilding of England, 1940–1980* (London 1981), pp. 140–6
33. R. Hewison, *The Heritage Industry*, (London 1987); P. Wright, *On Living in an Old Country* (London 1985).
34. H.J. Dyos and M. Wolff (eds), *The Victorian City*, to see this at its finest.
35. R. Pahl, *Whose City?* (London 1970); P. Abrams, 'Towns and economic growth: some theories and problems', in P. Abrams and E.A. Wrigley (eds), *Towns in Societies. Essays in Economic History and Historical Sociology* (Cambridge 1978).

other history, he suggested: 'The town is a social form in which the essential properties of larger systems of social relations are grossly concentrated and intensified – to a point where residential size, density and heterogeneity, the formal characteristics of the town, appear to be in themselves constituent properties of a distinct social order.'[36]

The early 1970s was also a period which saw the disappearance of those political and economic units to which many historians had directed attention and loyalty. Local government reorganization replaced many towns and cities with districts and regions and was complemented by the collapse of many locally specific family firms. New names for local authorities further undermined urban identities. Energy once directed towards understanding the city was increasingly directed towards the wider projects of social history – gender, nationalism, cultural dimensions of industrialism, racial and sectarian identities and relationships. These influences have left an urban history literature which is dominated by the two themes which play a crucial part in this collection, namely the attempt to describe and account for the development of the built environment, and an examination of urban social structures, an enquiry now much broader than the initial interest in political and class structures.

THE BUILT ENVIRONMENT AND PROPERTY RELATIONS

Early interest in the physical fabric of British towns was a by-product of an intellectual debate among economic historians concerned with the workings of the capitalist system and the implications of an increasingly integrated international economy.[37] Studies of specific towns and urban processes were undertaken as local empirical tests of a broader model of urban development which stated that international and domestic economic activity were inversely related. House-building thereby acquired a pivotal role in the emerging controversy surrounding international factor flows of capital and migrants – itself linked to the nature of nineteenth-century British imperialism – and was connected also with arguments advanced to explain the malfunctioning of the late Victorian economy.

36. Abrams, op. cit., p. 10; this was a direct reference to Wirth's article, see note 1.
37. A.K. Cairncross, *Home and Foreign Investment* (Cambridge 1953); B. Thomas, *Migration and Economic Growth* (Cambridge 1954).

Whether a developing international economy held the building sector hostage to serious demand fluctuations and to periodic starvations of capital supplies, thus adversely affecting the standard of living for the majority of Britons, was at the heart of the matter. Periodic waves of emigrants from Britain reduced the pressure on living space since additional household formation would otherwise have intensified the problems of overcrowding, public health and urban mortality. But such an exodus was also systematically related to the export of capital, the depletion of which within Britain was claimed to exacerbate the inherent instability of the building industry. Construction in Dalmarnock, it was argued, was dependent on the Dakotas, that of Oldham on Oklahoma.[38] This hypothesis, that British housing and, by extension, the quality of the urban infrastructure was the pawn of international capital movements was effectively rebutted by demonstrating the diversity of regional experience and emphasizing the role of local conditions on changes in the quality and character of the local housing stock.[39] Studies of house-building in north-east England and in Scottish burghs subsequently nailed the mechanistic 'Atlantic economy hypothesis', since they showed that variations in the pace and timing of house-building were closely correlated with variations in local levels of employment which were not themselves particularly determined by overseas influences.[40]

To a certain extent this interest in house-building, which in effect constituted an early examination by economic historians of the 'urban variable' in the context of business cycles, was already undergoing a reformulation in the early 1960s with H.J. Dyos's pioneering study of the growth of Victorian Camberwell.[41] Local considerations and characteristics internal to the building industry were accorded a primacy in the explanation of urban development. More significantly, and as a direct consequence of a movement away from a theoretically derived explanation of urban expansion

38. H.J. Habakkuk, 'Fluctuations in house-building in Britain and the United States in the nineteenth century', *Journal of Economic History*, **22** (1962): 198. A.K. Cairncross, *Home and Foreign Investment*, p. 25. Habakkuk's alliterative purpose would have been better served by selecting Ohio, given that much of Oklahoma was Indian Territory until 1907 and unlikely to have been the recipient of major overseas investment.

39. S.B. Saul, 'Housebuilding in England 1890–1914', *Economic History Review*, **15** (1962): 119–37; J.P. Lewis, *Building Cycles and Britain's Growth* (London 1965).

40. A.G. Kenwood, 'Residential building activity in north-eastern England 1863–1913', *Manchester School*, **31** (1963): 115–28; R.G. Rodger, 'Speculative builders and the structure of the Scottish building industry 1860–1914', *Business History*, **21** (1979): 226–46.

41. H.J. Dyos, *Victorian Suburb: a Study of the Growth of Camberwell* (Leicester 1961).

as offered by the 'Atlantic economy' hypothesis, a host of cognate research issues was generated. How important were the roles of landowner and developer? What was the contribution of the town council, of improvement schemes, of philanthropic organizations, and of other regulatory mechanisms? Elite formation, class relations, spatial and social segregation, and related dynamic elements of urban change were researched as the 'city as a laboratory' became the subject of enquiry for historical geographers, town planners, and urban sociologists focusing on contemporary issues yet aware of the historical dimension. Contemporary policy, derived from the nascent post-war planning paradigm and Keynesian theories of macro-economic management, was of necessity directed towards the cities due to war damage, changing industrial structures, and technological changes wrought by road transport. Altered axes of contemporary communications combined to focus research interest in the legacy of the Victorian city.

Encouraged by Dyos's eclecticism, urban historians eschewed theory. Urban history was 'a field without a single academic focus' in which 'catholicity [was] positively healthy'. And if there was 'a need to extend . . . technical capacity', Dyos considered that it would come from 'beyond the purely documentary' by drawing on studies of the townscape and of urban imagery rather than through a body of theory. It was precisely this diversity and lack of coherence which prompted a vigorous assault upon urban history in the 1970s based on the composite argument that, since 80 per cent of Britain was urbanized by 1914, then social history was synonymous with urban history, that cities were simply the locus of social interactions and did not themselves make a discrete contribution to the historical process, and that the field of study lacked any unifying theory.[42] Curiously, though a response might have been mounted along the lines that urban history represented a nineteenth-century British version of '*histoire totale*' with a strong blend of annalist and analyst, none has been forthcoming.

'The most fundamental obligation of urban history', Dyos claimed '. . . is to undertake a task no one else will and make plain how the land was built upon in the way that it was.'[43] In this responsibility historical geographers were, contrary to the Pahl – Abrams – Hobsbawm critique, adept at introducing a theoretical dimension. Concerned principally with spatial change in the nineteenth-century city, geographers readily embraced the land-use models of the Chicago school in which specialized land uses particular to each of retail, commercial and residential uses required sites at varying

42. See note 35.
43. H.J. Dyos, 'Editorial', *Urban History Yearbook* (1974, 1976).

distances from the central business district.[44] Location and central place theory, carefully adapted in 1960 by Alonso[45] in conjunction with users' ability to pay rent, provided a conceptual basis for doctoral theses in the 1960s. This somewhat static approach to the urban morphology of nineteenth-century cities was taken a stage further in numerous articles by J.W.R. Whitehand who explained that land-intensive house-building alternated with the land-extensive requirements of non-residential building, the latter taking place in the trough of house-building cycles.[46] As with most theoretically derived explanations, those of historical geographers have encountered criticisms based on their descriptive and static features, their detachment from historical reality, and their inability to incorporate cultural and political variables.[47] Yet they remain useful in identifying certain common principles, and if the concentric rings were never regular, or if suburban building did take place simultaneously with public and institutional building, these theoretical approaches clarify many of the issues involved when considering the revisions to the built form – buildings, streets, and physical characteristics – and land use in the nineteenth-century city.

A schematic model of urban development informs most geographers' interpretations as to how historical information could be presented in visual form using charts and maps. The susceptibility of nineteenth-century data to systematic analysis, and increasingly from the 1970s, to computerized manipulation and mapping, owes much to the efforts of historical geographers to communicate their research results in a visual medium. In a useful synthesis of geographical research Lawton conveys a sense of what Joe Banks called 'the contagion of numbers',[48] the social stresses and strains which developed in association with the built environment of the nineteenth century city under conditions of rapid population growth. Both in terms of presentation and methodology, therefore, Lawton typifies the historical geographer's approach of the 1970s with its heavy intel-

44. For useful summaries of these geographical theories see H. Carter, *An Introduction to Urban Historical Geography* (London 1983) Part IV, and H. Carter and C. R. Lewis, *An Urban Geography of England and Wales in the Nineteenth Century* (London 1990).
45. W. Alonso, 'A theory of the urban land market', *Papers and Proceedings of the Regional Science Association*, **6** (1960): 149–57.
46. J.W.R. Whitehand, *The Changing Face of Cities: a Study of Development Cycles and Urban Form,* (Oxford 1987) provides a useful summary in chapters 2 and 3, and for more detailed citations on fringe belts see his bibliography, pp. 182–3.
47. See for example M. J. Daunton, 'The building cycle and the urban fringe in Victorian cities: a comment', *Journal of Historical Geography*, **4** (1978): 175–91.
48. R. Lawton, 'An age of great cities', *Town Planning Review,* **43** (1972): 199–224, and J.A. Banks, 'The contagion of numbers' in H.J. Dyos and M. Wolff (eds), *The Victorian City.*

lectual dependence on an essentially ecological model of urban development.

Through numerous studies of estate development historical geographers made telling contributions to the spatial dimensions of urban growth, and to residential and social segregation. Some tested historical evidence against the hypothesis that in the transition from early modern town to post-industrial city concentric circles emerged with multiple nuclei.[49] Others examined the degree of consolidated landownership, and another cluster of studies addressed the patterns of inter- and intra-urban migration, successfully isolating the highly localized nature of these and the importance of kinship links.[50]

If land use and related models of urban space were a central strand of geographical research into the nineteenth-century city, a parallel approach developed almost independently. It was essentially Weberian in character, that is, the underlying dynamic was based on the city as an integral element in a system of domination and ongoing conflict. Virtually no arena of urban social, political and cultural relations was exempt from such an interpretation. Housing was the locus of conflict between landlord and tenant, and between private builder and municipal regulation; poverty and the relief of social distress was contested terrain between ratepayer and philanthropist, and between local and central government; leisure activities divided sabbatarians and entrepreneurs. Slums and suburbs, church and chapel, different fractions of the urban élite, and many other antitheses appeared more pronounced as the nineteenth century proceeded. Conflict, control, manipulation and domination were central elements in the language of class increasingly used to analyse urban relations in the nineteenth century. The actions of individuals, groups and institutions were each viewed as having consequences for other parties, both directly and indirectly. Particular strategies, whether of builders, politicians, industrialists, property-owners or labour revolved to some extent around externalizing the costs of a specific policy or decision and passing them

49. C.R. Lewis, 'A stage in the development of the industrial town: a case study of Cardiff 1845–75', *Trans. of the Institute of British Geographers*, **4** (1979): 129–52. This special issue was devoted entirely to spatial aspects of the Victorian city.
50. H. Carter and S. Wheatley, *Merthyr Tydfil in 1851: a Study of the Spatial Structure of a Welsh Industrial Town* (Cardiff 1982); R.J. Dennis, 'Distance and social interaction in a Victorian city', *Journal of Historical Geography*, **3** (1977): 237–50; J. Springett, 'Landowners and urban development: the Ramsden estate and nineteenth century Huddersfield', *Journal of Historical Geography*, **8** (1982): 129–44; C.G. Pooley, 'Residential mobility in the Victorian city', *Trans. Institute of British Geographers*, **4** (1979): 258–77; G. Rowley, 'Landownership in the spatial growth of towns: a Sheffield example', *East Midland Geographer*, **6** (1975): 200–13; K. Cowlard, 'The urban development of Wakefield 1801–1901', unpublished Ph.D. thesis (Leeds 1974).

on to another interest group.[51] Leverage and urban influence, or as captured in the title of Derek Fraser's book,[52] power and authority, were part of a normally implicit Weberian framework.

Vested interests took many forms. Detailed studies of landownership considered the building process and estate development as both an extension of the spatial models previously mentioned and a further examination of the Camberwell case study in diverse urban settings. An over-simplification of the importance of tenure[53] – leaseholding rather than freeholding was advanced as a likely cause of high density building with its associated environmental implications for mortality and morbidity – was the point of departure for several studies of estate development. However, the role of the landowner as a primary influence on the quality of the built environment formed the springboard for studies of Glasgow, London, Leeds and Birmingham, as well as of boroughs lower in the urban hierarchy such as Huddersfield, Belfast, Cardiff, Eastbourne, Cleethorpes and Skegness.[54] Though various authors showed that covenants or in Scottish burghs, feu charters, affected the detailed character of building development[55] and Harold Perkin demonstrated that parks and exclusivity were deployed to defend the social tone of seaside resorts, overall, as David Cannadine concludes in the extract reprinted here, 'the great estates were ultimately constrained by forces of the market'.[56]

51. Recently some of these ideas have been consolidated by R.J. Morris, 'Externalities, the market, power structures and the urban agenda', *Urban History Yearbook*, **17** (1990): 99–109.
52. D. Fraser, *Power and Authority in the Victorian City* (Oxford 1979).
53. M.J. Mortimore, 'Landownership and urban growth in Bradford and environs in the West Riding conurbation 1850–1950', *Trans. Institute of British Geographers*, **46** (1969): 105–19.
54. D.J. Olsen, 'House upon house: estate development in London and Sheffield' in Dyos and Wolff (eds), *The Victorian City*, pp. 333–57; J.R. Kellett, 'Property speculators and the building of Glasgow 1780–1830', *Scottish Journal of Political Economy*, **8** (1961): 211–32; M. Beresford, *East End, West End. The Face of Leeds during Urbanization, 1684–1842*, (Leeds, Thoresby Society, 1988); D.N. Cannadine, *Lords and Landlords: the Aristocracy and the Towns 1774–1967* (Leicester 1980); M.J. Daunton, *Coal Metropolis: Cardiff 1870–1914* (Leicester 1977); W.A. Maguire, 'Lord Donegall and the sale of Belfast: a case study from the Encumbered Estates Court', *Economic History Review*, **24** (1976); R. Gurnham, 'The creation Skegness as a resort town by the ninth Earl of Scarborough', *Lincolnshire History and Archaeology*, **7** (1972); P.J. Aspinall, 'Speculative builders and the development of Cleethorpes 1850–1900', *Lincolnshire History and Archaeology*, **11** (1976).
55. Kellett., op. cit., Cannadine, op. cit.; R.G. Rodger, 'The Victorian building industry and the housing of the Scottish working class', in M. Doughty (ed.), *Building the Industrial City* (Leicester 1986). pp. 151–206.
56. H.J. Perkin, 'The "social tone" of Victorian seaside resorts in the north west', *Northern History*, **11** (1976): 180–94.

What emerged from these studies of land tenure and land-ownership? Were these influential factors as regards housing design and urban form? In 1914 about 60 per cent of urban tenures in the United Kingdom were freehold with the remainder various types of leasehold.[57] Though a blend of tenures existed in most boroughs, some geographical concentrations existed. For example, Leeds, Bradford and West Riding towns were dominated by freehold and Lancashire by long leases. Nevertheless, defective housing was not confined to one type of tenure or location. Poorly drained areas were developed for industrial purposes or working-class housing irrespective of who owned the land, how concentrated the ownership was, or the nature of the tenure. By the same token freehold-dominated Leeds and overwhelmingly leasehold Birmingham produced almost identical middle-class suburbs: Headingley and Edgbaston. In London, fractured landownership in Hampstead did not impede homogeneous housing development.[58] Short-lease development was used for high-status housing by the Bedford estate and for low-income housing by the Norfolk estate in Sheffield.[59] Nor was 'feuing' – the peculiarly Scottish combination of freehold and leasehold tenure systems – associated exclusively with middle- or working-class tenement dwelling.[60] Geographical variations in rent levels bore no simple relation to the concentration of landownership, or to levels of overcrowding, or to type of tenure. Different systems of tenure, therefore, simply employed different time periods to realize a yield from an asset – one involved outright sale and immediate cash (freehold), the other an annual income (leasehold). Thus the landowners' ability to shape the built environment was contingent upon other factors, for example, the responsiveness of builders and the composition of demand.

The building industry attracted considerable academic attention not only because qualitative changes in living standards were themselves an element in the politically contentious interpretations surrounding the standard of living of the working classes, but for three further reasons. Firstly, because of its size – building constituted approximately 10 per cent of the workforce and as much as 30 per cent of gross fixed capital formation – and thus the multiplier effects on local employment levels

57. A. Offer, *Property and Politics 1870–1914: Landownership, Law, Ideology and Urban Development in England* (Cambridge 1981), p. 118.
58. F.M.L. Thompson, 'Hampstead', in M.A. Simpson, and T.H. Lloyd (eds), *Middle-Class Housing in Britain* (Newton Abbot 1977), p. 110.
59. Olsen, op. cit., p. 365.
60. R.G. Rodger, 'The "invisible hand" – market forces, housing and the urban form in Victorian cities', in D. Fraser and A. Sutcliffe (eds), *The Pursuit of Urban History* (London 1983), p. 200.

were both considerable and volatile; secondly, because the various skilled labour elements within the building industry were central to issues of compliance and the role of the labour aristocracy;[61] and thirdly, because speculative builders were regarded as potential culprits in the creation of slums. To identify builders as such has recently been challenged by Englander, Bedale, Rodger, Damer and Melling, each of whom have identified the modest record of many housing managers in relation to expenditure on repairs and maintenance.[62] These elements of landlords' profitability,[63] in conjunction with the organization and structure of the building industry contributed significantly to the poor quality of the built environment. Empirical studies have confirmed that the house-building was largely undertaken by a host of small firms. For example, in the second half of the nineteenth century, 70 per cent of Leicester house-building was in projects of five or fewer units, 50 per cent of Sheffield builders put up no more than three houses. In Scottish burghs, 54 per cent of builders undertook only a single project, a size distribution not dissimilar to that in Nottingham at the end of the eighteenth century, or London at the end of the nineteenth century.[64] However, the dependence of small enterprises on steady supplies of finance and the imperative of achieving a final sale induced cash flow crises and ultimately bankruptcies which had a prejudicial impact on the quality of house-building.[65] Organizationally, an important change in the building industry transpired around 1790 with the emergence of the general contractor,[66] but with their permanent workforces, they, too, increasingly discovered that to ensure full capital and labour utilization it was essential to build ahead of demand. In the last third of the nineteenth century builders experienced additional pressures and financial uncertainties from four directions: the need to

61. R.J. Price, *Masters, Unions and Men: Work Control in Building and the Rise of Labour 1830–1914* (Cambridge 1980).
62. D. Englander, *Landlord and Tenant in Urban Britain 1838–1918* (Oxford 1983); J. Melling (ed.), *Housing, Social Policy and the State* (London 1980); R.G. Rodger, 'The Victorian building industry'.
63. N.J. Morgan and M.J. Daunton, 'Landlords in Glasgow: a study of 1901', *Business History* **25** (1983): 264–81; D. Englander, *Landlord and Tenant*
64. P.J. Aspinall, 'The internal structure of the house-building industry in nineteenth century cities', in J.H. Johnson and C.G. Pooley (eds), *The Structure of Nineteenth Century Cities* (London 1982), p. 4; R.M. Pritchard, *Housing and the Spatial Structure of the City: Residential Mobility and the Housing Market in an English City since the Industrial Revolution* (Cambridge 1976), p. 39; C.W. Chalklin, *The Provincial Towns of Georgian England: a Study of the Building Process 1740–1820* (London 1974), p. 232.
65. G.S. Jones, *Outcast London: a Study in the Relationship between Classes in Victorian London* (Oxford 1971); C.G. Powell, 'He that runs against time: life expectancy of building firms in nineteenth-century Bristol', *Construction History*, **2** (1986): 61–7.
66. E.W. Cooney, 'The building industry', in R. Church (ed.), *The Dynamics of Victorian Business: Problems and Perspectives to the 1870s* (London 1980), pp. 142–60; R. Price, op. cit.

conform to stipulations in local building by-laws; the growth of building trade unions and their wage-bargaining powers; the introduction of conciliation and bargaining; and the escalating involvement of municipalities in building and housing management.[67] Their confidence and managerial autonomy undermined, builders of working-class housing with only local exceptions, virtually ceased operations in the decade before the First World War.

In what respects did such supply influences affect shapes on the ground? Such factors were just as important under conditions of modest population expansion as they were under the pressure of rapid population expansion in the Welsh valleys or Lancashire mill towns. In Oxford, as Morris shows below, the combination of landowning and building interests resulted in a congested, unhealthy and unregulated urban environment with serious implications for the well-being of all residents. Piecemeal and pragmatic development reinforced existing arrangements. However, though there can be little doubt that the street plan of the late eighteenth century was substantially retained throughout the Victorian period, and was only substantially amended in the twentieth century by the advent of the motor car, the character of the buildings, their colour, scale, densities and architecture underwent considerable adaptation. The Georgian terrace became the generic house type, vernacular versions reflecting hierarchical divisions in income and social status. As sewer connections and building regulations were increasingly adopted by municipal authorities – 568 did so between 1858 and 1868 alone [68] – and were compulsory after 1877, then the monotony of urban form, grid-like geometric rows of terraced houses, ensured a homogeneity of residential living relieved only somewhat by the colour and pattern of bricks, limited external ornamentation, and minor geographical variations.[69] The trend towards standardization was accelerated by a uniquely Victorian feature, mass-produced building materials, with the ubiquitous London Brick Company and other manufactured bricks as well as grates, plumbing and other fixtures, and a small but increasing volume of woodwork, being undertaken in workshops rather than customized on the building site.

In terms of middle-class housing, the flight to the suburbs meant that both detached and the previously uncommon semi-detached villas assumed a dominance in the nineteenth-century urban landscape. The relocation of significant proportions of the urban population increasingly absorbed neighbouring villages or created entirely

67. J. McKenna and R.G. Rodger, 'Control by coercion: employers' associations and the establishment of industrial order in the building industry of England and Wales 1860–1914', *Business History Review*, **59** (1985): 203–31.
68. S.M. Gaskell, *Building Control: National Legislation and the Introduction of Local Bye-laws in Victorian England* (London 1983), pp. 21, 37.
69. S. Muthesius, *The English Terraced House* (New Haven, Connecticut 1982).

new suburban ones with limited allegiance to the central district. Parks and private gardens, gated carriage drives and tree-lined roads inserted zones of quiet and tranquillity which formerly had been rarities but in the second half of the nineteenth century became the norm. This redefinition of space, underpinned by a Victorian preference for privacy and accelerated after 1870 by tramway development,[70] elevated the domestic ideal and encouraged a more introspective approach to the house.[71] Indeed, the cliché of a house as an Englishman's castle to a degree captured the increasing individuality of English domestic life and contrasted sharply with the robust tradition of communality as reflected in Scottish tenement living.

As centrifugal forces replaced centripetal ones in shaping residential patterns for all but the very poor, opportunities for reconstructing the central district also existed. In so doing, geometric shapes and monumentality increasingly dominated the new, regulated, urban fabric. Civic pretensions were physically located in conspicuous town buildings, the language of regulation and control being represented architecturally in the scale and impenetrability of new town halls, art galleries and libraries. Public building phases, workhouses and infirmaries in mid-century and schools from the 1870s, introduced a grand scale of public building. So too did philanthropic housing where large tenement blocks, most commonly found in London, were constructed as model dwellings for builders and landlords to copy.[72] Tenants were by no means unanimous in respect of the virtues of block dwellings, and later council housing inherited some of the tenants' antipathy towards this style of dwelling. In the larger towns, retailing and commercial interests replaced residential buildings in the final third of the century with office blocks and department stores. Even such public utilities as gasworks and, later, electrical power generating firms were frequently located in central areas, though exceptions to this clustering of monumental public buildings were to be found in slaughterhouses, infectious diseases hospitals and lunatic asylums where remoteness was considered to have a premium. Baths and wash-houses, Poor Law hospitals and workhouses, school buildings, charitable institutions and the proliferation of places of worship, in addition to buildings to locate the apparatus of civic administration interposed buildings of a scale and solidity unknown in previous

70. A.D. Ochojna, op. cit.
71. M.J. Daunton, *House and Home in the Victorian City: Working-Class Housing 1850–1914* (London 1983), pp. 11–37.
72. J.N. Tarn, *Five Per Cent Philanthropy: an Account of Housing in Urban Areas between 1840 and 1914* (Cambridge 1973); S.M. Gaskell, *Model Housing: from the Great Exhibition to the Festival of Britain* (London 1986).

generations. And the parks, botanical gardens, cemeteries, and recreational grounds introduced acres of public space from the 1850s which redefined festivals and leisure, as well as reconfiguring the mental maps of residents.

Perhaps the most important single influence on the spatial arrangements in the Victorian city was the railway. John Kellett's powerful analysis[73] (see below) based on exhaustive studies of five major cities – London, Liverpool, Birmingham, Glasgow and Manchester – demonstrated that as the owner of some 5–9 per cent of the urban area, the railway was a truly significant force for change. The public statement of confidence and solidity attributable to the grandeur of St Pancras station is well known, but at Stoke, Bristol Temple Meads, and a multitude of lesser locations, the station and the neighbouring railway hotel represented a landmark for residents, whether they were passengers or not. The mental map of residents was changed for ever once the railway had arrived. With their marshalling yards, deep cuttings, and multiple tracks, the former lines of urban communication, of access, neighbourhood and proximity were redefined. Areas became impenetrable. Urban zoning was rigidly defined, and as Dick Lawton commented, 'its legacies are still with us in the landscape and society of the present day'.[74] For Victorians this transition, rapidly achieved in most major towns in the 1840s and 1850s, represented a new urban frontier in some respects no less fundamental than in the plains states of the American Midwest. In redefining the distributional core, in removing areas of congested housing, in amending employment opportunities and in other respects, too, the railway reorientated the axes of urban development.

The railways, like the Improvement Commissioners' slum-clearance activities in Glasgow and in London from the 1860s,[75] themselves contributed to urban congestion in adjacent neighbourhoods. To make way for access their demolitions were not normally accompanied by rehousing for those displaced – up to four million people by 1914 according to one estimate[76] – despite the official obligation to do so. Private or company benefits transcended public costs. The second half of the century was devoted to containing or reversing the environmental consequences of uncontrolled development since pragmatic decisions by individuals and institutions alike had produced unfavourable consequences for others. The jumble of buildings typical

73. J.R. Kellett, *The Impact of Railways on Victorian Cities* (London 1969).
74. R. Lawton, 'An age of great cities', first sentence.
75. J.A. Yelling, *Slums and Slum Clearance in Victorian London* (London 1986); C.M. Allan, 'The genesis of British urban redevelopment with special reference to Glasgow', *Economic History Review*, **17** (1965): 598–613.
76. P.J. Waller, *Town, City and Nation: England, 1850–1914* (Oxford 1983).

of the early modern town succumbed to a more systematic arrangement induced not by town planning but by a combination of the economics of building, and the civic search to regulate pavement and street alike by insisting on building alignment.

Occasionally complemented by a variety of Marxist approaches,[77] the Weberian perspective has examined class relations, if not in entirely value-free terms, at least in matter-of-fact language. Nowhere was this better demonstrated than by Dyos and Reeder in their impressive analysis of the tensions between slum and suburb.[78] In contrast to the socially mixed areas of Georgian towns, the suburb was quintessentially a Victorian phenomenon. Michael Thompson (see below) succinctly summarizes the explanations which have been advanced to explain the growth of suburbs, examining in turn the role of transport developments, emulation of upper-class living, the emergence of privacy and domesticity as values reinforcing segregation, architectural fashion, and minimum threshold size of towns beyond which specialized zones develop.[79] All such explanations have some relevance, but Dyos and Reeder synthesized these in a way which has not been surpassed. They argued that middle-class economic power itself contributed precisely to those adverse city-centre living conditions from which they fled by deriving a *rentier* income from slums, and by redirecting business profits away from environmental improvement and into housing investment in the suburbs. Accordingly suburbs were a logical extension of nineteenth-century capitalism, part of an unending search for new investment outlets and profits. Thus suburbs provided an integrated, self-sustaining capitalist mechanism from the 1820s by generating custom for property developers, suppliers of building materials, furnishers, for transport operators, retailing and entertainment interests, and by providing opportunities for water and gas companies, not to mention new outlets for lenders and landlords, and the professional activities of solicitors, bankers, savings institutions and others associated with property transactions. A veritable 'bonanza' of new horizons, suburbs also offered opportunities for the 'manipulation of social

77. D. Harvey, *Social Justice and the City* (London 1973), and 'The urban process under capitalism: a framework for analysis', in M. Dear and A.J. Scott (eds), *Urbanization and Urban Planning in Capitalist Society* (London 1981), pp. 91–121; J. Foster, *Class Struggle and the Industrial Revolution: Early Industrial Capitalism in Three English Towns* (London 1974); P. Joyce, *Work, Society and Politics: the Culture of the Factory in Later Victorian England* (London 1980); J. Melling (ed.), *Housing, Social Policy and the State* (London 1980).
78. H.J. Dyos and D.A. Reeder, 'Slums and suburbs' in Dyos and Wolff (eds), *The Victorian City*, pp. 359–86.
79. F.M.L, Thompson, 'Introduction' to his *The Rise of Suburbia* (Leicester 1982). See also R.G. Rodger, *Housing in Urban Britain, 1780–1914: Class, Capitalism and Construction* (London 1989), pp. 38–43.

distinctions to those most aware of their possibilities and most adept at turning them into shapes on the ground'. An 'ecological marvel', suburbs distanced the threat of social change, and offered a spatial device which inoculated the middle class against the hazards of the city without requiring them to relinquish their political control over it.

The centrality of the suburb to the urban experience of the nineteenth century was, therefore, revealed by Dyos and Reeder. Middle-class urban management had to be sustained under the potentially disruptive conditions associated with rapid industrialization, urbanization itself and the growing power of organized labour. The middle class not only displayed a cultural and residential unity, but they also sought to control the political and administrative apparatus which shaped the suburbanizing process. They sought representation on the town councils and committees which were responsible for by-laws and related regulatory codes. The suburbs were seen as a safe haven in the face of the broadening franchise and the threats which the middle classes perceived in Chartism and trade unions.

A Marxist interpretation of the suburbanizing process argues that the tensions between slum and suburb were a deliberate perpetuation of the *status quo* in social relations through the mechanism of low wages with profits reinvested so as to derive productivity gains and further profits, a process dependent upon low-priced labour abundantly replenished by natural increase and urban immigration.[80] Capital accumulation and reinvestment therefore neglected environmental improvements unless it directly impaired the workers' health and efficiency, or threatened the landlords' rental income.[81] Capitalist accumulation thus generated two urban crises. One was the deterioration of significant portions of the capital stock, to which suburbs contributed and from which cities never recovered. The second was the creation of homogeneous inner-city neighbourhoods in which working-class consciousness ultimately ran counter to capitalist interests.[82]

Examinations of the nature and quality of the built form intersected with important occupational studies of wide-ranging significance for an understanding of the city.[83] Occupational and social structures

80. M. Castells, *The Urban Question* (London 1977), p. 263.
81. J. Foster, 'How imperial London preserved its slums', *International Journal of Urban and Regional Research*, **3** (1979): 93–114.
82. D. Rose, 'Accumulation versus reproduction in the inner city: the recurrent crisis of London revisited' in M. Dear and A.J. Scott (eds), *Urbanization and Urban Planning* pp. 339–81.
83. J.H. Treble, *Urban Poverty in Britain 1830–1914* (London 1979); Jones, *Outcast London*; R.G. Rodger, '"The invisible hand" – market forces, housing and the urban form in Victorian cities' in D. Fraser and A. Sutcliffe (eds), *The Pursuit of Urban History* (London 1983), pp. 190–211.

frequently overlapped, and one instrument in this was housing, since the development of neighbourhood and community identities were commonly based on proximity. Accordingly, the level and regularity of working-class incomes and of expenditure patterns were crucial to workers' ability to pay rent, and since the reconciliation of demand and supply for housing space was largely through price levels, the rental bargain between landlord and tenant has been subjected to close scrutiny in recent years. Several studies[84] have revealed the perennial friction between landlord and tenant as reflected in rent arrears, wilful damage and flitting, and landlords' consequential attempts through the courts to enforce evictions and to empower bailiffs to obtain personal possessions in lieu of rent. By showing that these types of hostile housing strategies permeated nineteenth-century property relations, and that confrontation between housewives and rent collectors was ongoing and not simply confined to a few wartime years on Clydeside, property issues have assumed a more important role as part of the Weberian analysis. That property relations also formed a significant launch-pad for socialist and feminist politics at the beginning of the twentieth century, and contributed much to an explanation of the distinctive political ideology of Scotland, was further evidence of their enhanced status.

Landlordism was substantially dependent on the safe investment preferences of small property-owners, a group which has been identified as of critical importance to the survival of the private rental market before 1914.[85] Estimates of the percentage of owner-occupied property in England and Wales have been revised upwards recently, to $c.14$–23 per cent of all tenures on the eve of the First World War,[86] so clearly rented accommodation represented the typical experience. Though the daily management of property was vested frequently in the hands of professional house factors, a group which was well represented on town councils and influential committees,[87] the declining power of ratepayers and of property interests generally has been located from at least the 1890s.[88] In the municipal fiscal

84. D. Englander, *Landlord and Tenant in Urban Britain 1838–1918* (Oxford 1983); J. Melling, *Rent Strikes: People's Struggle for Housing in West Scotland 1890–1916* (Edinburgh 1983); and, 'Clydeside rent struggles and the making of Labour politics in Scotland 1900–39', in R. Rodger, (ed) *Scottish Housing in the Twentieth Century* (Leicester 1989), pp. 54–88.

85. B. Elliott and D. McCrone, 'Urban development in Edinburgh: a contribution to the political economy of place', *Scottish Journal of Sociology*, **4** (1980): 1–26

86. M. Swenarton and S. Taylor, 'The scale and nature of the growth of owner-occupation in Britain between the wars', *Economic History Review*, (1985): 373–92, recalculate Cleary's guess of 10 per cent and upwardly revise it to 14–23 per cent for owner occupation in 1914.

87. N.J. Morgan and M.J. Daunton, 'Landlords in Glasgow: a study of 1901', *Business History*, **25** (1983): 264–81.

88. Offer, op. cit., pp. 210–33; Waller, op. cit.

crisis which developed from *c*.1890 as a result of escalating civic responsibilities and corresponding increases in expenditure levels, the narrow tax base put property interests under immense pressure. Indeed this was a matter of national political importance. Liberals, particularly the more radical elements, sought to tax both the unearned component of rising land values and undeveloped land as a means to resolve both the fiscal and housing crises, while Conservatives chose to deploy central taxation in the form of block grants to alleviate municipal fiscal problems. Urban property issues, thus, were a central element in Lloyd George's 'People's Budget' of 1909, and though these proposals were defeated, this nonetheless reflected a reordering of political priorities with property interests receiving lower status.[89]

Builders, landowners, landlords, factors, tenants, individually and in their collective groups and associations, exerted pressure on one another as they sought to gain some advantage for their particular interest. As such the built environment and property relations occupied a central place in the nineteenth-century urban experience, spilling over into the political arena, as well as through cultural characteristics and associational life into the social relations of the city.

SOCIAL STRUCTURE

British towns and cities were a natural location of class formation in the nineteenth century. They were the focus of important economic changes which were the basis of class relationships, and local political action was increasingly focused at a municipal level which itself formed an object and part of the substance of class action. These urban places also concentrated flows of information and ideas which provided the basis upon which class relationships might become class consciousness with the possibility of class organization and action. The massing of urban populations and resources were enabling factors in the organization of a variety of social groups and alliances. While urban places provided a site for class formation, it must be remembered that at all levels the process was an integral part of wider national and international developments. At this level technological change, market pressures and alterations to the organization of

---

89. B. K. Murray, 'The politics of the "People's Budget"', *Historical Journal*, **16** (1973): 555–70; B. B. Gilbert, 'David Lloyd George, the reform of British landholding and the budget of 1914', *Historical Journal*, **21** (1978): 117–41.

production based on what contemporaries called 'competition' were redefining class structures, as did campaigns for the reform of Parliament in 1832 and the Chartist demands for universal suffrage a decade later.

In the 1820s and 1830s observers such as the Scottish minister Thomas Chalmers and the young Manchester surgeon James Kay had realized that class relationships were changing and that the nature of the change varied with the specific nature of the economic structure and relationships of the towns concerned. Chalmers compared 'the general blandness and tranquillity' of the 'provincial capitals' like Edinburgh, Bath and Oxford with the 'disjointed' relationships of rich and poor which made manufacturing towns like Glasgow 'an arena of contest'.[90] By 1950 historians were beginning to explore the complexity of the relationship between the universal pressures for class formation and their outcome in specific towns and cities. Asa Briggs published a comparative analysis of the parliamentary reform campaigns of 1830–32 in three provincial cities: Birmingham, Manchester and Leeds. At a national level these campaigns represented a successful 'middle-class' challenge to the aristocracy. The success was clearest for the urban middle classes who gained a substantial share of parliamentary power through the redistribution of seats and the extension of the franchise. A noisy and articulate campaign by and on behalf of the working class for a wider extension of the franchise and a secret ballot to protect voters from the influence of property owners and employers failed in its objectives. The Birmingham Political Union, led by men such as currency reformer Thomas Attwood and radical lawyer Edward Parkes, conducted a confident and public campaign which united substantial portions of middle- and working-class opinion. In Manchester, the radical middle-class newspaper editor Archibald Prentice failed to generate a movement of this kind because class divisions were too great. Leeds lay between these two extremes with a more fragmented reform campaign and a substantial Tory-led campaign for factory reform.

Explanation of political activity was related to local economic structures. In Birmingham, small units of production reduced class tension and opportunities for social mobility blurred class distinctions. Manchester was the commercial and political centre for the cotton district. Three features of this industry produced deep and antagonistic class divisions. In the large factories wage labour saw no chance of improvement other than by class action through trade unions. The poverty of the handloom-weavers was a threat to public

---

90. T. Chalmers, *The Christian and Civic Economy of Large Towns*, 3 vols. 1821–26, vol. 1, pp. 27–29; J. Kay, *The Moral and Physical Condition of the Working Classes* (London 1832).

order and an indictment of the commercial system. Finally, cotton was an industry exposed to the full force of world trade fluctuation and competition, so that there were few opportunities for what Chalmers called 'kindliness' between masters and men.[91] Later work on Chartism was based upon the same principles. Birmingham with its small units of production was much less militant than single-industry cotton towns such as Stockport.[92] Subsequent work has modified the details of this. Behagg, for example, has showed that that small producers of Birmingham increasingly worked in labour, material and product markets which were dominated by a few large producers.[93] The central principle set by Briggs has remained: that the complex nature of class relationships and outcomes can be explained by the interaction of general movements and changes with the specific nature of local urban economic and social structures.

The work on urban class structure was influenced by the rapidly developing literature on English class structure which emphasized the variety of class-based responses to social change in the period between 1790 and 1830.[94] John Foster, working in a fairly rigid Marxist–Leninist tradition, tested the progress of these responses in three towns. The Lancashire cotton town of Oldham was chosen because of its reputation as a radical centre and because the cotton industry represented the most advanced form of capitalism within the British economy. South Shields and Northampton were chosen because they had 'contrasting forms of economic development'. Foster traced social development from sporadic resistance to oppression in the early years of the nineteenth century, through a trade union-based response, to a 'revolutionary class consciousness' guided by a vanguard of radical leaders. Not only was 'the town more or less permanently under the control of the organized working class' for the bulk of the 1830s and 1840s but these organizations were directed by a view of an alternative form of society based on co-operative production. He explained the 'exceptional militancy' of Oldham by the dynamic of its economic organization, dominated by factory-based production and a declining rate of profit in the cotton industry. Equally importantly for the urban historian, he saw the class consciousness of these two decades as 'essentially local and generated inside the labour movement'.[95] Although this study

91. A. Briggs, 'The background to the English parliamentary reform movement in three English cities', *Cambridge Historical Journal*, x (1950–52): 293–317.
92. A. Briggs, *Chartist Studies* (London 1959).
93. C. Behagg, *Politics and Production*.
94. E. P. Thompson, *The Making of the English Working Class* (London 1963); H. J. Perkin, *The Origins of Modern English Society, 1780–1880* (London 1969).
95. J. Foster, *Class Struggle and the Industrial Revolution. Early Industrial Capitalism in Three English Towns* (London 1974), p. 253.

recognized the importance of national developments such as the reform campaigns of Owenism and Chartism, evidence was drawn from local activities and organizations. Special attention was drawn to the struggle to control the minor agencies of local government, such as the Poor Law, police commissioners and magistracy.

A wide-ranging debate, initiated by the research of David Gadian (whose article is reprinted here), suggested that substantial reinterpretation of the Oldham evidence was necessary. Gadian agreed that Oldham was a powerful centre of radical influence but it was a radicalism of class collaboration. Half the leadership was middle class and the ideological content of its politics emphasized the conflict of interest between the 'productive classes' (workers and middle class) against the 'parasites' – landlords, financiers and fundholders. When Oldham was compared against other Lancashire centres the most characteristic feature of its economy was the small size of the units of production. The average number of employees in each factory was only seventy-six compared to 276 in Stockport and 281 in Blackburn. Gadian does not claim that class-based activity and consciousness was unimportant in working-class Lancashire. He showed the variety of levels of success and forms of expression and the manner in which this related to the structure and history of each town. In Stockport, middle-class opposition to working-class activity was vigorous and effective, and was dominated by a few large employers who used the blacklist and charity as effective sanctions. Ashton-under-Lyne, a town with a strong radical leadership and no unity among its employers, produced a militant working-class movement with a vigorous message of conflict. In Blackburn, apathy was a product of effective paternalism; in Bolton, a Unitarian-dominated middle class led the working class into Chartism but kept them out of the anti-Poor Law movement.[96]

Case studies and comparative studies made by urban historians contributed to two major debates within the history of class relationships in Britain. The first, outlined above, concerned the nature and chronology of class formation. Urban historians showed clearly that the pace and nature of class formation depended on the nature of local economy and society. They directed attention towards the 1830s and 1840s rather than to the earlier period, and showed the variety and complexity of local responses.

The second debate focused on the nature and explanation for the relative social calm of the 1850s and 1860s. This was closely associated with the development of a 'labour aristocracy', a group

---

96. D. Gadian, 'Class formation and class action in north-west industrial towns, 1830–50', in R.J. Morris (ed.), *Class, Power and Social Structure in British Nineteenth-Century Towns* (Leicester 1986), pp. 23–60; R. Glen, *Urban Workers in the Early Industrial Revolution* (London 1984).

of skilled men whose ideology of respectability was believed to have led to co-operation with the middle classes. Foster finished his account of Oldham with an account of 'liberalization' in which the owners of capital worried by the challenges of the previous decades used specific bribes, notably legislation on factory hours, to bring about an alliance with the working population which had threatened their power. Two other studies chose towns which were especially influenced by the culture of the skilled artisan, namely Edinburgh, Deptford, Woolwich and Greenwich.[97] These studies explored the logic of the artisans through the detail of local organization and social action. They found that the respectability of the artisan implied an independence from other social groups and a co-operative ideology which was probably easier to live with than Chartist demands and demonstrations, but did not amount to simple class collaboration. The urban basis of these studies was important for several reasons. The urban economies considered were ones in which large numbers of skilled men were employed. Urban population concentrations made a detailed differentiation of the built environment possible. As artisan incomes and town sizes grew, discrete and distinctive areas of artisan housing were created, separate from the middle classes whose dominance was rejected, and from the unskilled labourers whose life style was despised. Together, concentration and differentiation enabled the artisans to create and sustain a wide variety of formal organizations – friendly societies, building societies, literary clubs and co-operative societies – through which they expressed and developed their ideology.

This literature and the debates it contained has an importance for understanding class relationships and their development. Its importance for understanding urbanization itself is less obvious. There are two important ways in which these studies contributed to understanding urban life as such. In all the case studies class action seized upon the variety of formal institutions which were created in the towns and cities of Britain during this period.[98] These institutions provided a variety of experience and choice which was characteristic of urban organizations. They provided a basis upon which groups and individuals could experiment with limited commitment as they selected the directions which suited their perception of their class interest. They provided a basis upon which class interests could move from the often physical confrontations of the 1830s to the

---

97. G.J. Crossick, *An Artisan Elite in Victorian Society. Kentish London 1840–1880* (London 1978); R.Q. Gray, *The Labour Aristocracy in Victorian Edinburgh (Oxford 1976)*.

98. R.J. Morris, 'Clubs, societies and associations', in F.M.L. Thompson (ed.), *The Cambridge Social History of Britain, 1750–1950: vol. 3. Social Agencies and Institutions* (Cambridge 1990).

calmer negotiations of the 1850s and 1860s. Secondly, historians informed by a variety of theoretical viewpoints have, in the 1970s and 1980s, come to give increasing autonomy to cultural and ideological influences in the interaction of class and economic relationships. Thus the institutional structures and histories of specific towns have come to play an increasing part in accounts of class outcomes.

Large towns with a complex structure of mediating institutions were much more able to control class-based conflicts. In the early period, according to Lynn Lees, the corporate towns like Liverpool and Newcastle were better equipped, while places like Birmingham in the 1790s and Manchester in 1819 saw major breakdowns in class relationships. By the 1840s most of the large towns had acquired mediating institutions, which varied from ratepayer – elected corporations and resident magistrates to voluntary societies. Thus it tended to be smaller and medium-sized places which saw breakdowns of order in a decade of tense class relationships. By the 1880s institutional mediation was widely developed, through trade unions and trades councils, employers' organizations, and in some places, conciliation boards.[99] All this did not eliminate conflict over economic interest, but it did enable that conflict to be handled with less disruption. It was urban population concentration with the consequent opportunity for a variety of formal organizations which made this possible. In a comparative study of Birmingham and Sheffield Dennis Smith showed that the degree of integration between different aspects of urban social and institutional structure was important. Both towns were characterized by small units of production which by mid-century were joined by a few very large employers. Yet the outcome was very different. Birmingham supported a powerful local bourgeoisie with an active civic pride and consciousness; Sheffield began the nineteenth century as a centre of aggressive radicalism and early in the twentieth became the first major city with a labour administration. Smith showed that Sheffield was strongly integrated at a neighbourhood level around the chapels and workplaces of the cutlers' settlements which made up the economy of Sheffield, whilst at town level integration was weak. Since the mid-eighteenth century, Birmingham had built a strong structure of urban institutions, some like its Anglican church and grammar school inherited from the past, others like its resident magistracy and integrated radical politics were created in response to a particular crisis of social order like the Church and

99. L.H. Lees, 'The study of social conflict in English industrial towns', *Urban History Yearbook* (1980): 34–43; J.A. McKenna and R.G. Rodger, 'Control by coercion: employers' associations and the establishment of industrial order in the building industry of England and Wales 1860–1914', *Business History Review*, **59** (1985): 203–31.

King riots of the 1790s. Birmingham, like Leeds, was able to build a stabilizing institutional structure through the activities of a well-organized middle class with an innovative leadership of professional and mercantile people.[100]

The structure of the urban middle class and its variations have been increasingly related to the development of urban social relationships. The variety and nature of the economic positions occupied by the urban middle class is now better understood. The intensive use of trade directories and poll books has shown the importance of shopkeepers. During the 1830s, they represented over 30 per cent of the middle classes of places like Leeds, Manchester and Glasgow, and around 45 per cent of the middle classes of smaller manufacturing centres like West Bromwich and Bilston.[101] The merchants and professional men were small by comparison but played a strategic part in local government and voluntary societies. The share of manufacturers in the middle classes varied from 10 per cent to just under 40 per cent, though in the larger towns they were under-represented in public activity. By the 1850s and 1860s these manufacturers were beginning to take a more active and confident part in local political and cultural activity. Patrick Joyce showed the manner in which the cotton manufacturers of towns like Blackburn and Bury were able to dominate local politics and culture through the careful paternalistic management of their labour-force.[102] By the 1860s manufacturers dominated the local politics of many small boroughs.[103]

The rise of party and sectarian politics among these middle classes was evident in many urban areas in the 1830s and 1840s. This was related to two features of national urban development. The first was the increase in Nonconformists among the urban middle classes who were mostly excluded from the traditional structures of urban local government. These self-electing corporations derived from seventeenth-century charters, and their influence varied and was shared with a number of other agencies of local government such as ratepayer-elected improvement commissioners and overseers of the poor who were often linked to local church government. The

100. D. Smith, *Conflict and Compromise. Class Formation in English Society, 1830–1914* (London 1982); R.J. Morris, *Class, Sect and Party. The Making of the British Middle Class, Leeds, 1820–1850* (Manchester 1990).
101. R.H. Trainor, 'Authority and social structure in an industrialized area: a study of three Black Country towns, 1840–1890', unpublished Oxford D. Phil. thesis, 1981; S. Nenadic, 'The structure, values and influence of the Scottish urban middle classes: Glasgow, 1800–1870', unpublished Glasgow Ph.D. thesis, 1986.
102. P. Joyce, *Work, Society and Politics. The Culture of the Factory in Later Victorian England* (Brighton 1980).
103. J. Garrard, *Leadership and Power in Victorian Industrial Towns, 1830–80* (Manchester 1983).

Corporation could also be important because many were linked to the selection of members of parliament in those boroughs which possessed parliamentary seats. This changed in the 1830s. In 1832 most boroughs of any size were given seats in parliament with a franchise dominated by ten-pound householders, in other words, by the middle classes. In 1835 those boroughs with corporations were affected by the Municipal Reform Act which created ratepayer-elected councils which steadily gathered the agencies of local government under their control. The parliamentary seats and most of the councils rapidly became objects of party contest. These parties were more alliances led by the Whig and Tory aristocracies who fought for control of national government rather than disciplined parties in the modern sense. They were identified with, though not identical to, the sectarian split between Nonconformists and Anglicans.

Party and sectarian identity played an important role in directing the actions of the urban middle classes. These identities structured much of the battle for the institutions of urban local government. In the 1820s this involved the minor agencies which had an open franchise, such as the Improvements Commissioners. After the reforms of the 1830s opened the Corporation to a ratepayer franchise the main contest centred on these bodies.[104] Indeed, in Leeds the main change brought by reform was not in the socioeconomic composition of the Corporation, but in its party and sectarian identity which moved from Tory Anglican to Whig Nonconformist.[105] Religious identity played an important part in the creation of a middle-class urban culture of voluntary societies and charities. At times the contest was so disruptive that many of these societies adopted rules which excluded religion and politics from their discussions in order to avoid splits.[106] The noisy public contest of party should not obscure the importance of class relationships in local politics and culture. Although the battle for seats and votes was 'party' and these parties were closely related to religious identities, the issues which they debated were often class issues. The Poor Law, public health, public order, the regulation of housing, the demolition of unfit property, and even the placing of street lighting were all issues which involved the relationship of middle-and working-class people. This is not to deny that many issues were specifically party or sectarian, such as the appointment of paid Poor Law officials (should they be Whig or Tory?) or the extension of a local burial ground (should it be controlled by the Anglican Church?). Equally important were local

104. D. Fraser, *Urban Politics in Victorian England. The Structure of Politics in Victorian Cities* (Leicester 1976).
105. E.P. Hennock, *Fit and Proper Persons. Ideal and Reality in Nineteenth-Century Urban Government* (London 1973).
106. R.J. Morris, *Class, Sect and Party*, Chapter 11.

issues which might split the urban middle class such as the support for rival local railway bills or the power and authority of a local landowner or employer.[107]

The interaction of class relationships and the pressures of urbanization showed most clearly in matters of control and regulation. Because of the density and complexity associated with urban life it tends to require a tight framework of control and regulation. In a number of arenas, this control was developed in a manner which served to enhance the authority of the middle classes over the working classes. Daunton's analysis of building regulations shows this clearly. These regulations became increasingly elaborate during the century. From the 1840s a series of local by-laws imposed minimal standards on working-class housing; this not only priced housing out of the reach of a greater number of working-class incomes but shifted the physical form of that housing to a more open plan. The street was easier to police and light than the enclosed courts which had been banned.[108] This collection includes another example of this control process at work, the development of the police force in the industrial towns of northern England. The new, disciplined police forces of the nineteenth century began to be introduced in the industrial cities in the 1840s. They provided some control of crime and a more finely graded response to urban disorder than previous military interventions. They were also incorporated into middle-class efforts to control and change working-class social behaviour. Traditional freedoms such as assembly in the street were attacked. The police were expected to act against the whole evangelical cannon of 'sins', cruelty to animals, obscene songs, street drunkenness and the rest. The immediate outcome was conflict rather than suppression. By the 1880s assaults on the police were beginning to decline but the overall outcome was not one of control, but rather a continuous process of bargaining through which middle class leaders sought to influence working class behaviour.[109] Efforts to create a civic culture which would incorporate the working classes became more subtle and elaborate as the century progressed. By the 1840s most towns had Mechanics Institutes and Temperance Societies which served selected portions of the middle and working classes. By the 1850s the first parks and open spaces were being laid out to be joined by public libraries and art galleries. The mission of the middle-class activists

107. T.J. Nossitor, *Influence, Opinion and Political Idioms in Reformed England. Case Studies from the North-East of England, 1832–1874* (Brighton 1975).
108. Daunton, *House and Home*.
109. J. Davis, 'From "rookeries" to "communities": race, poverty and policing in London, 1850–1985', *History Workshop*, **27** (1989); R. Swift, 'Urban policing and social control in early Victorian England, 1835–86: a reappraisal', *History*, **73** (1988).

was to 'civilize' rather than control.[110] These influences were only one factor in the increasing complex of opportunities available in the growing towns. The authorities and middle classes never gained the totality of influence which some of the theories of 'social control' imply.[111] Growing working-class incomes and leisure in the last forty years of the century provided both problems and opportunities. Street football and bull-running had largely disappeared in the 1840s, but by the 1880s other urban activities, a little more contained and disciplined but equally open to popular innovation, were appearing. St Giles's Fair in Oxford (see Sally Alexander in this collection) was largely a creation of the nineteenth-century commercialization. The fair with its mixture of utility and entertainment became an important part of the working-class year. Like the development of the new football grounds with their professional teams and paying spectators, control was imperfect but the expansion of choice and opportunity was great.[112]

The nineteenth-century city was increasingly a middle-class place. Property ownership was dominated by a middle class of shopkeepers and petty capitalists. Even where aristocratic owners owned and tried to develop areas of towns, like the Calthorpe's in Birmingham or the Duke of Norfolk in Sheffield, their success was limited by the incomes and taste of the middle classes.[113] The town became the focus around which the middle classes developed a varied culture of voluntary societies, church and chapel, and family networks. The town was the arena in which middle-class political influence was felt while national politics was still dominated by an aristocracy only partly controlled by the middle-class votes created in 1832.[114] Working-class culture tended to operate at a neighbourhood level, often taking advantage of the villages which were engulfed by the expanding cities. The public house, the chapel and the street were the basis of clubs, sports activities and family networks.[115] It was the middle-class political and cultural leaders who made claims to represent the city.

The notion of a middle-class city and a working-class neighbour-

110. H.E. Meller, *Leisure and the Changing City, 1870–1914* (London 1976).
111. See, for example, A.P. Donajgrodski, ed. *Social Control in Nineteenth-Century Britain* (London, 1977); F.M.L. Thompson, 'Social control in Victorian Britain', *Economic History Review*, **34** (1981): 189–208.
112. R. Holt, *Sport and the British. A Modern History* (Oxford 1989).
113. D.N. Cannadine, *Lords and Landlords*
114. R.J. Morris, 'The middle class and British towns and cities of the industrial revolution 1780–1870' in D. Fraser and A. Sutcliffe (eds), *The Pursuit of Urban History*, pp. 286–305.
115. G.S. Jones, 'Working-class culture and working-class politics in London, 1870–1900: notes on the remaking of the English working class', *Journal of Social History*, **7** (1974); D. Smith, *Conflict and Compromise*.

hood is a crude but useful characterization of the urban places that had developed by the end of the nineteenth century. Can towns and cities equally be identified as male places? The growing literature on gender provides some guidance. Urban leaders, mayors, members of Parliament, chairmen and committee men of voluntary societies, parsons and ministers, were almost all male, but this was simply a reflection of the male dominance of society as a whole and had little to do with urban change.[116] This male dominance was being continually renegotiated throughout the century. Urban change played an important part in two episodes of this negotiation. By the 1820s the middle classes were creating a notion of 'separate spheres' which entailed the separation of women from the public world of work and politics. The growth of the suburbs played an important part in this process. As the case of Cadbury's Bourneville showed, the move to the suburbs confirmed the exclusion of women from the physical and as well the social space of business. Some of the cultural assumptions involved not only helped shape the physical environment of the nineteenth century but also influenced the twentieth-century planning movement through Howard and Geddes.[117] By the 1860s, the growth of urban government and the view that women might be legitimately concerned with matters of family, notably child care, education and health, together with a failure legally to exclude women from local politics, meant that a small but persistent group of women began to enter local politics and become members of school and Poor Law boards. By 1914 groups of women had gained a minor foothold in the welfare agencies of urban government.[118] Work by Ellen Ross showed that working-class women played a central part in creating and sustaining the working-class neighbourhood networks.[119] By the 1880s and 1890s a small number of these women entered public life through the Labour movement. The Co-operative Women's Guild and the ILP (Independent Labour Party) were especially important for them,[120] as also were a growing number of powerful urban welfare institutions which provided a foothold for the early generation of Labour politicians seeking to increase working-class

116. L. Davidoff and C. Hall, *Family Fortunes. Men and Women of the English Middle Class, 1780–1850* (London 1987).
117. C. Hall in this collection; H. Meller, 'Planning theory and women's role in the city', *Urban History Yearbook*, **17** (1990): 85–98.
118. P. Hollis, *Ladies Elect: Women in English Local Government, 1865–1914* (Oxford 1987); H. Corr, 'An exploration into Scottish education', in H. Fraser and R.J. Morris, *People and Society in Scotland*, vol. 2.
119. E. Ross, 'Survival networks: women's neighbourhood sharing in London before World War One', *History Workshop*, **15** (1983): 4–27.
120. J. Liddington and J. Norris, *One Hand Tied Behind Us. The Rise of the Women's Suffrage Movement* (London 1978).

political influence in a situation where the franchise was still limited. The small numbers of women and working-class people who began to take part in urban public life during the last decades of the century were taking advantage of one of the major processes of nineteenth-century urbanization.

The century saw a steady increase in the extent, depth and density of urban governmental power. Two basic structures were laid in place during the 1830s. First was the reformed system of representation whereby urban property owners elected members of Parliament who would supervise the national legislation which created the agencies and powers of so much urban government. Second, and following rapidly, were the reformed ratepayer-elected corporations which consolidated and then extended the power of the local state. The pressures for this extension of power were exposed in the 1840s when the crisis of public health became the subject of a series of major national reports. This was not just a matter of the epidemic crisis of cholera and typhus but also the steady and rising attrition of endemic infections. Concern over public order was no less important. Developments in public health provision took place unevenly, and if the details of timing were specific in different localities, nonetheless several phases can be identified. The problem was recognized and initial investments in water and sewerage were made in the 1840s. By the 1850s, the financial effects of municipal initiatives were evident in terms of rising rates, and shopkeepers and small traders entered local politics to vote against further action. They were helped in their resistance since in the contemporary state of scientific knowledge it was not always obvious that expensive action would have any beneficial results.[121] This was followed by a period of civic consciousness in which cities like Birmingham, Glasgow and Edinburgh moved in three directions. First, investments in sanitation were increased: second, municipal governments took over public utilities like gas, water and tramways;[122] and third, these towns began extensive demolitions of crowded and unhealthy property with the dual motivation of improving public health and easing transport congestion. If, in some places like Leeds and Sheffield, civic consciousness was more delayed and selective than elsewhere, Hamish Fraser's article in this

---

121. C. Hamlin, 'Muddling in Bumbledom: on the enormity of large sanitary improvements in four British towns, 1855–1885', *Victorian Studies*, **32** (1988/9): 55–83.
122. A. Briggs, *History of Birmingham*, vol. 2, *Borough and city, 1865–1938*, (London 1952); J.A. Hassan, 'The growth and impact of the British water industry in the nineteenth century', *Economic History Review*, **38** (1985); M. Falkus, 'The development of municipal trading in the nineteenth century', *Business History*, **19** (1977).

collection shows just how extensive the direct intervention of many municipal authorities in their local economy and society became. By 1900 most places reached a point at which the local tax base could no longer bear the cost of extended civic responsibilities.[123] There was a pause before national government began extensive subsidies for local authority income, thus introducing a complex relationship between local and national government which has still to work itself out.

If urbanization resulted in the expansion of state power, the relationship with religion was much more equivocal. Traditional accounts link the industrial city to the decline of religion. The growth of rational patterns of thought, necessary for urban life, and the break up of traditional communities, it is suggested was part of this decline of religious behaviour and belief.[124] Recent research and reassessment has shown this to be wrong or at best simplistic. As Kent suggests in this collection, the imperfect evidence available places the start of any decline, relative or absolute, after the 1860s, and maybe even after the 1880s. No clear link with urbanization is available. The pattern is something as follows. There was some dislocation in periods of rapid expansion in the early years of the century. This was the basis of loud complaints from people such as Thomas Chalmers, and was followed by a massive growth in religious provision and activity in all towns. The number and size of dissenting sects grew, and the established churches responded with church-building and missions. As already stated, sectarian identity gained a growing importance in politics and cultural activity, reaching a peak in the 1840s. In other words, the growth of religious activity and identities was part of the response to the growth of the cities. By the 1860s, many congregations were moving to the suburbs where an increasing number gained a clear middle-class identity,[125] though, as Hillis has shown for Glasgow, working-class people still formed the majority of members in many congregations.[126] The activities of these congregations expanded. In the 1830s they had sponsored bible societies and Sunday schools; by the 1900s many had boys brigades, men's fellowships and women's guilds, each with an increasingly secular content to their activities, and epitomized by the expansion of church football and cricket clubs. It is at this point that a real crisis of confidence for religious organization in the towns becomes clear. It may have some origin in the expansion and

123. E.P. Hennock, *Fit and Proper Persons*.
124. E.R. Wickham, *Church and People in an Industrial City* (London 1957); C.G. Brown, 'Did urbanization secularise Britain?', *Urban History Yearbook* (1988): 1–14.
125. H. McLeod, *Class and Religion in the Victorian City* (London 1974).
126. P. Hillis, 'Presbyterianism and social class in mid-nineteenth-century Glasgow', *Journal of Ecclesiastical History*, **32** (1981).

suburbanization of cities or in the commercialization of leisure, for the same sort of problems seem to have affected other organizations such as, the Philosophical and Literary Societies and Mechanics' Institutes which had dominated urban life in the 1840s.[127] This crisis was certainly not caused by something called 'urbanization'. Abrams' warning against the reification of the city is very relevant here.

CONCLUSION

During the nineteenth century British urban society became more complex, stratified and regulated than ever it had been. The contagion of numbers brought a huge massing of people, and an acute awareness of their interaction. An increase in physical scale dominated urban consciousness. This was not just a matter of the size of city-centre buildings, town halls, office blocks, warehouses, bridges and factories; it was also spatial and perceptual. Urban spatial dimensions altered fundamentally as zoning became more rigidly defined, and as suburbanization proceeded, choice and freedom in the city were perceived differently. The sense of threat felt by many, especially those with authority to defend, was countered by an imperfect control, and by attempts to redefine social identity. Paradoxically, it was the initial stimuli to urban concentration, the proximity, density, and social interaction of city life, which contributed to a slowing down and even to a reversal of the process, as commuters, facilitated by the tram (and around London by suburban lines), sought alternative life-styles. The urban place was a site upon which specific and local social economic processes interacted with national and international processes. By 1900 'urbanization' affected the bulk of the British population, so curiosity about towns becomes curiosity about social and economic history as a whole. The study of towns thus draws together many aspects of the lives of men and women living in an expanding industrial society. Urbanization was one of many processes shaping the lives of those people.

127. S. Yeo, *Religion and Voluntary Organizations in Crisis* (London 1976).

Part One
THE CITY AND ITS PEOPLE

Chapter 2

URBANIZATION

R.J. Morris

[from J. Langton and R. J. Morris (eds), *Atlas of Industrializing Britain 1780–1914* (London 1986), pp. 164–79.]

Historical geographers have provided important spatial analyses of the Victorian city. In mapping distributions of population, migrants and ethnic groups, social and residential segregation, land use and other variables, geographers have provided a leading analytical edge for their own and other disciplines concerned with historical change in towns. In this selection of maps, Morris synthesizes material easily available from British Parliamentary Papers and other published sources to show how visual representations of change in the city suggest lines of research enquiry which can be undertaken both at the city level, or at a smaller scale of analysis – the street, neighbourhood or district. Though critics have claimed that mapping the city only captures a picture of urban development at a specific moment, this has been countered by the development of a series of snapshots to provide a dynamic account of urban change. In addition, rendering historical material into map form has propelled urban historians towards identifying features held in common by cities, and thus into thinking systematically about the processes which produce slums, suburbs, retail and industrial districts, ethnic quarters and social segregation generally. Though the two-dimensional maps produced here capture many characteristics of the nineteenth-century city, contemporaries carried more sophisticated three-dimensional or, even four-dimensional versions of the city, based on their own mental maps of 'no-go' areas and similar boundary demarcations.

Industrialization in Britain as in many other economies included not only a change in economic structure and a sustained increase in population and per capita income, but also changes in the spatial

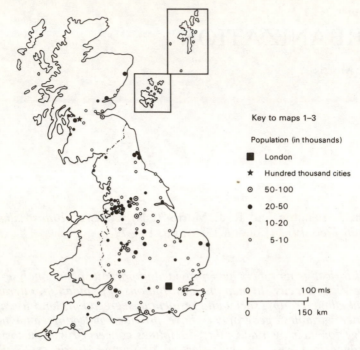

Key to maps 1–3

Population (in thousands)

■   London

★   Hundred thousand cities

⊙   50-100

●   20-50

•   10-20

○   5-10

Map 1   Town size in 1811

organization of that population which included both urban growth (an increase in the size of towns) and urbanization (an increase in proportion of the population living in towns). Maps 1–3 show the location of the urban places involved in this change. These maps use data developed by C.M. Law and Brian Robson[1] which accord well with the traditional definition of urban places as agglomerations of population of relative size, density, and heterogeneity. Three modifications have been made. Scottish data have been added from the printed census. The changing scale of urbanization has been recognized by changing the lower limit of the operational definition of urban from 5000 in 1801 to 10,000 in 1861 and 20,000 in 1911 (the modern UN definition of an urban place). The characteristic of towns as places for the organization of power emphasized by Max Weber has been recognized by re-dividing places like Manchester

1. B.T. Robson, *Urban Growth: an Approach* (London 1973); C.M. Law, 'The Growth of Urban Population in England and Wales, 1801–1911', *Transactions of the Institute of British Geographers*, **41** (1967): 125–43.

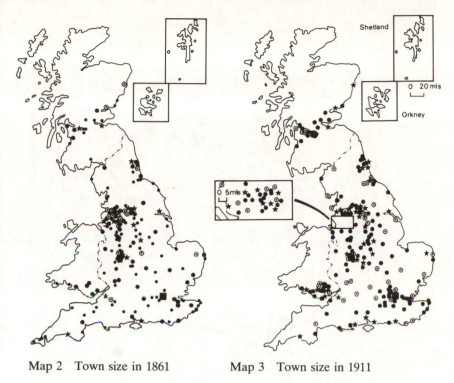

Map 2   Town size in 1861   Map 3   Town size in 1911

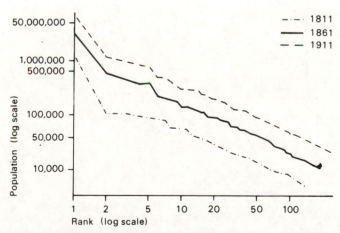

Map 4   Rank-order size, 1811, 1861 and 1911

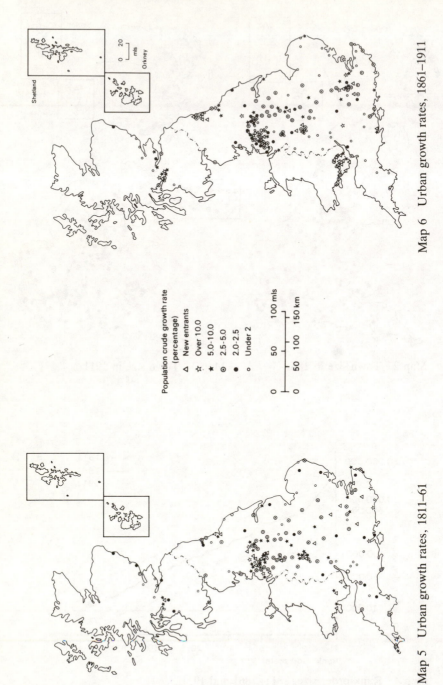

Map 6   Urban growth rates, 1861–1911

Map 5   Urban growth rates, 1811–61

Population crude growth rate
(percentage)

△ New entrants
☆ Over 10.0
★ 5.0–10.0
◉ 2.5–5.0
● 2.0–2.5
○ Under 2

and Salford which had an independent political character. There is a natural and very real conflict between the geographical concept of contiguity and agglomeration, and the sociological and historical concept of independent political and social identities.

Maps 1–6 show clearly the increasing size and number of urban places. New entrants were places with a population below 2000 at the start of the time period. The growth rates were the simple mean annual increase as a percentage of the population at the start of the time period. The rank order size chart (Map 4) plots size against rank order. If the relationship was one of proportionality (i.e. the second largest town was half the size of the largest, the third largest, a third the size and so on), then the results of the log scale graph would be a straight line. Although some older theorists asserted that such proportionality indicated a developed urban system (after all the USA was like that), such a standard should only be used for descriptive purposes. In this case the continued dominance of London is clear. The historical emphasis given to the provincial capitals was due to the newness of the 100,000 cities and their rapid growth. Any apparent decline in London was only in relation to previous massive dominance. In 1811 London was twelve times its nearest rival, in 1861 five and a half times, with a slight recovery to six times in 1911. Britain retained a metropolitan urban system throughout the nineteenth century, dominated by its primate city. There were other patterns. In the first half of the century growth was dominated by the resource-based textile and metal goods towns of Lancashire, Yorkshire and the west Midlands. St Helens, Burnley and Bradford grew at over 10 per cent a year. In addition there was a ring of towns around London like Luton and Enfield, and a group of leisure, residential and retirement towns, like Brighton, Cheltenham, Hastings and Torquay, mainly along the south coast, that attested to the strength of the service and commercial economy. The second half of the century witnessed growth in the capital goods and coal exporting areas of south Wales, north-east England and the west of Scotland. Clydebank, Jarrow, Middlesbrough, Cardiff and Mountain Ash represent this group. A large number of coal communities, like Ashington and Rhondda, were involved here. They have the size and density of urban communities but not always their heterogeneity. Perhaps they should be thought of as urban places, but without the means of organizing power possible in places more broadly based in history, culture and the economy. The ring around London thickened with places like Harrow, Woking and Watford joining the system. Such grouping always misses the isolated and specialist places like railway Swindon and fishport Grimsby.

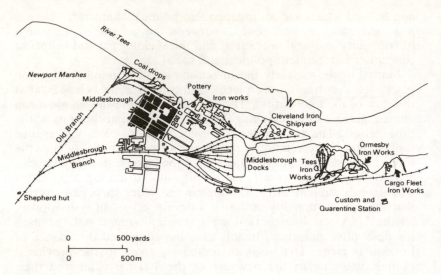

Map 7   Middlesbrough, 1853

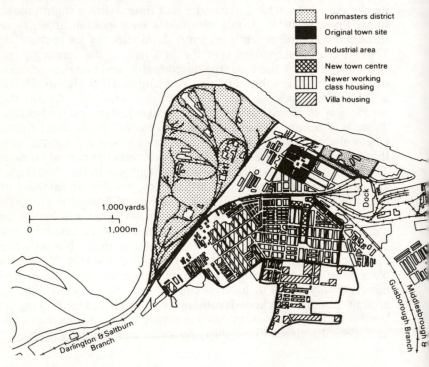

Map 8   Middlesbrough, 1891–3

This growth involved very few 'new towns' after the fashion of the planted medieval boroughs or the American frontier. In 1800, Britain was already well endowed with population centres and growth involved the development of those nuclei. The few new towns were related either to resource exploitation or were leisure resorts. Their nature revealed a great deal of the processes shaping nineteenth-century urbanization. Middlesbrough was laid out in 1830 as an extension of the better-known Stockton and Darlington coal-exporting system. By 1853 (Map 8), the original town layout had been filled. It was a regular grid with a central market square that would have suited an Irish plantation town. This gave Middlesbrough a very different focus from the medieval borough centres like High Street, Glasgow or Briggate in Leeds. During the 1840s, Middlesbrough acquired a dock, an Improvement Act, a pottery, shipbuilding and ironfounding industries. There were several elements here characteristic of urban formation: local merchant enterprise, London capital and professional expertise, a local resource base, railways and the compelling efficiency of the grid in allocating land use. By 1891–3 (Map 9), the railways had linked Cleveland iron ore to Durham coal, and Middlesbrough, 'this infant Hercules, the youngest child of England's enterprise'

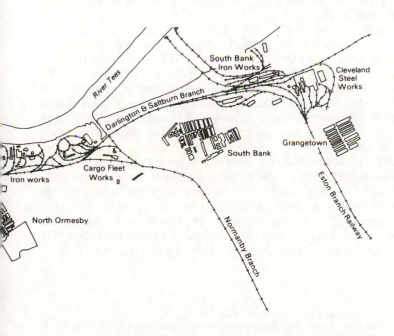

(Gladstone) experienced explosive growth from 7431 people in 1851 to 75,532 in 1891.[2] The resulting shape of the town revealed further aspects of British urban development. The logic of the grid despite several attempts to reassert itself had been disrupted by the railway and by the property boundaries of the old agricultural economy. Working-class housing had spread west along the tracks. More spacious villa housing spread south towards a newly donated park. The town centre had jumped the tracks and reformed around new municipal buildings. The placing of the new industrial iron and steel establishments was most significant. The shepherd's hut and Newport Marsh were replaced by the ironmasters district, whilst to the east was a series of works, each tied to its own settlement of working-class housing, such as Cargo Fleet (1852) and Ormesby (1854). The major industrial sites were placed around the periphery of the existing urban centre, seeking cheap land and access to the new transport system of rail and dredged river, little different in their logic from the modern industrial estate by the motorway. There was little tidy logic in British urban development. Britain lacked strong government direction in land allocation and rarely had a strong local unified landownership, so that the untidy logic of previous land boundaries, access to transport, and competition for desirable environments by a population with dramatically unequal incomes, produced these varied patterns even on the *tabula rasa* of the south bank of the Tees.

Eastbourne, on the south coast, was created for a very different purpose with a much more unified landownership structure dominated by the Dukes of Devonshire and the Gilbert family. By 1898 (Map 7), development showed several characteristic features.[3] To the west of the central business and leisure district was an area controlled by the Duke. His control plus its pleasant position ensured a uniform development of high-quality villa houses standing in large gardens. In outline it was very like the high-status middle-class housing of the large towns. Gilbert's land, slightly less desirable but equally well controlled, was laid out in well-appointed terraces. Mixed ownership south of the railway produced meaner working-class terraces. Strict control and oligopolistic ownership patterns accentuated the social differentiation of the town, whilst the area under fragmented ownership became the less socially prestigious area. Such an area was in any case necessary to provide labour for the construction and service sectors of the local economy. Gilbert

2. Asa Briggs, *Victorian Cities* (London 1963), pp. 241–76.
3. David Cannadine, *Lords and Landlords: the Aristocracy and the Towns, 1774–1967* (Leicester 1980).

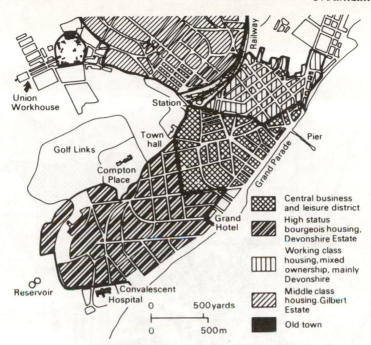

Map 9 Eastbourne, 1898

Legend:
- Central business and leisure district
- High status bourgeois housing, Devonshire Estate
- Working class housing, mixed ownership, mainly Devonshire
- Middle class housing. Gilbert Estate
- Old town

Map labels: Union Workhouse, Station, Pier, Town hall, Golf Links, Compton Place, Railway, Grand Parade, Grand Hotel, Reservoir, Convalescent Hospital, 0 500 yards, 0 500 m

and Devonshire between them prevented the creation of boarding houses like those in far away Blackpool.

Most British cities grew by accretion around an existing urban core. Glasgow must stand as an example of this process. By 1800, the old centre based upon Glasgow Cross and High Street had become increasingly unpleasant under the impact of population pressure and industrial activity. The wealthy and middle classes migrated west to the gridiron terraces of the 'new town', followed by the commercial centre.[4] Beyond Glasgow Green, the east end became a mixed area of working-class tenements, textile factories and transport facilities (Map 10). There was no sense of Chicago-school concentric rings in these cities. The traditional British analysis of east end, west end and central business district was only partially adequate. Like Middlesbrough, Glasgow was surrounded by a ring

4. S.G. Checkland, 'The British Industrial City as History: the Glasgow Case', *Urban Studies*, **1** (1964).

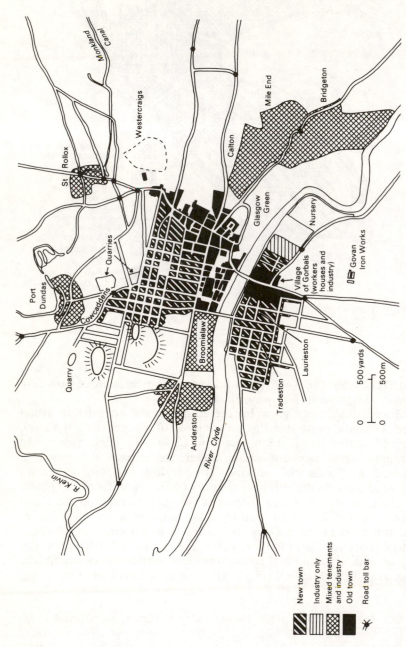

Map 10 Social and economic structure of Glasgow, 1825

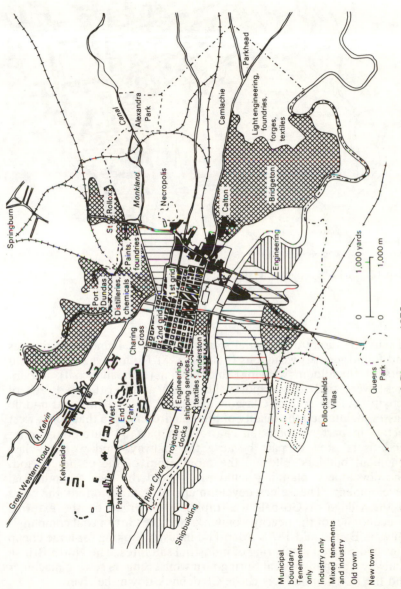

Map 11   Social and economic structure of Glasgow, 1875

Municipal
boundary
Tenements
only
Industry only
Mixed tenements
and industry
Old town
New town

Springburn
Canal
Alexandra
Park
Parkhead
Camlachie
Light engineering,
foundries,
forges,
textiles
Monkland
St. Rollox
Necropolis
Bridgeton
Calton
Port
Dundas
Paints,
foundries
Distilleries,
chemicals,
1st grid
2nd grid
Engineering
Charing
Cross
Engineering,
shipping services,
textiles   Anderston
West
End
Park
R. Kelvin
Kelvinside
Great Western Road
Patrick
River Clyde
Projected
docks
Shipbuilding
Pollockshields
Villas
Queens
Park

1,000 yards
1,000 m
0
0

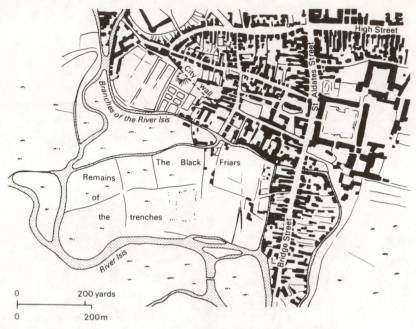

Map 12   St Ebbe's parish, Oxford, 1817

of partially discrete industrial settlements: Port Dundas (distilleries and foundries), Cowcaddens (quarries), St Rollox (chemicals), Anderston (handloom weaving) and Govan (iron and coal). Again, these were tied to transport (the canal) and existing patterns of activity. As the area of Glasgow expanded, the wealthy and middle classes maintained the quality of their environment in that north-west sector, in part by their feu charters, in part by outbidding other land users, and in part because the railways and working-class tenement builders followed the momentum of the earlier period. The developers' planning could rarely hold the logic of industrial development. The select development of Laurieston to the west of the village of Gorbals was rapidly submerged by the external diseconomies of the nearby ironworks and the Govan coal company's railway. By the mid-1870s (Map 11), industry looking for large cheap sites had created a new ring of industrial satellites. The North British Railway Company was at Springburn whilst Singers sewing machines and the iron shipbuilders chose Clydebank down the river.

Working-class housing was created in three basic ways – subdivision of existing properties, infilling and new building. All three

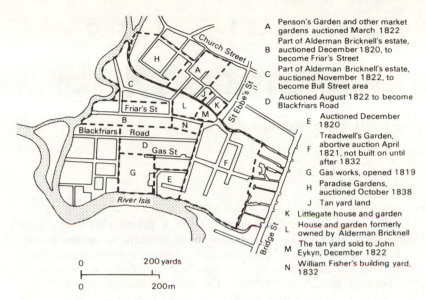

A Penson's Garden and other market gardens auctioned March 1822

B Part of Alderman Bricknell's estate, auctioned December 1820, to become Friar's Street

C Part of Alderman Bricknell's estate, auctioned November 1822, to become Bull Street area

D Auctioned August 1822 to become Blackfriars Road

E Auctioned December 1820

F Treadwell's Garden, abortive auction April 1821, not built on until after 1832

G Gas works, opened 1819

H Paradise Gardens, auctioned October 1838

J Tan yard land

K Littlegate house and garden

L House and garden formerly owned by Alderman Bricknell

M The tan yard sold to John Eykyn, December 1822

N William Fisher's building yard, 1832

Map 13   Building estates of St Ebbe's, 1819–38

processes were guided by the profit motive in a free market. The first example comes from Oxford, a town central to the service and agricultural economy. Map 12 shows the St Ebbe's area of the city in 1817.[5] It was a frequently flooded meadow, still marked by the defences of the civil wars. Around its fringes were market gardens and a tan-yard, characteristic of early nineteenth-century peri-urban land use. Between 1811 and 1821 Oxford's population increased by over 20 per cent. Building began in 1820 after the auction of Alderman Bricknell's estate (B and C, Map 13). In the next decade the area was laid out in streets and parcelled into small house-sized lots. The boundaries of the lots and direction of the streets reflected the old meadow boundaries and the watercourses. The lots were purchases and built upon in ones and twos by local men of small capital, many of them in the building trade: a mason, a college servant, a tailor, a bookbinder, and a carpenter who became a publican. In 1840, nearly half the houses were owned by those who lived in St Ebbe's. There were two major results of dividing this space into lots and building the houses in twos and threes.

5. R. J. Morris, 'The Friars and Paradise, an essay in the Building History of Oxford, 1801–61', *Oxoniensia*, **36** (1971).

Map 14   Houses in Blackfriars Road, Oxford

Visually, there was infinite variety upon a theme (Map 14). Each house or group of houses varied in small details, in the choice of brick or in the height or absence of cellars below the houses. This gave considerable relief to the potential dullness of some of the poorest streets in Oxford. The other result was less happy. When Henry Wentworth Acland, Lee's Reader in Anatomy at the University, wrote about the cholera epidemic of 1854 he produced a map (Map 15) which directed special attention to the recently built houses of St Ebbe's. The black dots and squares which represented the deaths in that and previous epidemics were concentrated in those new houses. What had happened was that each developer had behaved with impeccable logic within the boundaries of his own plot. A well was sunk for water supply. A soak hole was dug for human waste. However, St Ebbe's was a low-lying, waterlogged area liable to flooding. That was why the cost of the land was low enough to make it profitable for low-income housing. Now cholera is principally a waterborne disease, so that the environment of St Ebbe's was ideal for carrying infection from soak hole to water supply to new victim. Rational decisions taken by individuals under the constraint of the free market added up to the collective disaster recorded on Acland's map.

The example of infilling comes from the textile metropolis of Leeds.[6] William Lupton had been in financial difficulties before his death but left his widow with land at the north end of Leeds. The long narrow closes of the enclosed fields to the manor of Leeds were already occupied by a woollen mill and its reservoir and with the house and outbuildings of a gentleman merchant. As often happens, incidents in the family history of individuals, in this

6. M.W. Beresford, *East End, West End. The Face of Leeds During Urbanisation, 1648–1842* (Leeds, The Thoresby Society, vols. 60 and 61, 1989).

Map 15   St Ebbe's parish, 1854

case Mrs Lupton's widowhood, triggered the building at local level. It was only at the aggregate level that the overall pattern of building cycles appeared. In the early 1830s the property was divided into lots and advertised for sale (Map 16). Again a selection of builders and tradesmen were the developers. The result was an untidy variety of property, despite the attempt of Mrs Lupton and her advisers to impose order by laying out Merrion and Belgrave Streets. Map 17 shows the variety of property, back-to-back and through houses, an independent chapel and the increasingly cramped merchant houses.

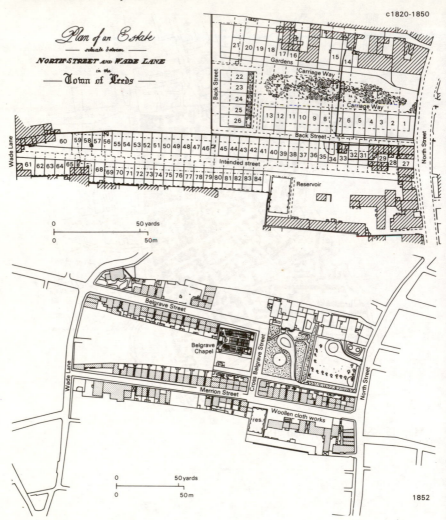

Maps 16–17 Building development of Mrs Lupton's estate, Leeds, 1820–52

An important shift in the spatial organization of this housing has been pointed out by Martin Daunton.[7] It is well illustrated by the maps of working-class housing in Nottingham drawn from the 1844–5 Health of Towns commission (Maps 18–19). Whilst towns have always had streets, the poorer housing was grouped

7. Martin Daunton, *House and Home in the Victorian City: Working Class Housing, 1850–1914* (London 1983).

58

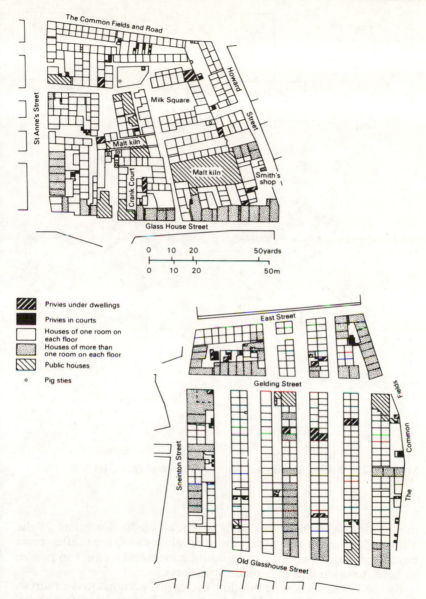

Maps 18–19   Nottingham housing, 1844

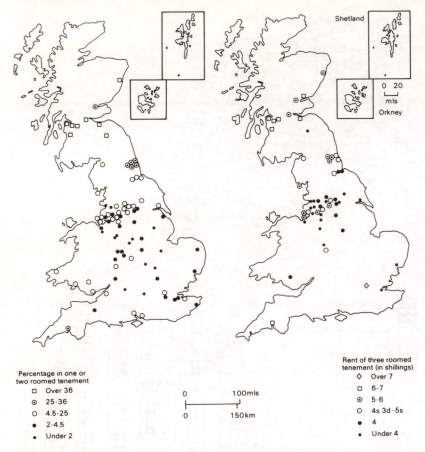

Percentage in one or
two roomed tenement

□ Over 36
⊙ 25-36
○ 4.5-25
● 2-4.5
• Under 2

Rent of three roomed
tenement (in shillings)
◇ Over 7
□ 6-7
⊙ 5-6
○ 4s 3d -5s
● 4
• Under 4

0   100mls
├──────────────┤
0   150km

Maps 20–21   British housing acccommodation and rents, 1905

in a disorderly manner in courts and fold yards. Sometime in the 1820s, often under the influence of local by-laws, town after town began building its working-class housing in streets – easier to police, to light, to drain and to provide with services.

By the 1900s, successive building cycles had accumulated hundreds and thousands of working-class dwellings in British cities. Industrialization did not bring uniformity. We do not yet know enough about regional building styles to map them with precision; although the broad outline of tenements in Scotland, back-to-backs in the north and Midlands are clear, details such as the Tyneside flats and Lancashire yarded houses are not. The information gathered for

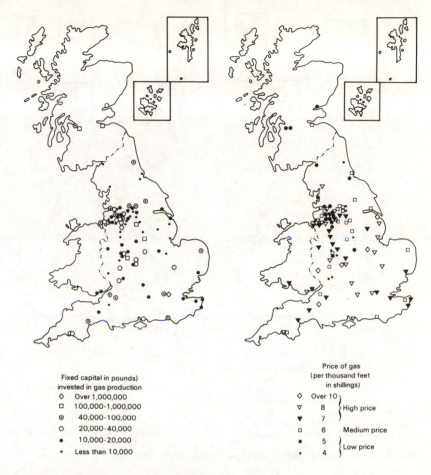

Maps 22–23   Urban public utilities: gas, 1847

the Board of Trade cost of living enquiries in 1908 showed the results of regional variation (Maps 20–21). Scotland was a high cost, overcrowded area. The north was overcrowded and low cost, whilst London was a high-cost focus.

British towns involved large accumulations of fixed capital in services and infrastructure. By 1850, nearly £12 million at historic cost had been invested in the fixed capital of the gas industry.[8] Most

8. M.E. Falkus, 'The British Gas Industry before 1850', *Economic History Review*, 2nd series, **20** (1967).

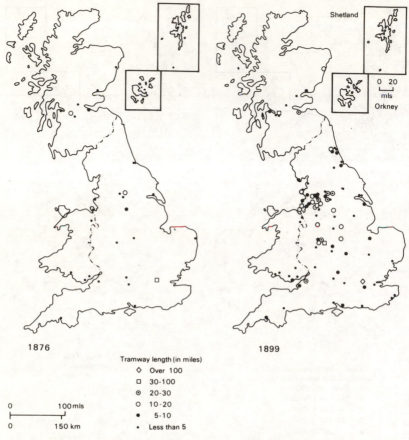

1876   1899

Tramway length (in miles)

◇   Over 100
□   30-100
⊙   20-30
○   10-20
●   5-10
·   Less than 5

Maps 24–25   Urban public utilities: trams, 1876–99

towns over 2500 in population were supplied. It was used mainly for lighting streets and business property. The major agglomerations had been incorporated by Act of Parliament (Map 22). The distributive pattern of gas prices (Map 23) was in part a regional one reflecting access to suitable coalfields and to the cheap transport costs of the coastal route, and, in part a reflection of town size, company age and management efficiency. Tramways also needed parliamentary approval. The first wave (Map 24) showed that London, Scotland and Yorkshire were areas of innovation; by 1899 (Map 25), the overall pattern of large urban centres had begun to assert itself.

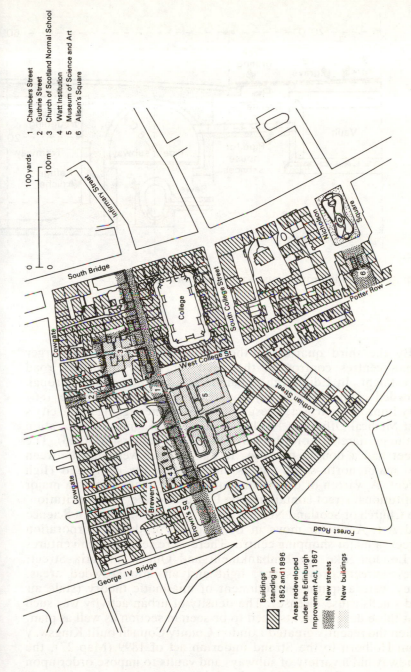

Map 26 Urban improvements: Edinburgh, 1852 and 1896

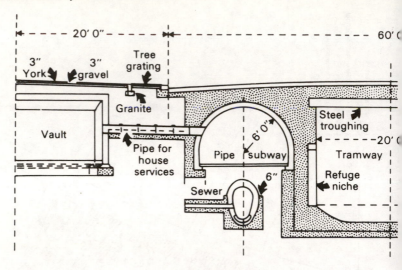

Map 27   Urban improvements: Kingsway, London, 1903

By the third quarter of the nineteenth century, the larger urban centres confronted the need for major inner-city road investment. In Edinburgh, Chambers Street was driven through crowded eighteenth-century squares and wynds under the 1867 City Improvement Act, a result of the constant nagging of the city's first Medical Officer of Health, Dr Littlejohn, and the inspiration of the patriarchal Lord Provost, William Chambers (Map 26). The street had a double purpose. It was an east–west link between two major north–south routes and avoided the congested High Street. A warren of courts and squares was changed into a major institutional street containing the University, the Watt Institution, the Church of Scotland Normal School and the Museum of Science and Art. A similar move in Birmingham produced Corporation Street, a major shopping centre. There were several such ventures in London, like the Embankment and Queen Victoria Street. These streets drove space, light and air into crowded areas. They were a spatial embodiment of miasmatic theory (stale air and smells cause disease). The density of urban activity was such that these developments need to be seen in section as well as plan. When the recently created London County Council built Kingsway from Holborn to the Strand under an act of 1899 (Map 27), the roadway hid a variety of subways and vaults to impose order upon the service and transport needs of the new street.

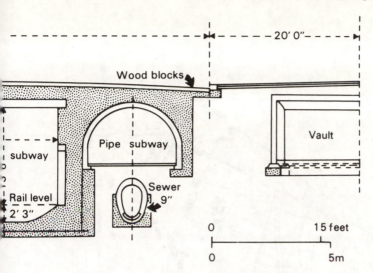

These services and new forms of transport were themselves a means of transforming the shape and use of cities. The British pattern was that of Edinburgh in which the tram and train followed the builder and by doing so stimulated further advance within walking distance of the terminus. The 1895 map (Map 28) showed the fingers of new building in the suburbs of Morningside and Newington. The stations of the suburban railway provided another link to the centre. The London 1905 map (Map 29) showed the massive rent gradient that was developing in the expanding cities. This meant that those with adequate income and regular work could use the new forms of transport to make dramatic improvements in the space and quality of their environment. The electric trams from Greenwich to Waterloo or from Enfield to the City cost a shilling a week at the early-morning workmen's fare.

During the nineteenth century the social characteristics of the population began to assume distinct spatial patterns, although historians are not as sure as they once were about the exact nature of these distributions. David Ward's analysis of status in Leeds showed that simple class-segregation was an inadequate account.[9] There were areas of high status especially in the west end and west suburbs, but most other areas contained significant proportions of high-status residents (Map 30). More detailed analysis of neighbourhoods and their patterns is necessary before surer statements can be made. Nor

9. David Ward, 'Environs and neighbours in "Two Nations", *Journal of Historical Geography*, **6**, (1980).

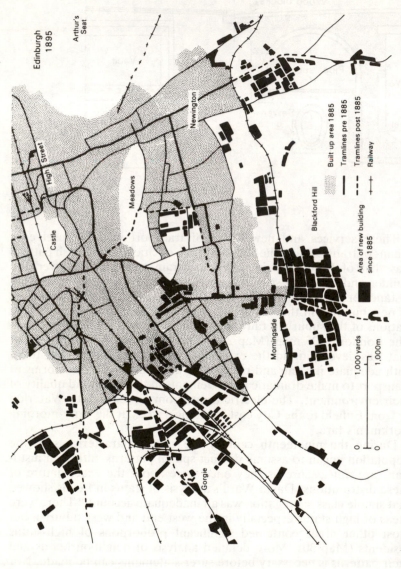

Map 28 Tramways and building in Edinburgh, 1885–95

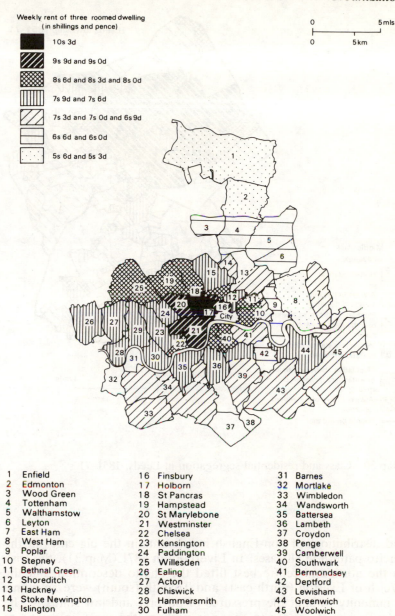

Weekly rent of three roomed dwelling
(in shillings and pence)

■	10s 3d
▨	9s 9d and 9s 0d
▩	8s 6d and 8s 3d and 8s 0d
▥	7s 9d and 7s 6d
▧	7s 3d and 7s 0d and 6s 9d
▤	6s 6d and 6s 0d
⸭	5s 6d and 5s 3d

0		5 mls
0	5 km	

1	Enfield	16	Finsbury	31	Barnes
2	Edmonton	17	Holborn	32	Mortlake
3	Wood Green	18	St Pancras	33	Wimbledon
4	Tottenham	19	Hampstead	34	Wandsworth
5	Walthamstow	20	St Marylebone	35	Battersea
6	Leyton	21	Westminster	36	Lambeth
7	East Ham	22	Chelsea	37	Croydon
8	West Ham	23	Kensington	38	Penge
9	Poplar	24	Paddington	39	Camberwell
10	Stepney	25	Willesden	40	Southwark
11	Bethnal Green	26	Ealing	41	Bermondsey
12	Shoreditch	27	Acton	42	Deptford
13	Hackney	28	Chiswick	43	Lewisham
14	Stoke Newington	29	Hammersmith	44	Greenwich
15	Islington	30	Fulham	45	Woolwich

Map 29   Rents in London, 1905

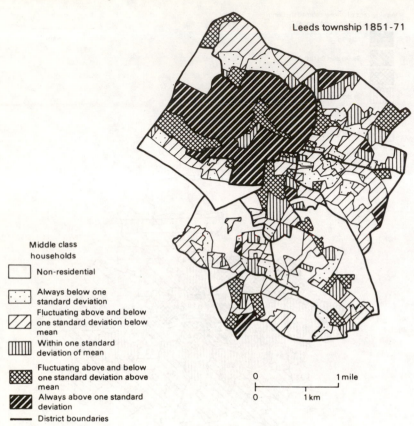

Leeds township 1851-71

Middle class
households

☐ Non-residential

⠿ Always below one
standard deviation

▨ Fluctuating above and below
one standard deviation below
mean

▥ Within one standard
deviation of mean

▨ Fluctuating above and below
one standard deviation above
mean

▨ Always above one standard
deviation

━━ District boundaries

0 ━━━━ 1 mile

0 ━━━━ 1 km

Map 30   Class and residential segregation in Leeds, 1851–71

did distributions of non-English immigrants in the big cities fit the
ghetto pattern in all cases. In Liverpool in 1871 (Map 31), the Irish
in the north and centre best fitted the ghetto description, but the
Welsh of Everton (north-east) and Toxteth (south) were an ethnic
community without the pressures of poverty and low status.[10] The
relationship of gender to space is perhaps the most enigmatic to
historians. Leeds in 1841 (Map 32) shows that higher proportions

10. Colin Pooley, 'Migrants in mid-Victorian Liverpool', *Transactions of the Institute
of British Geographers*, n.s.**2** (1977)

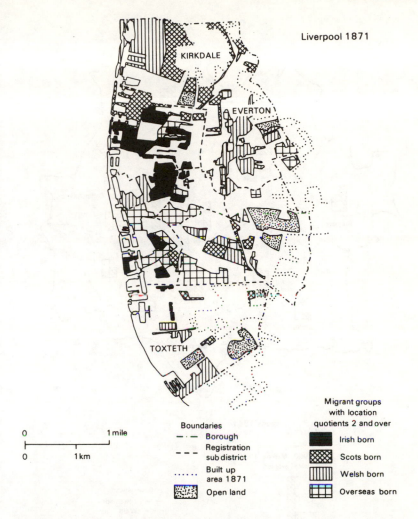

Map 31   Ethnicity in Liverpool, 1871

of women were found in high-status areas. These were areas full of female servants but also with many middle-class widows and spinsters. There was also a slight tendency for the female proportion to rise in the lowest-status areas, perhaps reflecting the low-paid female labour in textiles.

69

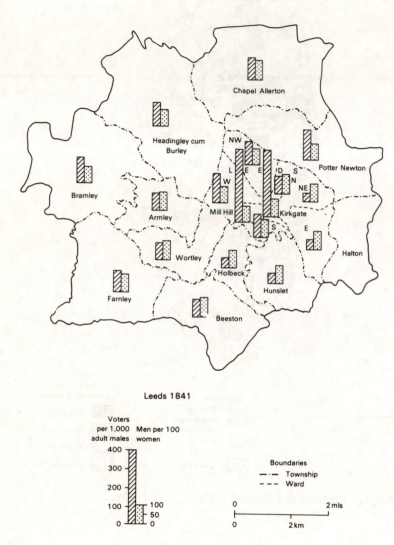

Leeds 1841

Map 32   Gender and status in Leeds, 1841

of women were found in high status areas. These were 'new'
of Leeds suburbs and areas with annual rental of houses and
suburbs. There is also evidence to suggest the reverse proportion
ratios in the lower-status areas, or that a certain class, few had
female labour to exploit.

SOURCES OF MAPS

Maps 1–6 Derived from the data set used by Robson (1973). I am grateful to Professor Robson for allowing me to use this data.

Map 7 Derived from Ordnance Survey 1:10560, Yorkshire Sheet 6, surveyed 1853 and published 1857.

Map 8 Derived from Ordnance Survey 1:10560, Yorkshire (North Riding) Sheet 6. SW and SE divisions, surveyed 1892–3 and published 1895.

Map 9 From Cannadine (see Note 3) and Ordnance Survey map 1:10560, 2nd edn, 1900, Sussex (East) Sheet 80 SW.

Maps 10–11 From Checkland (see Note 4), 44 and 47. My thanks to Professor Checkland for permission to use his work.

Map 12 From *A New Map of the University and City of Oxford*, 1812, published by R. Pearse, High Street, Oxford.

Maps 13–14 From the map and drawing prepared by Barbara Morris for Morris (see Note 5).

Map 15 From H.W. Acland (1856) *Memoir of the Cholera at Oxford in the year 1854*, London.

Map 16 From Business Archives, Lupton 127, Brotherton, Library, University of Leeds. My thanks to Mr P. Morrish for showing me these papers.

Map 17 Derived from Ordnance Survey 1:1056 Leeds, Sheet 11, surveyed 1847 and published 1850.

Maps 18–19 *First Report of the Commissioners for Inquiring into the State of Large Towns and Populous Districts*, BPP (HC) 1844, XVII, appendix, 143.

Maps 20–21 *Report of an Enquiry by the Board of Trade into Working Class Rents, Housing and Retail Prices . . . in the Principal Industrial Towns of the United Kingdom*, 590–3. BPP (HC) 1908, CVII.

Maps 22–23 *Returns from Gas Companies Established by Act of Parliament*, BPP (HC) 1847, XLIV.

Maps 24–25 *Return of Street and Road Tramways Showing the Amount of Capital Authorized and the Length Opened for Public Conveyance from the Passing of 'The Tramways Act, 1870' down to the 30th June 1876*, BPP (HC) 1877, LXXIII.

Map 26 Derived from the Ordnance Survey five-foot plan of Edinburgh, Sheets 35 and 36, published 1852, and five-foot plan of Edinburgh, sheets 111.8.16 and 21, resurveyed 1893–4 and published 1895.

Map 27 *Royal Commission on London Traffic*, vol. 5, BPP (HC) 1906, XLIV, plate XVIII.

Map 28 *Royal Commission on London Traffic*, vol. 7, BPP (HC) 1906, XLII, appendix J, diagram 12.

Map 29 As for Maps 20–21 but pp. 6–7.

Map 30 Derived from Ward (see Note 1), 152. My thanks to Professor Ward for permission to use this material.

Map 31 From Pooley (see Note 10). My thanks to Colin Pooley for permission to use his work.

Map 32 From the *Census Abstract* of 1841 and *The Leeds Parliamentary Poll Book*, Leeds 1841.

Chapter 3

EMPLOYMENT, WAGES AND POVERTY IN THE SCOTTISH CITIES 1840–1914

Richard Rodger

[from G. Gordon (ed.), *Perspectives of the Scottish City* (Aberdeen: Aberdeen University Press, 1985), pp. 25–63]

This study shows how, despite the spread of industrialization and the pace of urbanization, the character of urban areas remained distinctive in socioeconomic terms due to the varied nature of local employment opportunities. It was not simply a matter of the type of work, though for example, the professional and service sector of Edinburgh contrasted starkly with the staple employment in Dundee's jute industry, or the heavy industrial base of engineering and allied metal-working together with textiles in Glasgow. It was that these sectoral patterns themselves introduced many other subtleties – the proportion of working women, married single and widowed, varied according to types of employment, and specific branches of manufacturing for both men and women were susceptible to short time, seasonality and differential levels of unemployment during economic recession. Perhaps more significantly, this meant pronounced contrasts in absolute levels of wages, with consequences for patterns of consumption. Rodger shows that expenditure patterns were linked to the quality and quantity of affordable accommodation, and that housing standards in turn were correlated positively not just with predictable indicators such as infant mortality and life expectancy, but with child development generally. Employment characteristics and not just wage or skill levels, thus connect the economic base of urban areas with behavioural patterns, bonding those with common daily routines. The study shows four things: the continuing variety of employment experiences throughout the nineteenth century; some explanations for a distinctive Scottish urban culture; the oversimplification of analyses along class lines which refer to an undifferentiated middle or working class;

*and that the house, street and shop were important in forging
local identities, since trade unions and other formal associational
activities and institutions were mainly male spheres.*

I

At the dawn of the Victorian age Scotland had already achieved a
place among the elite in the industrial league table.[1] In the slipstream
of the English economy Scottish cotton textiles and the iron industry
projected Scottish industry to international eminence, based not only
on an amalgam of accumulated advantages – developed banking
structure, educational attainment, agricultural and intellectual en-
lightenment, social mobility – but also on real economic leverage,
lower unit costs of production. This leverage was in fact two-
fold: firstly, labour costs conspicuously lower than in her major
competitor, England; secondly, locational advantages, geological in
the coal and iron industries, geographical in the cotton industry, both
of which conveyed a sufficient edge to secure a Scottish foothold in
the industrialization of western Europe. Technological solutions to
the metallurgical problems of coke smelting in the iron industry and
to the mechanization of cotton textile production, pioneered in the
main in England and only adopted haltingly in eighteenth-century
Scotland, experienced a rapidity of diffusion in the nineteenth
century which contributed to a technical leadership with possibilities
for self-sustaining growth and expansion in late Victorian Scottish
industry. Underlying the transmission of an initial forward impulse
to the Scottish economy was a favourable, partly fortuitous, factor
endowment. Cotton textiles, coal and iron working proceeded on the
basis of standardized, mechanized and thus unskilled or semi-skilled
labour fused with low priced raw materials – cheap cotton imports,
suitable, accessible and abundant coal and iron deposits.

Factor endowments, both raw material and labour, proved not
inexhaustible. Urban immigration and natural increase slowed while
emigration accelerated; ore and coal seams encountered geological

---

1. For accounts of the industrial revolution in Scotland see for example R.H. Campbell *Scotland Since 1707* (Oxford 1965), and *The Rise and Fall of Scottish Industry
   1707–1939* (Edinburgh 1980); A Slaven *The Development of the West of Scotland
   1750–1960* (London 1975); S. G. E. Lythe and J. Butt *An Economic History
   of Scotland, 1100–1939* (Glasgow 1975); B. Lenman *An Economic History
   of Modern Scotland 1660–1976* (London 1977); C.H. Lee 'Modern Economic
   Growth and Structural Change in Scotland: the Service Sector Reconsidered'
   Scottish Economic and Social History 3 1983, pp. 115–35 provides a critique of
   these and other approaches to Scottish economic growth.

difficulties and diminishing returns; cotton imports were subject to interruptions and fluctuations, and output to increasing foreign competition. The balance of responsibility for continued industrial expansion passed after the 1870s increasingly to the specialized and highly skilled heavy engineering and shipbuilding sectors. But while this blood transfusion to the Scottish industrial economy sustained the aggregate performance in the intervening years before World War I, it simultaneously generated immense problems of adjustment for those workers previously at the spearhead of the economy.

This picture is, of course, the 'authorized version', the textbook treatment of Scottish industrialization. And yet it is really a Clydeside/Clydesdale version. Lip-service is paid to minor aberrations, pockets of industrial non-conformity – Dundee jute, Kirkcaldy linoleum, Dunfermline linens. To music hall comedians and general public alike the archetypal Scot is a Glaswegian. The assumed homogeneity could not be further from reality and the variance between the four principal cities of Scotland, viewed through their employment structure which is central to this chapter, offers some light on the economic and social diversity in Victorian Scotland. Nonetheless, some common denominators such as the causes of poverty and attitudes to it are briefly examined because of their general relevance to each of the Scottish cities.

II

Scottish middle-class attitudes to unemployment reflected for much of the Victorian age prevailing responses to poverty and urban discipline in general.[2] Intemperance, idleness and moral degeneracy were interpreted as character defects, remediable only through denial of relief and the recognition that no institutional long-stop existed to cushion the impact of unemployment. Personal revelation and individual resurrection in the biblical sense of rediscovery and rebirth were central pillars in attitudes towards the disadvantaged in Victorian society. Understandably, middle-class concern surrounded falling church attendances, evident even in the 1850s, and with this instrument of moral rearmament structurally weakened at an early

---

2. A Paterson 'The Poor Law in Nineteenth Century Scotland' in D. Fraser (ed.) *The New Poor Law in the Nineteenth Century* (London 1976), pp. 171–93; O. Checkland *Philanthropy in Scotland: Social Welfare and the Voluntary Principle* (Edinburgh 1980), pp. 30–64, 90–191; A.S. Wohl *The Eternal Slum. Housing and Social Policy in Victorian London* (London 1977); W. Logan, *The Moral Statistics of Glasgow* (Glasgow 1844).

stage, philanthropic gestures offered limited short-term palliatives to the unemployed and poor, whilst simultaneously appeasing middle-class consciences. Whether motivated out of evangelical ardour, concern for safety on the streets, or the containment of disease and moral contamination, cleansing the moral environment was complementary to cleansing the physical environment of burghs, and Scottish pamphleteers missed few opportunities to exhort constant vigilance in the campaign for improved urban behaviour. Entirely consistent with such fears and aspirations, middle-class attitudes to unemployment, as reflected in editorial columns, letters to news-papers, societies, official enquiries and committee reports, stressed non-intervention from officialdom on the grounds that fundamental character reform was the only enduring solution. Any other approach not only failed to offer a long-term solution, but made it more remote by rewarding indiscipline and idleness.

In a Scottish urban context it has been noted that this Victorian self-help stance on unemployment, and poverty in general, under-went some revision in the 1890s.[3] As the Tory chairman of a Glasgow Parish Council stated in 1901, 'Hitherto the administrators of the Poor Law have had to accept final results, and act without regard to causes; but the relief of this class (unemployed) cannot be satisfactorily undertaken without breaking that ancient policy. Now the time would seem to have come when power should be transferred on Parish Councils to take causes of pauperism into account.'[4] Almost certainly the philosophical debate and startling sociological research of Mearns, Mayhew, Booth, Rowntree and others had some role in this regard, arguing as they did that 27–43 per cent of primary poverty was directly attributable to sickness, old age, widowhood, and family size, that is, irrespective of the will to work.[5] More recently Rose has confirmed the upper estimates of contemporaries as more accurate.[6] Nowhere better illustrated the triangle of employment–poverty–morality than both the rag trade, which depressed Sherwell sufficiently to conclude in 1897 that 'morals fluctuate with trade',[7] and port employment, where Drage's study of dockers showed that between October 1891 and

3. J. H. Treble *Urban Poverty in Britain 1830–1914* (London, 1979), p. 52, and 'Unemployment and Unemployment Policies in Glasgow 1890–1905', in P. Thane (ed.) *The Origins of British Social Policy* (London 1978), pp. 147–72; I. Levitt, 'The Scottish Poor Law and Unemployment, 1890–1929' in T.C. Smout, (ed.), *The Search for Wealth and Stability: Essays in Economic and Social History presented to M.W. Flinn* (London 1979), pp. 263–8.
4. I. Levitt *op. cit.* pp. 266–7.
5. J.R. Hay *The Origins of the Liberal Welfare Reforms, 1906–14* (London 1975) and references cited.
6. M.E. Rose *The Relief of Poverty 1834–1914* (London 1972), pp. 15–16.
7. A. Sherwell *Life in West London* (London 1897), p. 146.

March 1892 employment exhibited severe volatility, the numbers ranging in London in each month from 1,350 to 4,000.[8] English parallels did not go unremarked in Scotland.[9] The social conditions of neighbourhoods in London St Giles and Seven Dials, other provincial cities and Scottish burghs were compared, especially with reference to the unsafe nature of the streets, and related to the intensification of problems associated with irregular employment in Scotland from about 1860 to 1900.[10]

That the role of the Christian church in the reformation of character was central to the remedial efforts to deal with poverty in Scottish burghs remained unshakeable. 'It is essentially the function of the Christian church to organize such agencies and to bring to bear such influences as shall move the poor to live decent and clean lives in the decent and clean houses provided for them', argued the Presbytery of Glasgow in their Report on the Housing of the Poor in 1891.[11] The acceptance of their responsibility and that of the town council was explicit: 'The work of the Corporation and the work of the Church must go hand in hand.'[12] If this moral rearmament did no more than reassert the central tenets of Victorian social policy, one important departure gave the key to the direction opinion, and ultimately policy, was moving. The report noted that, 'sheer poverty has much to answer for',[13] a conclusion based upon employment patterns. One witness, Glasier, when asked, 'You are of opinion (*sic*) that poverty is the chief, if not the only cause of the crowded and insanitary dwellings of the poor?', replied emphatically, 'Exactly', and referred particularly to labourers, foundry workers, warehouse porters, cobblers and, significantly, 'old and debilitated workmen, widows with little children and women and girls without male support' as the sources of poverty.[14] More specifically and in relation to immigrants, it was 'the fact that the bulk of them are not craftsmen' and that 'they get very uncertain work' that consigned them, their families and succeeding generations to poverty. In general, it was both the employment structure and remuneration levels which created poverty, and Glasier concurred with his questioner 'that there are many families whose position is not due in any measure to drunkenness or sloth, or any other form of

8. G. Drage *The Unemployed* (London 1894), pp. 130–1.
9. O. Checkland *op. cit.* p. 338.
10. Presbytery of Glasgow *Report of Commission on the Housing of the Poor in Relation to their Social Condition* (Glasgow 1891), p. 10, and Evidence of J. Morrison p. 54.
11. *Ibid.* p. 22.
12. *Ibid.* See also S. Mechie *The Church and Scottish Social Development 1780–1870* (London 1960).
13. Presbytery of Glasgow Report *op. cit.*
14. *Ibid.* Evidence of Glasier, pp. 178–9.

personal misbehaviour'.[15] In 1890 Glasier identified in Glasgow 4,500 dock labourers, 3,144 tailors, 4,850 carters and 5,293 iron workers, themselves totalling nearly 18,000 workers but representative of a much larger pool of 50,000 adult men 'who do not average more than 20s. a week'. This accounted for 27 per cent of the occupied adult male workforce and took no account of thousands of vagrants, of the irregularly employed, or of customarily low-paid female workers. What Glasier demonstrated conclusively was that with wages of £1 per week, or £52 over the year, 27 per cent of Glasgow workers were expected to feed, clothe and house their families on less than it cost the City Poor House (£55 9s 2d) or the Prison (£62 13s 3½d) per year for an equivalent number of inmates in their care. Telling, informed and quantified, such bald inconsistencies did much to loosen the mortar of the character deficiency argument though its adherents still managed to reassert the theme to enquiries in 1902–3, 1911 and 1911–17.

If economic theory, social investigations and philosophical debate were from the 1880s undermining the unanimity of character deficiency as an explanation of poverty, a faltering industrial performance and declining military capability accelerated the process. Within the space of fifteen to twenty years of Glasier's remarks, workmen's compensation for accidents, old age pensions, sickness and unemployment insurance, welfare entitlements ranging from school meals to milk and medical inspections, further restrictions on the length of the working day judged prejudicial to health, minimum wages in sweated trades, and early closing and general restraints on shop hours reflected a tacit acceptance of the fundamental causes of poverty – inadequate income.

Such diversity of legislative initiatives implicitly recognized that inadequate income stemmed from several sources – irregular work, casual and seasonal, low-paid sweated work, often female, and domestic circumstances, such as large family size, widowhood, interrupted earnings due to disablement or disease. However hesitantly, the distributional implications of industrialization were in receipt of some attention, though these industrial casualties were in no way considered in a socialist, Marxist or paternalist framework, but more in keeping with entrenched liberal views of assisting individuals to get back on their financial feet.[16]

15. *Ibid*. p. 179.
16. For an interesting view of housing provision on this aspect see J. Melling, 'Employers, Industrial Housing and the Evolution of Company Welfare Policies in Britain's Heavy Industry: West Scotland 1870–1920', *International Review of Social History* 26 1981, pp. 255–301.

III

The number of low and irregularly paid workers, and equally important their susceptibility to trade fluctuations, was crucial to the depth and extent of poverty in the Scottish cities. Put another way, the stability of employment prospects, the dependability of work allowed predictability and continuity of consumption patterns at above minimum levels. Table 1 shows that the occupational composition of the four Scottish cities was dissimilar in some essentials.[17]

Logically, in an urban setting, agriculture and fishing maintained only a minimal presence. If anything its importance declined after mid-century as the sophistication of the Scottish urban economy eroded agricultural opportunities within urban boundaries. Exceptional to this pattern was Aberdeen. The third quarter of the nineteenth century saw a sustained expansion in east coast herring fishing, with Aberdeen gaining an important role as a fishing station.[18] Thereafter, with occasional interruptions, the availability of transport and credit facilities assisted Aberdeen to attain a position of paramountcy in the expansion of the herring fishery. Curing, gutting and packing offered sizeable if seasonal employment for women, as reflected in the 1911 figures.

Commercial employment – merchants, dealers, bankers, accountants, valuers, clerks, insurance agents, salesmen, railway, road and other employees in distribution – displayed rather different characteristics. Firstly, consistent with a developing economy and

---

17. The occupational classifications used throughout this chapter are essentially those of W.A. Armstrong 'The Use of Information about Occupation' in E.A. Wrigley (ed.), *Nineteenth Century Society: Essays in the Use of Quantitative Methods for the Study of Social Data* (Cambridge 1972), pp. 191–310. Adaptations in a Scottish context are explained in R.Q. Gray *The Labour Aristocracy in Victorian Edinburgh* (Oxford 1976), Appendix II. In the interests of brevity a full explanation of Scottish occupational classification in the Scottish cities is not given here but is available from the author. Though relegated to a footnote, two methodological points should be made. Firstly, classification of the 1841 Census is acknowledged to be weak. Secondly, the classification of female employment, particularly in relation to textile and domestic work, is problematical. Orders of magnitude and trends are more appropriate in this census than precise percentage measures of occupational activity. Occupational data have been extracted from the following censuses of Great Britain, and Scotland: *PP 1844 XXVII*; *PP 1852–53 LXXXVIII Pt. II*; *PP 1862 L*; *PP 1873 LXXII*; *PP 1883 LXXXI*; *PP 1893–94 CVIII*; *PP 1904 CVIII*; *PP 1912–13 CXIX*; *PP 1913 LXXX*.
18. M. Gray 'Organisation and Growth in the East Coast Herring Fishing 1800–1885' in P.L. Payne (ed.) *Studies in Scottish Business History* (London 1967), pp. 206–13, and *The Fishing Industries of Scotland 1790–1914: a Study on Regional Adaptation* (Aberdeen 1978), pp. 166–80.

TABLE 1 Occupational structure in Scottish cities 1841-1911[a]

| | | | | | | | | % Employment by sector, sex | | | |
| | Professional | | Domestic | | Commercial | | Agriculture and fishing | | Industrial | |
	M	F	M	F	M	F	M	F	M	F
1841										
Glasgow (+ suburbs)	4.53	0.57	2.03	31.60	15.09	2.87	4.43	0.37	73.92	64.59
Edinburgh (+ suburbs)	13.34	1.93	6.53	70.36	14.10	2.71	2.77	1.39	63.26	23.61
Dundee	4.98	0.88	1.95	27.30	13.70	2.79	2.80	0.38	76.57	68.65
Aberdeen	6.46	2.24	4.05	40.37	14.57	2.44	6.21	0.97	68.71	53.98
1851[b]										
Glasgow	4.89	0.65	0.95	25.45	14.55	2.31	2.08	0.38	77.53	71.21
Dundee	3.61	0.73	0.43	14.98	11.28	1.12	1.92	0.30	82.76	82.87
Aberdeen	13.99	2.98	1.15	32.41	14.72	2.70	6.76	1.05	63.47	60.86
1871										
Glasgow	4.77	1.62	2.05	21.35	19.42	5.13	0.95	0.17	72.80	71.74
Edinburgh	12.71	4.17	3.73	55.22	16.44	5.32	3.18	0.97	63.93	34.31
Dundee	3.87	1.05	1.68	10.28	14.10	0.86	1.80	0.20	78.54	87.62
Aberdeen	9.86	2.67	1.97	34.11	18.92	2.81	5.52	1.05	63.74	59.36
1881										
Glasgow	5.18	4.63	1.13	20.66	19.71	2.31	0.69	0.21	73.29	72.19
Edinburgh	14.86	10.76	3.93	49.32	16.43	2.67	1.56	0.64	63.23	36.62
Dundee	4.20	2.64	1.21	8.38	14.54	0.53	0.91	0.09	79.14	88.36
Aberdeen	8.91	9.93	2.09	32.39	17.24	1.99	3.52	1.08	68.25	54.61

TABLE 1 *(cont.)*

		Professional		Domestic		Commercial		Agriculture and fishing		Industrial	
		M	F	M	F	M	F	M	F	M	F
						% Employment by sector, sex					
1891	Glasgow	5.18	4.55	2.03	21.26	21.70	4.42	0.47	0.20	70.63	69.57
	Edinburgh	15.64	10.70	2.61	45.87	18.80	3.80	1.51	0.28	61.45	39.35
	Dundee	4.93	3.53	0.92	10.04	15.53	0.91	1.20	0.12	77.43	85.40
	Aberdeen	9.15	9.50	0.83	31.45	21.33	3.12	4.07	0.18	64.63	55.75
1901	Glasgow	4.56	5.30	0.74	21.61	23.84	7.65	0.37	0.16	70.50	65.28
	Edinburgh	11.08	8.00	1.89	42.53	22.75	6.79	1.29	0.28	62.61	42.40
	Dundee	4.02	2.90	0.77	8.00	18.59	2.15	0.82	0.07	75.80	86.87
	Aberdeen	6.09	6.99	0.98	25.63	23.75	6.10	4.13	0.23	65.05	61.04
1911	Glasgow	10.03	7.51	0.73	19.67	19.59	3.24	0.40	0.11	69.25	69.47
	Edinburgh	15.54	9.65	2.50	39.82	15.94	2.43	1.79	3.14	64.23	44.96
	Dundee	8.23	3.58	0.89	8.54	14.56	0.93	1.13	0.07	75.19	86.88
	Aberdeen	10.16	9.26	1.10	23.75	19.27	2.61	11.16	6.02	58.31	58.36

Notes [a] Dependants included in 1861 Census.
[b] Edinburgh and Leith data combined in 1851 and therefore omitted from Table 1.

Sources See note 17.

the rise of a tertiary sector, there was a long run tendency for male employment to expand in these areas from about one in seven male workers to one in five between 1841 and 1901, though this expansion was weakest in Dundee. Secondly, the level of employment in commercial and distributive activities was in two sets of pairs throughout 1841–1911, with Glasgow and Aberdeen both similar and above Dundee and Edinburgh, which were themselves similar. Even within this broad pattern of commercial employment there were significant differences with implications for the pattern of consumption. In Edinburgh, financial prowess meant that the contribution to commercial employment from middle-class and petit-bourgeois elements was roughly equivalent to that from the transport sector with its heavier reliance on manual and unskilled workers. By contrast, in Glasgow, Aberdeen and Dundee transport workers were twice as numerous as white-collar workers in the banking, insurance and merchanting classifications. Thirdly, female commercial employment exhibited considerable instability between censuses, albeit at a low level. Although the census dates were not cyclical turning points themselves, sizeable intra-cyclical variations in commercial travelling, messengering, selling, and even telegraphy and telephones existed. Women employees in commerce and distribution were, therefore, prone to short-term shifts in employment prospects.

Interestingly, the four Scottish cities do not seem to have participated in a 'white-blouse' revolution, a secular expansion in female commercial employment opportunities in telephone exchanges, office work and related employment after 1870.[19] Nor does scrutiny of the professional tier of employment, despite rising rapidly in 1881, suggest a marked proliferation of women's work opportunities. In fact, the increase in female professional employment in 1881 is attributable to the inclusion of students in the work-force. Women students were numerically equivalent to the remainder of female professional workers – principally schoolteachers, governesses, nurses, musicians and artists – and if the percentages for professional female employment are halved in the three university towns to take account of the inclusion of students, the expansion is understandably more gradual.[20] Even so, female professional work was, in the last third of the nineteenth century, expanding, most noticeably in Edinburgh and Aberdeen and if hardly of 'revolutionary' proportions, the number of women students was at least a portent of future involvement.

Male professional employment in Aberdeen and Edinburgh was

19. P. Branca *Women in Europe since 1750* (London 1978), pp. 51–65 explains the concept. *See also* D. Garrison 'The Tender Technicians: the Feminization of Public Librarianship, 1876–1905', *Journal of Social History* 6 1972, pp. 131–59.
20. *PP 1893–94, XXI* Table LVI.

TABLE 2   Stability of employment: professional occupations 1881

| | *Percentage of occupied population* | | | | |
	Glasgow	Edinburgh	Dundee	Aberdeen	UK
Law	0.42	2.51	0.39	1.26	0.56
Medicine, dentistry	0.48	2.09	0.48	1.17	0.40
Arts, entertainment, music	0.80	1.66	0.63	0.82	0.60
Civil service	0.59	1.61	0.50	0.51	0.60
Army, navy	0.21	1.43	0.33	1.26	1.60
Teaching	0.45	0.97	0.47	0.74	0.61
Church	0.36	0.95	0.40	0.57	0.56
Police, municipal officers	0.86	0.90	0.61	0.59	0.65
Science, engineering	0.20	0.36	0.08	0.16	0.22
Total professional	4.37	12.47	3.60	7.10	5.79

Sources   Census of England and Wales 1881, *PP 1883 LXXX*; Census of
Scotland, *PP 1883 LXXXI*; C. Booth, 'Occupations of the People
of the UK, 1801–81', *Journal of the Royal Statistical Society 49
(1886): 414.*

until 1911 decisively more important than in Glasgow and Dundee.
Until 1911 some 12–15 per cent of employment in Edinburgh was
in the professions, the order of importance, for example in 1881
showing the entrenched position of legal, medical, cultural and
administrative occupations. Indeed, only in the representation of
the armed forces did Edinburgh fall below the national average and
overall the percentage of professional workers was 215 per cent that
of the UK.[21] In the most numerous branches of professional work
the Edinburgh proportion was 450–500 per cent above the national
average and the self-sustaining nature of this employment structure
can be seen by the fact that Edinburgh students were equivalent to
2.3 per cent of the workforce.[22] Comparative figures are given in
Table 2 for the other Scottish cities.

21. C. Booth 'Occupations of the People of the UK, 1801–1881', *Journal of the
    Royal Statistical Society* 49 1886, p. 414. Booth quotes the total professional
    occupied population as 5.6 per cent, rather than 5.79 per cent obtained using
    census data, *PP 1883 LXXX*.
22. *PP 1893–94, XXI* Table LVI reveals the different involvement of the city
    population in education in 1891. In Aberdeen 22.62 per cent of males, 17.85
    per cent females were in education; in Dundee 19.94 per cent males, 16.03
    per cent females; in Edinburgh 21.01 per cent males, 16.42 per cent females;
    in Glasgow 16.83 per cent of males, and 15.98 per cent of females were in
    education.

These illustrate the emphatically more stable employment base in Edinburgh with one worker in eight in professional work. Representatives of the professional middle classes in Dundee and Glasgow were not only far fewer than in Aberdeen and Edinburgh but were also below the national average. Even so, in Glasgow and Dundee some areas of professional work were better represented than in national terms – medicine and entertainment, for example, and significantly employment of police, prison and municipal officials, that is the agents of environmental and social control.

Salaried employment was synonymous with security of employment. Security of employment meant stability of income, predictability of domestic expenditure. The salary 'bargain', in contrast to the wage bargain, implied not only higher income and different terms of engagement – regular hours, notice of termination, payment in lieu of notice, pension entitlements in certain professions, an element of discretion regarding deductions for unpunctuality, and censure rather than sacking over other minor misdemeanours – but also greater security of employment. In fact a degree of regulated entry ensured insulation against the machinations of the labour market. Educational standards, articles, ordination, and medical assistantships served to regulate the professional labour supply as effectively, if not more so than the apprenticeship system for skilled manual workers. This cyclical insulation was enhanced by secular growth. The maturing industrial economy attached increasing importance to the service sector, and the professions participated in this trend. Booth calculated a rise from 3.6 per cent to 5.6 per cent between 1841 and 1881, and this upward drift with occasional interruptions and different intensity was replicated in the Scottish cities, the percentage rising from 6.9 per cent in 1841 to 7.7 per cent in 1881 and 11.02 per cent in 1911.[23] The importance of this salaried component in each city cannot be underestimated. In late Victorian Edinburgh one in seven male workers was in the professional grouping and if some such as municipal officials and entertainers lacked the status or income flow of lawyers and clerics there were other non-professional salaried occupations, as for example previously noted in the commercial sector, who compensated for them. As early as 1865 the Edinburgh Medical Officer, Henry Littlejohn, observed this peculiar occupational structure. In his famous medical report on health in Edinburgh he noted, 'Edinburgh has no pretensions to be a manufacturing city . . . the establishment of a University and of the highest courts of judicature appears to have diverted the attention of the inhabitants from mercantile pursuits.'[24] Littlejohn also noted

---

23. C. Booth *op. cit*; *PP 1844 XXVII*; *PP 1883 LXXXI*; *PP 1912–13 CXIX*.
24. H.D. Littlejohn *Report on the Sanitary Condition of the City of Edinburgh, with Relative Appendices, etc.* (Edinburgh 1865), p. 45.

the attraction of Edinburgh to the gentry. Leisure and amusements, soirées and concert parties, artistic and other cultural pursuits derived substantial patronage from such a heavily represented class, and as Lee noted, 'There can be no doubt that it was the metropolitan role of Edinburgh which gave the Lothian economy its structural similarity to the South East of England and that mixture of professions, commerce, personal services and consumer goods industries such as printing and publishing.'[25] Dundee, at the other end of the spectrum, offered professional employment to no more than one male worker in twenty during the Victorian era, and the stabilising, counter-cyclical consumption patterns were correspondingly weak.

The importance of this hard core of professional occupations was not confined to the middle classes themselves. The size and stability affected the strength of demand locally for a broad range of goods and services. The aggregate effect of a higher marginal propensity to save amongst the middle classes was more than offset by the regularity and scale of expenditure, and this injection of purchasing power sustained ancillary occupations to varying degrees in the four Scottish cities. Retailing, housing maintenance and clothing were amongst those branches of employment in which middle-class patronage cushioned variations in the volume of overall business. Just as professional employment was important in Edinburgh for its stabilising qualities, so the reduced presence of the professional element was of major significance to the employment structure of Dundee and Glasgow, denying a counterweight to the volatility of manufacturing employment.

Closely associated with the purchasing power of the middle class was the demand for domestic service (Table 1). This was pre-eminently a female sphere of work; employment for male servants, mostly coachmen, grooms and gardeners, though most resilient in Edinburgh, diminishing from 3.3 per cent of the occupied workforce of the four cities in 1841 to a nadir of 1.0 per cent in 1901. Widely divergent patterns of female employment existed in the four cities. In Edinburgh, the concentration of middle-class demand patterns generated unprecedented opportunities for women, 70 per cent of the female workforce in 1841 being in domestic service, four out of five of whom were indoor servants in private houses. Although this ratio of indoor servants remained much the same over the mid-Victorian censuses, by 1871 female domestic service in Edinburgh

25. C.H. Lee *op. cit.* p. 22; J. Heiton *The Castes of Edinburgh* (2nd edn Edinburgh 1860), p. 37. *See also* T.C. Smout *A History of the Scottish People 1560–1830* (London 1969), pp. 366–79; G. Gordon 'The Status Areas of Edinburgh in 1914' in G. Gordon and B. Dicks (eds) *Scottish Urban History* (Aberdeen 1983) pp. 168–96; R.Q. Gray *op. cit.* p. 20.

had declined to a still formidable 55 per cent of employed women.[26] Thereafter there was a 10 per cent reduction 1871–81, and three successive 7 per cent decennial reductions to 1911, so that on the eve of war 40 per cent of female employees in Edinburgh were in domestic service. The pattern was not replicated elsewhere. In Aberdeen domestic service accounted for 30–40 per cent of female employment between 1841 and 1891 and slipped to about 25 per cent in the twentieth century. The decline to 25 per cent was registered as early as the 1840s in Glasgow; thereafter it hovered around 20 per cent during the years 1871 to 1911. In Dundee, in sharp contrast to Edinburgh and Aberdeen, though echoing Glasgow at a lower level, domestic service was halved in the 1840s and following a more gradual fall in mid-century contributed a fairly steady 8–10 per cent of women's employment in the years 1871 to 1911. In each burgh, however, indoor service remained the dominant occupation; in 1911 it still accounted for seven out of ten servants.

Several features are worth stressing in relation to female employment generally. Firstly, there is some reason to believe that there was pressure on the household economics of the Scottish urban middle class. The proportion of female domestic indoor servants fell between 1881 and 1911 – from 85 per cent to 70 per cent in Edinburgh, from

TABLE 3 Female employment in Scottish cities by marital status, 1911

Age groups	Glasgow		Edinburgh		Dundee		Aberdeen	
	A	B	A	B	A	B	A	B
15–19	10.2	–	17.5	–	54.6	–	6.1	–
20–24	7.5	69.0	7.3	72.0	41.1	71.4	3.3	81.8
25–44	5.3	54.1	5.0	56.7	25.2	74.6	2.9	52.7
45–64	5.6	30.0	5.2	31.4	18.8	48.2	3.2	27.2
65–69	3.8	16.9	3.5	18.0	8.1	27.3	3.7	18.4
70+	2.8	6.5	1.8	6.8	3.9	10.1	1.1	5.3
All ages	5.5	26.5	5.1	26.4	23.4	39.0	3.0	22.6

A = % married and working B = % widowed and working
Source PP 1912–13 CXIX, Table XXIII B, pp. 35, 76, 112, 152.

26. T. McBride *The Domestic Revolution* (London 1976) argues that the apogee of domestic service was in 1891. Scottish data would confirm the rather earlier high water mark of 1871 suggested by F.K. Prochaska 'Female Philanthropy and Domestic Service in Victorian England', *Bulletin of the Institute of Historical Research* 54 1981, pp. 79–85, and M. Ebery and B. Preston, *Domestic Service in Late Victorian and Edwardian England 1871–1914* (Reading 1976). *See* E. Higgs 'Domestic Servants and Households in Victorian England', *Social History* 8 1983, pp. 201–10 for a wider discussion of these issues and the basis of census classification of domestic servants.

86 per cent to 76 per cent in Aberdeen, 77 per cent to 69 per cent in Dundee, though the proportion remained static, 74 per cent, in Glasgow. Thus in Edinburgh and Aberdeen, until the twentieth century, there was a greater reliance on indoor servants; conversely, the emphasis on occasional female work as chars and washerwomen was more pronounced in Glasgow and Dundee. Secondly, the age structure of domestic servants divided roughly equally into thirds, in the age groups 15–19, 20–24, and 25–44. Widows in domestic

TABLE 4   Ratio of widowed to married women in principal industries, 1911

	Glasgow	*Edinburgh*	*Dundee*	*Aberdeen*
Sick nurses	2.4	2.5	3.5	5.9
Domestic indoor servants				
– not hotels	1.8	2.1	2.3	1.7
– hotels		0.7		
Caretakers		2.1		3.1
Charwomen, cleaners	2.1	2.4	2.3	4.3
Laundry workers	1.1	1.1	1.6	1.9
Flax, linen manufacture			0.4	1.2
Jute manufacture			0.4	
Cotton manufacture	0.8			
Dressmakers	1.1	1.4	1.7	1.7
Shirtmakers, seamstresses	1.2	2.0		4.0
Provision dealers				1.5
Fish curers				1.1
Fishmongers, poulterers				1.3
Grocers			2.1	3.7
Greengrocers, fruiterers	1.0	1.3		
Eating house keepers				2.1
Lodging house keepers	4.1	3.9		4.8
Hawkers, street sellers	0.7	0.7	0.6	0.7
Canvas, sailcloth, sacking			0.3	
Carpeting, rugmaking			0.7	
Bakers, confectioners	1.3	1.0	1.1	
Teachers		1.9		
India, rubber, gutta percha		0.5		
Printing, bookbinding		0.8		
Paper manufacture		0.5		
Milksellers	1.1	1.4		
Shopkeepers	0.8	1.0		
Cooks (not domestic)	1.6			
Ironmongers, hardware	1.4			
Jam, preserves	0.7			

Source PP 1912–13 CXIX, Table XXIIIA, pp. 35, 76, 112, 152.

work outnumbered married women by a ratio of approximately 2:1 in each of the Scottish burghs in 1911. Thirdly, with the exception of Dundee which is discussed later, marriage was virtually synonymous with withdrawal from the labour force.

In earlier Victorian years the frequency of pregnancy and child-birth did much to impose this pattern; latterly rising real wages of the husband, if employed, enhanced emphasis on family life and the emulation of middle-class child-rearing attitudes, and diminished prospects for re-entry into a domestic sector which had stabilized or was even contracting slightly maintained married women's employ-ment at very low levels. From age twenty the proportion of working married women changed very little, a reflection of the social ac-ceptability in certain occupations and of the number of childless marriages. Finally, faced with the prospect of poverty, widows vigorously sought and obtained employment. Married women in employment exceeded widows by a ratio of at least 3.5:1 in each of the cities, but certain occupational areas were firmly associated with widows. These are shown in Table 4 where the ratio exceeds 1.0.

For example, even though in Glasgow there were four times more married than widowed working women in 1911, there were 2.4 times more widowed than married sick nurses. Thus as nurses, and teachers, shopkeepers, lodging and eating housekeepers, caretakers, chars, and laundry workers, in shirt-making and as seamstresses widows could obtain an income, however insufficient to support themselves and their families. If it did have to be supplemented by charitable societies' and distress committees' payments, it did keep them out of the workhouse. By contrast, manufacturing industry and food processing attracted more married women, and reflected their work experience as single women and as newly-weds before they had a family, and is borne out by the drop of employed married women between the 15–19 and 20–24 age groups (Table 3).

IV

For most Scottish women at the opening of the twentieth century, however, industrial work was the most common sector of employ-ment, even in Edinburgh (Table 1). Throughout the period 1841–1911 a steady 65 per cent to 72 per cent of employed Glaswegian women pursued industrial work, and in Aberdeen, too, the female industrial workforce remained consistently in the 55–60 per cent range during the Victorian and Edwardian period. In Edinburgh, with the lowest proportion of women industrial workers in 1841, approximately one in four, a mid-century expansion continued with a 10.7 per cent increase in each census between 1871 and 1901, and a further 6 per cent increase during 1901–11. Thus over the half century female industrial employment in the capital expanded by an average 1 per cent per annum, so that on the eve of war 45 per cent were in this sector – printing, bookbinding, food processing and clothing accounting for the majority. For Dundee, the 1840s were 'a prosperous period' for the textile industry.[27] Female employment already reflected this emphasis – 69 per cent of working women were textiles hands in 1841 and this jumped to 83 per cent in 1851. The outbreak of the Crimean War in 1854 'marked an unprecedented acceleration in the expansion of Dundee's already prosperous economy'[28] and from 1871 until 1911 a virtually static 85 per cent of Dundee women obtained work in textile manufacturing, despite the adversity created by foreign competition from the 1880s. No wonder Collins concluded that it was 'an almost wholly working class town'.[29]

Although the composition of male industrial employment exhibited marked differences both between the four cities and in the balance of its constituent elements, the absolute size of the industrial workforce remained remarkably constant throughout the period 1841 to 1911. Industrial employment as a percentage of the occupied workforce wavered by only one or two points either side of 77 per cent in Dundee, 72 per cent in Glasgow, 64 per cent in Aberdeen and 63 per cent in Edinburgh over the Victorian and Edwardian years (Table 1). Divergent industrial emphasis, partially reflected longstanding locational advantages in each city and the comparative advantage in costs of production in the selected specialisms of each city – centralized government, judiciary and administration in Edinburgh, accumulated textile expertise in Dundee, the cotton–iron–engineering complex of Glasgow, and fishing, quarrying and regional economic servicing in Aberdeen. Tables 5(a)–(d) show these and other branches of industrial employment for each city, and their changes over the period 1841–1911.

Certain general characteristics of industrial employment in the Scottish cities stand out. First, and most conspicuous, is the early dominance of textiles and clothing in 1841. Even in Edinburgh, though far more pronounced in the other three cities, this was the

27. B. Lenman, C. Lythe and E. Gauldie *Dundee and its Textile Industry 1851–1914* (Dundee 1969), p. 23.
28. *Ibid.*
29. B.E.A. Collins 'Aspects of Irish Immigration into Two Scottish Towns (Dundee and Paisley) during the Mid-Nineteenth Century'. Unpublished M. Phil thesis Edinburgh University 1978, p. 184.

TABLE 5(a)   Composition of Industrial Employment: Glasgow 1841–1911[a]

	1841 %	1851 %	1871 %	1881 %	1891 %	1901 %	1911 %
Printing and Publishing	1.12	1.38	1.90	2.21	2.58	2.37	2.82
Engineering, Toolmaking and Metalworking	7.17	8.67	14.08	12.81	14.17	14.84	16.86
Shipbuilding	0.35	0.14	1.33	0.68	0.72	0.84	1.80
Coachbuilding	0.40	0.13	0.48	0.46	0.62	0.63	0.72
Building	5.84	5.64	7.42	6.30	5.47	6.71	4.83
Furniture and Woodworking	1.06	1.41	1.17	1.79	1.77	2.03	3.18
Chemicals	1.22	1.00	1.17	0.64	0.60	0.79[b]	1.89[b]
Food, Drink and Tobacco	5.24	6.41	5.63	7.65	7.85	9.75	12.41
Textiles and Clothing	37.56	41.86	31.97	25.42	20.75	17.16	16.86
Other manufacturing[c]	2.90	3.36	3.32	3.21	3.37	3.45	3.34
General labouring	8.40	2.90	4.41	3.92	4.31	3.72	2.23

TABLE 5(b)   Composition of Industrial Employment: Edinburgh 1841–1911[a]

	1841 %	1871 %	1881 %	1891 %	1901 %	1911 %
Printing and Publishing	3.88	4.89	5.16	5.02	5.14	6.69
Engineering, Toolmaking and Metalworking	6.07	6.85	5.86	5.88	6.51	6.16
Shipbuilding	0.17	0.05	0.06	0.10	0.09	0.08
Coachbuilding	0.92	0.80	0.64	0.66	0.46	0.56
Building	5.73	9.64	9.28	6.92	8.98	6.24
Furniture and Woodworking	2.73	2.37	2.38	1.69	1.74	2.22
Chemicals	0.24	0.27	0.46	0.62	1.50[b]	3.22[b]
Food, Drink and Tobacco	8.31	7.36	8.54	9.34	10.40	11.57
Textiles and Clothing	13.04	14.64	11.17	11.49	10.00	11.00
Other manufacturing[c]	3.02	4.06	4.34	4.25	3.73	3.10
General labouring	3.69	2.32	1.90	2.63	1.67	1.69

largest employer. By 1911, however, the general wastage of the textile sector singled out Dundee as exceptional in the retention of this area of industrial employment.[30] A second general characteristic, to be expected, was the developing specialization of the industrial

30. A.J. Robertson 'The Decline of the Scottish Cotton Industry, 1860–1914', *Business History* 12 1970, pp. 116–28; B. Lenman *et al. op. cit.* pp. 23–42.

TABLE 5(c)   Composition of Industrial Employment: Dundee 1841–1911[a]

	1841 %	1851 %	1871 %	1881 %	1891 %	1901 %	1911 %
Printing and Publishing	0.56	0.55	0.58	0.73	0.71	1.02	1.56
Engineering, Toolmaking and Metalworking	5.59	4.38	5.63	6.11	6.10	6.54	5.62
Shipbuilding	1.14	0.91	1.08	1.24	2.24	1.64	1.89
Coachbuilding	0.21	0.15	0.20	0.23	0.35	0.20	0.25
Building	6.05	4.04	5.64	4.38	3.48	5.56	3.46
Furniture and Woodworking	0.77	0.90	0.63	0.78	0.84	0.94	1.86
Chemicals	0.19	0.21	0.16	0.12	0.23	0.17[b]	0.62[b]
Food, Drink and Tobacco	5.27	4.62	4.38	5.53	6.27	6.93	7.59
Textiles and Clothing	50.54	61.36	61.81	54.42	52.28	51.73	53.52
Other manufacturing[c]	1.29	0.97	1.54	1.22	1.82	0.85	0.91
General labouring	3.84	3.60	3.15	3.24	2.27	1.65	1.32

TABLE 5(d)   Composition of Industrial Employment: Aberdeen 1841–1911[a]

	1841 %	1851 %	1871 %	1881 %	1891 %	1901 %	1911 %
Printing and Publishing	0.91	1.03	1.42	1.62	1.89	2.04	2.51
Engineering, Toolmaking and Metalworking	6.32	5.04	5.89	5.76	6.02	6.50	5.78
Shipbuilding	1.24	1.14	1.37	1.01	1.24	1.19	2.54
Coachbuilding	0.34	0.19	0.56	0.57	0.72	0.76	0.78
Building	5.99	5.06	7.81	7.90	6.74	7.80	4.72
Furniture an Woodworking	0.87	0.95	1.03	1.29	1.19	1.52	2.92
Chemicals	0.37	0.22	0.70	0.52	0.52	1.81[b]	1.65[b]
Food, Drink and Tobacco	4.66	6.89	7.07	8.61	7.65	11.00	10.13
Textiles and Clothing	34.68	35.08	25.45	17.38	17.43	15.56	16.16
Other manufacturing[c]	3.18	4.69	7.23	6.16	5.81	3.13	3.12
General labouring	6.87	4.32	4.13	4.91	4.75	3.30	1.81

Notes   [a] Data for 1861 includes dependants and for purposes of comparison is excluded.
[b] Includes rubber;
[c] glass, paper, pottery, oil, cane, gum, grease.
Sources   See note 17.

base, of which mechanical engineering and metalworking in Glasgow, and printing and publishing in Edinburgh are the most obvious examples. A third feature was the effect of rising real incomes on the food, drink and tobacco industries, where the proportions employed in each burgh in 1871 were much the same as in 1841, but by 1911 had doubled.[31] Fourth, the cyclical effect of building was apparent in for example the upswing of the early 1870s, sustained into 1880–1 in Edinburgh and Aberdeen and a further example of their eclectic employment bases with stabilising and countercyclical properties.[32] The cyclical decline, post 1905, which brought a virtual cessation to housebuilding and was so serious as to warrant a special report in the 1911 census, was represented by the lowest ever recorded percentage of building workers in each burgh in 1911.[33] Woodworking offered countercyclical employment by way of compensation to some. Fifth, the 'other manufacturing' base was largest in Aberdeen and Edinburgh where diversity represented an insurance premium against trade cycle downturns. By the same token the upswing also had a reduced dynamic. Finally, the general labouring category supplemented this pattern, the pool of unskilled labour being deepest in Glasgow, and, surprisingly, Aberdeen. The implications of this casual employment of which general labouring is only a part are examined later.

Attention to changes in employment structure over time within each of the burghs should not obscure the comparative importance of a particular branch of industry at any one time. Appendix 1(a)–(g) allows a static analysis whereby for each census date, 1861 excepted, the proportionate contribution of a particular industry to the occupied workforce of a burgh is presented, and can be contrasted with the proportionate contribution in another city. While this has been done for industrial employment, a more detailed analysis of 53 occupational headings, male and female, in 1911 is presented in Appendix II and permits a static, end of period view of the relative importance of various types of employment for each city. These 'location quotients' indicate the degree to which in comparison to its proportionate contribution to Scottish employment as a whole, any one occupational grouping was represented in each of the cities. A ratio of 1.00 indicates that a particular occupation was as important proportionately to the city as it was to the country as a whole. For example, in category 12, banking (males), the ratio for Edinburgh was 2.00; there were proportionately twice as many male employees in the banking sector of the capital as there were in Scotland as a whole. In Dundee, the ratio was 0.50; banking employed proportionately half as many males in 1911 as nationally. In Glasgow,

---

31. W.H. Fraser *The Coming of the Mass Market 1850–1914* (London 1981).
32. R.G. Rodger 'Scottish Urban Housebuilding, 1870–1914'. Unpublished PhD thesis, Edinburgh University 1975, table 3.4, fig. 3.1.
33. *Ibid.* and table 5. The percentage employment in Edinburgh building trades in 1841 was in fact below that of 1911.

the ratio was 1.58; male banking employment in Glasgow was three times more significant for the composition of the workforce than it was for Dundee, was one and a half times more important than for Scotland as a whole, but made only threequarters the contribution to employment as it did in Edinburgh. Thus, the higher the ratio the more important that area of work for the city; the lower the ratio the less the significance for the composition of city employment.

In Glasgow, (Table 5(a)), traditional industries with high skill components – printing, woodworking, coachbuilding for example, enjoyed slight growth of employment at low levels. It was this trend of regular and gently expanding employment which most differentiated the aristocracy of labour for it was on this that the distinctive cultural, educational and recreational activities depended. Though intercensal variations reflected the instability of the industry, there was no long term upward or downward trend in building, and much the same applied to the 'other manufacturing' category. The chemical industry, until 1911, meant declining labour opportunities. By contrast the surge of engineering and the metal trades from the 1860s, which has been extensively covered elsewhere,[34] and food and drink industries in the 1870s compensated for the continuous decline of textiles, lower in each census after 1851.

'Edinburgh', Helen Kerr commented in 1912, 'is not an industrial centre.'[35] After finding it 'startling to discover that Edinburgh's principal occupation is that of service', Kerr observed that, excepting the service sector, 'the principal occupations would be found in printing and publishing, for which Edinburgh has always had a very high reputation, rubber works, distilling and brewing, together with the building industry and its allied trades'.[36] Presumably Kerr did not consult the censuses. Textiles and clothing and food, drink and tobacco remained the most important industries, accounting for one-fifth of all employment together, though the rankings changed with textiles and clothing conceding primacy by the turn of the century (Table 5(b)). Fragmented into small workshops and retailing concerns, Kerr could be forgiven for thinking the areas she identified as the most important, though rubber attained prominence only in the last Victorian decade, and engineering and metalworking retained its position throughout the years 1841 to 1911, employing about one worker in sixteen. As a reflection of the class composition of the capital, previously noted, the importance of the consumer

34. A. Slaven *op. cit.*; R.H. Campbell *op. cit.*; T.J. Byres 'Entrepreneurship in the Scottish Heavy Industries, 1870–1900' in P.L. Payne (ed.) *op. cit.* pp. 250–96.
35. H.L. Kerr 'Edinburgh' in H. Bosanquet (ed.), *Social Conditions in Provincial Towns* (London 1912), p. 55.
36. *Ibid.* pp. 54–5.

industries – furniture, printing, publishing and coachbuilding – was in the main greater than in the other Scottish cities, and this applied to the building industry, too, where in each census, 1841 to 1911, the proportion of the labour force in this sector was higher than in any of the other cities.[37] The same was true of the percentage employed in food, drink and tobacco. In mid-century Edinburgh this sustained about eight out of every 100 in the workforce, compared to five or six per 100 in the other cities, though the differential was eroded somewhat over the course of the Victorian period, and eventually overhauled in twentieth-century Aberdeen and Glasgow. Greater stability of demand not just for food and drink, but other essentials too, shelter and clothing, meant improved opportunities for regular manual work in the lee of Edinburgh's professional middle-class expenditure patterns. Reinforcing this regularity were two other influences. Firstly, the demand preference for high quality and thus hand-made, skilled craftsmanship. As Bremner described this in the case of jewellery, 'All the work done is of a superior kind'.[38] Consequently the labour aristocracy was heavily represented in Edinburgh, with associated implications for greater continuity of employment, higher average earnings and the growth of small savings.[39] Secondly, the size of philanthropic efforts in Edinburgh – some 150 charities disbursing £250,000 annually in the 1900s[40] – was itself a measure of comfortable life-styles in the capital, and indicated middle-class efforts to improve the comfort of others. Even this weekly buffer of approximately £7,000, like all transfer payments, gave some support to consumption levels and with marginal propensities to consume virtually 1.0 the re-circulation of this cash injection had wider employment implications for shopkeepers, landlords and small business in general.

Of the other Scottish cities, the employment, income and poverty structure of Aberdeen most closely approximated that of Edinburgh. Where national administration, bank and company headquarters, and supreme judicial functions were discharged in Edinburgh, local

---

37. R.Q. Gray *op. cit.* p. 24; I. Levitt and T.C. Smout *The State of the Scottish Working Class in 1843* (Edinburgh 1979), p. 9 note the Edinburgh-Glasgow income and wealth differential at the start of the Victorian period.
38. D. Bremner *The Industries of Scotland* (Edinburgh 1869), p. 131.
39. R.Q. Gray *op. cit.* pp. 26–7, 28–42, and 'Thrift and Working Class Mobility in Victorian Edinburgh' in A.A. MacLaren (ed.), *Social Class in Scotland: Past and Present* (Edinburgh 1976), pp. 128–42 and 'Styles of Life, the "Labour Aristocracy" and Class Relations in Later Nineteenth-Century Edinburgh', *International Review of Social History* 18 1973, pp. 428–52.
40. H.L. Kerr *op. cit.* pp. 56–8; S. Blackden 'The Poor Law and Health: A Survey of Parochial Medical Aid in Glasgow, 1845–1900' in T.C. Smout (ed.) *op. cit.* p. 262 notes that until the 1870s Edinburgh enjoyed three times as much medical treatment per 1000 population as Glasgow.

and regional responsibilities for the north-east and eastern highlands were executed from Aberdeen.[41] Coupled with an industrial base of important proportions until textile contraction, linens and woollens, in the 1850s reduced this element to half its former significance by 1881, Aberdeen enjoyed a balanced economy (Table 5(a)). This complementarity distinguished Aberdonian employment from that of Edinburgh, but conveyed a similar advantage – reasonable stability. Consumption patterns reflected this. Additionally, three other features supported the occupational balance. Firstly, the 'other manufacturing' category was more pronounced than in any other Scottish city. This diversification, associated with small workshop production, offered a degree of insurance against recession and bankruptcy in any one branch of employment. Secondly, it offered a larger pool of potential industrial developers, the 'springs of technical progress'.[42] Thirdly, Aberdeen enjoyed some industrial expansion to compensate for contraction. To offset the mid-century textile peak, food and drink, and chemicals were areas of industrial expansion after 1870, though the increase of female professional employment also from that decade was hardly likely to be accessible to unemployed linen workers. Skilled male employment by contrast was fairly steady after 1851, though there was an employment surge in coachbuilding in the 1880s, chemicals and food processing in the 1890s, and shipbuilding, woodworking and fishing related industries in the 1900s gave an impetus to skilled and unskilled alike. Employment prospects were further diversified with the presence of an important quarrying industry.[43] Amongst unskilled labourers in quarries and skilled workers in masons' and granitecutters' yards, an increasing percentage of the occupied Aberdonian male workforce found their employment, rising from 0.44 per cent in 1841 to 3.77 per cent in 1881 and to 5.23 per cent in 1911. The granite industry in fact contributed a countercyclical force, for a substantial volume of its output found its way to London, with its sustained building levels

41. R.C. Michie 'Trade and Transport in the Economic Development of North East Scotland in the Nineteenth Century', *Scottish Economic and Social History* 3 1983, pp. 66–94; M. Gray *The Fishing Industries, op. cit.* pp. 78, 179; A.A. MacLaren 'Class Formation and Class Fractions: the Aberdeen Bourgeoisie, 1830–1850' in G. Gordon and B. Dicks (eds) *op. cit.* pp. 112–29, and, *Religion and Social Class: the Disruption Years in Aberdeen* (London 1974), pp. 1–25.
42. R.S. Sayers 'The Springs of Technical Progress in Britain 1914–39', *Economic Journal*, 60 1950, pp. 275–91.
43. W. Diack *Rise and Progress of the Granite Industry in Aberdeen* (Aberdeen 1950), p. 77; T. Donnelly 'The Development of the Aberdeen Granite Industry 1750–1939'. Unpublished PhD thesis, Aberdeen University 1975.

in the 1880s, and to a wide range of civic buildings which also tended to ignore the normal trade cycle timing.[44]

In the sharpest possible contrast to this balance and diversity it was clear by 1900 that the economic base in Dundee 'was dangerously lopsided'.[45] Dundee Social Union, the Town Council and the Chamber of Commerce recognized that the burgh's fortunes were hostage to the production and market penetration of new Calcutta jute mills and random influences such as tariff barriers and wars, for example in America and Argentina.[46] Well established as a jute centre by 1841, peak expansion took place during 1861–68, in association with the American Civil War demand for bagging. The conclusion of this conflict and the Franco-Prussian War, a trade cycle downturn in 1873, and a Scottish banking and credit crisis in the late 1870s meant an abrupt reduction in jute employment. But the absence of alternatives meant that the percentage associated, however intermittently, with jute and linen employment in Dundee remained almost unchanged until World War I (Table 5(d)). In the 1900s, the sale of two shipping fleets, the migration of another to the Tyne, the decline of the whaling industry and the liquidation of Gourlay's shipbuilding yard in 1908 served to narrow further this industrial base and more than compensated for the nascent developments in electrical engineering, biscuit making, stationery and postcard manufacture.[47] Hence the absence of virile 'other manufacturing' was critical, narrowing the skill and work experience base and limiting the development options. This eclectic 'other manufacturing' grouping actually fell by 50 per cent in the 1890s. Heavy reliance on unskilled female labour meant few industries were attracted to Dundee, and the generally low and interrupted wage levels and scarcity of middle-class occupations depressed the consumer industries to levels well below those of the other Scottish

44. M.J. Daunton 'The Building Cycle and the Urban Fringe in Victorian Cities: a comment' and J.W.R. Whitehand 'The Building Cycle and the Urban Fringe in Victorian Cities: a reply', both in *Journal of Historical Geography* 4 1978, pp. 175–91; and R.G. Rodger 'The Building Cycle and the Urban Fringe in Victorian Cities: another comment', *Journal of Historical Geography* 5 1979, pp. 72–8.
45. B. Lenman *et al. op. cit.* p. 37.
46. *Ibid.* pp. 23–40; D.R. Wallace *The Romance of Jute: a Short History of the Calcutta Jute Mill Industry, 1855–1927* (London 1927).
47. S.G.E. Lythe *Gourlays of Dundee: the Rise and Fall of a Scottish Shipbuilding Firm* (Dundee 1964) and 'The Dundee Whale Fishery', *Scottish Journal of Political Economy* 11, 1964, pp. 158–69; R.C. Michie 'North-East Scotland and the Northern Whale Fishing, 1752–1893', *Northern Scotland* 3 1979, pp. 62–85; B. Lenman *et al. op. cit.* p. 38.

cities.[48] Textile wages were 20 per cent below those in Glasgow in the 1870s,[49] and in 1905 the Dundee Social Union reported that only 8 per cent of male textile workers received wages of more than £1 per week, and mostly they were mechanics and overseers, not operatives.[50] No women earned £1 a week in the jute industry. Flax and jute spinners' wages, hovering around 6–7 shillings per week in the 1850s reached a peak in the 1870s at about 12–14 shillings and then fell back to 7–10 shillings per week, 1880–1900, depending on the grade and stage of production. In 1905 the Social Union report recorded 12 shillings per week for women rovers, reelers, winders and weavers, with shift mistresses earning the highest wage of 14 shillings. Spinners (10s 4d), twisters (10 shillings) calenders, tylers and bundlers (9 shillings) were all paid at lower levels. At such rates it was more than most workers could expect to have sufficient for food and shelter, and demand for other manufactured goods and services was unresponsive to even quite large price changes.[51]

Throughout the period 1841–1911 more than 50 per cent of employment was in jute and linen textiles, and clothing, itself not noted for high wages or regular work.[52] One study reported Dundonians poorly nourished in comparison to Lancashire textile workers.[53] Almost certainly, steadier employment between 1853 and 1872 brought improving and more regular wages. But the pattern of interrupted time and lengthy unemployment thereafter were more significant determinants of health and poverty than a declining cost of living index.[54] In any event, the retailing habits and the pressure on rents caused by casual workers' need for proximity to the place of work pushed the cost of living in Dundee beyond that of any

48. J.C. Gilbert *A History of Investment Trusts in Dundee 1873–1938* (London 1939) and W.G. Kerr, *Scottish Capital on the American Credit Frontier* (Austin Texas 1976), pp. 169–89 show that the Dundee middle class were present in certain areas.

49. B. Lenman *et al. op. cit.* p. 70; Corporation of the City of Glasgow, *Glasgow Municipal Commission on the Housing of the Poor, Minutes of Evidence*, Irwin, p. 523.

50. Dundee Social Union *Report on Housing and Industrial Conditions and Medical Inspection of School Children* (Dundee 1905).

51. J.H. Treble *Urban Poverty op. cit.* p. 149 states that 'weaving households in Dundee were devoting eighty per cent of their meagre incomes during 1834 to acquire the limited range of foodstuffs which comprised their inadequate diet'.

52. J.A. Schmiechen *Sweated Industries and Sweated Labor: the London Clothing Trades, 1860–1914* (London 1984) investigates the general problems associated with employment in sweated industries.

53. J. Lennox 'Working Class Life in Dundee 1895–1903'. Unpublished PhD thesis Dundee University, quoted in B. Lenman *et al. op. cit.* p. 66.

54. B.R. Mitchell and P. Deane *Abstract of British Historical Statistics* (Cambridge 1972) gives data on cost of living in Britain generally.

other Scottish city, indeed beyond the cost of living in London.[55] Even without low wage levels the cost of living index itself throttled the volume of demand in the consumption industries of Dundee. The final quarter of the nineteenth century, therefore, witnessed intensified pressure on living standards, and the mortality rates in Dundee, which were substantially above those in the other cities, reflected this.[56] Low and irregular pay killed Dundonians by reducing affordable nutritional and accommodation standards to such minimal levels as to expose large numbers of workers, and weaken their resistance, to environmental diseases.

V

In what respects then did this employment and wage structure influence poverty and prosperity in the four Scottish cities? At the commencement of industrialization labour costs were substantially lower than in English boroughs. In the 1870s the differential, which had already narrowed somewhat, was some 10–15 per cent lower in a wide range of Scottish industries.[57] R. H. Campbell's measured judgement of the relative Scotland-UK wage levels in 1886 was of 'an unequivocal interpretation of Scotland as a low wage economy'.[58] Though high wages existed in certain sectors of the Scottish economy, rarely were these more than a few points above the national average and even then in some industries, such as silk, which employed very

55. Board of Trade *Report of Enquiry into Working Class Rents and Retail Prices with the Rates of Wages in Certain Occupations in Industrial Towns of the United Kingdom in 1912* 1913, Cd 6955, pp. xxxvi–xxxvii.
56. B. Lenman *et al. op. cit.* pp. 77–99. Dundee Dean of Guild Court responsibilities for environmental and building control were confined in the mid-nineteenth century to the central city areas. The expansion of tenement building to house the population influx associated with textile expansion was thus unsupervised and considerable structural and sanitary problems ensued. This administrative control in Dundee was far weaker than in the other cities.
57. R.G. Rodger 'The "Invisible Hand": Market Forces, Housing and the Urban Form in Victorian Cities' in D. Fraser and A. Sutcliffe (eds) *The Pursuit of Urban History* (London 1983), pp. 194–7; A.L. Bowley 'The Statistics of Wages in the United Kingdom in the Last Hundred Years', *Journal of the Royal Statistical Society* 62 1899, pp. 708–15; 63 1900, pp. 297–315; 64 1901, pp. 102–12; 68 1905, pp. 563–614; E.H. Hunt *Regional Wage Variations in Britain 1850–1914* (Oxford 1973); *PP 1887, LXXXIX*, Returns of Wages Published between 1830 and 1886; *PP 1893–94, LXXIII* (ii), Wages of the Manual Labour Classes; Industrial Remuneration Conference *Report* (London 1885) pp. 142, 515.
58. R.H. Campbell (1980) *op. cit.* p. 80.

few Scots. In fact even though the gap had narrowed further by 1912, the unweighted mean wage in the Scottish economy was 94.8 per cent of the UK wage. This position continued beyond World War I and had parallels in the salary structure too, as A.D. Campbell concluded, 'Income per head has been lower in Scotland fluctuating between 87 and 96 per cent of the United Kingdom average.'[59] This lower figure was more in keeping, with an extensive regional survey of wages undertaken by the Board of Trade in 1905.[60]

Lower wages in the four Scottish cities would have been of no great import had prices been correspondingly lower. In fact, as the Board of Trade noted in 1912, they were not.[61] Scottish urban price levels were consistently above those of English boroughs, and would have been much higher had not Scottish fuel prices been below those in the English cost of living basket of goods. Irrespective of earnings, especially prone though they were in Glasgow and Dundee to interruptions, wage rates in the four cities were appreciably lower and costs of living higher than in English boroughs. For an identical basket of food Dundonians paid 10.2 per cent more, and Glaswegians 5.7 per cent more than Mancunians, a differential which had already narrowed by 1912. Taking rent into account also, which with food represented 80 per cent of working-class weekly expenditure, and again compared to Manchester (though the same applied to Leeds, Sheffield or Nottingham) Glasgow residents paid a further 5.3 per cent, in Aberdeen the cost of living was 7.4 per cent above the English boroughs, and in Edinburgh and Dundee these inflexible elements of weekly expenditure required respectively 9.6 per cent and 10.6 per cent more than in the English cities and were on a par, or even above, the cost of living in London.[62]

But whereas the poverty implications of the adverse living costs are self-evident, the impact of the structure of industrial production was less obvious, but no less adverse. Labour productivity in Scotland remained below the national average. Across the 97 branches of employment the unweighted mean of Scottish labour output registered only 96.6 per cent of UK labour productivity. With wages at 94.8 per cent of the UK level and labour productivity at 96.6 per cent Scottish employers in aggregate rationally preferred labour intensive

59. A.D. Campbell 'Changes in Scottish Incomes 1924–49' *Economic Journal* 65 1955, pp. 225–40.
60. Board of Trade *Report of Enquiry into Working Class Rents, Housing and Retail Prices, etc.* 1908, Cd 3864, xl.
61. Board of Trade *Report of Enquiry into Working Class Rents and Retail Prices with the Rates of Wages in Certain Occupations in Industrial Towns of the United Kingdom in 1912* 1913, Cd 6955, p. xxxvi, concluded, 'The index numbers for the Scottish towns . . . are considerably higher on the whole than those for English and Welsh towns'.
62. Calculated from *Ibid.*

to capital intensive production where that choice was technically available to them.[63] The leverage of low labour costs so significant in the early phase of Scottish industrialization found an echo therefore until World War I, and while this sustained Scotland's position in the pre-war industrial league table, lack of capital deepening and industrial diversification meant relegation to the second division in the inter-war years, and problems of structural adjustment even now.[64]

If the long-term production structure favoured labour-intensive methods short-run adjustments to manufacturing output were in the main translated into adjustments in labour inputs. The reservoir of labour was the mechanism by which employers reduced total costs in recession, that is, by cutting variable costs. By increasing shifts, hours and piece rates in the upswing, in other words by avoiding additions to fixed costs through capital expenditure in a boom which might prove temporary and long-term increments to capacity unnecessary, employers again varied labour inputs. With raw material or semi-manufactured prices exogenously determined and final prices increasingly pressurised by foreign competition, employers chose to impose the burden of adjustment to variations in their order books upon the volume of employment available to the workforce. The trade cycle was no more than an employment cycle by another name.

This is not to argue that technical development and capital expenditure were stagnant. Clearly the engineering expansion post-1870 in west central Scotland belied this, though the long-run stability of engineering in the other cities is equally striking. More, it stresses that both the nature of industrial products and the lower labour costs in Scotland conspired to reassert labour-intensive production methods. Ultimately this meant that variations in business conditions would be felt more acutely in cities where an unskilled labour force was more conspicuous or where that workforce was subject to substantial variation in the demand for the product of its labours.

For many Scottish city dwellers, then, even though wage rates were below and the cost of living above national levels, the cause and course of poverty was determined by another consideration –

63. R.H. Campbell 'Introductory Essay' in Campbell (ed.) *Scottish Industrial History: A Miscellany* (Edinburgh 1978), p. xxxix.
64. H. W. Singer and C. E. V. Leser 'Industrial Productivity in England and Scotland', *Journal of the Royal Statistical Society* III 1948, p. 309; N.K. Buxton 'Economic Growth in Scotland Between the Wars: the Role of Production Structure and Rationalization', *Economic History Review* 33 1980, pp. 538–55; A.D. Campbell *op. cit.*; T. Dickson 'From Client to Supplicant: Capital and Labour in Scotland, 1870–1945' in *Scottish Capitalism: Class, State and Nation from before the Union to the Present* (London 1980), p. 284.

irregular employment. Several authors have shown that technical change and the expansion of a mass consumer market revived many part-time opportunities for the self-employed.[65] The sewing machine rekindled dress-making, tailoring and the clothing trades in the last third of the nineteenth century. Jam, lemonade and confectionery consumption generated new areas of occasional employment for women; and brewing achieved the same for men. And the advent of advertising created opportunities for handbilling, bill posters, sandwich-board men, newspaper vendors and postal workers for whom a revolution in Victorian information technology spawned opportunities for casual work. All of this added to already well-established, numerically significant, irregular employment in portering, messengering, carting, street-selling and general labouring for men, and sporadic employment as chars, washer-women and paper bag, box-makers and other factory and workshop employment for women. Treble has done much to illuminate these developments in a Glasgow setting.[66]

Amongst male workers in Scottish cities one in four (25.49 per cent) were in employment subject to interrupted time. Some were engaged in seasonal trades – dock workers with mid-winter doldrums (even more pronounced in the sailing ship era), building workers' slack time in winter, contrasting with peak employment for gas workers, and the most noted and seasonally varied branch of employment, the garment trade. Seasonality meant erratic wages for all but the artisan elite, a short cut to deprivation and poverty. In Glasgow, Treble's calculations show that between 1891 and 1911 20–23 per cent of male and 26–29 per cent of female employment was in occupations closely associated with seasonal variations.[67]

In comparison to the 26.1 per cent of female employment susceptible to seasonal employment in Glasgow in 1911, the percentages based on identical occupations in Edinburgh and in Aberdeen were 20.3 per cent and 18.6 per cent. For Dundee seasonality in these

65. B.S. Rowntree and B. Lasker *Unemployment: a Social Study* (London 1911); D. Bythell *The Sweated Trades: Outwork in Nineteenth Century Britain* (London 1978); J.A. Schmiechen 'State Reform and the Local Economy', *Economic History Review* 28 1975, pp. 418–22; J.H. Treble *op. cit.* pp. 67–70; J.A. Schmiechen *Sweated Industries op. cit.* p. 185 states that 'sweating was the result of growth not stagnation'.

66. J.H. Treble 'The Market for Unskilled Male Labour in Glasgow, 1891–1914' in I. MacDougall (ed.), *Essays in Scottish Labour History: a Tribute to W.H. Marwick* (Edinburgh 1979), pp. 115–42. For his data for Glasgow unskilled male and female workers irregularly employed (and also comparable classifications for Edinburgh, Dundee and Aberdeen) see Ch 2, table 9 in G. Gordon (ed.) *Perspectives of the Scottish City* (Aberdeen 1985).

67. J.H. Treble 'The Seasonal Demand for Adult Labour in Glasgow, 1890–1914', *Social History* 3 1978, pp. 43–60.

trades was 7.8 per cent, though in fact virtually the entire textile sector in Dundee could be said to be seasonal.

Many workers were, however, subject to the same characteristic, irregular income, but from a less visible direction. Trade cycle variations generated sizeable changes in the demand for labour in a society still heavily reliant on animate energy sources – portering, navvying, messengering, carting. Elasticity of demand for such occupations, engaged on an hourly or half-daily basis, presented considerable scope for accommodating changes in output, with none of the risk borne by the entrepreneur. The adjustment was through labour costs only. With a large reservoir of unskilled labour supplemented by what Samuel called 'comers and goers'[68] vagrants and migrants, output variations were achieved by laying off, or in the upswing, engaging labour. Stockpiling, cocooning plant, scrapping and updating policies, whatever the technical disposition of management, could not be easier than hiring and firing unskilled labour. Such elasticity in both demand and supply schedules for labour meant frequently interrupted incomes, albeit often for short periods only. Not surprisingly, therefore, in Glasgow 27 per cent, in Edinburgh and Aberdeen 24 per cent, and in Dundee, 20 per cent of male workers were prone to such influences.

There were opportunities for dovetailing seasonal work; family income sources might be phased complementarily, cyclical downswing in one sector could be offset by buoyancy in another, and so on, and for some this counteracted the effect of interrupted income. With diligent household economy, income could be spread through spells of short time and short run unemployment, and lay-offs did offer a respite to arduous toil for unskilled workers. And only some of the 27 per cent in Glasgow, 24 per cent in Edinburgh and Aberdeen, 20 per cent in Dundee were affected by interrupted work at any one time, though all might well experience it at some stage of an employment year. Although the percentage of city workers potentially exposed to irregular work did not vary very greatly between the four cities, the actual experience of interrupted time could and did differ appreciably, and in this respect the industrial balance and the scale of professional work substantially determined the extent, frequency and duration of irregular work. The more stable the employment and expenditure base of the city, the less the actual experience of interrupted time of those exposed to the possibility.

This susceptibility was indeed the crucial influence on living standards. It was the average weekly income taken over the duration

68. R. Samuel 'Comers and Goers' in H.J. Dyos and M. Wolff (eds) *The Victorian City: Images and Realities*, vol. I (London 1977 edn), pp. 123–60.

of an employment year which dictated consumption patterns.[69] Wage rates, and earnings when in employment were lesser considerations than the average affordable levels of expenditure throughout the year. In this respect Scottish rental leases were particularly decisive.[70] Commonly the long-let, a one year rental from Whitsunday was contracted up to four months before the commencement of the lease.[71] In the context of variable employment prospects the standard of accommodation affordable over the duration of one year's lease had to take account of interrupted earnings. English short lets allowed a tenant *in extremis* to move to cheaper accommodation. In Scotland, a very large segment of the working population, 25.5 per cent in the cities, was prone to interrupted income yet committed for up to 16 months to a rental component of their weekly expenditure from which it was difficult to escape, and even then only with financial penalties. Not surprisingly the letting and ejectment system produced unusually hostile landlord–tenant relations before World War I and rent strikes during it.[72] In this uncertain climate of household accounting many tenants understandably chose a level of accommodation at such minimal levels that they felt reasonably confident that whatever the nature of seasonal and casual employment in the ensuing twelve-month period they should be able to maintain rental payments. It was a delicate balancing act. For 20,000 Glaswegians per annum evicted for non-payment of rent it was clearly beyond them.[73] Many achieved some equilibrium in the phasing of domestic income and expenditure, though, to do so meant settling for a standard of accommodation – typically a one- or two-roomed tenement flat with minimal and shared amenities – at a level prejudicial to health and life expectancy.

In Edinburgh and Aberdeen one-third, and in Glasgow and Dundee, one-half of the population lived in a one- or two-roomed

69. R.G. Rodger 'The "Invisible Hand" . . .' *op. cit.*
70. R.G. Rodger 'The Law and Urban Change: Some Nineteenth Century Scottish Evidence', *Urban History Yearbook* 1979, pp. 85–6; *see also PP 1907 XXXVII*, and *PP 1908 XLII*, Report of the Departmental Committee on House-Letting in Scotland, vols I and II for characteristics of tenancies in Scotland.
71. D. Englander *Landlord and Tenant in Urban Britain, 1838–1918* (Oxford 1983), pp. 167–70 and M.J. Daunton *House and Home in the Victorian City: Working Class Housing 1850–1914* (London 1983), pp. 132–9 give accounts of the house-letting system in Scotland.
72. J. Melling *Rent Strikes: People's Struggle for Housing in West Scotland 1890–1916* (Edinburgh 1983); S. Damer 'State, Class and Housing: Glasgow 1885–1919' in J. Melling (ed.) *Housing, Social Policy and the State* (London 1980); D. Englander 'Landlord and Tenant in Urban Scotland – the Background to the Clyde Rent Strikes', *Journal of Scottish Labour History Society*, 15 1981, pp. 4–16.
73. M.J. Daunton *op. cit.* p. 136.

house, and at an overcrowded density of more than two per room.[74] Even then such accommodation was palatial for many tenants.

The distinction between the unskilled and others in housing was evident elsewhere. Mortality and morbidity reflected similar patterns.[75] For example the mean death rate of the Old Town, was 52.8 per cent above that of the southern suburbs of Edinburgh between 1875 and 1900.[76] But perhaps the most striking instance of class difference was in the anthropometric data collected by the Dundee Social Union, the Edinburgh Charity Organisation Society and, in the largest survey of its kind ever undertaken, by the School Board of Glasgow.[77] An emphatic empirical link was forged between income and health, or as the official report put it, 'The numbers examined are so large, and the results are so uniform that only one conclusion is possible, viz.: – that the poorest child suffers most in nutrition and in growth.'[78]

In Figure 1 this connection is presented according to room size, a reflection of employment and affordable income, although it could be presented equally effectively according to skill and residential location. Broughton School in Edinburgh was 'attended by children of small shopkeepers, of skilled artisans, and of clerks'.[79] The mean heights of these children of the lower middle and prosperous upper working classes, compared to children of equivalent occupations in the North Canongate School, 'the old, central working class area . . . serving the poorest parts of the city . . . (where) the skilled trades are underrepresented compared to the industrial population of the city generally at the 1901 census'[80] showed that the children were between one and three inches taller than the children of north Canongate. Despite genetic and migratory influences, Gray concluded, 'The children of the semi- and unskilled sample have the largest mean difference from all Broughton School' and that

74. Scottish Land Enquiry Committee Report *Scottish Land* (London 1914), pp. 350–1.
75. C. Pennington 'Tuberculosis' in O. Checkland and M. Lamb (eds) *Health Care as Social History* (Aberdeen 1982), pp. 90, 96–7.
76. H. MacDonald 'Public Health Legislation and Problems in Victorian Edinburgh, with Special Reference to the Work of Dr Littlejohn as Medical Officer of Health'. Unpublished PhD thesis, Edinburgh University 1972, vol. 2, graph A.
77. Dundee Social Union *Report on Housing and Industrial Conditions and Medical Inspection of School Children* (Dundee 1905); City of Edinburgh Charity Organization Society *Report on the Physical Condition of Fourteen Hundred Schoolchildren in the City together with Some Account of their Homes and Surroundings* (London, 1906); Scotch Education Department, *Report as to the Physical Condition of Children Attending the Public Schools of the School Board for Glasgow* (HMSO 1907), Cd 3637.
78. SED *Report op. cit.* p. v.
79. R.Q. Gray *op. cit.* p. 85.
80. *Ibid.* pp. 83–4.

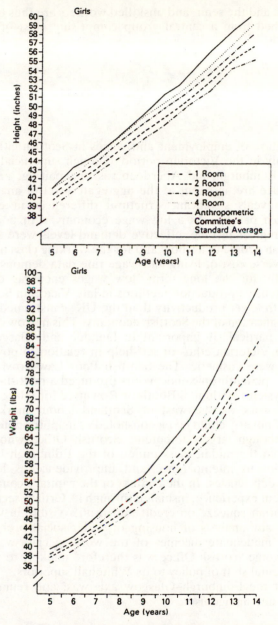

Fig. 1 Glasgow Children compared to the National Average, 1904; height and weight according to house size. (Scotch Education Department, *Report as to the Physical Condition of Children Attending the Public Schools Board for Glasgow* (HMSO, 1907) table VIIIA–B)

105

'engineers and the semi- and unskilled workers are thus both sharply distinguished from a central group comprising most of the skilled workers'.[81]

VI

The structure of employment and wages in Scottish cities diverged appreciably in the Victorian period. Though superficial similarities between Edinburgh and Aberdeen, as one pairing, and Glasgow and Dundee are apparent at the aggregate level of analysis, closer scrutiny reveals significant structural differences in employment within each pairing. As a low-wage economy with pockets of intensely irregular income, effective demand levels were subdued for the Scottish people as a whole and for the working class in particular, as the adverse cost of living and wage rate data demonstrate. More significantly for the long term, low wages encouraged continued labour-intensive production methods in late Victorian Scottish cities which, with lower productivity than the UK, constrained the growth and diversification of the Scottish economy. This narrow employment base was particularly important in Dundee and Glasgow and the prevailing Victorian ethos of self-help in relation to poverty meant solutions were cosmetic. The Scottish Poor Law provided a basic minimum; philanthropic endeavours produced a multi-faceted social support system. Without a Booth or Rowntree for Glasgow, without empirical work on the west of Scotland labour market, English surveys of poverty could be pigeon-holed as inappropriate by a newly created, though largely impotent, Scottish Office whose officials, drawn from the middle-class milieu of the Edinburgh bourgeoisie, could point to intemperance and improvidence as longstanding character deficiencies. In the context of the capital's counter-cyclical employment experience, insulated through its tertiary sector from the late Victorian squeeze on credit and profits visible in west central Scotland, any analysis of housing or wider social problems which identified inadequate incomes of the working class was heretical. An embryonic Scottish Office was therefore unlikely to recommend a fundamental shift of policy to its Whitehall superiors.[82] No wonder then, that the Edinburgh–Glasgow axis was, and remains, one of suspicion and antagonism.

81. *Ibid.* p. 86.
82. D. Milne *The Scottish Office* (London 1957), pp. 15–17; K. Burgess 'Workshop of the World: Client Capitalism at its Zenith, 1830–1870' in T. Dickson (ed.) *op. cit.* pp. 230–4.

106

Appendix I

The structure of industrial employment in the Scottish cities

Percentage of workforce in	Glasgow	Edinburgh	Dundee	Aberdeen
(a) *1841*				
Printing and Publishing	1.12	3.88	0.56	0.91
Engineering, Toolmaking an Metalworking	7.17	6.07	5.59	6.32
Shipbuilding	0.35	0.17	1.14	1.24
Coachbuilding	0.40	0.92	0.21	0.34
Building	5.84	5.73	6.05	5.99
Furniture and Woodworking	1.06	2.73	0.77	0.87
Chemicals	1.22	0.24	0.19	0.37
Food, Drink and Tobacco	5.24	8.31	5.27	4.66
Textiles and Clothing	37.56	13.04	50.54	34.68
Other manufacturing[a]	2.90	3.02	1.29	3.18
General labouring	8.40	3.69	3.84	6.87
(b) *1851*[b]				
Printing and Publishing	1.38		0.55	1.03
Engineering, Toolmaking and Metalworking	8.67		4.38	5.04
Shipbuilding	0.14		0.91	1.14
Coachbuilding	0.13		0.15	0.19
Building	5.64		4.04	5.06
Furniture and Woodworking	1.41		0.90	0.95
Chemicals	1.00		0.21	0.22
Food, Drink and Tobacco	6.41		4.62	6.89
Textiles and Clothing	27.60		53.82	21.19
Other manufacturing[a]	3.36		0.97	4.69
General labouring	2.90		3.60	4.32
(c) *1871*				
Printing and Publishing	1.90	4.89	0.58	1.42
Engineering, Toolmaking and Metalworking	14.08	6.85	5.63	4.23
Shipbuilding	1.33	0.05	1.08	1.37
Coachbuilding	0.48	0.80	0.20	0.56
Building	7.42	9.64	5.64	7.81
Furniture and Woodworking	1.17	2.37	0.63	1.03
Chemicals	1.17	0.27	0.16	1.70
Food, Drink and Tobacco	5.63	7.36	4.38	7.07
Textiles and Clothing	31.97	14.64	61.81	23.65
Other manufacturing[a]	3.32	4.06	1.54	7.23
General labouring	4.41	2.32	3.15	4.13

Appendix I (*cont.*)

Percentage of workforce in	Glasgow	Edinburgh	Dundee	Aberdeen
(d) *1881*				
Printing and Publishing	2.21	5.16	0.73	1.62
Engineering, Toolmaking and				
Metalworking	12.81	5.86	6.11	5.76
Shipbuilding	0.68	0.06	1.24	1.01
Coachbuilding	0.46	0.64	0.23	0.57
Building	6.30	9.28	4.38	7.90
Furniture and Woodworking	1.79	2.38	0.78	1.29
Chemicals	0.64	0.46	0.12	0.52
Food, Drink and Tobacco	7.65	8.54	5.53	8.61
Textiles and Clothing	25.42	11.17	54.42	17.38
Other manufacturing[a]	3.21	4.34	1.22	6.16
General labouring	3.92	1.90	3.24	4.91
(e) *1891*				
Printing and Publishing	2.58	5.02	0.71	1.89
Engineering, Toolmaking and				
Metalworking	14.17	5.88	6.10	6.02
Shipbuilding	0.72	0.10	2.24	1.30
Coachbuilding	0.62	0.66	0.35	0.72
Building	5.47	6.92	3.48	6.74
Furniture and Woodworking	1.77	1.69	0.84	1.19
Chemicals	0.60	0.62	0.23	0.52
Food, Drink and Tobacco	7.85	9.34	6.27	7.65
Textiles and Clothing	20.75	11.49	52.28	17.43
Other manufacturing[a]	3.37	4.25	1.82	5.81
General labouring	4.31	2.63	2.27	4.75
(f) *1901*				
Printing and Publishing	2.37	5.14	1.02	2.04
Engineering, Toolmaking and				
Metalworking	14.84	6.51	6.54	6.50
Shipbuilding	0.84	0.09	1.64	1.19
Coachbuilding	0.63	0.46	0.20	0.76
Building	6.71	8.98	5.56	7.80
Furniture and Woodworking	2.03	1.74	0.94	1.52
Chemicals[c]	0.79	1.50	0.17	1.81
Food, Drink and Tobacco	9.75	10.40	6.93	11.00
Textiles and Clothing	17.16	10.00	51.73	15.56
Other manufacturing[a]	3.45	3.73	0.85	3.13
General labouring	3.72	1.67	1.65	3.30

Appendix I (*cont.*)

Percentage of workforce in	Glasgow	Edinburgh	Dundee	Aberdeen
(g) *1911*				
Printing and Publishing	2.82	6.69	1.56	2.51
Engineering, Toolmaking and				
Metalworking	16.86	6.16	5.62	5.78
Shipbuilding	1.80	0.08	1.89	2.54
Coachbuilding	0.72	0.56	0.25	0.78
Building	4.83	6.24	3.46	4.72
Furniture and Woodworking	3.18	2.22	1.86	2.92
Chemicals[c]	1.89	3.22	0.62	1.65
Food, Drink and Tobacco	12.41	11.57	7.59	10.13
Textiles and Clothing	16.86	11.00	53.52	16.16
Other manufacturing[a]	3.34	3.10	0.91	3.12
General labouring	2.23	1.69	1.32	1.81

Notes   [a] Glass, pottery, earthenware, paper, gum, grease, cane.
       [b] Edinburgh and Leith are only available as a combined urban population, and for the sake of comparability with other censuses, have been omitted.
       [c] Includes rubber.
Sources See note 17.

Appendix II

Employment in Scottish cities, 1911: location quotients*

Census category	Occupation	Location quotients: Males				Location quotients: Females			
		G	E	D	A	G	E	D	A
1	Civil Service	0.97	2.61	0.80	1.26	0.82	0.96	0.26	0.58
2	Local Government service	1.64	1.21	1.22	1.28	0.90	0.78	0.45	1.18
3	Naval and Military services	0.45	1.49	0.65	0.53	-	-	-	-
4	Clerical Profession and service	0.72	1.46	0.78	0.80	0.61	1.44	0.72	1.83
5	Legal Profession and service	0.79	3.84	0.65	1.65	0.85	2.41	0.44	1.61
6	Medical Profession and service	1.11	2.56	0.94	1.31	1.17	1.66	0.30	1.25
7	Teaching Profession and service (not under Local Authority)	1.06	3.69	2.13	2.94	0.83	1.45	0.62	1.30
8	Other Professions and their services	1.43	2.24	1.11	1.49	1.43	1.61	0.88	1.45
9	Domestic and Institution service	0.33	1.12	0.40	0.49	0.73	1.40	0.32	0.88
10	Hotel, Eating-house service	1.57	1.85	1.25	1.05	1.29	1.54	0.47	1.07
11	Commerce	2.04	2.10	1.03	1.40	1.69	1.23	0.53	1.42
12	Banking and Insurance	1.07	2.25	0.96	1.56	1.58	2.00	0.50	1.17
13	Railway service	1.30	1.33	0.77	0.79	1.55	1.09	0.18	0.73
14	Road transport service	1.51	1.84	0.99	1.15	1.33	1.50	0.33	0.83
15	Railway, Road, Canal, Harbour construction	0.76	0.59	0.45	0.55	-	-	-	-
16	Coach, Motor Cycle building	1.30	1.08	0.56	1.47	1.29	1.29	0.29	1.29

Appendix II (*cont.*)

Census category	Occupation	Location quotients: Males				Location quotients: Females:			
		G	E	D	A	G	E	D	A
17	Shipping and Docks	1.52	0.38	1.26	2.06	2.00	0.75	0.38	1.25
18	Shipbuilding	0.61	0.28	0.79	0.89	0.50	0.00	0.00	0.60
19	Agriculture	0.03	0.13	0.09	0.16	0.20	0.70	0.01	0.30
20	Fishing	0.04	0.15	0.06	4.00	0.00	0.00	0.00	5.27
21	Coal Industry	0.20	0.21	0.13	0.15	0.20	0.31	0.08	0.14
22	Shale Industry	-	-	-	-	-	-	-	-
23	Other mining industries	0.13	0.13	0.00	0.00	-	-	-	-
24	Quarrying	0.24	0.23	0.42	6.08	1.50	0.00	0.50	8.50
25	Iron manufacture	1.76	0.43	0.70	0.56	1.67	0.38	0.22	0.33
26	Metal manufacture other than iron	2.21	1.83	1.21	0.90	1.86	1.36	0.68	1.23
27	Precious metals, jewels, musical and Scientific Instruments manufacture and sale	1.58	3.59	0.76	1.31	2.03	1.83	0.14	1.90
28	House, &c., Building and Decorating	1.13	1.61	1.02	1.16	1.68	2.05	0.45	1.27
29	Wood and Furniture industries	1.74	1.41	1.44	1.83	2.31	1.01	3.53	1.08
30	Brick, Cement, Pottery, Glass industries	1.42	1.46	0.18	0.32	1.91	0.59	0.16	0.22

G = Glasgow; E = Edinburgh; D = Dundee; A = Aberdeen

* For method of calculation see G. S. Jones, *Outcast London*, Appendix 2, Table 5.

Source *PP 1913 LXXX.*

Appendix II (*cont.*)

Census category	Occupation	Location quotients: Males				Location quotients: Females			
		G	E	D	A	G	E	D	A
31	Chemical and Rubber industries	1.60	2.35	0.70	1.65	1.12	3.02	0.17	0.44
32	Leather and Leather goods manufacture	1.85	1.83	0.98	0.76	2.00	1.88	1.31	0.50
33	Paper and Stationery manufacture	1.05	1.42	0.49	1.51	1.58	1.24	0.27	2.67
34	Printing, Publishing and allied industries	1.73	4.92	1.53	1.61	1.95	3.38	0.47	1.58
35	Cotton Industry	2.39	0.06	0.06	0.09	2.62	0.19	0.19	0.21
36	Wool Industry	0.18	0.25	0.02	1.69	0.17	0.08	0.01	1.33
37	Silk Industry	0.67	0.67	0.00	0.00	0.64	0.21	0.00	0.00
38	Linen Industry	0.06	0.06	1.77	1.69	0.03	0.01	0.70	1.89
39	Hemp, Jute, Rope, Mat Industries	0.12	0.07	22.84	0.57	0.05	0.00	11.91	0.50
40	Thread, Hosiery, and other textile industries	1.16	0.27	0.67	0.30	0.89	0.21	0.12	0.33
41	Bleaching, Dyeing and allied industries	0.72	0.11	2.07	0.18	0.65	0.35	0.41	0.20
42	Dealing in Drapery and Textiles	1.91	1.30	1.01	1.48	1.50	1.26	0.80	1.37
43	Hat-Making and Selling	2.33	2.50	1.00	1.33	1.31	1.30	0.62	1.35
44	Tailoring, Dressmaking	1.37	1.83	0.94	1.32	1.31	1.23	0.40	1.08
45	Bootmaking	1.20	1.10	1.01	1.21	1.36	0.94	0.42	0.83
46	Other dress industries	1.81	1.44	1.26	1.30	2.96	0.39	0.22	1.14

Appendix II (cont.)

Census category	Occupation	Location quotients: Males				Location quotients: Females:			
		G	E	D	A	G	E	D	A
47	Preparation and Sale of Provisions	1.30	1.46	1.24	1.48	1.51	1.06	0.71	1.17
48	Tobacco Manufacture and Sale	2.60	2.00	1.20	1.40	2.53	1.60	0.66	0.49
49	Brewing, Distilling	1.25	3.94	0.71	0.50	2.14	0.59	0.77	0.36
50	Gas, Water, Electricity Supply (not under Local Authority)	0.45	0.25	0.09	0.18	-	-	-	-
51	Drainage and Sanitary Service (not under Local Authority)	0.20	0.20	0.00	0.00	-	-	-	-
52	General Shopkeeping and Dealing	1.25	1.12	1.17	1.29	1.09	0.96	0.52	1.03
53	Other and undefined industries	1.26	1.21	0.96	1.44	1.73	1.18	0.49	1.66

G = Glasgow; E = Edinburgh; D = Dundee; A = Aberdeen
* For method of calculation see G. S. Jones, *Outcast London*, Appendix 2, Table 5.
Source PP 1913 LXXX.

Chapter 4

VICTORIAN CITIES: HOW DIFFERENT?

David Cannadine

[from *Social History*, **2** (1977): 457–87][1]

The problematic central to Cannadine's article is how urban space was redefined under the twin processes of industrialization and urbanization so that residential zones for rich and poor became transposed. The concentration of the rich in the centre of the pre-industrial city was in stark contrast to their preference for the periphery in the 'modern' city; simultaneously, the poor experienced the reverse, centripetal force. Such a transposition was not accidental, as explained by H.J. Dyos and D.A. Reeder in their pathbreaking paper, 'Slums and suburbs', in H.J. Dyos and M. Wolff (eds), The Victorian City, *vol. 1 (1973), but was based on the inequalities inherent in a mature capitalist system. Cannadine dismisses the claims by D. Ward, 'Victorian cities: how modern?',* Social History, **1**, *no. 2 (1975) and others, that in their unsystematic and confused land use early- and mid-Victorian cities continued to resemble pre-industrial cities. That segregation, both social and residential, existed is reasserted by reference to three key features of British urbanization: firstly, that population growth was most rapid in the first half of the nineteenth century and that suburbs pre-dated transport developments; secondly, that the continued existence of large landowners in British cities significantly affected the geography of urban growth; and thirdly, that middle-class attitudes unequivocally endorsed segregation. Unlike American cities, transport did not liberate the middle class; it truly threatened their established and exclusive suburbs. Thus a spatial dynamic is imparted, with tension and pressure inherent components of land use at any given time. Territoriality,*

1. An earlier draft of this paper was presented at an S.S.R.C. seminar on human geography and economic and social history held at the University of Hull on 5 and 6 September 1975. I am most grateful to the other participants for their stimulating and constructive criticism.

114

not narrowly defined in terms of the physical partitioning of urban space but in relation to its symbolism of contested terrain, emerges as the organizing motif in analysing nineteenth-century cities. The Birmingham suburb of Edgbaston forms the basis of Cannadine's study. Family life in Edgbaston is considered in Chapter 11.

The study of residential segregation patterns in nineteenth-century towns grows increasingly complex. Once it all seemed easy. There was Sjoberg's pre-industrial city, easily recognized, simply defined and universally valid.[2] Then came the Industrial Revolution, bringing with it 'an entirely new pattern for disposing of space'.[3] Its urban result was equally ubiquitous: the 'modern' city of Engels and Booth in the nineteenth century and of the Chicago School in the twentieth.[4] In Sjoberg's city, the rich dwelt at the centre and the poor at the periphery, while for the majority in between, in so far as there was a pattern of residential segregation, it was on the basis of ethnicity and occupation rather than socio-economic status.[5] In the 'modern' city, the position is reversed. Segregation, which is much more widespread, is by status and income.[6] The poor, whatever their occupation, huddle together on the edge of the central business district, whilst those with time and money to spare flee to the periphery.[7] And between these extremes are the increasingly segregated lower and middle classes, in a variety of overlapping zonal, sectorial and clustered residential patterns. Thus, the collective and cumulative impact of growing population, increased scale of organization, revolutionized mass transport and separated home and workplace combined to produce the spatially differentiated, residentially segregated city.[8]

2. G. Sjoberg, *The Pre-Industrial City: Past and Present* (Glencoe, Illinois, 1960), 5.
3. O. Handlin, 'The modern city as a field of historical study' in O. Handlin and J. Burchard (eds.), *The Historian and the City* (Cambridge, Mass, 1963), 10.
4. F. Engels, *The Condition of the Working Class in England* (trans. and ed. by W.O. Henderson and W.H. Chaloner, Oxford, 1958), 54–6; Charles Booth, *Labour and Life of the People* (1889–91), II, pt. iii, 406; E.W. Burgess, 'The growth of the city: an introduction to a research project' in R.E. Park and E.W. Burgess (eds.), *The City* (5th impression, Chicago, 1968), 47–62. For a recent re-statement of this view, see B.T. Robson, *Urban Analysis: A Study of City Structure With Special Reference to Sunderland* (Cambridge, 1969), 98.
5. Sjoberg, *op. cit.*, 91–103.
6. O.D. Duncan and B. Duncan, 'Residential distribution and occupational stratification', *American Journal of Sociology*, LX, 5 (March 1955); T.R. Anderson and J.A. Egeland, 'Spatial aspects of social area analysis', *American Sociological Review*, XXVI, 3 (June 1961).
7. L.F. Schnore, 'Problems in the quantitative study of urban history' in H.J. Dyos (ed.), *The Study of Urban History* (1968), 200.
8. H. Perkin, *The Origins of Modern English Society, 1780–1885* (1969), 172–5; E. Lampard, 'The urbanizing world' in H.J. Dyos and M. Wolff (eds.), *The Victorian City: Images and Realities* (1973), 1, 29, 40.

I

Although this clear view of relatively rapid transition and sudden segregation still persists, it has recently been modified, as the wisdom and utility of seeing the nineteenth-century city as the Chicago of Burgess *et al.* in past time has been increasingly challenged. This has been especially true in North America, where historians have investigated the patterns of residential segregation in ostensibly 'modern' towns such as mid-nineteenth-century Boston, Philadelphia, Milwaukee, Toronto and Hamilton. They have shown them to be essentially 'walking cities', rarely more than two miles in radius, with small-scale business predominating, and with houses of all sizes, shops, factories and offices mixed up together.[9] Goheen's description of Toronto applies to most North American cities: 'By comparison with the end of the century the city was a jumble of confusion in 1860. Commerce, industry and high-class residential properties were tightly intermixed.'[10] In so far as residential segregation did exist, it was more in accordance with Sjoberg's model than Burgess's: an affluent core and a poorer periphery.[11] It was the advent of mass transport towards the end of the nineteenth century, rather than the more amorphous process of industrialization at the beginning, which reversed this situation.[12] The metropolitan area was progressively increased in size, reaching to between ten and fifteen miles from the city centre.[13] Commuters replaced pedestrians; the 'tracked city' superseded the 'walking city'.[14]

9. S. Bass Warner, jr., *Streetcar Suburbs: The Process of Growth in Boston, 1870–1900* (Cambridge, Mass., 1962), 1–3, 15–17; *idem, The Private City: Philadelphia in Three Periods of its Growth* (Philadelphia, 1968), 50, 53, 56–8; S. Blumin, 'Mobility and change in *ante-bellum* Philadelphia' in S. Thernstrom and R. Sennet (eds.), *Nineteenth-Century Cities: Essays in the New Urban History* (New Haven, 1969), 187–90; K. Neils Conzen, 'Patterns of residence in early Milwaukee' in L.F. Schnore (ed.), *The New Urban History: Quantitative Explorations by American Historians* (Princeton, 1975), 151–9; P.G. Goheen, *Victorian Toronto, 1850 to 1900: Patterns and Processes of Growth* (Chicago, 1970), 7–10, 84–5, 115–54; M.B. Katz, 'Social structure in Hamilton, Ontario' in Thernstrom and Sennet, *op. cit.*, 239–41.
10. Goheen, *op. cit.*, 84.
11. Although Knights' survey of *ante-bellum* Boston suggests that the poor as well as the rich were to be found in the centre: P.R. Knights, *The Plain People of Boston, 1830–1860: A Study in City Growth* (New York, 1971), 89–90.
12. Goheen, *op. cit.*, 3, 10, 194–201; Warner, *Private City . . .*, 169–73, 177; *idem, The Urban Wilderness: A History of the American City* (New York, 1972), 60, 62, 86–101.
13. *Idem, Streetcar Suburbs . . .*, 65, 153.
14. K.H. Schaeffer and E. Sclar, *Access for All: Transportation and Urban Growth* (Harmondsworth, 1975), chs. ii and iii, for a fuller summary of the arguments advanced in the works cited in this paragraph.

Recently, David Ward has argued that what was true of nineteenth-century America also held for nineteenth-century England, namely that 'both the kind and level of residential and social differentiation in those cities which had attained a substantial size by the early and mid-nineteenth-century were somewhat different from those displayed by the same cities at the turn of the century'.[15] In particular, he pointed out how many features of early and mid-nineteenth-century cities were survivals from 'pre-industrial' times, such as the practice of some of the rich of living out of town, the division between banking and trading areas in the centre, and the existence of large mixed areas of industry and housing.[16] In addition, he argued that the gap between the most rapid period of population growth (in the first three decades of the nineteenth century) and the revolution in mass transport (in the last quarter of the nineteenth century and first decade of the twentieth) meant that for the majority of people who could not afford transport, any attempt at lengthy journeying from home to workplace was by definition impossible.[17] How, then, could such towns be extensively segregated? In support of this argument, he cited Chorley, an industrial town in Lancashire where in 1851 as in 1806, home and workplace were relatively close together, segregation was more by occupation than status, and the rich and powerful tended to congregate at the centre.[18] As in England, so in America, it was only the revolution in mass transport which ushered in the 'modern' city. Accordingly he suggested that 'the retrospective application of many of the generalizations and methods of the contemporary social sciences to . . . nineteenth-century cities' should be undertaken with more caution than has sometimes been the case.[19]

Inevitably, so bold an argument is bound to stimulate discussion and provoke dissent. Certainly his general picture of nineteenth-century urban growth finds corroboration in several case-studies of English towns. For example, detailed investigations of Hertford, York, Exeter and Lincoln have shown the extent to which 'walking cities' survived in England in the nineteenth century.[20] Their 'pre-

15. D. Ward, 'Victorian cities: how modern?', *Journal of Historical Geography*, 1, 2 (April 1975), 137.
16. *Ibid.*, 138–43.
17. *Ibid.*, 144.
18. A.M. Warnes, 'Early separation of home from workplace and the urban structure of Chorley, 1780 to 1850', *Transactions of the Historic Society of Lancashire and Cheshire*, CXXII (1970), 130–3; *idem*, 'Residential patterns in an emerging industrial town', *Institute of British Geographers Special Publication*, 5 (1973), 175–83.
19. Ward, *op. cit.*, 135, 138, 151.
20. E.R. Roper Power, 'The social structure of an English county town', *Sociological Review*, XXIX, 4 (Oct. 1937), 395–8; A. Armstrong, *Stability and Change in an English County Town: A Social Study of York, 1805–51* (Cambridge, 1974), 16–46, 74–6, 94–5; R. Newton, *Victorian Exeter, 1837–1914* (Leicester, 1968), XIX, 10, 60; Sir Francis Hill, *Victorian Lincoln* (Cambridge, 1974), 2, 5.

industrial' economies and high-status central areas put them un-equivocally closer to Sjoberg's model than Burgess's. Indeed, they can be described in exactly those words which Thernstrom used about early nineteenth-century Newburyport: 'The distinct class-segregated neighbourhoods of the modern city did not yet exist. There were no working-class ghettos, nor had the merchant and professional class abandoned the central business district as a place of residence.'[21] Nor indeed were they to do so, until the 1870s in York and the 1880s in Lincoln and Exeter.[22]

Like Chorley, however, these towns shared one characteristic which makes them inadequate supporting evidence for Ward's argu-ment: none can be described as being 'of a substantial size by the early and mid-nineteenth century'. In Chorley, for instance, it was hardly surprising that home and workplace should have been in close proximity, given that its population in 1806 was 6,000, and had only reached 12,700 by mid-century.[23] In the same way, the 'integrated and stable' social structure of Hertford is more easily understood when it is recalled that between 1800 and 1900 its population only rose from 3,000 to 9,000.[24] Likewise, at mid-century, Lincoln's population had not yet reached 20,000, and neither York nor Exeter had topped 40,000. Even in 1900, York was still below 80,000, Lincoln and Exeter less than 50,000 apiece.[25] Such towns tell us little of the conditions prevailing in those larger urban areas conventionally labelled 'Victorian cities', with whose residential patterns the remainder of this paper is concerned. In particular, it will be suggested that distinct patterns of segregation did prevail in mid-nineteenth-century English towns, not as extensively as they did after the coming of the tram, but still considerably more so than was *apparently* the case in contemporary America, or had been the case in England hitherto. Accordingly, however strong may be the arguments against applying the concepts of 'modern' social science to *ante-bellum* Philadelphia, it will be maintained that, in England, the case, for applying them to Engel's Manchester remains largely intact.

21. S. Thernstrom, *Poverty and Progress: Social Mobility in a Nineteenth-Century City* (Cambridge, Mass., 1964), 37.
22. P. M. Tillott (ed.), *The Victorian History of the County of York: The City of York* (1961), 286–7; B. Hutton, *Clifton and its People in the Nineteenth Century* (York, 1969), 26–8; A. Vernon, *A Quaker Business Man: The Life of Joseph Rowntree, 1836–1925* (1958), 18–25, 158; Hill, *op. cit.*, 302; Newton, *op. cit.*, 134.
23. Warnes, 'Early separation . . .', III, 120.
24. Power, 'The social structure . . .', 395, 398.
25. Hill, *op. cit.*, 306; Newton, *op. cit.*, 134, 315; Armstrong, *op. cit.*, II, 77; Tillott, *op. cit.*, 254.

II

Contemporaries in early and mid-Victorian England had little doubt that their largest towns were segregated.[26] The rise of 'the language of class', the practice of equating working-class areas with 'darkest Africa', and the fear of the unknown and irreligious masses who inhabited these regions, all bear witness to the residentially segregated society which had evolved by the middle of the nineteenth century.[27] McCulloch, for instance, writing of Sheffield, noted the contrast between the 'dingy, mean appearance' of the town as a whole, and the 'extreme beauty of the surrounding country, embellished as it is, in every direction, by the numerous villas of the opulent bankers, merchants and manufacturers of Sheffield', a description almost identical to Engel's more famous contemporary piece on Manchester.[28] James Smith, reporting on the sanitary state of Leeds in 1845, described it thus: 'Streets more recently formed are more ample in width, and there are many very cheerful open streets where the better classes reside. The lower classes, here as elsewhere, inhabit the less comfortable and less healthy localities.'[29]

26. It is also true that, whatever may be the case for Chorley, other recently expanded but still relatively small towns showed considerable signs of residential segregation. In some predominately working-class towns, such as Crewe and Coventry, where the middle-class element was small, segregation *between* different groups of the working-class inhabitants was quite marked. (See J. Prest, *The Industrial Revolution in Coventry* (Oxford, 1960), 40–2, and W.H. Chaloner, *The Social and Economic Development of Crewe, 1780–1923* (Manchester, 1973), 48.) Similarly, 'exclusive' resorts such as Bath and Leamington depended for their success and reputation on keeping their considerable population of servants, builders and beggars at a discreet distance from the dwellings and public buildings constructed for the enjoyment of the 'leisured' classes. (See G. Hart, *A History of Cheltenham* (Leicester, 1965), 196, 323–5, 341; R. Chaplin, 'Discovering lost new towns of the nineteenth century', *The Local Historian*, x, 4 (Nov. 1972), 187–8.)
27. A. Briggs, 'The language of class in early nineteenth-century England' in A. Briggs and J. Saville (eds.), *Essays in Labour History* (1967), 43–73; *idem, Victorian Cities* (Harmondsworth, 1968), 59–64; G. Stedman Jones, *Outcast London: A Study in the Relationship between the Classes in Victorian Society* (Harmondsworth, 1976), 179–80. For contemporary opinions other than those subsequently quoted in this paragraph, see Perkin, *op. cit.*, 172–5; Stedman Jones, *op. cit.*, 30, 166; D. Olsen, 'Victorian London: specialization, segregation and privacy', *Victorian Studies*, xvii, 3 (March 1974), 268, 272–4. For a full list of contemporary 'condition of England' literature, see H.J. Dyos, 'The slums of Victorian London', *Victorian Studies*, xi, 1 (Sept. 1967), 11–13.
28. J.R. McCulloch, *A Dictionary, Geographical, Statistical and Historical, of the Various Countries, Places and Principal Natural Objects in the World* (1851), ii, 678. See also his similar description of Glasgow in *ibid.*, 1, 904–5.
29. B.P.P., *2nd Report of the Commissioners for Inquiring Into the State of Large Towns and Populous Districts*, 1845, xviii, 313.

Indeed the whole contemporary 'condition of England' question was nothing if not the discovery by 'the rich' of the existence and plight of 'the poor', the 'two nations' of Disraeli's memorable phrase.[30] The comments of Edwin Chadwick on his experiences among the poor of Glasgow and Edinburgh have often been quoted in support of this view.[31] Less well-known, but even more apposite, were the 'general remarks' made by J.R. Martin three years later:

> What is socially true of London, is so in great part of all provincial towns; the occupants of the better quarters, with a few individual exceptions only, know absolutely nothing of the state of the worst quarters. Owing to the vastness of London – owing to the moral gulf which there separates the various classes of its inhabitants – its several quarters may be designated as assemblages of towns, rather than as one city; and so it is, in a social sense, and on a smaller scale, in other towns; the rich know nothing of the poor; – the mass of misery that festers beneath the affluence of London and of the great towns is not known to their wealthy occupants.[32]

What aspects of the urbanization process in England had brought about this greater degree of segregation? Why should mid-century Manchester, rather than mid-century Philadelphia, anticipate early twentieth-century Chicago? First, the rates of population growth on each side of the Atlantic differed. English cities expanded most rapidly in the decades before the Great Exhibition, whereas in America the 1880s and the 1890s were the years of greatest growth. So, in England the population explosion antedated the revolution in mass transport by fifty years, whereas in America these two phenomena coincided.[33] Thus, while the relatively simple

30. See, for example, the surveys of Nottingham and Brighton referred to in R.A. Church, *Economic and Social Change in a Midland Town: Victorian Nottingham, 1815–1900* (1966), 185–6; R. Smith, 'Early Victorian household structure', *International Review of Social History*, xv, 1 (April 1970), 70; E.W. Gilbert, *Brighton: Old Ocean's Bauble* (1954), 187–9. It will be noted that one observer described Brighton in terms of concentric rings, with the riches in the middle and the poor on the periphery. But Brighton was neither a 'pre-industrial' nor a 'commercial' city. As a seaside resort, it was only natural that the prime sites on the sea front should be assigned to the upper and middle classes.

31. Edwin Chadwick, *Report on the Sanitary Condition of the Labouring Population of Great Britain* (edited by M.W. Flinn, Edinburgh, 1965), 397; Armstrong, *op. cit.*, 75–6; Perkin, *op. cit.*, 172.

32. B.P.P., *2nd Report of the Commissioners for Inquiring into the State of Large Towns and Populous Districts*, 1845, XVIII, 298.

33. Briggs, *Victorian Cities*, 79–80, 86; A.F. Weber, *The Growth of Cities in the Nineteenth Century* (New York, 1899), 52; H. Perkin, *The Age of the Railway* (1970), 123–4; D. Ward, 'A comparative historical geography of streetcar suburbs in Boston, Massachusetts and Leeds, England: 1850–1920', *Annals of the Association of American Geographers*, LIV, 4 (Dec. 1964), 477.

description of American towns as developing from 'walking cities' to 'tracked cities' may suffice, it seems unlikely that it will do full justice to the complexities of the English case. Here, from the 1800s until the 1870s, those who could afford private or public transport left the exploding cities more rapidly and more numerously, thereby creating segregated, surburban areas on a scale which contemporary American cities could not rival.[34]

Much of the land thus utilized was owned in large blocks by gentry, aristocrats, or corporate bodies,[35] and the existence of such estates, along with the elaborate provisions of land law, family settlements and primogeniture under which they were necessarily held, was a second feature of the urbanization process in England to which there was no exact American equivalent.[36] On this side of the Atlantic, however, neither historians nor urban geographers have any doubt as to its importance.[37] For, while it would be imprudent

34. It is important to stress that, while the boundaries, both municipal and 'walking', of most English provincial cities were limited (in 1861, no provincial town except Newcastle had a municipal area in excess of 6,000 acres), those who could afford it often lived anything up to ten miles out, well served by omnibus services. While some Americans left the centres of their towns in a similar way, it does not seem to have been in sufficient numbers to reverse the basically 'pre-industrial' zoning pattern. See A.D. Ochojna, 'Lines of class distinction: an economic and social history of the British tramcar, with special reference to Edinburgh and Glasgow' (Edinburgh Ph.D., 1974), 1, 2, 10–11; Warner, *Streetcar Suburbs* . . ., 12–13, 41, 106–9; C.G. Kennedy, 'Commuter services in the Boston area, 1835–1860', *Business History Review*, XXXVI, 2 (Summer 1962), 153–70; K.T. Jackson, 'Urban deconcentration in the nineteenth century: a statistical enquiry' in Schnore, *op. cit.*, 130–2.
35. D. Spring, 'English landlords and nineteenth-century industrialism' in J.T. Ward and R.G. Wilson (eds.), *Land and Industry: The Landed Estate and the Industrial Revolution* (Newton Abbot, 1971), 39–40, 42–3. The definition of what precisely constitutes a 'large' urban landowner is not easy to give in terms of size, since the great estates tended to be smaller in London than in the provinces. The Bedfords' entire holding in nineteenth-century London, for instance, was a mere 119 acres, whereas in Birmingham the Calthorpes held in excess of 2,000 acres. (See D. Spring, *The English Landed Estate in the Nineteenth Century: Its Administration* (Baltimore, 1963), 13, and *infra*, section iv.) The best description, therefore, is in terms of the *behaviour* of the owners, in particular in terms of their desire to draw up a coherent long-term plan for their estate, their ability to implement it, and their capacity to preserve it. (See D. Olsen, *Town Planning in London in the Eighteenth and Nineteenth Centuries* (1965), 8–10; F.M.L. Thompson, *Hampstead, Building a Borough, 1650–1964* (1974), 74.)
36. Warner, *Streetcar Suburbs* . . ., 124–5; *dem, Urban Wilderness* . . ., 15–27.
37. Olsen, *op. cit.*, 8; Thompson, *op. cit.*, 73; H. Hobhouse, *Thomas Cubitt: Master Builder* (1971), 109; H.J. Dyos, 'A castle for Everyman', *The London Journal*, I, 1 (May 1975), 130–1; D.C.D. Pocock, 'Landownership and urban growth in Scunthorpe', *The East Midland Geographer*, V, 1 (June 1970), 52–61; G. Rowley, 'Landownership in the spatial growth of towns: a Sheffield example', *The East Midland Geographer*, VI, 4 (Dec. 1975), 200–13.

to accept Frank Banfield's picture of urban landowners, the evidence emphatically supports Dr Kellett's conclusion that 'it was the ground plan formed by property titles' which was 'the key to explaining the whole course of development of certain types of urban area, and the emergence of characteristic residential and industrial zones'.[38] Or, as Broadhurst and Reid put it:

> If we suppose that one individual is the owner of an entire parish, or an entire town . . . he can, by means of the covenants he inserts in the leases, cause the inhabitants either to emigrate *en masse*, or to carry on their trade according to his pleasure for, say, one hundred years, so that there shall be just as many and just as few butchers' and grocers' and publicans' shops, and in just such quarters of the town as he and his successors may dictate.[39]

This pamphlet was written in 1885, and a contribution to the debate on leasehold enfranchisement. But beneath the polemics is described in essence the situation which had prevailed since the early years of the nineteenth century. Before then, only in London, Edinburgh, Dublin and the spa towns had urban expansion occurred to an extent which enabled the large-scale urban landowner to play a major role.[40] But the unprecedented growth from the 1800s enabled others to join in, many of whom sought to mould the urbanization process to suit their own preferences, which were, for the most part, to attract to their estates as permanent, suburban residents, the most important, wealthy and influential people which the town could provide.[41] Ralph Clutton's words spoken in 1885 were true of the century as a whole: 'There is a great tendency on the part of the people who have building estates rather to seek to develop them for dwellings for the middle class, and not to develop them in the first instance for dwellings for the labouring class'.[42] In so doing, the landowners added a further impetus to the process of residential segregation.[43] For, motivated as many of

38. F. Banfield, *The Great Landlords of London* (1890), 72, quoted in Olsen, *op. cit.*, 200. J.R. Kellett, *The Impact of Railways on Victorian Cities* (1969), 125, 419–24.

39. H. Broadhurst and R.T. Reid, *Leasehold Enfranchisement* (1885), 16.

40. I. Mumford, *The City in History* (Harmondsworth, 1966), 451–6; Sir John Summerson, *Georgian London* (1970), chs. iii, vii, xii; C.W. Chalklin, *The Provincial Towns of Georgian England: A Study of the Building Process, 1740–1820* (1974), 61–2; A.J. Youngson, *The Making of Classical Edinburgh, 1750–1840* (Edinburgh, 1966), ch. iv; C. Maxwell, *Dublin under the Georges, 1714–1830* (2nd ed. 1956), 73–7.

41. Kellett, *op. cit.*, 410–19; Olsen, *op. cit.*, 20–1; F. Sheppard, *London, 1808–1870: The Infernal Wen* (1971), 94.

42. Quoted in Kellett, *op. cit.*, 258, and Olsen, *op. cit.*, 21.

43. D. Olsen, 'House upon house: estate development in London and Sheffield' in Dyos and Wolff, *op. cit.*, 1, 339–40.

them were by long- rather than short-term considerations, concerned with status and prestige rather than mere profit, they were more likely to welcome 'respectable' tenants wanting large houses with big gardens who paid relatively low rents, than working-class or industrial residents who would pay more rent but look less decorative. In deliberately choosing not to maximize his profits, the large-scale urban landlord therefore became a major agent of residential segregation.[44] The development of respectable, middle-class suburban estates embodied a convergence of aristocratic preferences and middle-class needs.

Of course, it did not always work out quite this neatly. In some cases, the middle classes failed to appear or, having appeared, moved on almost at once, as was the case in Bloomsbury.[45] Some towns, such as Leeds and Manchester, were not surrounded by great urban estates, and in others, such as Cardiff and Sheffield, there was one landowner – in these cases the Marquess of Bute and the Duke of Norfolk respectively – so preponderant that there was no possibility of laying out the entire estate for middle-and upper-class tenants.[46] But even here, 'respectable' areas did none the less exist. The landowner might develop one part of his estate on an exclusive basis, as did the Marquess of Bute with the area known as Butetown in the 1820s and 1830s.[47] Or several middle-class people might form a company, buy up plots of land, and administer them on the same restricted lines which were so often the hallmark of aristocratic ownership, as was the case with Victoria Park near Manchester and the Kelvinside Estate near Glasgow in the 1830s.[48] Or, as in Hampstead, speculative builders themselves might provide the tone of elegant uniformity by constructing houses of a similar style and standard to those already standing close by, thereby anticipating by fifty years or more a process which only became widespread in America from the 1870s.[49] Thus by one means or another was

44. Dyos, 'A castle for Everyman', 130–1; Thompson, *op. cit.*, 369–70, 375; L. Stone, *Family and Fortune: Studies in Aristocratic Finance in the Sixteenth and Seventeenth Centuries* (Oxford, 1973), XVI; F. M. L. Thompson, 'The social distribution of landed property in England since the sixteenth century', *Economic History Review*, 2nd ser., XIX, 3 (Dec. 1966), 516; Olsen, *Town Planning* . . ., 8–10, 16; Rowley, *op. cit.*, 206.
45. Thompson, *Hampstead* . . ., 73–4; Chaplin, *op. cit.*, 187, 189–93; Kellett, *op. cit.*, 250–1; Olsen, *Town Planning* . . ., 60.
46. J. Davies, 'Glamorgan and the Bute Estate, 1760–1947' (Wales Ph.D., 1969), 431–53; Olsen, 'House Upon House . . .', 341–5, 353.
47. Davies, *op. cit.*, 445.
48. M. Spiers, 'Victoria Park, Manchester: a study of its administration and its relations with local government, 1836–1954' (Manchester M.A., 1961), 28–31; M.A. Simpson, 'Middle-class housing and the growth of suburban communities in the west end of Glasgow, 1830–1914' (Glasgow B. Litt., 1970), 85–95.
49. Thompson, *Hampstead* . . ., 241; Olsen, 'House upon house . . .', 346–7; Warner, *Streetcar Suburb* . . ., 154, 156.

the overriding desire of middle-class people to leave the confines of Coketown indulged a desire which, in its intensity and its satisfaction, stands as the third aspect of the urbanization process in the early and mid-nineteenth century which neither previous English experience nor contemporary American practice could parallel.[50]

It was these combined influences of population growth, land-owners' preferences, and middle-class attitudes and actions, which created that unprecedented degree of residential segregation in mid-nineteenth-century England which contemporaries noticed and historians have endorsed. Thus at mid-century, a London suburb such as Poplar was almost devoid of any houses but those of the working class, whereas areas of Liverpool like Abercromby Square and Everton were almost exclusively 'better-class residential districts'.[51] Likewise, the élite of Leeds, after a false start in the Park, settled down to enjoy the suburban delights of Headingly and Chapeltown, areas which, at three to four miles from the town centre, required transport to reach them, thereby putting them effectively beyond the range of all but the wealthy.[52] And what was true of the merchant princes of Leeds also held good for their cousins in Oldham, Glasgow, Nottingham, Manchester and Liverpool who, sheltered behind the barriers of distance, toll gates, park keepers and restrictive covenants, were able to enjoy a life of segregated quietude, surrounded by parks, pleasure grounds, botanical gardens and exclusive schools.[53]

50. Mumford, *op. cit.*, 555–6; Kellett, *op. cit.*, 355, 357; Chalklin, *op. cit.*, 68; A. Harris, 'Changes in the early railway age: 1800–1850' in H.C. Darby (ed.), *A New Historical Geography of England* (Cambridge, 1973), 522–3; F.M. Jones, 'The aesthetic of the nineteenth-century industrial town' in Dyos, *The Study of Urban History*, 172–3; Simpson, *op. cit.*, 5–7, 58–61; Spiers, *op. cit.*, 3, 7, 12, 16.

51. F. Bedarida, 'Social structure in nineteenth-century Poplar', *The London Journal*, I, 2 (Nov. 1975), 161, 180–3; R. Lawton, 'The population of Liverpool in the mid-nineteenth century', *Transactions of the Historic Society of Lancashire and Cheshire*, CVII (1955), 96–7, 110–11, 117, 120. It is worth adding that for London as a whole, Stedman Jones believes segregation to have been 'practically complete' by 1861: Stedman Jones, *op. cit.*, 247.

52. Briggs, *Victorian Cities*, 143–4; R.G. Wilson, *Gentlemen Merchants: The Merchant Community in Leeds, 1700–1830* (Manchester, 1971), 198–206; M.W. Beresford, 'Prosperity Street and others: an essay in visible urban history' in M.W. Beresford and G.R.J. Jones (eds.), *Leeds and its Region* (Leeds, 1967), 191–2, 194; G.C. Dickson, 'The development of suburban road passenger transport in Leeds, 1840–95', *Journal of Transport History*, IV, 4 (Nov. 1960), 214–15, 219; G. Kitson Clark, 'The Leeds élite', *The University of Leeds Review*, XVII, 2 (1974–5), 232, 257.

53. J. Foster, *Class Struggle and the Industrial Revolution: Early Industrial Capitalism in three English Towns* (1974), 84, 182; Simpson, *op. cit.*, 49, ch. x, 428, 432–8; K.C. Edwards, 'The geographical development of Nottingham' in K.C. Edwards (ed.), *Nottingham and its Region* (Nottingham, 1966), 389–90; Spiers, *op. cit.*, 13–18; Lawton, *op. cit.*, 96–7; Ochojna, *op. cit.*, I, 10–11.

Thus the residential structure of large English and American cities was different at mid-century. In England, the majority of the rich were already at the periphery: the fundamental shift from 'pre-industrial' to 'modern' had already occurred.[54] But in America, the major alteration in residential patterns was still to come. Accordingly, it is scarcely adequate to dismiss Engels's Manchester as 'an exception to the normal nineteenth-century pattern'.[55] For if the 'normal pattern' of 'Victorian cities' is assumed to be the 'walking city' of *ante-bellum* Philadelphia, where 'the patterns of residential segregation were surprisingly weakly developed', then not only Manchester, but *all* major English cities come outside it.[56] And, reciprocally, if the more highly segregated cities of mid-nineteenth-century England are taken as the norm, then those in America are the aberration. If, therefore, the term 'Victorian cities' is assumed to apply to large, segregated towns in England rather than to those still-undifferentiated urban areas across the Atlantic, then the crucial question is not, 'Victorian cities: How modern?' but rather, 'American cities: How Victorian?'

Moreover, in so far as the city of Engels and McCulloch *can* be described in these segregated terms, it is clear that, ironically, it is closer in structure to early twentieth-century Chicago than were the cities of contemporary America. Assuredly, it was only in *some* English towns – Oldham, Manchester and Sheffield – that the zone of affluent houses encircled the city completely.[57] But that deviation from Burgess's idealized model was shared by many 'modern' cities in his own day. While the sensibilities of the urban geographer may be offended by the *incompleteness* of such patterns, the historian will seek to stress the fact that they existed *at all*. Indeed, to the extent that such patterns *did* exist, they were in the form of those very crescents, arcs, segments and wedges which another member of the Chicago School, Homer Hoyt, felt were a more realistic model for describing the 'modern' city than Burgess's concentric rings.[58] Accordingly, it seems possible to re-affirm three propositions about the nature of early and mid-nineteenth-century English cities: first, that they *were* residentially segregated into well-defined areas to an unprecedented extent; second, that the pattern of segregation

54. This, it should be stressed, is only with regard to *residential* patterns. Clearly, towns such as London and Birmingham retained their 'pre-industrial' *economic* structure well into the second half of the nineteenth century. See Stedman Jones. *op. cit.*, 159, 337, 346; Briggs, *Victorian Cities*, 186.
55. Jackson, 'Urban Deconcentration . . .', 126, note 44.
56. Ward, 'Victorian cities . . .', 138.
57. *Ibid.*, 137.
58. H. Hoyt, 'The pattern of movement of residential rental neighbourhoods' in H.M. Mayer and C.F. Kohn (eds.), *Readings in Urban Geography* (Chicago, 1959), 499–510.

did approximate towards that later found in early twentieth-century Chicago; and third, that as a result, the analytical tools evolved in other disciplines to analyse the 'modern' city *can* have useful and valuable retrospective application for Engels's England even if not for *ante-bellum* America.

III

This argument made for the first seventy years of the nineteenth century has implications for that subsequent period of urban growth characterized on both sides of the Atlantic by the advent of mass transport. It was not just that England differed from America in that its towns adopted the tram more slowly and on a smaller scale.[59] More important was the fact that this common technological innovation was imposed on cities whose residential structure was already very different. In America the tram accompanied and created segregation on a large scale for the first time; in England it merely accentuated a process under way for over half a century. The years from 1820 to 1870 had witnessed the golden age of exclusive, middle-class suburbia. Now the lower middle class and the labour aristocracy were able to follow suit. In England, therefore, unlike America, the tram and the people it brought with it did not so much *liberate* the middle classes from the town centre as *threaten* their exclusiveness on the periphery. It eroded rather than buttressed those relatively sharp lines of class distinction established in an earlier period, and gave rise to a degree of class tension and conflict inexplicable without reference to the earlier period of successful middle-class segregation.

First, there was conflict between the inhabitants of segregated suburbia and the social groups immediately beneath them, those lower middle classes and well-paid members of the labour aristocracy whom the tram (in the provinces) and the railway (in London) progressively liberated from the town centre, enabling them to head for the country which had hitherto been a middle- and upper-class preserve. Thus areas of lower quality housing came to encroach upon, and finally surround and breach, these bastions of middle-class exclusiveness. Tramways were built across them; commuters congested them; vociferous lower-class rate-payers demanded the removal of toll gates. During the closing decades of the nineteenth century and the first decade of the twentieth, the middle classes

59. Ward, 'Streetcar suburbs in Boston . . .', 477, 483, 485; Ochojna, *op. cit.*, 14–75.

were under attack, from workers, speculative builders and local authorities. At Kemp Town in Brighton, Kelvinside in Glasgow, Victoria Park in Manchester, the North and South Shores in Blackpool and Hampstead in London, it was the same story.[60] And while in each case there were some invoking the 'public interest', 'social justice' or just plain profit, who threw in their lot with the attacking army, in the main the middle classes manned their barricades with vigour.[61]

But rarely did they do so with success. Trams came to Hampstead in 1887; most of Kelvinside was annexed to Glasgow in 1891; a pleasure beach was established on Blackpool's South Shore a little later in the decade; tolls were exchanged for trams on the North Shore in 1899; cars began to pass through Victoria Park without paying in the 1900s, and trams arrived in 1920.[62] Pressed on all sides, the middle classes retreated to establish and defend new positions of exclusiveness further out, and to see their old haunts occupied in their absence by their pursuers.[63] So began the game of follow-my-leader, as the lower middle classes pursued 'their betters' towards the open country, to be followed in their turn, as pay improved, hours shortened and fares cheapened, by the labour aristocracy.[64] 'The middle classes were the first and the working classes the last to move, but they all kept on doing so.'[65] In Camberwell and in Paddington, the top people moved out and the lower classes moved in, a process still going on to this day in places such as Woodford.[66] What had been for over half a century segregated, secure suburban havens became transit camps with transient campers.[67] And as the central business district itself became enlarged, especially in the

60. A. Dale, *Fashionable Brighton, 1820–60* (1967), 88–9; Simpson, *op. cit.*, 73–6, ch. vi; Spiers, *op. cit.*, 65, 109, ch. vi; J.K. Walton, 'The social development of Blackpool, 1788–1914' (Lancaster Ph.D., 1974), 80–91; Thompson, *Hampstead . . .*, 351–65.
61. Walton, *op. cit.*, 89; Spiers, *op. cit.*, 116–17; Simpson, *op. cit.*, 171–85.
62. Walton, *op. cit.*, 82–3, 87–91; Spiers, *op. cit.*, 108–9, 126–34; Simpson, *op. cit.*, 20, 180–5, 390–1, 439–40; Thompson, *Hampstead . . .*, 364, 370–5.
63. Sheppard, *op. cit.*, 94; H.J. Dyos, *Victorian Suburb: A Study of the Growth of Camberwell* (Leicester, 1961), 105–9; J.T. Coppock, 'The changing face of England, 1850-circa 1900' in Darby, *op. cit.*, 659; H.J. Dyos and D.A. Reeder, 'Slums and suburbs' in Dyos and Wolf, *op. cit.*, 1, 360–1.
64. H.J. Dyos, *Urbanity and Suburbanity: An Inaugural Lecture* (Leicester, 1973), 15; *idem, Victorian Suburb . . .*, 76; Sheppard, *op. cit.*, 8–10, 109; Ochojna, *op. cit.*, 266–72; Thompson, *Hampstead . . .*, 361–4.
65. D.A. Reeder, 'Capital investment in the western suburbs of Victorian London' (Leicester Ph.D., 1965), 57.
66. D.A. Reeder, 'A theatre of suburbs: some patterns of development in West London, 1801–1911' in Dyos, *The Study of Urban History*, 261, 264–5; Dyos, *Victorian Suburb . . .*, 76, 191–3; P. Willmott and M. Young, *Family and Class in a London Suburb* (1960), ch. 1.
67. Dyos, *Victorian Suburb . . .*, 23.

inter- and post-war years, the great houses and their big gardens were converted into offices, nursing homes, hotels and departments and hostels for the local university.[68]

In those towns where the exclusive middle-class suburbs of the first three quarters of the nineteenth century had been sited on large urban estates, this development introduced a further element of conflict, between the tenants who, after defeat, were often eager to leave, and the landlord who, under these circumstances even more than before, wanted to prevent them from doing so. As Donald Olsen has noted: 'If the great task of the estate plan was to entice respectable tenants, the great task of management during the terms of the leases was to keep them there.[69] But leases ran conventionally for ninety-nine years, whereas the period of exclusiveness for these early middle-class suburbs – assuming the landlord had been successful in getting the preferred 'respectable' tenants in the first place – terminated in a shorter time. As the nineteenth century neared its close, the desire of landlords to preserve their exclusive urban estates inviolate was increasingly at odds with those 'anonymous economic and social forces' which went to make up the process of urban expansion.[70]

As Asa Briggs has noted, 'There was plenty of movement in the Victorian city – it was founded on it', and in so far as that was true for the late nineteenth century, that movement was both a cause and a consequence of class conflict.[71] When belligerently defending their suburban oases, the middle classes antagonized the approaching classes beneath; when self-interestedly fleeing from them, they annoyed their landlord above. Both types of tension were absent from those American cities already referred to, only Roxbury on the outskirts of Boston affording a parallel example of encirclement and decay.[72] Given the explanation for this conflict advanced here, the lack of a similar response in America will come as no surprise. The same transport innovation superimposed on cities whose residential structure was already different, would necessarily produce different results.[73]

68. Spiers, *op. cit.*, 146–61; P.H. Mann, *An Approach to Urban Sociology* (1965), 84.
69. Olsen, *Town Planning . . .*, 21–2.
70. *Ibid.*, 215.
71. Briggs, *Victorian Cities*, 73.
72. Warner, *Streetcar Suburb . . .*, 106–16.
73. Recent work on Latin American and Australian cities in the age of the tram suggests that they, too, did not develop in exactly the same way as cities in North America. See L.F. Schnore, 'On the spatial structure of cities in the two Americas' in P.M. Hauser and L.F. Schnore (eds.), *The Study of Urbanization* (New York, 1965), ch. x; J.R. Scobie, *Buenos Aires: Plaza to Suburb, 1870–1910* (New York, 1974), 114–20, 158–9; J.W. McCarty, 'Australian capital cities in the nineteenth century', *Australian Economic History Review*, x, 2 (Spet. 1970), 117.

IV

The remainder of this paper examines one particular exclusive suburb, the Calthorpes' Edgbaston Estate in Birmingham, a classic example of landlord influence and middle-class preference combining to produce a segregated neighbourhood, and an equally fine instance of late nineteenth- and early twentieth-century conflict and decline. It is also offered as an example of the way in which the techniques of the social sciences may be modified and used to illuminate the events and experiences of the past. Thus it is a case-study both in terms of its facts and its methodology.

The estate was bought by Sir Richard Gough, a retired East India merchant, in 1717.[74] It was a small, rural manor, at its closest one mile from the centre of Birmingham, measuring 1,700 acres. It was extended by subsequent purchases to over 2,000 acres, or rather more than four-fifths of the entire parish, at which size it remained until sales and donations this century reduced it to slightly less than its original size.[75] Although nine building leases were granted on land in the north-east corner nearest to the town during the years 1786–96 (the family by then having ceased to reside on the estate), it was not until the time of Sir Richard's great grandson, George, the third Lord Calthorpe, who held the title from 1807 to 1851, that the decision was taken to develop the estate systematically by granting ninety-nine year building leases. The details of the scheme were outlined in 1811–13 by John Harris, Lord Calthorpe's agent, and were immediately accepted and implemented. He proposed 'a general and well-considered plan' in order to attract 'the gentlemen and tradesmen . . . at the expense of the farmer', on the grounds that such people would take land 'rather for amusement than profit'.[76] That residential accommodation might be given to people of lower status was not even considered. Speculative building was to be discouraged, the preferred type of tenant being 'those people who, having acquired a moderate competence, wish to retire to a small country house and therefore take just as much land as would be sufficient for the purpose'.[77] In short, at the very time when it was becoming increasingly fashionable for growing numbers of wealthy people to quit town centres and seek more congenial surroundings,

74. *Edgbaston Estate Office Mss.* (subsequently *E.E.O. Mss.*), Release of the Manor of Edgbaston in the County of Warwick, 16 April 1717. I am grateful to Brigadier Sir Richard A.-G.-Calthorpe for permission to consult these papers.
75. A. Sutcliffe and R. Smith, *The History of Birmingham*, III (1974), 457.
76. Hampshire County Record Office, *Calthorpe Papers* (subsequently H.R.O. *Cal. Mss.*), Boc 35, John Harris, Observations for Lord Calthorpe's Correction, 1811.
77. H.R.O. *Cal. Mss.*, F/C/157, Harris to Calthorpe, 14 June 1813.

the Calthorpes sought to meet this demand in Birmingham by creating, in Lewis Mumford's words, 'a green ghetto dedicated to the élite'.[78]

How did they do it? What steps did they take to create and maintain a distinctive image for their estate so as to attract such high-class tenants? They were given a flying start by environmental advantages which the area enjoyed. First, the estate was situated on the south-western side of the town and, since the prevailing wind came from the west, it was spared the smoke and pollution which hung over the rest of the town throughout the nineteenth century.[79] Moreover, unlike the lands to the south-east, the estate was located on relatively high, well-drained, undulating land. To open up this attractive area for building, the Calthorpes spent over £47,000 during the course of the nineteenth century on 'fine roads . . . and ornamental walks, which present an aspect of beauty and picturesqueness in striking contrast to the old parts of Birmingham'.[80] These roads were wide, sewered and laid far apart. In addition they were beautified by the planting of trees which, along with those already existing, were zealously protected by the estate so that its sylvan appearance should remain intact.[81]

This pleasant prospect was complemented by 'the encouragement of a wide range of amenities' so as to establish the appropriately lofty 'tone' – a common practice among estate developers at that time.[82] Accordingly, land and money were given for churches: for St George's in 1833, St James' in 1852, and St Ambrose and St Mary's in 1898.[83] In addition, the estate established its reputation as 'patron of the charities of life' by letting land on favourable terms to those local voluntary associations anxious for clear air and sylvan surroundings – the Deaf and Dumb Asylum in 1814, the Botanical and Horticultural Society in 1836, and the General Institution for the Blind in 1851.[84] Although in part such generosity was motivated by genuine philanthropic concern, the Calthorpes also had their eye very

78. Mumford, *op. cit.*, 561.
79. For a general model which, on the basis of looking at Sheffield, Nottingham and Huddersfield, suggests that the western side of towns was more likely to be the high-class area, given a westerly prevailing wind, see Mann, *op. cit.*, 96.
80. *E.E.O. Mss.* Box 1, G. Edwards, written evidence for the *Select Committee on Town Holdings*, 1888, 2; *Edgbastonia Directory for 1883* (Birmingham, 1883), 41.
81. For detailed evidence, see D.N. Cannadine, 'The aristocracy and the towns in the nineteenth century: a case study of the Calthorpes and Birmingham, 1807–1910' (Oxford D. Phil., 1975), 267–8.
82. Sir John Summerson, foreword to Dyos, *Victorian Suburb* . . ., 8; J.R. Kellett, 'Property speculators and the building of Glasgow, 1780–1830', *Scottish Journal of Political Economy* VIII, 3 (Oct. 1961), 224.
83. Cannadine, *op. cit.*, 86–7, 92, 109.
84. *Ibid.*, 77–9, 92.

firmly on business. 'Such an establishment will generally promote the interests of the estate', wrote Harris when urging that favourable terms should be given to the Botanical and Horticultural Society.[85] To this list of benefactions may be added the provision of land for a public park in 1857 and its donation to the town in 1894, as well as two grants of land for the site of the new Birmingham University in 1900 and 1907.[86] Here again, altruism and self-interest were mixed. 'It will open up a large area of building land which is at present not available', wrote the Edgbaston agent of the time.[87]

On the negative side, the tone was set by the almost complete exclusion of industry, trade and commerce, 'which tends to make the neighbourhood respectable and genteel', as one commentator noted as early as 1819.[88] 'It has hitherto been understood', wrote Harris to Calthorpe in 1830, 'that no steam engine or manufactories were admissable into the parish.'[89] Half a century later, the same policy still held. In 1888, George Edwards, the then Edgbaston agent, claimed that he had rejected an application for land at eight pence a yard 'for a site on lease without restrictions, and have afterwards let the same land with restrictions suitable to the character of the neighbourhood at two pence a yard'.[90] When land was given for Calthorpe Park and the University, it was on condition that it should never be used for commercial or industrial purposes. Indeed, of all the 1,284 building leases granted between 1786 and 1914, only eleven were for non-residential purposes, and even these were explicitly restricted to small-scale undertakings, such as a stone mason's works or a carpenter's shop.[91]

This consistent policy of exclusion was naturally accompanied by the insertion of 'stringent covenants as to the purpose for which the land may be used'[92] in the building leases. The list of prohibitions explicitly excluded both poverty and industry:

> Any small dwelling house or houses of the description of labourers' or poor persons' houses or which shall be occupied by labourers or poor persons, nor any workshop or workshops or other kind of shop

85. H.R.O. *Cal. Mss.*, F/C/1217, Harris to Calthorpe, 9 Sept. 1830.
86. Cannadine, *op. cit.*, 95, 109, 112–13.
87. *E.E.O. Mss.* K/5, Davies to the Hon. Walter Gough-Calthorpe, 16 July 1900. For an account of the Calthorpes' philanthropic activities which sets them in the context of social and political change in the city, see D. Cannadine, 'The Calthorpe family and Birmingham, 1810–1910: a "conservative interest" examined', *Historical Journal*, XVIII, 4 (Dec. 1975), *passim*.
88. C. Pye, *Description of Modern Birmingham* (Birmingham, 1819), 190.
89. *E.E.O. Mss.* Box 5, Harris to Calthorpe, 16 Jan. 1830.
90. *E.E.O. Mss.* Box 1, G. Edwards, written evidence for the *Select Committee on Town Holdings*, 1888, 2.
91. Cannadine, 'Aristocracy and the towns . . .', 249.
92. W. Barrow, 'The town and its industries' in J.H. Muirhead (ed.), *Birmingham Institutions* (Birmingham, 1911), 47.

or shops, nor any place or places for carrying on any trade or manufacture, nor any beer shop, ale house, tea garden, public strawberry
garden or any other place of public resort or amusement whatsoever.[93]

In addition, all building plans were vetted before construction was
authorized, the estate reserved the right to inspect each house twice
each year, and there were strict covenants to ensure that buildings
were maintained in good condition, both inside and out. As the
century drew on, and as some tenants tried to convert houses into
fish shops, dressmaking establishments and consulting rooms, estate
agents spared no effort in enforcing these covenants zealously.[94]

The final aspect of management which merits attention was sustained hostility to attempts to promote public transport across
the estate. The tendency of canals, railways and trams to bring
with them warehouses, factories and slums was as well known to
contemporaries as to historians.[95] To such decay the Calthorpes
were indefatigably opposed. Their policy was set in 1791 when Sir
Henry Cough-Calthorpe, first Lord Calthorpe, uniquely among all
Birmingham landowners similarly threatened, had clauses inserted
protecting his property when a canal (the Birmingham and Worcester) was projected across his estate. Industry, the making of
reservoirs and the taking of water from streams on his estate were
all explicitly prohibited.[96] This policy was continued throughout the
nineteenth century. In 1866 the line of the railway to Harborne was
opposed. Between 1871 and 1881 a protracted battle was fought
against what was initially the Birmingham and West Suburban
Railway to Kings Norton, which later became the Midland Railway
to Bristol. And as the new century dawned, repeated, if slightly
less energetic attempts were made to ward off the threat by the
Corporation to lay tramlines down the Harborne and Hagley Roads
in 1901, 1906–7 and 1911–12.[97] On the second of these occasions, the
Calthorpes' legal charges came to over £600.[98]

V

This policy of estate management, carefully evolved, consistently
applied and zealously enforced, at least until the last decades of the
nineteenth-century, exemplifies to perfection the static and élitist

93. *E.E.O. Mss.* Box 6, Building lease to Thomas Clowes, 25 March 1828. The
    covenants became even stronger as the century progressed.
94. Cannadine, 'Aristocracy and the towns . . .', 264–5.
95. Kellett, *Impact of Railways*, 349–50.
96. The Birmingham and Worcester Canal Act (1791), clauses iv, v, xiii.
97. Cannadine, 'Aristocracy and the towns . . .', 288–98, 300–5.
98. *E.E.O. Mss.* Letter Book IV, Balden to Calthorpe, 2 July 1907.

preference of nineteenth-century urban landlords, more anxious to maximize prestige than profit, and thereby acting as major agents of social segregation. And, given the Calthorpes' success in attracting 'the opulent inhabitants of Birmingham', 'those who have basked in the sunshine of commercial prosperity',[99] it is clear that for a long period they were providing exactly what the new, enlarged industrial élite of Birmingham wanted. 'Edgbaston is unquestionably the most important suburb in Birmingham', observed *Edgbastonia* on the occasion of its first issue in 1881. It was 'the favourite place of residence for the professional men, merchants and traders of the busy town which it adjoins. With a population more numerous and wealthy than those of other suburbs.'[100] Such an immodest claim would have been ridiculously conceited, had it not been truc. In 1882 the same magazine began a series on 'Edgbastonians past and present'. It read like a Birmingham *Who's Who*. Among the first to be featured were Arthur Ryland, George Dawson, Charles Sturge, E.F.M. MacCarthy, Thomas Avery, H.W. Crosskey, J.H. Chamberlain, Thomas Martineau, Joseph Chamberlain, Joseph Sturge, Samuel Timmins and Timothy Kenrick.[101] And as the old century faded, the civic élite showed no inclination to move away: Charles Gabriel Beale, Sir George Kenrick, Sir Oliver Lodge, Charles Gore, Austen and Neville Chamberlain were all sheltered beneath the Calthorpes' residential umbrella. As the table shows, Edgbaston was but the Council House at home:

TABLE 1   Members of Birmingham Town Council resident in Edgbaston

Year	Aldermen	Councillors
1866–7	10/16	17/46
1877–8	11/15	18/47
1881–2	11/16	22/48
1891–2	11/18	19/55
1901–2	10/18	15/53

Note   The second figure gives the total membership of the Town Council.
Source   Kelleys Directories of Birmingham: 1868, 436; 1878, 585–6; 1882, 673–4; 1892, 732–3; 1902, 974–6.

 99. Pye, *op. cit.*, 191; W. Hutton, *History of Birmingham* (6th ed., Birmingham, 1835), 457–8.
100. *Edgbastonia*, May 1881, 1.
101. *Edgbastonia*: May 1882, 76–9; Sept. 1882, 140–3; Nov. 1882, 172–4; Apr. 1883, 49–52; Aug. 1883, 113–17; Oct. 1883, 145–8; Nov. 1883, 161–6; Jan. 1884, 1–4; Mar. 1884, 33–6; Apr. 1884, 49–54; Sept. 1884, 129–37; Mar. 1885, 33–6. Joseph Chamberlain had actually left Edgbaston for Highbury in 1880. But, as the issue featuring him pointed out: 'Many of his family connections are still amongst the most respected of our inhabitants.' (*Edgbastonia*, Mar. 1884, 33.)

In other words, having successfully established its reputation during the first fifty years of slow development, for the rest of the nineteenth century the Calthorpe Estate housed that 'small knot of Nonconformist families, who knew each other well, frequently inter-married and continued until the middle of the twentieth century to dominate local social life'.[102] Beales, Chamberlains and Kenricks were united in the past by common ancestors as in the present by corporate activity. What, then, could be more natural than that they should live in close proximity?[103] And who could then be surprised that they should constantly inter-marry?[104] Here was the epicentre of that 'great village' which Dale believed Birmingham to be.[105] The history of Birmingham in its most heroic period was very largely the history of the public lives and group consciousness of Edgbaston's most famous inhabitants.

If the landlord gave Edgbaston its roads, its trees and its distinctively exclusive planning, and if the appropriate people had moved in bringing the desired residential tone, these families also gave it something more, which the Calthorpes' policy made possible, but could never itself provide. For it was these families who gave Edgbaston a specific set of cultural values, who invested the area with sentiment and symbolism in the same way that the great families of Boston did on Beacon Hill.[106] In both cases, among the residents, there was the same self-conscious group identity, the same 'complex network of blood relationships', the same civic zeal, and the same pride in having been born or having lived in one area of the town.[107] A generation ago, Walter Firey described Beacon Hill as being

> located some five minutes' walking distance from the retail centre of Boston. This neighbourhood has for fully a century and a half maintained its character as a preferred upper class residential district, despite contiguity to a low rent, tenement area . . . During its long history, Beacon Hill has become the symbol for a number of sentimental associations which constitute a genuine attractive force to certain old families in Boston.[108]

102. Briggs, *Victorian Cities*, 204.
103. E.M. Hoover, 'The evolving form and organization of the Metropolis' in H.S. Perloff and L. Wingo, jr (eds.), *Issues in Urban Economics* (Baltimore, 1968), 237, 246, 264; Warner, *Streetcar Suburbs . . .*, 75, 157; W. Ashworth, 'Types of social and economic development in suburban Essex' in R. Glass (ed.), *London: Aspects of Change* (1964), 80; Thompson, *Hampstead . . .*, 241.
104. D. Timms, *The Urban Mosaic: Towards a Theory of Residential Differentiation* (Cambridge, 1971), 13.
105. Briggs, *Victorian Cities*, 204.
106. W. Firey, 'Sentiment and symbolism as ecological variables', *American Sociological Review*, x, 2 (April 1945). For a similar idea set in a European context see: E. Jones, *A social Geography of Belfast* (1960), 272–80.
107. W. Firey, *Land Use in Central Boston* (Cambridge, Mass., 1947), 97, 108.
108. Firey, 'Sentiment and symbolism . . .', 141.

If Birmingham is substituted for Boston, Edgbaston for Beacon Hill, the description is perfect. In both cases, 'a wide range of sentiments – aesthetic, historical, familial – . . . acquired a spatial articulation'.[109] Why otherwise did the civic élite of Birmingham at the end of the nineteenth century continue to reside where their predecessors had? They did so because Edgbaston stood both for a pleasant environment and for group solidarity. The attitudes of landlord and residents coincided perfectly. The Calthorpes gave Edgbaston its careful planning and élitist orientation. These families gave a specific set of cultural values. The coincidence of needs could not be more precisely demonstrated, making Edgbaston a classic example of 'a geographical area characterized by physical individuality and by the cultural characteristics of the people who live in it'.[110]

VI

Thus, the Edgbaston Estate ranks as a classic example of early and mid-nineteenth-century suburban residential segregation, more unified in its pattern of landownership than Hampstead, greater in area than Victoria Park, and more coherently managed than Kelvinside. But the pattern of segregation was never quite that simple. For while the ban on industry was as good as absolute, in terms of housing Edgbaston was characterized by a much less homogeneous and exalted social tone than its unitary planning and lofty corporate cultural values would suggest. As the table shows, by 1914 the majority of its inhabitants were not the hardware princes just described, but the lower middle class and even the labour aristocracy.

Although the table is biased downwards, since all values are in money not real terms, and since a £500 house in 1810 was clearly for a higher social group than a £500 house in 1910, the overall picture of a pyramid is undoubtedly correct. Less than one-third of all the leases and only one-seventh of the houses permitted were those relatively lavish dwellings, costing £1,000 or more, which gave Edgbaston its reputation as 'the Belgravia of Birmingham', and were

109. *Ibid.*
110. H.W. Zorbaugh, 'The natural areas of the City', *Publications of the American Sociological Society*, xx (1926), 197. Quoted in Timms, *op. cit.*, 6. The best account of life among the Edgbaston élite, from both an admiring and a satirical standpoint, is to be found in the highly allusive novels of Francis Brett Young, especially *White Ladies* and *Dr Bradley Remembers*. See also: M. Bantock, *Granville Bantock: A Personal Portrait* (1972), ch. viii.

TABLE 2   Value of houses built on Edgbaston Estate, 1786–1914

Size of house (£)	No. of leases granted	No. of houses authorized
1500+	165	189
1000–1499	180	247
500–999	468	944
0–499	471	1,461
Total	1,284	2,841

Source   E.E.O. Mss., Lease Books, I–VIII.

the physical embodiment of the cultural values of its Nonconformist élite. Slightly more than one-third of the leases, and also about one-third of the houses, were for the solid and respectable middle classes. The remainder – one-third of the leases and no less than half of the houses – were for the lower middle class and the labour aristocracy. Dr Reeder's analysis of the census figures for the whole parish for 1851 and 1861 corroborates this picture.[111] Only 10 per cent of the households could afford to keep three or more servants, and while, in 1851, 58 per cent of heads of household had occupations of a professional and managerial nature, that left nearly half who were petty producers, travellers, clerks, labourers, or even unemployed.

It is clear what had happened to the estate as it had expanded. As with many other initially exclusive developments, the preferences of the landlord had melted before the irrefutable fact that even in a town the size of Birmingham, there were simply not enough well to-do people to fill up so large an estate with villas. Consequently, the Calthorpes were forced to take tenants lower down the social scale, and to house them in dwellings constructed by those speculative builders whom they had initially sought to discourage. Accordingly, it became necessary to zone the estate so as to separate the welcomed wealthy and the tolerated tradesmen. In Edgbaston, segregation meant not only keeping industry out, but keeping tenants of different socio-economic status apart. Although the slowness of the estate development made this hard, in that it was difficult to designate whole areas for one type of housing when they might not be filled up for fifty years or so, the fact that the estate was wedge-shaped, and bounded on the north side by Hagley Road, and on the south-west side by the Bristol and Pershore roads, made it possible to

111. D.A. Reeder, 'The making of a garden suburb: Edgbaston in the nineteenth century' (unpublished conference paper, Urban History Group, 1970), 7–8.

evolve a plan which was simple yet effective.[112] Where the estate owned land on the far side of these roads, abutting directly on to the town, the working-class and lower-middle class houses were

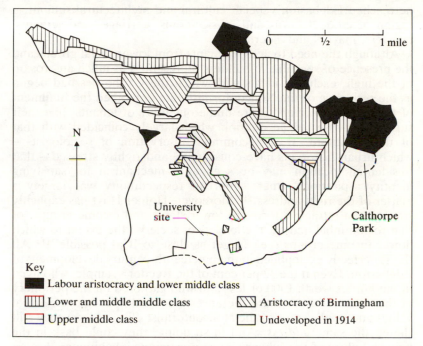

Fig. 1 Edgbaston estate zoning pattern, *c.* 1914.

tucked discreetly away. Then, acting in conjunction with these three main roads as a buffer against the pressure of the expanding and adjacent town, there was a crescent of middle-middle-class houses, extending from Hagley Road, via Calthorpe, George, Frederick and Wheeleys roads to the Bristol and Pershore roads. Finally, in the centre of the wedge, sheltered from the cheapest Calthorpe houses and the hostile, proximate urban environment, were those expensive dwellings – fewer in number but much greater in area – which were responsible for the estate's exalted status, mansions such as 'Whetstone' in Farquar Road, where one branch of the Kenrick family lived, 'Westbourne' in the road of the same name, where Neville Chamberlain took up residence after his marriage in 1911, and 'Mariemont' in the same road, home of Sir Oliver

112. See Fig. 1.

Lodge, first Principal of the new University of Birmingham. Thus, as the map shows, a visitor approaching the estate at any time after 1880, from either its northern or south-western border, would pass through successive layers of housing until, in the centre of the wedge, he reached Edgbaston's social, cultural and architectural summit, a region of croquet lawns and music rooms, carriages and servants' quarters, mayors and aldermen.

Although the need to accept tenants from lower social groups and the presence of speculative builders represented as much an erosion of the high, exclusive ideals with which the Calthorpes had begun as the residence of the Nonconformist élite embodied the fulfilment of them, this lower and more numerous body of tenants, like their superiors, possessed an outlook which largely coincided with that of their landlord. It is a common observation of sociologists – which urban historians have consistently and rightly stressed – that 'residential location may be seen as a mechanism for satisfying identity aspirations', that 'suburban respectability was largely a matter of the right address.[113] Moreover, Homer Hoyt has explicitly stressed the attractive force, to lower status and income groups, of that region inhabited by 'the leaders of society', the extent to which 'lower income groups seek to get as close to it as possible'.[114] All this is perfectly exemplified in the nineteenth-century development of Edgbaston. Even if the 42 per cent of the Reeder's sample, who lived in the houses worth £500 or less and who gathered on the periphery of the estate, did not share the ancestors, wealth, religion, cultural values and public spirit of the Nonconformist élite, at least they still shared the same *address*. And in so doing, they could bask in the reflected glory of the suburb's most prestigious inhabitants.

Edgbaston was thus a neighbourhood in both senses in which that word has meaning for the sociologist. If the Nonconformist élite is taken, then it was as Dale saw, a face-to-face community, where the residents enjoyed close social contact, familial, personal, professional, religious and cultural.[115] But, at the same time, if the second definition is taken, namely that of a statistical aggregate contained within a recognizable physical area, in which the inhabitants share certain specific social characteristics, but impersonally, then that description is clearly valid also.[116] Accordingly, regardless of their exact social level, the majority of tenants tended to be as anxious to safeguard Edgbaston's famed and unique qualities as was

113. Timms, *op. cit.*, 251; Dyos, *Victorian Suburb* . . ., 23, 82–3.
114. Hoyt, 'Pattern of movement . . .', 501.
115. R. Glass, 'The structure of neighbourhoods' in Max Lock (ed.), *The County Borough of Middlesbrough: Survey and Plan* (Middlesbrough, 1947), 156.
116. *Ibid.*

the landlord. The occupants of the great houses naturally wished to preserve them inviolate. And the lower-class tenants wanted that too, in order to maintain that reflected glory in which it was their ambition to bask.

So it is possible to detect a tenant consciousness independent of, but collaborating with, the landlord. In 1866, when the Harborne line was projected, the Estate Office consulted the tenants whose houses might be affected, and found that sixteen opposed the scheme of whom six subsequently lent their support to the Calthorpes' opposition to the bill.[117] Against the line to Kings Norton the tenants were even more aggressive, thirty-six lessees promoting their own separate petition to supplement that of the Calthorpes in 1879.[118] But it was when the Corporation attempted to lay trams that the tenants' collective consciousness was most effectively roused, so much so that it was they, rather than the landlord, who took the initiative. In 1901, when trams were first seriously threatened along the Harborne and Hagley roads, an *ad hoc* tenants' committee was set up. A poll was conducted among the Edgbaston residents, and of the 429 who voted, 383 were against.[119] Opposition took the same form in 1906–7, when the Calthorpes, increasingly reluctant to go to the expense and trouble of opposition, were dragged along by the vigour of their tenants' campaign.[120] By 1911–12, the landlord, worried by problems of death duties and reversion, had all but given up. On the two previous occasions, the Calthorpes had petitioned separately from their tenants. This time the new tenant for life simply added her signature to the residents' petition, and donated £100 towards expenses.[121] The tenants had all but superseded the landlord as guardian of the amenities. Though made up of a wider social spectrum than Firey's Boston Brahmins, the vigilance of Edgbaston's tenants merits comparison with that of the residents of Beacon Hill.[122]

They were similarly concerned about the enforcement of covenants. The estate correspondence is littered with letters from irate tenants protesting against smoke from neighbouring greenhouse chimneys, the noise from boys playing football on undeveloped land close by, and the dire social consequences of an adjacent house being used as a dressmaking establishment.[123] Most tenants

117. Cannadine, 'Aristocracy and the towns . . .', 288–9.
118. *Ibid.*, 295.
119. *Ibid.*, 301.
120. *Ibid.*, 303–5.
121. *E.E.O. Mss.* Minute Book VIII, 121–2, 29 Dec. 1911; *E.E.O. Mss.* Box 7, the Hon. Mrs Rachel A.-G.-Calthorpe to Balden, 29 Jan. 1912.
122. Firey, 'Sentiment and symbolism . . .', 143; *idem, Land Use* . . ., 128–32.
123. Cannadine, 'Aristocracy and the towns . . .', 268–9.

built in Edgbaston 'without fear of detriment to the value of their property', because they believed the landlord would enforce the covenants.[124] It only needed the slenderest of evidence and outraged tenants were writing to remind the agent where his duty lay. Half the correspondence at the Estate Office was from the agent, urging the few wayward tenants to obey the covenants; the other half was from lessees reporting infringements. Indeed, given that there was no possible way in which the Office could keep an eye on all the 2,841 houses built by 1914, it was only with such co-operation from lessees, tenants and residents that covenant enforcement could be made effective at all. Ultimately the Calthorpes were dependent on the consent and co-operation of their tenants. And because the tenants had the outlook that they did, in the main, they got it.

VII

Like Victoria Park and Kelvinside, Edgbaston's golden age as a suburban retreat began in the 1830s (by which time the teething troubles of the two previous decades had been successfully over-come) and lasted for half a century or so.[125] Although the building booms of the 1850s, 1860s and 1870s resulted in a proliferation of small houses to a greater extent than either landlord or upper middle-class tenants would ideally have wished, the zoning plan evolved en-sured that exclusiveness was preserved, and this, combined with the international fame of Edgbaston's most illustrious civic dignitaries, meant that the estate retained both its integrity and its reputation largely intact until the 1880s. But what happened thereafter? How did it face the challenges which threatened other exclusive suburbs? How far was its segregated atmosphere preserved inviolate in the new century? One clue to this is provided by the fact that from the mid-1880s, new building practically came to a complete halt. In the next sixty years or so relatively few houses were built, and only two new major roads were laid down. Both the turn-of-the-century and the inter-war building booms passed Edgbaston by.[126] In 1914, over half of the land area was still unbuilt on.[127] If only in terms of its pace of development, Edgbaston's golden age was over by the mid-1880s.

This suggests that all was not well on other fronts. On the

124. *Edgbaston Directory for 1883*, 41.
125. For a detailed account of the chronology of Edgbaston's development, see Cannadine, 'Aristocracy and the towns . . .', ch. v.
126. *Ibid.*, 228–36; The Calthorpe Estate Company, *An Introduction to the Calthorpe Estate Re-development Proposals* (Birmingham, 1958), 3.
127. See Fig. 1.

contrary, despite the fact that for over half a century landlord and tenants had combined 'to resist developments which were socially unacceptable',[128] by the time the new century dawned, they were definitely on the defensive, seeking – unavailingly – to ward off the threats to its exclusiveness which were increasingly pressing. Indeed, even before its development had slowed down, Edgbaston had already been ravished by the construction of the Harborne line in 1874 and the Birmingham and West Suburban Railway in 1876. Much more important, however, were the consequences for the estate of the growth of new suburbs to the west of Edgbaston, at Quinton, Warley, Oldbury, Bearwood, Selly Oak, Bournville and Moseley from the 1880s.[129] Edgbaston, once a wedge with its western extremity open to the countryside had become, by 1914, an enclave surrounded by built-up areas on its borders.[130] The inhabitants of these new, distant suburbs, needing to cross Edgbaston to get to work in the city centre, created heavy commuter traffic along the once quiet and residential Hagley, Harborne, Bristol and Pershore roads.[131] Omnibus services were introduced, and tramways were constructed along Bristol Road as early as 1876 (when neither the estate nor the tenants protested),[132] and along Hagley Road itself in 1914. Protests and petitions had not been enough. The Corporation, even though composed of so many Edgbaston residents, championed the public interest rather than local loyalty.

The effect of the tramways was alarming. Noise and ugliness brought depreciation to houses already built, and effectively post-poned the construction of any more. On the Bristol Road, there were no building leases granted for twenty years after the trams came.[133] Whereas in 1872 there had been 47 prominent Birmingham men residing in that road, by 1906 there were only four.[134] Indeed, by the 1910s, they were not merely leaving the Bristol Road. The increased noise of the growing commuter traffic and the attraction of the new suburbs farther out meant that some were beginning to leave Edgbaston altogether, for the peace and greater distance of places such as Knowle and Solihull.[135] 'If the estate will only wait

128. Coppock, 'Changing face of England . . .', 670.
129. A. Briggs, *The History of the County of Warwick*, VII, *The City of Birmingham* (1964), 17–24; *Birmingham Daily Post*, Greater Birmingham Supplement, 22 May 1911.
130. See Fig. 2.
131. *E.E.O. Mss.*, Birmingham Corporation Bill, Minutes of Evidence, 7 Mar. 1907, 28; *E.E.O. Mss.* Letter Book IV, Balden to Calthorpe, 10 Dec. 1904.
132. It was not realized at this early date exactly what the consequences of trams would be.
133. *E.E.O. Mss.*, Birmingham Corporation Bill, Minutes of Evidence, 8 March. 1907, 77.
134. *Ibid.*, 11 March. 1907, 177.
135. Briggs, *History of Birmingham*, 140.

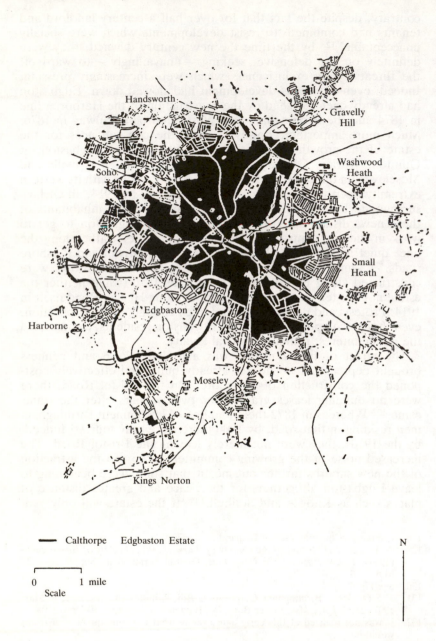

Handsworth

Gravelly
Hill

Soho

Washwood
Heath

Small
Heath

Edgbaston

Harborne

Moseley

Kings Norton

—— Calthorpe Edgbaston Estate

N

0   1 mile
   Scale

Fig. 2 Built-up area of Greater Birmingham, *c.* 1914

a little time, the migration on the part of the wealthier people will end', wrote the Bishop of Birmingham in 1914.[136] He was wrong. By the First World War, Edgbaston's seclusion and monopoly had both vanished. The game of follow-my-leader had begun.[137]

The attempts to enforce covenants present a similar picture of 'strategic retreats'.[138] In the centre, where stood the great palaces, and on many parts of the Bristol, Hagley and Pershore roads, all was well. But elsewhere on the periphery there were two problems. First, the oldest middle-class houses, at the north-east corner, near Five Ways, were by 1910 100 years old, 'with no modern conveniences . . . with no bathrooms at all, and really . . . quite out of date'.[139] And the landlord was powerless to force the tenants to modernize such houses, whose antiquity and lack of facilities only served to reinforce the flight to the new outer suburbs, filled as they were with houses in the latest style, fitted with modern conveniences.[140] Elsewhere, in the three largest working-class areas, there was the problem of metropolitan pressure on the lowest quality Calthorpe housing. Although the historian may feel *a priori* doubts about the 'ecological determinism' of E.W. Burgess's concentric zone model, its relevance here cannot be denied. By the early 1900s, despite the combined vigilance of most of the tenants and the Estate Office, these lower-class districts were definitely sinking in tone and appearance in the face of the onslaught of the adjacent inner zone.[141] And such decline, having once begun, did indeed prove to be irreversible, as private houses were taken over by lower income groups, then converted into lodging houses and workshops.

---

136. *E.E.O. Mss.* Box 9, the Bishop of Birmingham to the Hon. Mrs Rachel A.-G.-Calthorpe, 4 June 1914.
137. The continuation of Table 1 is as follows:

Year	Aldermen	Councillors
1909–10	8/16	18/53
1911–12	8/29	18/90
1921– 2	6/29	10/90

Note The second figure gives the total membership of the Town Council.
Source *Kelleys Directories of Birmingham*: 1910, 1119–20; 1912; 1135–6; 1922, 1286–7).

138. Olsen, *Town Planning . . .*, 215.
139. House of Lords Record Office, Minutes of Evidence, *House of Commons Select Committee on Birmingham Corporation Bill*, 16 Apr. 1912, 3.
140. For a more detailed analysis of the reasons why upper income groups move to new houses see: R.J. Johnston, *Urban Residential Patterns: An Introductory Review* (1971), 96–7, and references cited there.
141. Burgess, 'Growth of the City . . .', 50. See also Fig. 2.

143

Since the Second World War, decline has been complete, to red light areas and, most recently of all, to immigrant ghettos.[142] With the exception of the small and most recently developed artisan area on the western boundary of the estate, all areas marked black on Map I have been sold, so that the estate had retreated almost completely into an enclave behind the Hagley and Bristol roads. The first and smallest area, adjacent to the railway and the Worcester Canal, where decay was most advanced, was sold off in 1918.[143] The two remaining areas were disposed of to the Corporation in the 1950s and 1960s.[144] Since then, old houses have been completely demolished, and a systematic programme of urban renewal undertaken. That such drastic steps were necessary explains why the estate was glad to sell these embarrassing areas. That such squalor could exist at all was eloquent proof of the limits to a landlord's power, even when backed up by the majority of his tenants. Ultimately even this joint barrier was not impregnable.

In conclusion, it is worth drawing attention to two recent facets of Edgbaston's development. First, although Edgbaston still keeps its reputation as the 'graceful suburb',[145] spatially referred cultural values and social prestige have gone because, as with Beacon Hill, the families who provided them no longer play the role nor occupy the houses they once did. It was not just, as the Bishop of Birmingham said, that they had begun to leave Edgbaston, increasingly true though that was. It was also that, by 1940, *wherever* they lived, these families had ceased to dominate Birmingham as they once had. Neville Chamberlain's death in that year was symbolic in more ways than one.[146] Although the families still survive, their collective identity, their religious zeal, their civic influence, and their residential propinquity have gone. By 1945, the great Edgbaston houses were too old, too big and too expensive to maintain.[147] Houses and life-style, group solidarity and cultural values, sentiment and symbolism, have all vanished.

Simultaneously, the landlord's view has altered. The redevelopment plan of the 1950s was an overt acceptance of the fact that the estate could no longer survive so close to the town centre

142. Sutcliffe and Smith, *op. cit.*, 458; P.N. Jones, 'The segregation of immigrant communities in the City of Birmingham, 1961', *University of Hull Occasional Papers in Geography*, 7 (1967); map reproduced in H. Carter, *The Study of Urban Geography* (1972), 276.
143. *E.E.O. Mss.* Box 6, K/17, Sale Catalogue of 'outlying parts' of the Edgbaston Estate for auction 20 June 1918.
144. Sutcliffe and Smith, *op. cit.*, 459.
145. *Birmingham Mail*, 14 Sept. 1973.
146. Sutcliffe and Smith, *op. cit.*, 14.
147. Calthorpe Estate Co., *op. cit.*, II; Hoyt, 'Pattern of movement', 509.

as a purely residential development.[148] Since then, the north-east corner has been fully integrated into the central business district, with the construction of new shops and office blocks. The old middle-middle-class houses along the Hagley and Bristol roads have been adapted for use as offices, consulting rooms and hotels.[149] And in the area between, where once the great houses stood, there are now schools, colleges and integrated residential developments for young middle-class families. 'Whetstone' has been replaced by one such unit; 'Westbourne' is now the site of a preparatory school; and 'Mariemont' has been replaced by a hall of residence for a neighbouring college of education. Only the trees, walls and commemorative plaques speak of a bygone, more static and exclusive era. But both the landlord's policy, and the tenants' social status, which jointly created the old Edgbaston, have gone for good.

VIII

How far does this account of Edgbaston's growth and decline stand up as a case-study both in fact and method? As far as the general account of urban residential patterns is concerned, the evidence presented for Edgbaston seems to support it. By the middle of the nineteenth century the estate was a highly segregated area, with industry of any kind all but completely excluded, with schools, botanical gardens and churches, and with well-built houses – the smallest comfortable, the largest opulent – predominating. In so far as this had been achieved, it represented a convergence of landlord's and tenants' wishes. For, as Hugh Prince pointed out, 'Landowners decide what type of buildings are put up, but the character of a suburb is determined by the people who inhabit it'.[150] The vigour of the landlord's policy, and the strong corporate identity of Edgbaston's inhabitants, meant that the estate remained segregated and inviolate for over half a century, with pressure from without and decay from within being energetically resisted. Yet ultimately, even here, the attempt to deny the existence of the lower orders, retail trades and public transport ultimately failed.[151] At the turn of the

---

148. Calthorpe Estate Co., *op. cit., passim; idem, Windows on Edgbaston* (Birmingham, 1958), *passim*; Sutcliffe and Smith, *op. cit.*, 459–60.
149. For a similar transformation of Nottingham's Goose Fair district, see Mann, *op. cit.*, 84.
150. H.C. Prince, 'North-West London, 1814–1863' in J.T. Coppock and H.C. Prince (eds.), *Greater London* (1964), 84.
151. J.R. Kellett, review of Olsen, *Town Planning . . .*, in *Economic History Review*, 2nd ser., XIX, 1 (April 1966), 209.

century Edgbaston came under attack. Public transport and decay crept in; the top people crept out. The great families departed; the landlord's energy flagged. Segregation and co-operation were replaced by conflict and departure.

In showing this it is to be hoped that, on an admittedly modest scale, the detailed account had also exemplified the methodological approach earlier suggested. Concepts from the work of Firey, Hoyt and Burgess have all been used. Indeed, they greatly illuminate the residential patterns which have been under discussion. But, given their American orientation and their idealized form, they have only been used selectively, since none of them are completely applicable. Firey's work on cultural values has much in it of relevance to the Edgbaston élite, but it explains little about the social groups below. Hoyt's idea of the 'attractive force' of the 'leaders of society' is clearly of relevance, but Edgbaston's wedge shape was the result of the landownership pattern rather than any more general trends in Birmingham's urban expansion. Burgess's model of the pressure exerted by the expanding metropolis is helpful, but his grand schema of concentric rings does not apply.

So the result is an eclectic amalgam of themes which the historian has worked out for himself, and of modified and selected concepts from the social sciences. Naturally, the precise blend of researched fact and adapted theory will not be the same for an English social historian as for an American urban geographer, and much of the dissent registered in this article may be no more than a function of the different cultural and intellectual backgrounds of the writers. But given the scope of the problem under discussion, such a diversity of approach is surely both healthy and necessary.

Part Two
THE PHYSICAL FABRIC OF THE CITY

Chapter 5

THE RISE OF SUBURBIA

F.M.L. Thompson

[from F.M.L. Thompson (ed.), *The Rise of Suburbia* (Leicester University Press 1982)]

This elegant overview of recent research on suburbs begins with a generous acknowledgement to H.J. Dyos, Victorian Suburb: a Study of the Growth of Camberwell *(1982) as of seminal importance in understanding the physical development, and the social and political relations, of the nineteenth-century city. Thompson offers an insight all the more penetrating for his ability to set aside some of his own research on* Hampstead, Building a Borough 1650–1914 *(1974), in which patterns of landownership and estate development are given a central place, and marshalls an explanation of suburban expansion which shifts the emphasis to demand-based factors. These involved two major elements. There was a developing critical mass of middle-class effective demand which by the early nineteenth century was able to sustain suburbs in most large cities. The second element was an analysis of middle ideology and taste drawing heavily upon recent writing on the separation of home and work which was related to the creation of 'separate spheres', those gender specific areas of home and family life linked to privacy, seclusion and social distancing. The Victorian image of a rural idyll, as represented by gardens and open views, is also incorporated as a cultural explanation of suburban growth. The image of the suburb should not be exclusively drawn from middle-class experiences; the reality of suburbanization was of a social patchwork, with transport routes, notably tram services after 1870, piercing former cohesive suburban areas and creating a social patchwork of different types of suburbs. Railways were thus less important to the development of suburbs than trams were to their proliferation and diversity in the last quarter of the century.*

149

Suburbia rose between 1815 and 1939, an unlovely, sprawling artefact of which few are particularly fond. To be sure, there were suburbs long before the nineteenth century in the sense of places beyond city limits, the outskirts of towns hanging on to the central area physically and economically, for the most part composed of the ramshackle and squalid abodes of the poorest and most wretched of the town's hangers-on and its most noxious trades. Already, from the middle of the eighteenth century, the great suburban sea-change had started in London, the decisive social upgrading which made places distanced from the city centre desirable residential areas for those who could afford it rather than mere dumping grounds for the unfortunates unable to live in town houses. Nevertheless, while the idea of the residential suburb as an attractive emblem of material and social success and not as evidence of failure and rejection was in circulation before 1815, and its realization on the ground was already sprouting particularly in South London, it was not until the years after Waterloo that modern suburban development got properly under way on a significant scale. It is equally true that suburban expansion did not stop in 1939, never to be resumed. The Second World War certainly brought an abrupt and general halt, but much new building since 1945, particularly round provincial towns, has replicated the established suburban mode of attaching new building estates and complete fresh suburbs to the existing built-up area. By and large, however, what has persisted into the second half of the twentieth century is the commuting arrangement, the separation of residence and workplace despite the planners' efforts to reunite them in new towns. It has been expressed on the ground more in the shape of physically distinct dormitory towns, urbanized villages, and infilling and redevelopment in older suburbs, than in any massive suburbanization of the outer fringes of existing settlement. The great divide of the Second World War may be more visible as a distinction between the types of environment created than as a difference between the social complexions of the communities that live in them or the dependent relationship of those communities to mother cities, but it is a sufficiently clear distinction to make it sensible to view the sprawling phase of suburban growth as a completed process with as definite a beginning and end as any complex historical process ever has.

While it was going on, the process gratified landowners, developers, builders and the occupants of the new suburbs, or at least continued to lure them with prospects of profits, status, and happiness, but pleased practically no one else. Contemporary social and architectural critics were fascinated and appalled by the mindless, creeping nature of the sprawl with its apparently insatiable capacity for devouring land, destroying the countryside, and obliterating scenery for the supposed purpose of enabling more people to live in semi-rural surroundings. The ceaseless activity of the builders, the alarming rapidity with which they turned pleasant fields into muddy, rutted building sites, the confusion of hundreds of building operations going on simultaneously without any discernible design, the impression that little schemes were starting up everywhere at once and were never being finished, were in themselves frightening portents of disorder and chaos as if a machine had escaped from its makers and was careering wildly out of control. If the business of development was more than a little disturbing, its end product was generally viewed with distaste, ridicule, or contempt. The suburbs appeared monotonous, featureless, without character, indistinguishable from one another, infinitely boring to behold, wastelands of housing as settings for dreary, petty, lives without social, cultural, or intellectual interests, settings which fostered a pretentious preoccupation with outward appearances, a fussy attention to the trifling details of genteel living, and absurd attempts to conjure rusticity out of minute garden plots. 'A modern suburb', wrote a contributor to the *Architect* in 1876, 'is a place which is neither one thing nor the other; it has neither the advantage of the town nor the open freedom of the country, but manages to combine in nice equality of proportion the disadvantages of both.' And in 1909 Sir Walter Besant deplored 'the life of the suburb without any society; no social gatherings or institutions; as dull a life as mankind ever tolerated'.[1] It was this kind of perception of suburbia as little short of a social disaster, the blind creation of an aesthetic and cultural desert, which not only gave it a despised image in the minds of architects and town planners but also convinced them that it was the result of lack of system and control. The coincidence, since 1945, of a change in the direction of development with the imposition of reasonably effective planning regulations has further convinced them of the correctness of this diagnosis.

Urban historians and geographers arrived later on the suburban scene, after the frontier had been closed. They were led by Jim Dyos, who was born in one inner suburb, Kentish Town, and made his reputation with the history of another, Camberwell. In his pioneering *Victorian Suburb*, Dyos was chiefly concerned to rescue the suburb from historical oblivion and to show that its reputation for insignificant and uninteresting anonymity was unwarranted.[2]

1. *Architect*, XVI (1876), 33; Sir Walter Besant, *London in the Nineteenth Century* (1909), 262; both quoted in D.J. Olsen, *The Growth of Victorian London* (1976, 1979 edn), 200, 210, whose chapter 'The villa and the new suburb' contains an excellent account of attitudes towards suburbia.

Putting Camberwell under the historical microscope he demonstrated that the apparently random jumble of streets, house patterns, and neighbourhoods which made up the completed inner suburb of 1900 was in fact an intricate mosaic of building estates and developments, each piece with an identifiable and intelligible form created in an explicable and hence an orderly and rational, although not necessarily lovely or admirable, way. Each piece of the jigsaw had an identity and character shaped by the way in which a particular developer at a particular time visualized in terms of buildings the resolution of an equation involving the potentialities of the site and its location, building costs and current tastes in house types, and the nature of the likely demand for housing in the district. The solutions varied between districts at any one time, because individual decisions and the circumstances influencing them differed; but above all they varied over time, reflecting not merely changing tastes and expectations but also the changing general position of Camberwell itself, at one moment on the outer fringe and 50 years later well behind the suburban frontier. Chronological layers of development were therefore unravelled, of initial occupation and re-occupation and subdivision of houses, of social aspiration and social decay, within existing neighbourhoods and influencing the character of districts yet to be developed, plotting and explaining the progress, or decline, of Camberwell from sought-after suburb on the edge of the country to integral part of the fully urbanized central metropolis. The book is a triumphant demonstration that the suburb and the sub-districts of which it is composed, far from being featureless wastelands possess individuality and character in the distinctive layouts and buildings of their physical structure. Even more it is a demonstration of how property deeds, building leases, maps, estate papers, business records, and a great array of printed sources can be made to yield an understanding of the diverse influences which determined the timing of the making of the suburban environment and its physical and social shape, an understanding which shows that in the process of creating suburbs seemingly blind and mindless market forces were only translated into shapes on the ground through perfectly rational and orderly decisions by people.

At the same time as Dyos was publishing, urban geographers, many of them with historical interests, began in the early 1960s to turn their attention from urban morphology in general to suburban forms and suburban growth in particular. Much of this work adopts the same approach and essentially empirical method, uses the same sources, and tackles the same questions, as those favoured by urban historians, seeking to explain the detailed timing and configuration

2. H.J. Dyos, *Victorian Suburb: A Study of the Growth of Camberwell* (1961).

of specific suburban developments in terms of the pre-development structure of landownership, the pattern of tracks, paths, and field boundaries, the actions of individual owners and developers, the influence of the means of transport, and the operation of the drives and pressures of social class.[3] Other geographers, much influenced by the work of urban sociologists in America, adopted a more consciously theoretical and abstract approach in extending to suburban and fringe areas the analysis of land use patterns in terms of physical and social distance from the city centre, and in measuring the degree to which their study areas conform to the Chicago model of social segregation, itself no more than a generalized description of the spatial distribution of the industrial, commercial, and residential sectors of a particular city.[4]

The stiffening of historical research by the incorporation of a conceptual framework is all to the good, and while the labours of the 'factorial ecologists' among the geographers have done little to illuminate the suburban scene, if only because the census materials with which they work are both crude in relation to social classifications and in relation to recognizable suburban districts, in general the parallel and often converging streams of urban history and urban geography have set the course for the post-Camberwell study of suburban history. Studies have been published of the suburbs of metropolitan Essex,[5] Paddington and Hammersmith,[6] Hampstead,[7]

3. For example, J.T. Coppock and H.C. Prince, *Greater London* (1964), especially the chapters by Prince, 'North-west London, 1814–63', and J.H. Johnson, 'The suburban expansion of housing in London, 1918–39'.
4. The main American influences have been R. Park, E.W. Burgess, and R.D. Mackenzie eds., *The City* (1925); H. Hoyt, *The Structure and Growth of Residential Neighbourhoods in American Cities* (1939); G. Sjoberg, *The Pre-Industrial City* (1960); H.M. Mayer and C.F. John eds., *Readings in Urban Geography* (1964); P.M. Hauser and L.F. Schnore eds., *The Study of Urbanization* (1965). Among British applications see J.W.R. Whitehand, 'Fringe-belts – a neglected aspect in urban geography', *Trans. Inst. Brit. Geographers*, XLI (1967); and most recently, C. Roy Lewis, 'A stage in the development of the industrial town: a case study of Cardiff, 1845–75', *Trans. Inst. Brit. Geographers*, NS, IV (1979), and M. Shaw, 'Reconciling social and physical space: Wolverhampton, 1871', *Trans. Inst. Brit. Geographers*, NS, IV (1979).
5. W. Ashworth, 'Types of social and economic development in suburban Essex', in Centre for Urban Studies Report no. 3, *London, Aspects of Change* (1964).
6. D.A. Reeder, 'A theatre of suburbs: some patterns of development in West London, 1801–1911', in *The Study of Urban History*, ed. H.J. Dyos (1968).
7. D.J. Olsen, 'House upon house', in *The Victorian City*, I, eds. H.J. Dyos and M. Wolff (1973); F.M.L. Thompson, *Hampstead: Building a Borough, 1650–1964* (1974); and *idem*, 'Hampstead, 1830–1914', in *Middle-Class Housing in Britain*, eds. M.A. Simpson and T.H. Lloyd (1977).

Victoria Park, Manchester,[8] Kelvinside,[9] and Edgbaston,[10] as well as a general account of the interwar explosion of London's outer suburbia.[11] Since suburban history, appropriately enough, retains a semi-detached relationship to urban history and there is no clear line between town and suburb, the latter frequently becoming part of the central area as a result of later expansion, the histories of particular towns often discuss suburban development.[12] Even so, the tally of modern scholarly studies of suburbs is not a long one, and much more remains in unpublished theses. The publication of *The Rise of Suburbia* in 1982 included the distillation of theses on Bromley, Ealing and Acton, Bexley, and Headingley, Potternewton, and Chapel Allerton in north Leeds, and very nearly doubled the number of available studies of particular suburbs. It preserved the balance between the metropolis and provincial towns which had already been established, and added to our understanding of how and why the suburban environment came into existence.

Almost without exception suburban studies start with an outline of population growth since 1801, a statement of the relative and absolute increase in the size of the population living in towns, and a more detailed account of the size of the total population and its decennial rates of growth in the mother city or conurbation of the study area. There is an underlying assumption, sometimes made explicit, that the vast increase in the numbers of town-dwellers, or at any rate a high proportion of that increase in any town of considerable size, could in the nature of things – given that more people must occupy more space, and that the space within existing town limits whether defined administratively or geographically was already full – only be housed in suburbs established on the outskirts. Having provided some explanation of the growth in overall urban population, whether in demographic terms or in terms of the economy of the particular town and the sources of expansion in its employment and incomes, the questions for the suburban historian become those of which sections of the net increase in total population moved to the suburbs and why, and which parts of the surrounding space were turned into suburban residential areas, when, by what stages, by whom, and why in some particular shape rather than any other.

8. M. Spiers, *Victoria Park, Manchester* (1976).
9. M.A. Simpson, 'The West End of Glasgow, 1830–1914', in Simpson and Lloyd, *op. cit.*
10. D. Cannadine, *Lords and Landlords: The Aristocracy and the Towns, 1774–1967* (1980), part 2.
11. A.A. Jackson, *Semi-Detached London* (1973).
12. Most recently in M.J. Daunton, *Coal Metropolis: Cardiff, 1870–1914* (1977).

Indeed, it makes very good sense in the British context to consider population growth as fundamental, and to look for some threshold in town size beyond which a traditional urban structure of a unified and physically, socially, and economically integrated townscape gave way to a modern arrangement of central town and dependent suburbs. For the nineteenth century it is valid to see suburbanization as a facet of urbanization, a necessary part of and condition for the wider process. It would be hazardous to make any firm pronouncement without local knowledge of the history and topography of every large town, but by mid-century it is likely that every place with more than 50,000 inhabitants thought of itself as possessing some suburbs; Brighton had its Kemp Town and Hove, Newcastle its Jesmond and Gosforth, Hull its Cottingham when they reached about that size. Nevertheless, before accepting that suburban development was a necessary consequence of the scale of urbanization it is worth asking whether the connexion is as strong as the nineteenth-century experience suggests.

There were certainly theoretical alternatives to the suburban mode for accommodating expansion in urban populations, and other countries provide working examples of them in practice. The development of residential suburbs of distinctive appearance and distinctive class was one form of lateral expansion. Another form of lateral expansion was by simple accretion at the town edges of buildings and street patterns that reproduced and continued the character of the established town, in new quarters with mixed residential, commercial, and industrial functions, and with intermixed residents from different social classes. This, apparently, is what happened in most American cities until the 1870s; they remained compact 'walking' cities, despite considerable growth in size, with no pronounced social – as distinct from ethnic – segregation. It was only with the appearance of the new technology of mass transit by tramways that socially segregated districts began to develop, the vehicle of segregation being the suburb.[13] Towns could also expand upwards rather than sideways, throwing up vertical streets in tenement and apartment blocks. This was the way with most continental, and the large Scottish towns; by this means Paris and Vienna remained classically compact cities, in contrast to London, the scattered city, and one stepped outside Rome, for example, in the later nineteenth century literally into an empty surrounding desert.[14] That English towns did not follow these models was an act of choice, not of necessity.

13. The evidence and arguments are marshalled in D. Ward, 'Victorian cities: how modern?' *J. Hist. Geog.*, I (1975), and D. Cannadine, 'Victorian cities: how different?' *Social Hist.*, IV (1977). And see S. Bass Warner, Jnr. *Streetcar Suburbs: The Process of Growth in Boston, 1870–1900* (Cambridge, Mass., 1962).
14. S.E. Rasmussen, *London: The Unique City* (1937; Pelican edn, 1960), 13–14.

The largest English towns – Liverpool, Manchester, Birmingham, Leeds, and Sheffield, as well as London – were suburbanized, and socially segregated, half a century or so before the arrival of cheap mass transit, which was not developed effectively in the English setting before the 1890s. It can be argued that horse omnibuses and railways, if they chose to offer suburban train services, provided transport that was neither for the masses nor cheap but was nonetheless sufficient to carry the better-off minority out to suburbs. There is a great deal in this argument, but since the Americans possessed the same pre-tramway transport technology without using it to support the same style of living, omnibus and suburban train should be regarded as permitting, rather than creating, the suburb. In any case it was entirely possible for a place like Camberwell, one and a half to two miles from the City, to remain quite substantially a 'walking suburb' at least until the 1870s, and yet to be unmistakably suburban in character and function regardless of the degree of reliance on walking to work.[15] The high density, high rise development of continental and Scottish cities, on the other hand, has been explained by high building land values and, in some cases, stringent building regulations designed to prevent building outside municipal limits for reasons of internal security and social control. The building regulations were important, and were not paralleled in Britain; Scottish municipal regulations were generally tougher than English ones, which outside London tended not to exist at all until mid-century, but they acted to increase building costs through control of materials and structures and did not regulate the availability of sites. Where building was allowed building land values were markedly higher in continental towns than in England, and the ready availability of supplies of relatively cheap building land with a gradient of values generally descending from city centres was a prerequisite for suburban development. On the other hand, recent experience suggests that it requires a very sharp rise indeed in plot value in relation to building cost, raising the site element from a traditional 5 to 10 per cent of overall cost to one-third or even one-half, before high density tall buildings become the only economic use of building land. In Scotland, moreover, the generally higher building land values did not inhibit the development of Kelvinside with its suburban densities, suburban profiles, and suburban qualities, once a demand for that kind of thing appeared among the wealthier Glaswegian middle class.[16] High land prices encourage high buildings, and low land prices are favourable to suburban development, but neither can be regarded as decisive influences.

15. Dyos, *Victorian Suburb*, 69.
16. Simpson, *loc. cit.*

England's own pre-suburban experience, moreover, has to be taken into account. There was marked urban growth in the course of the eighteenth century, particularly after 1750, the proportion of the population living in towns increased from about one-fifth to around one-third, and the actual numbers of town dwellers roughly from one million to three million.[17] Some of this increase in urbanization was accounted for by an increase in the number of places which could be called towns, each of them still quite small in 1801. But much of it was the result of the growth of large towns: leaving London aside, by 1801 Liverpool, Manchester, Birmingham, and Bristol were well over the 50,000 mark, Leeds, Sheffield, and Newcastle upon Tyne were not far behind in the 30–40,000 range, and Norwich, despite having fallen back in the city league table, was of similar size. All these towns had grown up to this point without generating any true suburbs, although they had small settlements of town housing outside the central areas for the wealthy and a spattering of country houses for the wealthiest. What is more, attempts to build suburbs as places of defined appeal and status were generally unsuccessful before the 1820s. In Liverpool the plan to build a residential suburb for the well-to-do on the earl of Sefton's estate in Toxteth Park, to be called Harrington, was a flop in the 1770s and 1780s, and it was not until the 1820s, and then in a different direction at Everton, that the suburban idea began to take hold with Liverpool's wealthy merchants. In Manchester Ardwick was beginning to grow as a suburb for the wealthy perhaps just a few years earlier, while in Birmingham a grandiose scheme to create a new hamlet of some pretensions in Ashted hung fire in the 1790s, and development in Edgbaston was sporadic and unimpressive until the 1820s.[18]

Even eighteenth-century London, while obviously exceptional in sheer size and complexity, already at the beginning of the century a concentration of over half a million people and at its close a conurbation of nearly one million, was not unequivocally a special case of suburban precocity. Such an expansion in numbers clearly involved an expansion in the built-up area to house them, and successive stages in the growth of the town were plainly marked by new communications carried round the contemporary edges of settlement, for example the New Road, now Marylebone and Euston Roads, in the 1760s and the Regent's Canal in the 1800s; while new bridges across the Thames from mid-century signalled the spread of south London from Southwark into Newington, Walworth, and Lambeth. The great bulk of this expansion was urban in form, an

---

17. Figures for eighteenth-century urban population depend on the definition of 'town' which is adopted; those in the text are taken from C.W. Chalklin, *The Provincial Towns of Georgian England* (1974).
18. *Ibid.*, 90, 110–11, 88; Cannadine, *Lords and Landlords*, 91–3.

extension of established patterns of streets of terraced housing, of squares in the more fashionable parts, of close-packed courts and alleys and jumbles of tenements in the less favoured areas intermixed with industrial and commercial activities, a general growth in size of the environment for town life in the varied and evolving forms in which it already existed in the older inner areas of dense settlement. Beyond these districts of the expanding town a ring of satellite villages flourished and grew in the eighteenth century, linked to the metropolis by thin ribbons of substantial villa development and short strings of roadside terraces. In the backlands behind these ribbons several schemes of estate development were successfully launched in the later eighteenth century, conceived as new towns and accorded appropriate names to advertise their individuality: Hans Town, Somers Town, Pentonville, Camden Town, and so on. At the time these were geographically suburbs, in their distance and semi-detachment from the centre, and to a degree were socially suburban in being, for their élites, places of residence divorced from their places of work. Physically and architecturally, however, they were extensions of the town, laid out in streets and squares and built in repetitive three and four storey terraces whose plain regularity Victorians found so monotonous and unimaginative, and whose accommodation was often found too large and expensive for single family occupation.[19] The impression, derived from the shape and appearance of the built environment rather than any knowledge of how the inhabitants lived, which remains unresearched, is that the atmosphere of these new towns was more urban and akin to other socially and economically similar parts of older London than it was new and distinctively suburban. The overgrown villages which lay beyond, Hackney, Highgate, Hampstead, Clapham, or Camberwell, were a clear step closer to being prototype suburbs with the charms of their surrounding country and their local cream of successful merchants and professional men going up to town daily in their carriages. Even so, their mixed development of large individual houses in park-like grounds for the wealthiest, and small squares and short runs of terraced town housing for others, and their mixed use for family summer stations removed from the heat and stench of the city, and for holiday resorts, as well as for some permanent residence, gave them a pleasantly varied appearance and a diversified social life rather than an unmistakably suburban stamp.

There is, of course, a tautological trap in implying that the full stamp of suburban approval can only be given to that species of low density development of residential districts arranged in roads,

---

19. J. Summerson, *Georgian London* (1945), chapter 20, has no hesitation in classifying the outlying parts of 'Greater Georgian London' as suburban.

avenues, ways, and walks rather than streets and squares, studded with detached and semi-detached low rise houses set in individual garden plots, and peopled with middle-class commuters, which only appeared in the nineteenth century. It then becomes a matter of spatial definition, not of argument, that pre-nineteenth century methods of dealing with the expansion of towns and treating their outskirts were not truly suburban. Nevertheless architectural historians are in no doubt that detached and semi-detached houses built for single family occupation are of the suburban essence, and that such houses did not exist before the nineteenth century; heralded in the revolutionary plans for the Eyre estate in St John's Wood in the 1790s, they were first realized on the ground in the successful development of that estate from 1815 onwards, and became the origin, through much mutation and debasement, of virtually all suburban houses.[20] It is arguable, also, that it was only in the setting of this kind of house, where the family could distance itself from the outside world in its own private fortress behind its own garden fence and privet hedge and yet could make a show of outward appearances that was sure to be noticed by the neighbours, that the suburban life style of individual domesticity and group-monitored respectability could take hold. It has often been remarked that the key feature in the attractions of suburban living is that it offers a retreat from the noise and bustle of the metropolis to the privacy and seclusion of the family home. The daily retreat has to be made possible by some means of getting to work, and its security has to be insured against challenges and interruptions from different life styles by a high degree of social homogeneity and exclusiveness in the residential neighbourhood, but its core is the single family house where a private domestic life can be lived. 'The flight to the suburbs', writes Donald Olsen, 'involved the temporary rejection of the rest of society, of that part that extended beyond the immediate family of the householder: the most satisfactory suburb was that which gave him the maximum of privacy and the minimum of outside distraction.'[21] In a male-dominated society this was an essentially male view of the attractions of suburbia since it was the man who went out to work and then sought daily relief from the strains of business and the demands of relations with colleagues and strangers by escaping to the supposedly undemanding comforts of the family home, while his wife was left to make what she could out of day-long isolation in the cherished privacy and seclusion. The creation of an

20. *Ibid.*, 158–9; Olsen, *Growth of Victorian London*, 213.
21. *Ibid.*, 211; the section on 'Privacy', 210–16, is the best summary of contemporary, and twentieth-century views of the role of the pursuit of privacy in the creation of suburbia.

environment in which this division of middle-class male lives between a public world of work contacts and a private world of family life was what the rise of suburbia was all about. The question then is, why did the pursuit of privacy, or its realization in building forms, happen at this particular time?

At one level the answer is that someone in a position to influence the shape of building operations – urban estate owner, developer, architect-surveyor, or builder – invented the semi-detached house, and that once invented it caught on. The someone, moreover, can be precisely identified as John Shaw, the architect–surveyor to the Eyre estate, and his designs for the detached and semi-detached villas of St John's Wood were a stylistic event of far-reaching importance. Domestic architecture has its own traditions, its own processes of change, and its own internal logic, and it is possible to place this particular departure in a sequence of efforts to produce scaled down and watered down versions of aristocratic housing arrangements suited to smaller incomes: town terraces were imitations in gradations of compression and austerity of upper-class town houses, and the semi-detached was the ultimate reduction of the country house through intermediate layers of villas. Unless it is assumed, however, that designers and builders dictate to the housing market and that occupiers are obliged to live in whatever kind of house it pleases the builders to provide, a design-based explanation remains superficial. In a competitive world a new product is successful only if there turns out to be a demand for it.

It is unlikely that a potential demand for this type of housing had been around for many years without a supply to satisfy it appearing. It is not easy to see any decisive shifts in the factors controlling the supply of building land or of houses in the years before the suburban take-off which could support an explanation from the supply side. Admittedly, the trend over the eighteenth century was for the owners of sizeable building estates to make increasingly systematic and carefully organized efforts to regulate and supervise the layout and design of developments on their properties, and insofar as they and their advisers were cautiously conservative in their ideas they tended to legislate in their building agreements for tried and tested types of town housing and to try and prevent aberrations or experiments. It would be a mistake to suppose, however, either that competently and effectively controlled building estates exercised a stranglehold over supplies of building land, or that their owners had the power to frustrate market forces by autocratic decree. All the evidence suggests that there were plentiful supplies of building land much of which was available without any restrictions on what was to be built; that many urban landowners who did attempt to use building agreements and leases to impose their concepts of permissible development drew the terms carelessly and imprecisely, with many loopholes for builders to do undesirable things; and that even the most regulatory landowners were unable to enforce a character of development which the location and housing demand for the site would not sustain.[22] There were, therefore, no effective legal or political constraints on the availability of building land which could have prevented the erection of single family houses if there had been an effective demand for them, and while there has been little systematic work on the intractable subject of building land values there is nothing to indicate that land costs were so high in the eighteenth century as to inhibit low density development, or that there was any decisive drop as a precursor of suburban growth. What evidence there is suggests a rising trend for building land values through the nineteenth century, with cyclical variations, and contains no sign that the starting point of this trend marked any discontinuity from the eighteenth century; that, indeed, would have been inconsistent with the well-observed tendency of land values on the urban fringe to move smoothly from high agricultural values for accommodation land, prime hay or grazing land, or market gardening, to the bottom rungs of building values.[23]

If land would always have been available somewhere on the outskirts of the city for builders to build what they liked, it is equally unlikely that any changes in building costs or in the organization of the building industry made semi-detacheds possible where they had not been possible before. Building costs certainly rose during the French Wars as a result of rising prices for building materials, and then fell, but this was a cyclical rather than a secular movement. A short-term fall in costs, and plentiful supplies of cheap finance for builders, may have given an initial impulse to suburban building in the 1820s, but in broad perspective nineteenth-century suburban growth should be viewed as taking place in a context of slowly rising costs, if only because of the improving quality and equipment of the suburban house, rather than being pictured as a response to increasing cheapness.[24] The building industry itself did undergo major changes, with the emergence of a few large-scale contractors in the early nineteenth century and the transformation of the small building unit from a joint enterprise of building tradesmen headed by a senior craftsman as undertaker to the small capitalist building firm with a builder employing members of the different building trades as wage workers. The emergence of the building contractor,

22. These issues have been much discussed, for example in Thompson, *Hampstead*, 85–90, 365, and Cannadine, *Lords and Landlords*, 395–401.
23. See, for example, Thompson, *Hampstead*, 224–31. There is much detailed evidence on building land values in the contributions to this volume.
24. K. Maywald, 'An index of building costs in the United Kingdom, 1845–1938', *Econ. Hist. Rev.*, 2nd ser., VII (1954).

however, was not a precondition of suburban development, since the great bulk of this work was for long done by multitudes of small-scale and ephemeral speculative builders; and although it is possible that the small capitalist was better able to engage in speculative house-building than the craft enterprises he replaced, it is apparent that these eighteenth-century predecessors, headed perhaps by a carpenter or a mason, were perfectly capable of taking risks and building on speculation for the market as they saw it.[25]

Plentiful supplies of comparatively cheap building land and a building industry capable of producing speculatively for a range of incomes permitted the growth of suburbs, but there do not seem to have been any changes in these factors sufficiently sharp or pronounced to have caused that growth to get under way. It is possible, however, that the effective supply of building land was increased by transport improvements opening up fresh and more remote areas for settlement, without any change in the inclinations or policies of landowners being required. In a general sense modern suburbia could not have happened without the omnibus, commuter train, and tram, powerfully reinforced in the twentieth century by the motor; without such means the geographical spread and the growing distances between home and work could not have been supported. While transport improvements and extensions clearly sustained the general process of suburban expansion and intensification, this does not necessarily imply a causal connexion or indicate which way it operated. New transport ventures are rather more likely to be designed to cater for an established traffic than to create an entirely new one, even though once operating they have great potential for stimulating large increases. In any event when new railways did produce a clear suburban response, as they did in Bromley in the 1850s and in west London in the 1860s and 1870s, this happened long after the attractions of the suburban way of living had been successfully demonstrated, and the new transport promoted the development of an already tested product in a fresh locality. It is less easy to imagine new forms of transport poking their fingers out into the country in the hope of initiating a way of life that had not yet been tried and shown to be socially and commercially successful. On the other hand, flexible and adaptable forms of transport were at hand in the crucial period at the beginning of the nineteenth century that were capable of playing their part in enlarging the residential area through extension of their services, so soon as a demand for them arose.

25. H. Hobhouse, *Thomas Cubitt: Master Builder* (1971); F.M.L. Thompson, *Chartered Surveyors: The Growth of a Profession* (1968), 79–93.

By the early years of the century there was already a well-developed network of short-stage coach services in the London area, running between such peripheral villages as Paddington, Camberwell, Clapham, Islington, or Edmonton and the City and West End. Fares were high, coaches small, and journeys slow with long stops at the public houses which were the picking up points, so that this kind of passenger transport was not suited to the regular commuter who would have needed to use a private carriage or his own feet for a truly suburban daily journey to work. Nevertheless the short-stage provided the essential link with the centre for the more occasional traveller, for shopping, visiting, or entertainment, which permitted Paddington or Clapham families to evolve a suburban pattern of life. The horse-drawn omnibus, introduced in 1829 on the Paddington–City route, was a development of the short-stage concept, adding a larger capacity vehicle with rear entry for easy access, boarding and alighting at the passenger's wish, faster journeys, and lower fares.[26] Bus services expanded rapidly in the 1830s, freed from the previous prohibition of picking up or setting down in central London, and quickly became established as one of the most important determinants of the character of early suburban development. Buses made possible daily journeys to work at times of day, journey speeds, and fares which were convenient to the affluent to middling middle class of professional men, civil servants, merchants, bankers, larger shopkeepers, and perhaps some senior clerks. Buses, therefore, allowed families in such groups to live at a distance from work and dispense with private carriages, and permitted those who could never have aspired to own private carriages to do likewise. They permitted middle-class neighbourhoods to function without coach-houses or mews, households to be run with only female servants, and houses to be smaller and less expensive because quarters for male horse servants were not needed. These all became standard features of early Victorian suburbs, and they were all dependent on the horse bus.

The horse may rightly be credited with much influence over the form which the suburban environment took, and with permitting its colonization of growing territories in the 30 years or so before the 1850s, when suburban train services first began to have any significant effect in allowing or stimulating further suburban growth. It would be going too far, however, to suggest that the availability of horse-drawn public passenger transport was decisive in triggering the birth of the suburb. The sequence of events was that the suburb came first and the short-stage coach or omnibus followed once the potential passengers were established. It is true that this came to be such an

26. T.C. Barker and M. Robbins, *A History of London Transport*, I (1963), 4–22.

automatic development that people came to live in districts with very poor, or no transport services in the confident expectation that a new bus route would be opened as soon as there was a sufficient concentration of residents to furnish profitable customers, so that settlement in advance of transport was simply a matter of timing and the mechanics of business and no proof that settlement went ahead without regard to transport services.[27] This reasoning could, however, be applied with little modification to the pre-suburban world, in which the organization and equipment of the horse and coach trades were fully capable by the later eighteenth century of responding to the emergence of new bodies of customers by providing new services. While suburban development needed some form of transport services in order to take root and flourish, it is thus likely that in the initial phases at least it was the development which called forth appropriate kinds of transport, and unlikely that there had been any powerful but latent suburbanizing force held in check by any absence of enterprise or innovation in transport.

If, therefore, the building and occupation of districts of single family homes, and hence the origins of suburbia, cannot be satisfactorily explained by independent changes in the supply conditions, it is natural to suggest that the initiating impulse came from the side of changes in housing demand. The two possibilities are that the desire for a domestic life of privacy and seclusion was a new experience for any sizeable section of the middle class, only gathering force for the first time around the beginning of the nineteenth century; or that the desire had long been present and that what happened was some change in the means of satisfying it, a shift in effective demand. From the vantage point of the major provincial towns the origins of successful suburbs can be explained quite simply in terms of effective demand at the group rather than the individual family level. Before the 1820s or 1830s there simply were not enough comfortably off middle-class families in Birmingham or Manchester, Liverpool or Leeds, to populate an exclusive residential district as distinct from the occasional square or crescent, or individual mansions scattered in the surrounding country. The failure of earlier attempts to develop respectable or prestigious suburbs can be laid at the door of lack of demand because of the small size of the local bourgeoisie. Once this passed some critical level, which happened at different points between the 1820s and the 1850s according to the overall size, social structure, and prosperity of different towns, middle-class residential suburbs took hold, although the great provincial cities were still hard put to it to sustain more than one smart suburb at a time and, as

27. Thompson, *Hampstead*, 239, 251–2.

the case of Leeds shows, the limited size of the market made mixed character suburban development not uncommon.[28]

Middle-class numbers look like a sufficient explanation for the provincial case, without drawing on any analysis of middle-class ideology or taste. An argument from smallness of numbers, however, is unlikely to convince if applied to eighteenth-century London. Much work remains to be done before its social structure can be understood or depicted with precision, but it is tolerably clear that by the end of the century something like one-fifth of its population belonged to the middling ranks of society. In round numbers this means that there were 30,000 to 40,000 middle-class families, and although the group comprised a broad and varied range of occupations, social positions, and incomes, stretching from £80 to £100 a year at the lower end of the shopkeeper and small employer scale up to £500 to £800 a year of the wealthy merchants and prosperous professional men, at which level it shaded off into the upper classes where super-rich bankers, brewers, and large-scale traders were on terms with the aristocracy and gentry, it must nevertheless have contained several thousand families able to afford houses worth £40 to £50 a year or even more.[29] Single family homes with ample servant accommodation could well be provided at that sort of rent, and a total demand numbered in thousands could well have supported several suburban districts. The simple answer is to say that it did indeed do just that, and the Claphams, Newingtons, Camberwells, Islingtons, or Hackneys of the eighteenth century were precisely the type of suburbs that this upper middle class wanted.

Such a conclusion, however, merely prompts a rephrasing of the issue: if eighteenth-century upper middle-class Londoners wanted their suburban settlements to be reiterations of town housing in town formations, why did their early nineteenth-century descendants want something entirely different? The clue, it has been suggested, lies in the kind of life for which the detached or semi-detached house set in its own garden was the necessary physical setting. The clear separation of work and home, the insistence on social distancing, the treatment of the home as a feminine domain, the importance attached to domestic privacy and the exclusion of the vulgar prying multitude, can all be seen as parts of a code of individual responsibility, male economic dominance and female domestic subordination, and family-nurtured morality which served to give the bourgeoisie a social identity and mark them off from

28. See C. Treen, 'The process of suburban development in North Leeds, 1870–1914,' in Thompson (ed.), *The Rise of Suburbia* (1982).
29. L.D. Schwarz, 'Income distribution and social structure in London in the late eighteenth century', *Econ. Hist. Rev.*, 2nd ser., xxxii (1979); and G. Rudé, *Hanoverian London* (1971), 48–51.

the upper class and the lower orders. The separation of work from domestic life was occurring in the later eighteenth century as a result of changes in production technology and business organization which made the home an unsuitable or impossible place for many kinds of trade and manufacture; the emphasis on personal religious and moral responsibility and behaviour from the Clapham Sect and the Evangelicals, whose message was powerfully reinforced by the French Revolution and fears of disorderly, irreligious mobs, gave a central role to the family as the main instrument of moral education; and the socially segregated suburb of separate family houses shortly emerged to supply the ideal environment for practising the newly reformed life style incorporating these religious, moral, and social aspirations.[30]

There is great intellectual attraction in this ideological explanation of the launching of modern suburbia, since it grounds a new form of middle-class housing demand firmly in a set of ideas and ideals whose own origins have roots in changes in the economy and developments in religion, bypasses any enquiry into changes in real incomes and effective demand, and yet makes it possible to regard a shift in the character of demand as the decisive suburbanizing force. Some doubts need to be resolved, however, before this interpretation can be wholly accepted. Was the cult of privacy and regulated domesticity a class phenomenon, did its practice require a particular kind of housing, and does the chronology fit, so that the development of the ideals and conventions can be shown to have preceded suburban growth? The upper class, or some of it, cultivated the virtues of family life, propriety, and rectitude, and translated these values into elaborate arrangements to provide privacy, sexual segregation, delimitation of specialized spheres of activity, and separation from the servants, in the planning of their houses, at much the same time as the middle classes were developing their domestic rituals.[31] Within the working classes some sections of the skilled artisans and regularly employed developed ideas of respectability which included pride in the home and the cultivation of family life. It may well be that the conventional view is correct, which ascribes a conversion of aristocratic and upper-working-class minds and attitudes to the triumph of the bourgeois ideal, but such a conquest has not been conclusively demonstrated and it remains possible that groups in all classes were responding simultaneously

30. This is a highly simplified version of the thesis emerging from the research on the separation of spheres and the rise of domesticity which Leonore Davidoff and Catherine Hall of the University of Essex have in progress. There are hints of a similar theme in John Burnett, *A Social History of Housing, 1815–1970* (1978), 95–6, 102–3.
31. M. Girouard, *The Victorian Country House* (1979 edn), 15–31.

to a common set of influences on morals and manners.[32] This may not have much practical significance for the initiation of suburban growth: the aristocracy had town houses and country houses and did not need any more; skilled workers could not afford to live far from their work and were obliged to take what houses were available and adapt them as best they could to the needs of family life; only the more affluent members of the middle classes both required and could afford the new suburban houses as settings ideally suited to the practice of domesticity. It does, however, bear on the question of whether a specific type of house was essential, or much better suited than alternative types, to the realization of privacy and seclusion.

Long town streets of terrace houses without gardens were prone to stimulate a lively, public, gregarious street life, which bustled with noise, strangers, and external distractions, and perhaps most damagingly of all for internalized family discipline and self-sufficiency, encouraged the random and promiscuous mixing of children out of reach of parental control. Terrace housing was not, however, inherently inimical to a more inward-turning life of seemliness and propriety. While many terrace houses were, or became, multi-tenanted, this descent into multi-occupation by several households was largely the result of later nineteenth-century social deterioration of streets and neighbourhoods which had started life with reasonably high status, and the normal terrace house was not only perfectly capable of acting as a single family home but was in fact usually designed and initially occupied as such. It was, moreover, well adapted for a domestic regime of clearly separated spheres of activity, as a French visitor to London noted in 1817:

> These narrow houses, three or four storeys high – one for eating,
> one for sleeping, a third for company, a fourth underground for the
> kitchen, a fifth perhaps at the top for the servants – and the agility, the
> ease, the quickness with which the individuals of the family run up and
> down, and perch on the different storeys, give the idea of a cage with
> its sticks and birds.[33]

In addition there is no suggestion that the terrace house in any way encouraged the presence of workplace and residence in the same building, indeed it seems probable that most terrace houses were always exclusively residential. Suitably placed in quiet locations terraces were serviceable vehicles for sheltered middle-class living,

32. H. Perkin, *The Origins of Modern English Society, 1780–1880* (1969), chapters 8 and 9; a classic statement of the argument that the bourgeoisie imposed their ideology on the rest of society.
33. L. Simond, *Journal of a Tour and Residence in Great Britain*, I (1817), 64, quoted in Burnett, *op. cit.*, 104.

and although they were falling out of favour from the 1820s because of the superior merits and convenience of detached and semi-detached houses for privacy, this was a slow process and terraces were still being built in new middle-class suburbs well into the 1860s.[34]

Above all the crystallization of the ideas of privacy and domesticity and their general acceptance among the middle classes, and others, was also a long-drawn-out process, stretching from the 1780s to its culmination in the 1850s and 1860s. It is by no means clear that the development of the new domestic ethos preceded the new suburban growth, and if the two processes went on alongside each other it is at least as likely that the environment influenced the behaviour pattern as that the desired behaviour pattern helped to shape the environment. The spatial dispersion and separation of the suburban environment was, after all, highly likely to foster the further development and refinement of attitudes which emphasized the attractions and virtues of privacy, withdrawal of the family on to its own social resources, avoidance of embarrassing chance encounters with strangers, and peaceful recuperation from the worries of business. The suburban environment in itself had no moral qualities apart from those attributed to it by its inhabitants, and when these decided that suburbs were morally good because of their immunity from the wickedness and immorality of the city a fresh source of support was tapped to sustain the continuing suburban expansion. Certainly physical expansion and cultural development fed upon one another, but it would be hazardous to award causal primacy to either.

Work on the earliest nineteenth-century suburbs has concentrated on analysing the process of constructing the built environment and on explaining in detail why developments followed particular layout patterns and builders put up particular kinds and values of houses in specific places. If it were possible to match this level of research on the development and construction side with equally intensive study of the previous backgrounds, attitudes, and aspirations of the new inhabitants who constituted the demand for the kind of housing without which these ventures could not have succeeded, it might be possible to resolve the problem. Since the new suburban dwellers left no body of records of their life styles, their cultural outlook, or their motives in moving, this may never happen. Meanwhile it

---

34. Thompson, *Hampstead*, 276–80. Smart terraces were still being widely built in the 1870s, for example in Gosforth, Newcastle upon Tyne. On the other hand, a prime reason for the failure of the town-style development of Pimlico to find its intended middling-middle-class market in the 1850s and 1860s, and hence for its comparatively tarnished image, was the competition of the more modern villa suburbs being built at the same time.

would be sensible to look to the suburban garden for the roots of the demand for suburban living, something which brought the possibilities of privacy and seclusion with it but which was desired in a straightforward way for its own sake because it was a piece of tangible evidence, however minute, that the dream of being a townsman living in the country was something more than just an illusion. The essential quality of the new suburbs was that they were on the edge of the country with open views beyond, even if subsequent development leapfrogged past them and hemmed them in as inner suburbs. An essential attribute of the single family house was the garden, preferably one in front to impress the outside world with a display of neatly-tended possession of some land, and one at the back for the family to enjoy. It can be suggested that a desire for individual gardens was surfacing among the potential suburbanites as just about the time when building suppliers chose to put the article on the market. It was in the 1790s that the countryside was ceasing to be feared or despised as boorish, backward, or hostile and was coming to be admired by cultivated opinion as the home of all that was natural and virtuous. In 1810 John Nash outlined his scheme for the development of Regent's Park, using the well-tried and conventional building forms of Georgian London, terraces and crescents, but placing them in a new rural setting instead of in a gridiron of streets and squares, so that each resident should have the illusion of looking out on his own country park. Even more important, in 1824 Nash tacked Park Villages East and West on to the imposing formality of the elegant Park terraces, villages which were indeed an aristocratic garden suburb in miniature, rusticated cottages, each one different, each one in its garden, planted in an urban context.[35] Even here *rus in urbe* was realized on the ground for the fashionable aristocracy and very wealthy, a model not only for developers and builders to imitate but also a pattern for the ambitious middle classes to seek to emulate. An aristocratic fashionplate – and in its early contemporary, stage St John's Wood villadom was almost equally wealthy – it can be argued, transmuted middle-class yearnings for a whiff of the country, which had hitherto seemed unacceptable and inappropriate in town dwellers, into a positive and respectable demand. There were, after all, vast numbers of towndwellers who had come from rural backgrounds; some of them, presumably, hankered after the country they had left, and some of these had the means to indulge such nostalgia In late eighteenth-century London from one half to two-thirds of the adults had been born in the country; and it is probable that the mid-nineteenth-century pattern of internal migration which shows that at least two-thirds of the

35. A. Saunders, *Regent's Park* (1969), 86–7, 133.

residents of south London and Liverpool suburbs, and presumably other suburbs likewise, had moved to the suburbs from neighbouring and largely rural areas and had not moved out from the central zone, also applied earlier.[36]

Some portion of the new suburbanites undoubtedly did desert the old town centres, escaping from increasing dirt, noise, stench, and disease, dissatisfied with the social confusion of mixed residential areas and with the inconvenience of traditional town houses for the style of life they wanted to pursue. But if they were heavily outnumbered by those coming direct to the suburbs from rural and small town surroundings, it is to these that we should look for the mainspring of suburban housing demand, and there is little difficulty in supposing that they were more interested in clutching at some small reminder of country life than in seeking an environment suited to the practice of an ideology of which they were most likely not yet aware. All that was needed to release this pent-up demand, it seems, was a demonstration that moving to a town did not necessarily have to mean moving to a town house and accepting a fully urbanized way of life. Since terrace housing of the traditional town form continued to be built in middle-class suburbs into the second half of the nineteenth century, it is conceivable that this had mainly in view the demand from established towndwellers who wanted to move to something familiar but in more pleasant surroundings, while the market for detached and semi-detached houses lay among the new arrivals. In any event, if demand for the new kind of suburban housing was stirred by fashionable and aristocratic example it is likely that it showed itself mainly in those sections of the middle class which felt closest to the aristocracy, least antipathy to them, or most anxiety to model themselves on what they took to be gentlemanly habits, the groups least likely to be concerned to develop a distinctively and assertively bourgeois culture. It is arguable that suburban growth and the suburban life was set in successful motion by the more imitative and self-effacing sections of the middle class in pursuit of the illusion of bringing the country and gentrification into the urban setting, more intent on appearing to merge themselves unobtrusively into a superior class than on seeking means to express their own class identity.[37]

Much of this reasoning remains to be tested by further research. The results of recent research rest on the implicit assumption that

36. J.R. Kellett, *The Impact of Railways on Victorian Cities* (1969), 408–9.
37. This is consistent with what is known about the political conservatism of suburbia somewhat later in the nineteenth century: J. Cornford, 'The transformation of conservatism in the late nineteenth century', *Victorian Studies*, VII (1963–4).

once the commercial viability of the suburban process had been established and an effective demand for its product had been shown to exist, thereafter the creation of further suburbs became almost a self-sustaining activity, a consequence of urban population growth and the growth and changing distribution of real incomes, which continued indefinitely, subject to cyclical fluctuations, until at least partially arrested by political regulation. This point had been reached by the 1830s, and it is reasonable to argue that from that time those who controlled the necessary resources, landowners, developers, builders and their financers, would channel those resources into the construction of suburban estates confident – frequently over-confident – that a continuing demand existed for his general type of housing. Suburbia had caught on, it was developing its culture, its social rituals, its conventions; the lawnmower had arrived, for those with large enough lawns; it was becoming the ambition of all those who could afford it to live as close to the edge of the country as possible, preferably no doubt employing a gardener. The questions had become, on the supply side, to judge whether and when a particular town and a particular locality could sustain a piece of suburban development, and to decide how to trim and adjust the suburban type in layout and house size to suit the location and the local market, and on the demand side to judge between the reputations, attractions, and costs of the different suburban districts on offer. Demand, of course, changed over time, not merely as fashions in house styles changed or as the special character of older suburbs altered and declined as the frontier moved outward, but also in terms of the social and income groups which composed it; the social deepening of the suburban market in response to falling costs and rising real incomes, can be seen in both Acton and north Leeds, and was a feature of the 1880s and 1890s which brought the lower middle class into suburbia in a considerable way.[38] Variations in the level of demand over time, as well as changes in its social make up, were as important as changes in the conditions affecting new building, in determining the cycles of vigorous expansion and slackness which characterized suburban development; and at the level of the particular suburb or individual building estate within it they were of supreme importance in settling its success or failure. At the general level, however, the motives of suburbanites in wanting to be, or at least passively consenting to be, suburbanites had ceased to be a problem requiring investigation; the suburban way of life in a suburban environment ranging from costly and leafy to inexpensive and gimcrack, was plainly what was preferred by the majority of

38. S.M. Gaskell, 'Housing and the lower middle classes, 1870–1914', in *The Lower Middle Classes in Britain, 1870–1914*, ed. G. Crossick (1977).

171

those who could possibly afford it – it even came to be assumed by planners and policy-makers, with dubious justification, that it was what most of the working classes would want too if the means could be found to provide it for them.

The four case studies included in *The Rise of the Suburbs* did a great deal more than show how, when, and why shapes on the ground took the particular form they did in response to general impulses, although they do this in a way to satisfy curiosity about the influences which have moulded the local environment. Four general points stand out, which can only be made through studying the suburbanizing process in action in specific places: the importance of rural, pre-development features in influencing the shape, form, character, and timing of suburbanization, coupled with the limitations which market forces placed on the power of landowners and developers to decide what should be built; the varying role of transport services in different situations; the mixed social character of suburban districts, coupled with strong self-zoning tendencies; and the long drawnout and much interrupted nature of the process of growth in any particular neighbourhood.

It has frequently been observed that the fully built-up environment exhibits the marks and scars of its rural antecedents, and that field paths and boundaries, ancient tracks, and property boundaries show through in the pattern of roads, the territories of housing estates, and the social and chronological frontiers between distinct housing types of the urbanized scene. Recent studies confirm the observation with many local illustrations, but go much further in revealing the complex character of the shadows which pre-development features cast before them. The structure of property rights involved in taking the development process through from the open land of farming, market gardening, or country house park to the suburban street is most expressly and schematically formulated in Treen's approach.[39] At the level of the individual building estate or building plot the availability of the land for development depended on the readiness, and legal capacity of the landowner to release it; the identity of the pre-development landowner, and the mixture of financial and social influences on him, therefore played a critical part in determining the timing and type of building operations. What emerges, however, is that there was no one type of pre-development owner or pre-development situation which was specially prone to stimulate development. In Bromley, land transfers which brought in new, speculative owners were of great importance as preconditions of development, while in north Leeds long-established, absentee aristocratic landowners attempted, without great success, to act as

39. Treen, 'The process of suburban development in North Leeds', *op. cit.*, 160, table 14.

direct developers of their estates well in advance of any strong demand for villas in the area.[40] Ownership changes on the urban fringes might, indeed, indicate either the arrival of land speculators who would proceed to exploit the building potential they perceived, as happened with the north Leeds aristocratic estates from the 1870s onwards, or the settling of the wealthy on small residential country estates where they could hold development at bay for many years, until finally forced into retreat by the overwhelming pressure of suburban encirclement, as happened in parts of Bexley.

Readiness to speculate on rising land values and to release land for building was less a product of recent acquisition, or of the business connexions of a landowner, although these were important in some instances, than of non-residence and of the kind of advice on estate management a landowner was receiving. The social standing of the landowner and the strength of his links with the area could have a strong influence on the class of development favoured, the gentry, pseudo-gentry, and dignified corporate owners such as the Goldsmiths' Company with their estate in Ealing, aiming for the prestige of the upper end of the wealthy middle-class market, while owners and developers of lower status were likely to pursue the line of greatest profit through the most intensive type of available development regardless of its social class. The power of the landowner to translate his wishes into actual buildings, however, was tightly circumscribed by the commercial realities of each particular situation, its existing reputation, its immediate surroundings, and the strength of local demand. Many ambitious schemes failed through over-optimistic estimates of site potential, and on the whole the apparatus of landowner control through supervision of layout and design, and through stipulation of minimum values for houses to be erected, is best seen as providing effective reinforcement for general influences of place and status already working in the desired direction, but as being ineffective in turning back contrary tides.[41] The direction of these tides was frequently set by the first few pieces of new development in a neighbourhood, and the style of housing added casually to an existing village or settlement in an early phase of minimal growth could well determine the character of a much later phase of full-scale development. Thus the Stevens Town district of Ealing developed as an area of working-class housing in the 1870s and 1880s on the basis of a few workmens' cottages which had

40. J.M. Rawcliffe, 'Bromley: Kentish market town to London suburb, 1841–81 in Thompson ed. *The Rise of Suburbia, op. cit.*, 41; Treen, *op. cit.*, 163.
41. Rawcliffe, *op. cit.*, 50; M. Jahn, 'Suburban development in outer west London 1850–1900', and M.C. Carr, 'The development and character of a metropolitan suburb, Bexley, Kent', both in Thompson, *op. cit.*, 170 and 224 respectively.

been built there without much thought in the 1840s; a few lower-middle-class houses built in Acton in the 1850s set the tone for the whole district in the 1880s; some industrial development in Lower Burley, north Leeds, in the 1840s set the scene for covering most of the district with working-class back-to-backs in the 1860s; the handful of superior villa residences built near Bexley village in the 1880s and 1890s were still exerting their influence towards making this a high status area in the 1930s, while the initial lower class development further north in Welling was perpetuated in its later rapid growth.[42] In this way the first tentative, small-scale and often unplanned steps in development can be seen as themselves becoming pre-development features in relation to subsequent phases of comprehensive development, exerting strong influences on the social character of the final suburban product.

It has long been recognized that transport services played an important part among the general influences on suburban growth, but the exact nature of that part, and whether improved transport was an essential, causal, or permissive element in suburbanization, have been matters of dispute. Improved transport in the nineteenth century meant, above all, railways, and the prevailing view is that only in a few exceptional cases can railways be regarded as an important cause of suburban growth, and that generally 'the development of suburbs . . . preceded the provision of railway services, by periods of at least a decade or two for each of the larger cities'.[43] In part this view relates to the suburbs of the large provincial cities which at least until 1900 were little more than two to three miles from city centres, too short a distance for suburban trains to be practicable; the unimportance of railways in provincial suburban growth is confirmed in the study of north Leeds, where the intrusion of the Leeds–Thirsk railway was an impediment rather than an assistance to development. In part, however, the view concerns London's suburbs, and rests on the stringent assumption that railways only caused suburban growth when railway policy on fares and services took an actively promotional line, an assumption that virtually reduces the railway suburbs to Edmonton and Walthamstow, where the Great Eastern's workmen's fares and workmen's trains reluctantly but decisively promoted the rapid development of working-class suburbs after 1864. The outer suburbs at more than five or six miles from the centre could not have developed as dormitories without commuter rail services, however skeletal, and even if railway companies did little or nothing to encourage such growth through special fares or convenient services the presence

42. Jahn, *op. cit.*, 122; Treen, *op. cit.*, 171; Carr, *op. cit.*, 227.
43. Kellett, *op. cit.*, 354–76.

of a railway should be regarded as a necessary, although not a sufficient, condition for outer suburban growth. The building of railways preceded the development of suburbs in Bromley, Acton and Ealing, and Bexley, but the interval between opening a station and substantial suburban expansion varied between a few years and many decades, and the absence of any immediate railway-triggered expansion in Bexley confirms the proposition that railways made the outer suburban dormitories possible but did not create them.

Where other conditions were favourable – an attractive location, an established nucleus of village or small market town, landowners keen to act as developers, a handful of existing residents with city connexions, and a propitious moment in the trade cycle – the promotion of a railway could be the catalyst of expansion, producing a genuine railway suburb. This happened in Bromley, where local landowners were the chief promoters of the railway which was opened in 1858, ushering in a decade of rapid growth spearheaded by a small number of affluent middle-class households able to afford the high cost of commuting. Very soon, however, it became apparent that residential expansion was proceeding in spite of the inconvenience, inefficiency, and inadequacy of train services, and Bromley passed into the same situation as Ealing until the 1860s, where the Great Western completely neglected its suburban services, or Bexley in the 1930s, where headlong housing expansion ran well in advance of train services or access to stations, a situation in which transport services followed after development was under way.[44] A much more complicated statement about the relationship between transport and development emerges from the close analysis of railway promotions and train services in outer west London, and here it is possible to see the interdependence of the two, with the promotion of new lines in advance of suburban housing both by speculative landowners and by a railway company reliant on suburban traffic, the District, and the improvement of services by main line companies at hours and frequencies to suit the commuters' needs, acting as stimuli to revive building activity from a preceding depression. Here railway services acted as a chief instrument for communicating upswings in the building cycle to the district in the middle phases of its development, even if they had been of little importance in starting the initial development.[45]

In the inner suburbs where distances were too short for railway operation, and in the provinces, horse buses were of great importance to middle-class commuters and these were invariably

44. Rawcliffe, *op. cit.*, 38; Carr, *op. cit.*, 243.
45. Jahn, *op. cit.*, 114.

introduced only after suburban development had taken hold.[46] From 1870 onwards horse trams were being rapidly introduced, and as a means of cheap mass transit they had a much more widespread effect than workmen's trains and fares in enabling the lower middle class and the artisans to push out into suburbia and to threaten the exclusiveness of middle-class suburbs. The encroachment of trams was resisted in Ealing, as in Edgbaston, Hampstead, Kemp Town, Kelvinside, and Victoria Park, because it threatened to bring in a lower class of people and bring on social deterioration, and as in other places the resistance was in the end unsuccessful. By the early 1900s electric tramways were being projected into virgin territory, well ahead of suburban settlement.[47] While it is salutary to be reminded that in Leeds the horse trams did not run early enough in the morning for working-class commuters, and were largely used by the middle classes, in general they were a working-class form of transport and a reminder that suburbs did not remain exclusively middle-class.[48] Further research may well show that tramway suburbs were more significant than railway suburbs, not perhaps as entirely new settlements called forth out of green fields, for no transport service seems to have been capable of doing that save in exceptional circumstances, but as places which experienced a dramatic transformation in social character and physical scale as a direct result of tramway penetration.

The Bexley evidence shows clearly that the development of dormitory suburbs for the working and lower middle classes in Bexleyheath, West Wickham, and Welling was strongly boosted by the trams linking them to industrial employment on Thameside. Where workplaces remained within walking distance, as they did in the inner parts of north Leeds, workers could afford to live within the suburb and work outside it, and they were catered for in the fingers of back-to-back housing which intruded on the social homogeneity of the district. Elsewhere, in outer London, commuting to a job in the centre was out of the question for the working classes before the coming of cheap public transport, and yet pockets or even substantial neighbourhoods of working-class housing appeared in the outer suburbs long before the trams or workmen's trains. The nineteenth-century suburban dream was a middle-class dream; the nineteenth-century suburban reality was a social patchwork. Of course, whole building estates and entire sub-districts were successfully developed with solidly middle-class housing, finely attuned to the different grades of income and

46. G.C. Dickinson, 'Suburban road transport in Leeds, 1840–95', *J. Transport Hist.*, IV (1960).
47. Cannadine, 'Victorian cities: how different?', 467.
48. See Thompson ed., *The Rise of Suburbia*, 176, and 226.

status within that class; but the creation of a complete single class suburb was an illusion. In part this conclusion is an effect of the boundaries which are chosen to define the area of an individual suburb. It would be perfectly possible to take a district of single class housing and call it a suburb in itself, and indeed many sub-districts of unitary social standing did establish their own place-names which became essential elements in their identities, such as Bedford Park or Grove Park. There is perhaps no reason to suppose that administrative areas, entire parishes or townships such as Ealing, Bexley, Bromley, or Headingley, should be treated as potentially single suburbs. In the main, however, this conclusion does not rest on definitional ambiguities. It is not so much that each parish or township contained a multiplicity of separate, but related suburbs each of its own class, as that the very process of establishing a suburban community and the imperatives of building development produced some degree of social mixture.

Even in the purest middle-class suburban case, where the incomes to support the community were entirely generated by the minority of affluent commuters at the top of the social pyramid, these households required the support not only of indoor domestic servants but also of a considerable array of service activities to keep houses, gardens, clothes, linen, transport, roads and streets, and persons in good running order, and the workers in such industries, trades, and services needed to live locally. The pure case, uncluttered by other businesses and occupations inherited from a pre-suburban economy, probably did not exist in practice, but the small working-class districts of Bromley in the 1860s and 1870s appear to have come close to satisfying the requirements of this model. In the thoroughly mixed case lower grade housing was built far in excess of the size of a working and lower middle-class population in this directly and locally dependent and supporting role, and the extra labour force thus settled tended to attract employment to the area in a mutually supporting process which generated small-scale manufacturing, public utilities, and service industries in the suburb serving wider markets; this seems to have happened in Acton, with its laundries, dye works, and manure factory, in Hanwell with its light industry, and to a lesser extent in parts of Ealing. In the intermediate case a similar excess of working and lower middle-class housing was built, but industrial development within the boundaries of the suburb remained restricted and many of the residents were employed outside the district, in jobs which they could reach on foot; this seems to be broadly true of Lower Burley and parts of Headingley.

Three studies in *The Rise of the Suburbs* examined the building of districts of working-class housing before the coming of cheap public transport and were concerned to explain how this happened and why it happened in particular places. In general, workmen's cottages and lower-class terraced housing tended to go up on sites which developers and builders did not think sufficiently attractive to be eligible for anything of a better and more expensive grade, and these sites tended to be those nestling against some undesirable existing feature – a factory or workshop, a railway line, or a previous piece of lower class development.[49] Frequently these were also small parcels of building land, and the restricted possibilities of sites of only a few acres may have attracted the smaller, less ambitious, and more precariously financed builders who could only build the cheapest kind of houses. In this way fragmented ownership producing individual sites of small size may have encouraged lower-class development, a process reinforced by piecemeal development where one small island of working-class housing could set the tone for the whole adjoining area. Site size alone, however, was not a determining factor, since in Acton the British Land Company acquired a very large building estate of 70 acres and promptly set about creating a new working-class community on it.[50] There is indeed a suggestion that the freehold land societies and successor companies of the third quarter of the century may have directly contributed to the building of lower-middle-class and artisan housing in the suburbs, since they were primarily in business to create smallish building plots within the reach of potential owner-occupiers, who tended to be found more in those groups than higher up the middle class. This was not necessarily the case, however, for although the inconveniently shaped and placed part of the British Land Company's estate in Bromley was developed in this way, its prime part was successfully covered with prime villas which were occupied by representatives of the wealthy middle class.[51]

The most likely explanation, perhaps, hinges on the endemic over-optimism of developers and builders about the likely level of affluent middle-class demand for houses. They were forever setting out with high hopes for the demand for large and comparatively expensive houses, and forever finding that there were too few of the middle classes to go round. In this situation a developer or builder with strong financial resources and some personal commitment to a vision of the ultimate social complexion of his building estate might halt operations and wait to resume them at the same social level when the appropriate class of demand revived. An entrepreneur with no personal ties to the reputation of the neighbourhood, and perhaps a pressing need to turn over his capital rapidly and obtain some immediate returns, was, however, likely to take the obvious

49. *Ibid.*, 62, 98, and 171.
50. *Ibid.*, 64, 107, and 172.
51. *Ibid.*, 59, and 103.

course of shifting his target down market by going in for a lower and cheaper grade of housing. Small builders operating on tight margins, and land societies anxious to keep their sites moving so as not to have their assets locked up in undeveloped land, fitted this description, and maybe for these reasons were more frequently than others responsible for introducing the working classes and lower middle classes into districts that had initially seemed destined for superior middle-class settlement.

The recurrent optimism, or greed, of landowners, developers, and builders, lured on by the often illusory prospect of large gains to be made from speculation on development into providing an over-supply of building land and of houses was ever present. The result was that the development of individual estates was frequently a highly protracted and much interrupted affair, perhaps stretching over nearly half a century, and this in itself meant that the completed fabric might be a patchwork not only of successive architectural styles but also of social classes, as different layers of fashion and effective demand passed over and beyond a district.[52] It was this slowness of development which was likely to leave any particular estate raw and incomplete for years on end, that gave H.G. Wells the impression, fictionalized in *The New Machiavelli*, that Bromley in the mid-nineteenth century was the victim of 'an invading and growing disorder' that was replacing the social order and harmony of a neat little market town by a mindless, wasteful, anarchy which was suburbia:

> The outskirts of Bromstead were a maze of exploitation roads that led nowhere, that ended in tarred fences studded with nails . . . and in trespass boards that used vehement language. . . . It was a multitude of uncoordinated fresh starts, each more sweeping and destructive than the last, and none of them ever really worked out to a ripe and satisfactory completion. Each left a legacy of products – houses, humanity, or what not – in its wake. It was a sort of progress that had bolted; it was change out of hand, and going at an unprecedented pace nowhere in particular.[53]

After many years the ragged incompleteness disappeared, suburban neatness and tidiness colonized the builders' rubble and waste and turned it into gardens, and the underlying order and rationality of suburban development was finally embodied in a fully built environment. In Bexley in the 1930s, in a very different market situation and with the appearance of large-scale building firms exploiting economies of scale and capable of building a complete

52. *Ibid.*, 141.
53. H.G. Wells, *The New Machiavelli* (1911; Penguin edn, 1946), 33ff esp. 39.

semi-detached in three days, the process which had formerly taken decades was completed in a year or two.[54] Whether H.G. Wells would have been better pleased with the result because it was achieved rapidly without intervening years of chaos may be doubted. The suburban result, however attained, represented what a great many people wanted to live in; it is not necessary to admire it in order to wish to understand how it happened.

54. See Thompson ed., *The Rise of Suburbia*, 265.

Chapter 6

THE RAILWAY AS AN AGENT OF INTERNAL CHANGE IN VICTORIAN CITIES

J.R. Kellett

[from J. R. Kellett, *The Impact of Railways on Victorian Cities* (London 1969), pp. 287–95; 337–53)

The simplicity and elegance of Kellett's writing, supported by meticulously researched case studies of railway development in Birmingham, Manchester, Liverpool, Glasgow and London, made such an impact on urban history that few have sought since to write about transport and the city. In this pioneering study, Kellett not only explored and then downgraded the connections between transport and suburbanization, he also demonstrated the central role of railways both as a means of communication and distribution, and more significantly, as part of a dynamic urban process in which land values, compensation, and demolition interacted so as to redefine land use and initiate zoning. Embedded in the study are concepts of social costs and public regulation, and to some extent these reflect the historiography of economic history in the 1960s with its interest in the distributional impact of economic growth on living standards, and cost-benefit analyses of infrastructural investment. These motifs, and connected with them, the issue of the public regulation of private initiatives, are explored in their historical setting by Kellett, who brings another exceptional quality to the case studies of the nineteenth-century city, an ability to convey the hustle and bustle, the noise and grime of the street. In focusing on land and property rights Kellett is also able to convey the tense in-fighting of vested interests as they attempted to secure leverage over the location of terminals, industrial and other prime sites. In short, the coming of the railways intensified the land-use opportunities, exposed the raw workings of several interconnected markets in the Victorian city, and created a setting in which various interest groups sought to impose their influence and internalize financial gain. This tension between the public good and private rights is never far from the surface.

181

1. THE CITY CENTRE

INTRODUCTION

The rapid growth of the major Victorian cities was accompanied by internal changes in communications which, though not as dramatic as the arrival of the railways, were essential to sustain continued expansion throughout the nineteenth century.

The greatly increased internal circulation of people and goods, by day and night, in the expanding cities, had to be accommodated by expensive street re-alignments and improvements. The alterations in each town required no new techniques, and make a dull chronicle, but neither the investment effort nor the results should be underestimated. The sums involved in cutting new streets in Birmingham and London, where the most drastic alterations took place, ran to a million and a half per scheme in the 1870s; operations comparable in nature if not in total scale, with the urban railway works. The improvement of Victorian cities' internal roads kept pace, though only by the narrowest of margins, with the growing numbers of road vehicles, and provided them with variable routes for transit at approximately one-third to one-half of modern urban road speeds.[1] The new variety and number of public cabs and omnibuses, and the volume and increasingly specialized types of commercial vehicle which thronged the streets in mid-century, reflect a service industry which was growing as rapidly as any in Victorian cities.[2]

In London, for example, although the numbers employed in regular service for the railways, as clerks, porters, guards, drivers, and other officials, roughly trebled between 1861 and 1891 (from 8,300 to 24,800), the numbers employed as carmen and carters also trebled (from 14,700 to 43,800). The employment offered by the passenger cabs, omnibuses and coaches in 1891 added a further 48,200, so that the totals engaged in horse-drawn urban transport of passengers and goods were more than three times as large as those in regular metropolitan railway service. With their families and dependents they numbered, according to Charles Booth's calculations, some 260,000 people – one of the largest

1. From 3.28 to 4.55 m.p.h. (House of Commons, hereafter H.C., 1863, VIII, QQ. 1226–8) to between 5 and 10 m.p.h. effective speeds. R.J. Smeed, 'The Traffic Problem in Towns', *Town Planning Review* 35 (1964–5), 133–58.
2. John Hollingshead, *Odd Journeys in and out of London* (1860), 182–6, describes the great range and variety of horse drawn vehicle seen on the streets.

occupational groups in London.[3] It is true that many of the carters, cabbies and omnibus drivers were engaged upon cross traffic and feeder services connected with the railways, but others provided services which were sturdily competitive. Within a ten-mile radius of London by far the greater part of retail distribution was in the hands of the carters. Even Mr Seymour Teulon, an ex-director of the South Eastern railway company, who lived twenty-one miles out of town, found it more convenient to use a carter in the 1860s; and in 1900 the vans and carts had a virtual monopoly, 90 per cent or more, of the merchandise and shop goods, over a two-hour journey or ten-mile radius.[4] On the streets of London's inner district the horse buses, given a new profitability by the fall in imported feeding-stuffs, gained passengers at a faster rate than the railways in the fourth quarter of the century.[5]

The last quarter of the nineteenth century also saw the belated application of the railway principle to urban street traffic. Although at first introduced experimentally – in Glasgow, for example, the first horse tramways were intended to move coal and other goods by night and passengers by day – they were soon established as the only practical method of improving upon orthodox horse-power; doubling the stage lengths and trebling traction.[6] Using very limited technical means the street tramway provided the most substantial of all contributions to the Victorian cities' internal transport problems, conveying, by the end of the century – even in London, where the lengths of run favoured the railway – 45 *per cent* more passengers annually than local railways.[7] The tramcar played a role which was important enough to survive for many decades into the age of electricity and the petrol engine. It shared the drawbacks of a fixed-route system, seen so clearly in the urban surface-railway lines; but the force of these drawbacks was greatly reduced by the fact that the stops were frequent and easy of access, and the routes widely and cheaply dispersed.[8] In these ways the growing internal traffic of Victorian cities was accommodated, using simple techniques which had been available at the time early horse-railway pioneers like Thomas Hill had canvassed their ideas in the 1820s.[9]

3. Charles Booth, *Life and Labour of the People of London* (London, 1892), VII, 284.
4. H.C., 1867, XXXVIII, Q. 16441 (Teulon); H.C., 1904 (305) VII, QQ. 113–4.
5. T.C. Barker and Michael Robbins, *A History of London Transport* (London, 1963), 243, 261, 271.
6. House of Lords Record Office (hereafter HLRO), Min., H.C., 1872, 3 June, S.C. on Glasgow, Coatbridge and Airdrie Tramways.
7. H.C., 1905, XXX, 570.
8. Cost per mile: Tramways £40,000 (without street widening); tubes £250,000–£300,000; railways £1,000,000 (cut and cover); H.C., 1905, XXX, 590.
9. Manchester Reference Library (hereafter MRL), Political Tracts, P 3411, P 3486.

RAILWAY LAND HUNGER AND THE VICTORIAN CITY

Yet still, even after the other internal transport changes have been given their due weight, the most revolutionary of all the novel features of the mid-nineteenth century city were its new railway stations, and they exercised, over each city, both a general and a local influence. In the first place, the railway station stood as a symbol of the most recent of major advances in technology; the extension, to locomotion and distribution, of steam power, which had already revolutionised substantial sectors of industrial production. In the environment of the Victorian city the modernity of the railway station was outstanding: one arrived by mechanical transport, in a manner which differed only in degree from that of today, before stepping out into a world of horse-drawn vehicles. 'Wonderful Members of Parliament', wrote Charles Dickens, 'who little more than twenty years before had made themselves merry with the wild railroad theories of engineers, and given them the liveliest rubs in cross examination, went down into the north with watches in their hands, and sent a message before by the electric telegraph to say that they were coming.'[10]

The Victorian railway was also the most important single agency in the transformation of the central area of many of Britain's major cities. Unlike the ubiquitous horse omnibus, cab or tramcar, operating cheaply upon the public thoroughfare, it could only function if large areas of the town were exclusively set aside for its fixed routes and separate rights of way. Nor could its equipment be dispersed at night into scores of small yards and stables, located wherever a cheap and convenient space presented itself. Although, like the horse-drawn traffic, the railway was called into being primarily to serve the traffic needs of established business and residential areas, it was a noisy and obtrusive servant. Soon the space it required was comparable with that of any other single group of commercial or industrial land users.

It is not easy to present an undistorted measurement of the impact of railway land-hunger upon Victorian cities. For example, there is, as yet, no standard classification of the central business districts of British cities comparable to that carried out in the United States by J. E. Vance, R. E. Murphy and B. J. Epstein.[11] Nor are there, as

10. Charles Dickens, *Dombey and Son*, Ch. 6.
11. Raymond E. Murphy and J.E. Vance Jnr., 'Delimiting the Central Business District', *idem* 'A Comparative Study of Nine Central Business Districts', *idem* and Bart. J. Epstein, 'Internal Structure of the Central Business District', *Economic Geography*, 30 (1954). 189–222, 301–336, 31 (1955), 21–46.

yet, any published series of historical land use maps, although some work is now being undertaken in this field. Under the circumstances the most simple and practical definition of the comparable central districts of the five major Victorian cities has seemed to take the built-up area in 1840, when detailed maps of each are available, and to measure planimetrically the intrusions into this area made by the railways during the rest of the century.

Worked out upon this basis the central space requirements of the railways up to 1900 can be seen to vary between 5.5 per cent for London (where the legislative policy of exclusion has already been described) to 7.5 or 9 per cent for the port and terminal cities, Glasgow and Liverpool.

	Built-up area in 1840 (acres)	Railways in central zone in 1900 (acres)	% of central zone owned by railways in 1900
London	14,453	776	5.4
Birmingham	1,439	75.5	5.3
Liverpool	1,673	151	9.0
Manchester	1,886	137	7.3
Glasgow	1,117	84.5	7.6

Given the necessary correction factors, these results accord reasonably well with Harland Bartholomew's work on fifty-three cities in the United States, where the average land use claim staked by the railways was 4.86 per cent, rising to 12.76 per cent for a transfer point like Kansas City.[12] Bartholomew also reported, though unfortunately it is not possible in the present state of urban studies in this country to parallel his figures, that on average the American urban railways were second only to commercial and trading land users in the central area, and consumed approximately three-quarters as much area as heavy and light industry combined. In view of the absence of comparable information here no similar relationship between the railways and other central land users can be demonstrated, but it is perhaps reasonable to suggest, on *a priori* grounds, that proportions

12. Harland Bartholomew, *Land Use in American Cities* (Cambridge, 1955) 58–9. An example of the correction needed may be illustrated from a British city. J. Cunnison and J.B.S. Gilfillan, *The Third Statistical Account of Scotland: Glasgow* (Glasgow, 1958), 47, Table IV, gives modern land use figures, according to which 4.5 per cent of land within the City Boundary was used by railways in 1944–5. But the area included covers 39,725 acres, of which 40.3 per cent was undeveloped, 10.9 per cent open land. This is not inconsistent with the figure cited in the text above.

of at least a similar order might be expected in the major British cities.

The railways' land-hunger, however, could be seen to the greatest effect in the peripheral areas outside the central district of each city. Here land was consumed for marshalling yards, locomotive and carriage works and sheds, link and cut-off lines, and circumferential railways, at a prodigal rate. By 1900, for example, taking an average track width of 22 yards, as the amount usually allowed for the limits of deviation, Glasgow's urban lines and terminals, and the railways skirting the city, together with their associated yards and sidings, occupied over 820 acres – an area equal to three-quarters of the built-up acreage of the whole city in 1840.[13] In Liverpool and Manchester also, the lands in railway ownership in 1900 were half as large as the built-up areas of each city sixty years earlier; although in Birmingham, for reasons already suggested, and in London, where the city area was already very large by 1840, the railway's land acquisitions were not so disproportionate.

Reference to urban maps illustrates and explains this remarkable land hunger. In Glasgow the St Rollox – Sighthill – Springburn complex of engine works and goods yards covered over 190 acres to the north-east of the city; to the south, the Caledonian railway company's various coal depots, carriage sheds and marshalling yards covered another 160. North of the river, link railways skirted the town from east to west in a great semicircle. In Birmingham the Curzon Street and Vauxhall yards covered 120 acres to the east of the city. In Manchester the Ardwick yards covered nearly 90 acres, and the Central and Ship Canal yards covered a further 30 and 50 acres respectively; 100 acres more was laid out for the Lancashire and Yorkshire and L. & N.W. goods sidings, and the Windsor Bridge cattle yards in Salford; and a link railway skirted the east of the town to Miles Platting, where sidings and yards covered another 120 acres. In Liverpool the northern dock sidings, and those at Kirkdale and Sandhills covered 75 and 55 acres respectively; with the Aintree sidings, also to the north but a little further out of town, adding a further 40 acres of marshalling yards. A link railway running from Garston in the south skirted the built-up area, before curving in towards the coast again to the north of the town, connecting *en route* with the enormous sidings at Edgehill, which covered 150 acres. These features, as with the other towns mentioned, are so large as to stand out.

---

13. F.S. Williams, *Our Iron Roads* (1852), 93, 'exclusive of cutting or embankment'. The official view was that 34 yards, or 12.97 acres per lineal mile should be allowed, and even this was probably an underestimate on the urban approach lines. H.C., 1867–8, LXII, 275.

In London, north of the Euston Road, a series of depots and yards covered over 300 acres; and similar, though smaller, groups of railway depots, servicing, storage and marshalling areas marked the other major exit routes. As in the other cities, peripheral railways also skirted the town; the spectacularly unsuccessful West London (Punch's) railway; the timely and successful North London, which had started life as a mere dockside line with the northern trunk routes; and the East London, a contractors' line built by John Hawkshaw, Samuel Brassey and Lucas brothers.[14] In some of these cases the lines had originally run along the fringe of the urban frontier, but had later been surrounded by buildings; otherwise they were the nearest surface railway equivalents to the *ceintures* of the northern cities.

The space consumed by these years, for loading, storage, shunting, servicing, and even for building the engines and rolling stock, requires little comment or explanation, except once more to stress the very large total acreages set aside for this specialized use in each town's outer districts, and the barrier effect of these great unbridged urban clearances.

Examples of the barrier effect could be cited for any city but are difficult to discuss without illustration. Indeed the large-scale Ordnance Maps give a more graphic impression than any words of the effect of severance and isolation the intrusive railway sidings and ever thickening through routes had upon the districts in which they were located. The development of southern Laurieston and Tradeston, a district which was intended to be one of the finest residential areas in Glasgow by its projectors David and James Laurie, fell a victim to encroachments by industrial users, and was given the *coup de grâce* by the Caledonian, and the Glasgow and South Western railway companies.[15] Although only 1–1¼ miles from the Exchange and central business district, it was cut off, a resident complained, 'as if it were a walled city or something like that.'[16] Laurieston rapidly deteriorated between 1840 and 1900 into a slum annexe to the Gorbals; a useful overflow district (for some of the thousands displaced by more central railway demolition) with large houses capable of subdivision into warrens housing 150 people under one roof.

It would be an over-simplification to ascribe Laurieston's dilapidation to the railways alone. Anderston, at a similar distance to the west of the city centre, developed a similar pattern of shabby mixed

---

14. T.C. Barker and Michael Robbins, *op. cit.* 217 (Punch's); Michael Robbins, *The North London Railway* (South Godstone, 1953); *The Builder*, XXVII (1869), 630 (East London).
15. John R. Kellett, *Glasgow: a Concise History* (1966), 14–18.
16. HLRO, Min., H.C., 1846, 9 July, p. 272, S.C. on Caledonian Railway (Dunlop Street Station).

zoning and gross residential overcrowding during the same period, although the railways were excluded from the district. Clearly, the evolving 'twilight zones' of Glasgow, east London, and other Victorian cities, were no mere by-product of the railways' approach routes and sidings. The root cause, as those who took an interest in the urban working class from Pearson to Booth or Costelloe pointed out, was the usurpation of central space by business, commercial and railway users, combined with the sustained demand for casual labour in the central district. 'A slum, in a word', said Costelloe, 'represents the presence of a market for local casual labour.'[17] There were in London half a million who had to live close at hand to be 'on the spot at the lucky time'; in the Drury Lane slums for the Covent Garden market, at Tower Hill for the docks, in Soho for the West End tailoring trade.[18] Even in the skilled craft industries – where equipment might have to be borrowed three or four times per day – the pull of the central district was almost as strong as in the casual labour market. The opportunities for cheaper food on credit from local shopkeepers, and for the part-time employment of womenfolk in the central area, were among the other factors contributing to the overcrowding of the central area listed by the Royal Commission on the Housing of the Working Classes.[19] These factors applied with similar force not merely in London but in the other major Victorian cities.

The making of a slum is too large and general a process to be ascribed to the railways alone, but it is noticeable that districts divided and confined by the railways tended to be cast finally and irretrievably into the now familiar mould of coal and timber yards, warehousing, mixed light and heavy industrial users, and fourth-rate residential housing.

Apart from the yards and sidings, which filled an obvious operational purpose, however, there were also large tracts of cross-overs and connecting lines, the utility of which was far more questionable. Although built, on occasions, to serve an ephemeral or tactical purpose, these products of rivalry were just as permanent and immoveable as the sections of track with a durable function. They could not be rolled up when the occasion which had prompted them had passed; and yet the statute book is full of these short links and

17. B.F.C. Costelloe, *The Housing Problem* (1899), 48–9. A Reprint of pp. 41–63 of *Trans. Manch. Stat. Soc.*, 1898–9.
18. *Ibid.* 48. For these reasons those working in Shoreditch declined the offer of a cottage and garden at Potters' Bar on the railway which had trains running into a terminus near their old houses. 'They were offered housing and railway facilities for the same rent they paid in the slum. Yet not 5% of them would even look at the offer.'
19. H.C., 1884–5, XXX, 22–3.

extensions, often grouped wholesale under a discreet 'Additional Powers' bill. They were listed, at the close of the year in *The Times*, but in the smallest advertising type, and the driest legal style; 'and the result', John Hollingshead complained, 'is that projects more revolutionary in their effects upon persons than an Indian rebellion or a Parisian riot, are able to give that "preliminary notice" of their birth which is required by parliamentary regulations, without disturbing even the timidest and oldest inhabitant among us.'[20]

Every town can produce examples of these cross-overs, triangle junctions and link lines, but the most spectacular are the 'New Cross tangle' and the 'Battersea tangle' in south London. Originating at the time of the Victoria, and Bricklayers' Arms stations, and added to in succeeding generations, these networks of lines consumed over 300 acres of inner suburban land. They are large enough to stand out on any aerial photograph of London, and their complexities have inspired chapters in two recent books by O. S. Nock and Edwin Course, which unravel the historical intentions of each addition to the track in this vast network.[21] In this attempt they have been bolder than Mr Serjeant Sargood, who, perhaps speaking with the assumed ingenuousness which counsel sometimes affected, abandoned all attempt at explanation.

> There is such a network of railways I do not think there is any one person in England, unless it is perhaps Mr Allport, who knows what the different lines are. They run in such innumerable directions, and engines are passing along them at such angles at such various speeds, and with so much complication, that I do not think anybody who did not know that they will all be arranged safely but would suppose that they must all come to a general convergence and wreck, and that it will be the end of them all.[22]

The railway companies engaged in the struggle for Britain's major cities were not deterred by any such apocalyptic visions from pursuing a policy of building, at all costs, their own linkages. John Hawkshaw explained the very strong feelings upon this subject entertained in railway boardrooms.[23] There were four clear categories of railway independence. First, the ideal for which each company strove, was a line built, staffed and controlled by the promoting company. Second, a joint line, regarded as a poor substitute for

20. J. Hollingshead, *Underground London* (1862), 203.
21. O. S. Nock, *British Steam Railways* (1961), 109–26. Edwin Course, *London Railways*, (1962), 63–81, 105–177.
22. HLRO, PYB 1/579, 27 May 1873, p. 7.
23. HLRO, Min., H.L., 1866, 13 July, p. 227, S.C. on M.S. & L. (Central Station and Lines).

autonomy.[24] Even the Cheshire Lines Committee, supposedly an alliance, needed arbitrators to settle the disagreements which constantly arose between the constituent companies; and the extreme in disharmony was demonstrated on joint workings such as the Manchester South Junction line.[25] The operation of this urban link railway was controlled by a joint committee composed of an equal number of directors from the M.S. & L. and the L. & N.W., with chairmen alternating from each company. Since the directors' votes invariably cancelled each other out, it was by the casting vote of the chairman that decisions were made, and last quarter's decisions invariably countermanded.[26] Third in order of preference came the granting of running powers. This was essentially the action of a company whose own intentions had been frustrated, and had sought the alternative of an expensive appeal to Parliament for statutory rights to use sections of a competitor's track or station. Powers wrested by statute from a grudging competitor in this way tended to be greatly diminished in practice by the day-to-day possibilities for operational obstructiveness. Finally, and lowest on the scale, was the mere 'grant of facilities' on sufferance.

Given conditions of competition, and the fluctuating hot and cold relationships even between allied companies, it was inevitable that each railway company should, in addition to its immediate space requirements for running and marshalling, seek to make urban links, under its own direct control, duplicating competitors' approach linkages just as it duplicated their stations.[27]

24. Although it was better than nothing, and O.S. Nock describes it as 'a typical London, Chatham and Dover strategy' to induce large companies to share expenses. In this way the L.C. & D. became involved in line or station sharing with six major companies. However the result, once more, was 'an incredibly complicated series of connecting lines.' O.S. Nock, *op. cit.* 111.
25. HLRO, Min., (M.S. & L.), H.L., 1866, 13 July, p. 229.
26. *Manchester City News* (1881–2), 24, 'Notes and Queries' Supplement, MRL 9427 M 9 A.
27. For examples of this in London and Liverpool referred to by a railway manager see H.C., 1872, XIII, QQ.6681–3 (Cawkwell).

2. THE INNER DISTRICTS AND THE SUBURBS

PHYSICAL EFFECTS UPON THE INNER DISTRICTS OF THE CITY

The main effects of railways in the centre of the Victorian city were to add to the congestion of traffic and the overcrowding of working-class housing, and to contribute, both directly and indirectly, to the changes in land use and the rapid increase in land values. Their characteristic effects in the inner districts were to compress the areas which were within walking range of the city centre, to interrupt communications between them, to stabilize their land values for residential uses and reduce their improvement prospects. The fringe of the central district, comprising the inner areas of cheap housing, small trades, storage yards and dumps, into which the working classes overspilt in the 1860s, formed a region where the effect of urban railway building seems, at close quarters, to be more far-reaching than might initially be expected. Not merely did the many-tracked urban routes, with their fringe lands, act as formidable physical barriers, but they also produced a curious effect upon the inner districts through which they passed, freezing their value, and confirming their dereliction.

Two detailed examples may serve to illustrate the effect. The *Report for the Citizen's Association for the Improvement of Unwholesome Dwellings*, published in Manchester in 1903[28] was inspired by Booth's and Rowntree's surveys of London and York. It attempted to describe the situation of the 200,000 poor in Manchester, 75,000 of whom were living below the level of 'primary poverty', as defined by Rowntree. This report summarized available evidence at the end of the nineteenth century concerning the location of back-to-back houses, (the worst of all surviving slum properties), bye-law houses, industrial and commercial properties. 'Our purpose', wrote their secretary and editor, T.R. Marr, 'has been to get information which would enable those who reach Manchester by train to realise the condition under which people live in these streets.'[29]

The striking way in which the railways served to delimit the central business area by 1900 was clear. Except for a small quantity

28. T.R. Marr, *Housing Conditions in Manchester and Salford, 1903* (1904), Frontispiece.
29. *Ibid*. 64.

of dilapidated housing squashed between the new Cheshire Lines Committee Central Station, the Great Northern railway goods depot, and the old Liverpool Road terminus of the Liverpool and Manchester railway (now converted to a goods depot), and a few back-to-back houses between the approaches to Exchange station and the river Irwell, the whole central district of warehouses, shops and offices was by 1900 delineated by the railways running south-west from Victoria, and west from London Road stations. Less distinctly, the eastern boundary was defined by the area of mixed industrial and residential zoning running between the Lancashire and Yorkshire railway's Oldham Road, and the Midland railway's Ancoats, goods stations. Here, apart from a few shopkeepers in Ancoats Sanitary District No. 1, and some clerks, mechanics and artisans in the 11th district, lived the porters, labourers, hawkers, tramps, hurdy-gurdy men and people of no definite occupation, sandwiched between the railway sidings, dye works and cotton mills, iron and boiler works, gas and sanitary installations, and works making oil and grease.[30] The houses were of the cottage type with stone flags resting directly on a clay subsoil, unventilated, with defective drainage, a third of them occupied by more than one family. Altogether a particularly bad example of the type of no-man's land created by speculative building in the areas between railway sidings and industrial users on the outer fringe of an urban central district. 'In no other district do we find', reported the Manchester and Salford Sanitary Association, 'such an aggregation of extremely old, low, damp, filthy and dilapidated dwellings, nor any houses arranged so as to enclose so much that is noxious and offensive.'[31]

The railways cannot directly be blamed for creating or perpetuating these conditions. An extraordinarily detailed survey carried out in the 1880s by John Leigh, the Medical Officer of Health, illustrated the causes of acute distress among the working class in 'twilight zones' like Ancoats, and his evidence accords exactly with that of Charles Booth. They were places of resort for poorly paid casual labourers who were unable either to move from the district or to pay higher rent; therefore they were accommodated in shoddy and cheap housing, with defective sanitation and cramped space; finally, the precarious balance which might be maintained whilst in employment, good health and spirits, was upset by loss of work, sickness, bereavement or intemperance. Although there were some complaints to him about dense smoke and other industrial nuisances, the railways were not mentioned as a major factor in their discomfort.[32]

30. MRL, Reports of the M.O.H., 1884, p. 48 *et seq.*
31. *An Enquiry into the Causes of Excessive Mortality in No. 1 District, Ancoats* (1889), 38. MRL 614 RE 1.
32. Reports of the M.O.H., 1881–6 *passim.*

Yet the railways played an indirect part in concentrating population in these areas and in determining their locations. Their extensive central demolitions contributed to what a contemporary member of the Manchester Statistical Society described as 'the summary elbowing out' of residents into the outer areas.[33] Moreover, it can be demonstrated that the railways themselves marked out the inner districts through which they passed as suitable overspill areas for those 'elbowed out' of the centre.

Amongst the Medical Officer of Health's Reports in Manchester is a most unusual series of maps drawn by Richard Bastow, probably founded on Adshead's land use map of 1850, which is itself remarkably detailed. Bastow's maps show on a large scale, for all the central rating zones, not merely land uses, but also the varying ages of residential housing.[34] With their help it is possible to analyse the physical effect of the urban termini, and their approach and link lines, upon the surrounding urban fabric in greater detail for Manchester than for any other of the major cities chosen for study.

They show clearly, as is already well known, that once the demolitions which accompanied the driving of the railway into the city were over, the routes, for a considerable margin along both sides, tended to attract thick belts of industrial users, storage and constructional businesses and the like. They also show, however, that where residential housing was left standing, it was never renewed. Bastow's age groupings for houses are *'1850–1870'*, *'1830–1850'*, and *'Before 1830'*. In the whole of Manchester and Salford there was, with the exception only of the Miles Platting district, not one substantial area through which the railways ran which showed housing built or rebuilt after 1830; and many of the cottages past which the railways rattled at roof top level were a hundred years old at the time the Medical Officer wrote, derelict properties dating back even to the 1780s.[35] It is conspicuous that where the railways passed no residential replacement took place. They were frozen, as far as renovation or improvement was concerned, as completely as if time had stopped in 1830. Capital sunk in replacing residential housing in such an environment with a more up-to-date equivalent was obviously considered capital wasted. The best plan for a proprietor was to patch the properties up, accept a lower class of tenant, and wait until a further major alteration made it possible to abandon

33. H. Baker, 'On the Growth of the Manchester Population, Extension of the Commercial Centre of the City, and Pressure of Habitation, 1871–81', *Trans. Manch. Stat. Soc.* (1881–5), 9.
34. MRL 614.0942 M 4.
35. District No. 2, the area around Victoria station fell into this category. The warehouses were replaced, or they chose to remove, but some of the housing surviving off Hanover and Mills streets dated back to 1780.

193

residential use altogether: until a commercial or business offer was made, a corporation clearance or street widening scheme swept the district away, or the railways themselves enlarged their approaches.

Richard Bastow's unique series of maps shows only one prominent area in which modern cottage properties, under 20 years old, had been erected in substantial numbers adjacent to railway lines; those bordering on the Lancashire and Yorkshire railway at Miles Platting, occupied, in large part, by the relatively well paid railway workers.[36] Miles Platting, however, one and a half miles from the centre, was almost far enough out to be called a suburb, and was newly built. 'Whilst healthy zones of new growth match the annual expansion of the city, the rottenness at the core increases', wrote a contributor to the Manchester Statistical Society in 1871. 'Moreover it is not practicable', he continued, 'that all the labouring classes should live in the suburbs.' For the casual labourer in the city a walk of four or five miles a day would be 'a tax too burdensome to be borne'.[37] Given the demand for casual labour, the labourer's need for easy access to the daily-changing opportunities for employment, and reluctance to move away from the home meals and short walks of the inner districts, the house farmers found no difficulty in letting rooms there, no matter how dilapidated and ramshackle the buildings might be.

One is reminded of the passage in which Dickens describes the view from the viaduct as Mr Dombey's railway journey draws to its end. 'Everything around is blackened. There are dark pools of water, muddy lanes, and miserable habitations far below. There are jagged walls and filthy houses close at hand, and through the battered roofs and broken windows, wretched rooms are seen, where want and fever hide themselves in many wretched shapes, while smoke and crowded gables, and distorted chimneys, and deformity of brick and mortar pinning up deformity of mind and body, choke the murky distance. As Mr Dombey looks out of his carriage window, it is never in his thoughts that the monster who brought him there has let the light of day in on these things: not made or caused them. It was the journey's fitting end, and might have been the end of everything; it was so ruinous and dreary.'[38]

Dickens was perfectly correct to point out that the railways let the light of day in on such living conditions, by holding them before the eyes of those of the travelling public who looked out of the window as they approached the terminal. The railways did not cause the deficiency in the supply and quality of housing, nor the illness,

36. *Ibid*. Report, March 1883, 31.
37. G.T. Robinson, 'On Town Dwellings for the Working Class', *Trans. Manch. Stat. Soc.* (1868–72), 69.
38. Charles Dickens, *Dombey and Son* (1869), 176, Chap. XX.

intemperance and unemployment which marked the residents in these quarters. But similar views from the viaduct were all too characteristic of the final approaches to termini in most of the great cities. Indeed, to move on to the second detailed example, Charles Dickens himself has left a vivid description of an equally wretched area, isolated between the approach routes of the London and North Western and Great Northern railways at Euston and King's Cross. Agar Town and Somers Town formed an area of short leases and intermingled residential and industrial uses, dominated by the approach lines of railway termini, similar to Birmingham's Saltley, Manchester's Ancoats, Glasgow's South Laurieston or Liverpool's South Scotland and Vauxhall wards.

The north London area of dereliction differed from that of Ancoats, just described, in two ways. First, the houses were new and their life span only twenty-one years, instead of the fifty or more years for which the ramshackle terraces and back-to-backs of Ancoats had to serve.[39] But they were even more dilapidated, consisting of sheds and hovels run up by journeymen bricklayers and carpenters working on Sundays and in their spare time, an 'English Suburban Connemara', as Dickens described it.

There were the dog-kennel, the cowshed, the shanty, and the elongated match-box styles of architecture. To another, the ingenious residence of Robinson Crusoe seemed to have given his idea. Through an opening was to be seen another layer of dwellings at the back: one looking like a dismantled windmill, and another perched upon a wall, like a guard's lookout on the top of a railway carriage. Every garden had its nuisance – so far the inhabitants were agreed – but every nuisance was a distinct and peculiar character. In one was a dung-heap, in the next a cinder-heap, in the third, which belonged to the cottage of a costermonger, was a pile of whelk and periwinkle shells, some rotten cabbages and a donkey: and the garden of another exhibiting a board inscribed with the words 'Ladies School' had become a pond of thick green water.[40]

The centre of the district was occupied by the mountains of refuse from the metropolitan dustbins, and by the small-scale trades associated with such an area: rag collectors, knackers' yards, bone boiling, manure making, and soap manufacturing works, brick kilns and a gasworks.

The 'Ladies School' notice was a reminder of earlier days when a few larger houses, market gardeners and dairymen had occupied

39. An attempt was made to extend the leases, as John Hollingshead discloses, 'expecting no doubt to profit by the advance of railways on the metropolis.' John Hollingshead, *Ragged London* (1861), 130.
40. Charles Dickens, *Dombey and Son*, Chap. 6, quoted by H.C. Prince, in 'North West London', *Greater London* (ed. J.T. Coppock and H.C. Prince, 1964), 111–12.

the area, which was owned by the Church Commissioners. In 1841, a couple of years after the Euston railway station had been opened, William Agar, a lawyer who had taken a lease from the Church Commissioners, parcelled out the estate indiscriminately into 21-year building leases. When these fell in again in 1862 the whole area was demolished to make way for the St Pancras station of the Midland Railway company – which, because its scheme fell just outside the defined limits of the Metropolitan area, was allowed full powers of demolition without even the *quid pro quo* of cheap workmen's services, imposed in the same year upon the Great Eastern company in the terms of its Liverpool Street Station Act.[41]

The second way in which Agar and Somers Towns differed from Ancoats was that the former areas did not merely front the terminal approaches, they were actually sandwiched, after Thomas Brassey had completed the Great Northern's works to King's Cross (1852), between two of the largest terminal approaches for a distance of a mile and a half, up to Camden Town. This overlapping of the areas of dereliction left a zone, or wedge, in which all development was paralysed, and which formed a convenient and obvious route for the third great company to drive in its northern approach.

To a certain extent such densely occupied and makeshift inner suburbs were a product of the rapid growth of urban population itself, including the growth of a large class unable to pay for anything better, and were not the result of any action by the railway companies; but the railways might be said to have worsened the situation in two ways. First, they added substantially to the stream of dispossessed leaving the central district, without either providing alternative accommodation or really cheap fares. By these actions they produced the very opposite effect to that commonly ascribed to the railways; they increased the degree of overcrowding and compressed the mid-Victorian city rather than assisting it to expand. The immediate results of this pressure of overcrowding can be seen in the subdivision of existing tenements, the occupation of empty houses where these could be found, and the running up of 'temporary' housing of the type small builders or weekend entrepreneurs were prepared to supply, no matter how short the building lease. In areas where houses had stood untenanted the empties were taken up; and this side-effect of demolition was one which larger builders with stocks of empties on their hands openly welcomed. In fact the clearest way to trace the movement of population caused by railway demolition, John Leigh, the Manchester Officer of Health, suggested, was to note the rate at which empty houses were taken up in the adjacent reception areas. He

41. H.C., 1905, XXX, 568–9.

quotes, from his own experience, the example of how, after the destruction of the old three-storey houses which had occupied the site of the C.L.C.'s Central Station in Manchester, two or three of the sanitary areas in the upper part of St George's district began to show a marked increase in mortality.

> This led to a house-to-house visitation, for there was no epidemic at this time, nor apparent reason why the mortality should be of a higher rate than usual, or higher than in the neighbouring sanitary districts. It was ascertained that a considerable number of persons who had been displaced from some of the worst streets off Deansgate by the operations for the Central Station had migrated to these sanitary districts, carrying, of course, with them their bad habits and deteriorated health. They had been led to these localities by the fact that a number of the houses had long been empty, and were available at low rents. They raised the rate of mortality of the districts, but, benefiting by the change, had lowered their own.[42]

These reception areas were scattered, within walking distance of the casual labour markets, around the inner areas of the city, sometimes in the shadow of the station, sometimes in some other area of low residential amenity: on occasions the inflow was even accommodated by the rookeries surviving in the central area. But, and here was the second influence of the railways, they cramped and confined the inner districts into which migration from the centre took place, by their network of main lines, viaducts, yards and works, and, as it were, *suggested* areas where, because residential values had been frozen, the overflow might accumulate. Unlike other areas, for which the process of gradual improvement and residential replacement was always a possibility, however remote, the inner districts intersected by the railways were fixed in dereliction.

The effect upon amenity was combined with an effect upon communications. Ancoats was particularly bad in this respect. 'With a population equal to that of a large city', wrote John Leigh, 'it has not a single road or street enabling that vast population to communicate in a fairly straight line with the city with which its business chiefly lies. A series of zig-zags, along narrow streets, form its avenues to the city. Every year adds to its dismal character, and lessens the enjoyment of its inhabitants.'[43] Like the inhabitants of Saltley, the equivalent area in east Birmingham, the 48,000 inhabitants of Ancoats suffered from an interdiction of communications by the railway workings. Apart from the sheer difficulty and expense of bridging railway land, the routes themselves were often

---

42. MRL, Reports of the M.O.H., March 1884, 120.
43. *Ibid*. March 1884, 48.

raised on embankments or viaducts, crossing the street pattern at angles, with the minimum headroom and width; so that where road communications were poor, or incompletely formed, the possibilities of future widening and realignment were drastically curtailed.

In London similar effects were produced, both in the east and in the south, by railway approaches through the inner districts. Petitions against the London and South Western railway company's projected route from Waterloo to Thames-side at Clink Street summarize the objections. 'It will run direct across all the southern entrances to London, crossing at a low elevation, the important and leading thoroughfares of Waterloo Road, Blackfriars Road and Southwark Bridge Road, and enclosing as it were the southern part of the metropolis with a brick wall and preventing all future improvements.'[44] Such destruction of communications between the inhabitants and the central district was 'contrary to the feeling which has abolished city walls and gates as obstructions to business and recreation'.[45] Mr Charles Stephens, owner of a hundred and fifty acres freehold in Camberwell, and a hundred more in Lewisham, described a landowner's anxiety to the Royal Commission of 1846 in these words: 'Such a railway will place an impassable and hideous wall between the most important and populous parts of this parish – and will induce the building of houses, wherever that event shall take place, in a confined manner and of an inferior class.'[46]

Although on this occasion the protests were timely and effective, in other areas representations were not organized, were too late, or were directed to bodies not competent to deal with them. A few hundred yards from the line just rejected, the London and South Western company completed a viaduct to Waterloo, which caused, almost at once, the very effects predicted by the petitioners of St Saviour's, Southwark, and St Giles's, Camberwell.[47] 'A rapid deterioration followed the coming of the railways to Lambeth,' writes the Survey of London. 'Streets were cut up and buildings torn down or dismembered, while the series of dark, damp arches under the lines encouraged the more disreputable element of the population.'[48]

The railway arch was, of course, a functional necessity for many of the approach routes, if they were to avoid the wholesale street

44. H.C., 1846, XVII, App. 1, p. 249.
45. *Loc. cit.* p. 256.
46. *Ibid*. Q.2810.
47. 'This is an evil . . . in connection with the impassable boundaries of railway lines, as will be seen on the South Western map by tracing the course of the railway from Nine Elms to Clapham Junction.' 'The worst elements have for the most part taken refuge in blocks of houses isolated by blank walls or railway embankments or untraversed by any thoroughfare.' Charles Booth, *op. cit.*, (1892), I, 265, 281.
48. *The Survey of London*, XXIII (1951), 1.

closures and level crossings, against which Parliament had set its face. All the early hopes that arches might be turned to advantage miscarried, however, and within a few years they became symbols of all that was shabby and down-at-heel in Victorian urban life. Some of the central arches were let to people who lived on the premises, in spite of 'the difficulty of providing chimneys and such other little difficulties', and carried on a low class of trade.[49] Some of the arches of the Blackwall railway were bought by 'a very benevolent person, who has fitted them up as houses for the poorer class of people': and near the Minories station a clergyman's application for the use of the arches for an infant school was granted. 'The Committee were very happy to do all they could in granting them at a very moderate rent, and a large and very interesting school is carried on under those very arches.'[50] During the commercial crisis of 1866 unemployment relief at 9s a week was given to upwards of 400 men in Bethnal Green 'in three vacant railway arches which have been kindly let for the purpose'.[51] More casually, the arches were used as overnight shelter by the human derelicts of Victorian society; by spirit drinkers and unsuccessful criminals, by Gustav Doré's 'sleepers out'.[52] A railway arch was chosen as the symbol of ultimate degradation by the popular Victorian artist Augustus Egg, for his narrative paintings showing the fate of an unfaithful wife.[53]

Wherever the arches of railway viaducts appeared, the wretched flotsam of urban life followed. Complaints concerning their deteriorating effect were made against the London and South Western, the Eastern Counties, the Greenwich and the Blackwall railway companies in London: and repeated on similar occasions in the provinces. 'A viaduct', wrote one resident in east London, 'would not be tolerated in a respectable neighbourhood and undoubtedly renders a bad one worse.'[54] Nor, as time passed, was any improvement apparent. The first bad impressions were only confirmed by further experience.

'I travel something from 25,000 to 28,000 miles a year by railway', said an engineer in 1866, 'and have done so for the last 25 years. I have my eyes pretty well open generally and I know no railway passing through a town on arches . . . without it being to my mind a very serious detriment to the town property through which it passes.'[55] 'You see it in all towns', the Town Clerk of Manchester

---

49. HLRO, Min., (M.S. & L.), H.L., 1866, 16 July, pp. 8–12.
50. H.C., 1846, XVII, QQ.413–4 (Tite).
51. *Illustrated London News*, 15 February 1868, 156.
52. Gustav Doré and Blanchard Jerrold, *London: a Pilgrimage* (1872).
53. Graham Reynolds, *Painters of the Victorian Scene* (1953), Plate 49.
54. H.C., 1846, XVII, App. 16, pp. 273–4.
55. HLRO, Min., (M.S. & L.), H.L., 1866, 16 July, p. 78 (Bateman).

concurred, 'if you go along a railway with a viaduct; the very character of the property you look down upon shows that it is not the place where improvements may be looked for – the viaduct puts a stop absolutely to any improvement from the time it is constructed.'[56]

THE RAILWAYS AND THE LOCATION OF INDUSTRY

There was, however, another side to the coin. To residential property-owners and to industrial firms using road cartage the viaducts were a nuisance and obstruction, but to the heavier industrial firms in the suburbs the railway lines gave valuable linkages with suppliers and markets. In each of the major Victorian cities the same tendency for industry to disperse into the inner districts, to the river side, or to more distant suburbs is apparent.

It is difficult to know how much to assign to the influence of rail connections, in view of the other powerful influences working to produce the same result. The growing scale of the business units engaged in manufacture demanded acreages of floor space which could only be acquired by moving out from the city centre. The large urban factory in the central district was an anachronism by the 1860s, progressively squeezed out of the city centre by rising land values; though the small scale workshops specializing in the clothing, furniture, printing, precious metals and jewellery, watchmaking, precision engineering and the light metal trades, showed a surprising tenacity, particularly in Birmingham and London, and continued to multiply in the inner districts, or even in certain quarters of the city centre.

Again, it is difficult, in view of the supremacy of carting over short distances, to assess the significance of railway linkages in the redistribution of industry. For every factory with railway sidings there were a dozen without; but those which took advantage of direct rail connections tended to be the larger and more modern. Some, specially in heavy engineering, formed groupings of firms large enough to dominate employment in their district, as at Gorton, or Newton Heath, near Manchester, or Springburn near Glasgow.

56. British Transport Historical Records (hereafter BTHR) PYB 1/383, Q.2995.

The connection between the large firms in the areas just mentioned and the railways was unusually close because they were all suppliers of engines and rolling stock. The Manchester firm of Beyer, Peacock and Company, although at first it produced a variety of ironmongery in a centrally located factory, soon became identified with locomotive manufacture and with Gorton.[57] 'What a change has come over the scene', wrote John Higson in *The Gorton Historical Recorder*.

> The ancient trees are felled, the lanes are being superseded by roads and are assuming modernized appellations; pack horses are fled; their place is supplied by railway engines – In the course of time, the situations of our hedgerows and fields will become lost under the sites of streets and houses, and form a part of the vast city of Manchester.[58]

By the late 1860s over 40 acres was covered by the works and sidings at Gorton, and a further 45 acres and 13 miles of sidings covered part of Newton Heath.[59] Another Manchester firm, Sharp, Stewart and Company, which had originally made cotton machinery, and had also been located centrally (at the Atlas works, between Oxford Street and Great Bridgewater Road), performed a still more complex migration in 1885, not to the outskirts of Manchester, but to the specialized engineering suburb of Springburn in Glasgow.[60]

These engineering works form special cases, of course, because of their intimate business and sales connections with the railways, but they are important enough in themselves to be mentioned by name; and they produced the interesting phenomenon of extremely specialized areas in Glasgow, Manchester and east London which were virtually suburban versions of Crewe or Swindon.[61]

Evidence also exists of other large firms, not directly connected as suppliers and manufacturers to the railway companies, which built new premises adjacent to the railways or, if already established, sought rail linkages. Soho, near Birmingham, for example, one of the cradles of the Industrial Revolution, where Matthew Boulton's factory predated the railways by 70 years, secured early connections with the main line to Wolverhampton.[62] Some other established

57. *The Engineering and other Industries of Manchester and District* (1887), 47. 'Gorton Foundry', in the *Manchester Guardian*, 2 July 1925.
58. *Op. cit.* (Droylsden, 1852), p. v.
59. *Manchester of Today: an Epitome of Results* (Manchester, 1888), 149. 'Works visited etc.', MRL 620 94273 INI.
60. *Manchester City News*, 28 March 1903. Great Central Railway, *Official Album* (1902). Old Glasgow Club, *Transactions* 8 January 1951.
61. Stratford in east London occupied a position similar to that filled by Gorton in Manchester, or Springburn in Glasgow. R. Glass et al, *London: Aspects of Change* (London, 1964), 64, states that 6,800 workmen were employed there at one time, compared with 17,000 at Gorton.
62. D.C. Eversley, 'Industry and Trade, 1500–1880', *A History of the County of Warwick* (Victoria County History, 1964), VII, 132–40.

Birmingham firms moved out of the central area in a similar manner to that seen in Manchester. Tangye's, for example, left the small factory at Clement Street, where they had made the hydraulic rams and pulley blocks upon which the firm's fortunes had been founded, and moved to an eleven acre site half-way between the G.W. railway Handsworth, and the L. & N.W. railway Soho stations.[63] The entirely new factory of the B.S.A. company likewise set up its works and colony at Small Heath on the Oxford line.[64] All three of these were also engineering works, though not connected with locomotives or rolling stock; but at King's Norton other light manufacturers, from paper to india-rubber making, were established near the railway line.[65]

An assessment of the importance of rail connections to the suburban industrialist must await a more detailed study. It will not be an easy task, for although the relative costs of alternative modes of transport for supplies and finished goods must have been carefully considered by entrepreneurs, particularly at the height of the railway rates controversy in the 1880s yet published business histories are disappointingly silent on this point.[66]

However, in lieu of contemporary information, a great deal can be sketched in *ex post*, from the geographical distribution of industrial works spreading outwards from the great towns, and this has been done, in convenient form and with great local knowledge, by the surveys carried out for the British Association, at Birmingham, Manchester, Glasgow and Liverpool.[67] At London, although a great deal of similar material has been gathered in original theses, only one, by P.G. Hall, has been published.[68] To avoid the repetition

63. *Birmingham Mail*, 13 July 1880.
64. D.C. Eversley, *loc. cit.* 132–3.
65. G.C. Allen, *The Industrial Development of Birmingham and the Black Country* (1929), 291 *et seq.* M.J. Wise and P.O'N. Thorpe, *loc. cit.* 222–4.
66. Modern work, taking the form of questionnaires to industrial firms, suggests that whilst transport costs and facilities rank very high in most firms' calculations, other considerations receive only slightly less weight. Some of these – planning permission, the incidence of local taxes – have received new significance in the twentieth century; but one consideration often mentioned as critical, and which applied with undiminished force in the nineteenth century, is the availability of low priced units of land, located where future expansion would be practicable. T.E. McMillan Jnr, 'Why Manufacturers Choose Plant Locations', *Land Economics*, XLI (1965), 239–46.
67. *Birmingham and its Regional Setting: a Scientific Survey* (British Association, Birmingham, 1950); *The Glasgow Region: a General Survey* (ed. R. Miller and J. Tivy, Glasgow, 1958); *A Scientific Survey of Merseyside* (ed. W. Smith, Liverpool, 1953); *Manchester and its Region* (ed. C.F. Carter, Manchester, 1962).
68. P.G. Hall, *The Industries of London since 1861* (1962). See also J.E. Martin 'Three Elements in the Industrial Geography of Greater London', *Greater London* (ed. J.T. Coppock and H.C. Prince, 1964), 246–65.

of much that is already familiar, and requires extremely detailed topography, the reader is referred to these well illustrated studies. From them and from other local sources, the emergence by the late nineteenth century of Manchester's 'industrial collar', of the wide belt of industrial building in the Midlands from Birmingham towards Wolverhampton, and of Liverpool's and Glasgow's changing districts of industrial specialization, can be approximately traced on the ground. But the course of industrial history in each great town, its successes in certain fields of manufacture, and abandonment or failure in others, the extent of diversification in its manufacturing base; these are matters which cannot be linked by any simple causal chain to the coming of the railways. The railways are merely one element in the whole network of external economies which bound together the areas of regional specialization associated with each great city.

As part of the growth of interdependent industries, physical proximity, or cheap and easy access to fellow-manufacturers engaged on other stages of the production process, was obviously of cardinal importance; but it could be achieved by means other than rail linkages, and the more closely concentrated the region, the less use were main line railways within it. This applied even to large-scale manufacturers, but for the small scale producers operating on short runs and small quantities from ready built factories or workshops in the Victorian cities' inner districts the linkages between them were of a complexity which made them quite unsuitable for short-haul by the railways. The small, miscellaneous loads of the Birmingham or London manufacturer, the frequent need for trans-shipment for further processing after a short journey, the heavy terminal charges, made the railways slow and uneconomic for the local movement of goods. In his study of London's industries in the later nineteenth century, Peter Hall has given a fascinating picture of the small trades, depending upon close connection with component suppliers and associated skills, and constituting 'incomparably the major industrial area of London'. 'With this type of productive organization', he points out, 'the real assembly line runs through the streets; a journey around the Victorian manufacturing crescent (of inner north and east London) on any typical weekday reveal the extraordinary congestion of goods vehicles, hurrying in all directions about their business.'[69] Clearly railway goods trains were not suited to the maintenance of such local and rapid linkages.

If we are looking for what Colin Clark has dubbed 'micro-locational factors', it could be argued that we find them rather

69. *Greater London*, 227–8.

more in the case of the canals than the railways.[70] The industrial concentration around the Port Dundas canal basin, in the north of Glasgow, is far more striking than any rail-based concentration.[71] In Birmingham the two-mile stretch of canal between Bordesley and Aston had already 124 works and wharves along its bank 25 years before the railways were constructed; and the 'tongues of industrial development' out to Smethwick and towards Derby were also located along the Birmingham and Wolverhampton and Fazeley canals.[72] These routes were later reinforced by railways, which followed the canals closely, but the prior locational impulse was that of the canals. In Manchester the Ashton and Rochdale canals, built at the turn of the eighteenth century, attracted over a hundred textile mills, breweries, chemical works and foundries; and other industrial users spread along the Bolton, Bury and Junction canals.[73] In Liverpool the industrial grouping along the canals was less marked. The Leeds and Liverpool canal, which entered from the north, accumulated a few mills, vitriol and gasworks along its banks; but the other major canals all entered the Mersey upstream, and their effect was lost in the general port and river traffic; and in London the effect of urban canals was necessarily limited.[74] Where canals had been established, however, even in London, they continued – like the Regent's Canal and Hertford Union canals in East London – to attract industry to their sides throughout the nineteenth century. Eight-ninths of the traffic on these canals was simply for local transfer by the end of the century, and soap, varnish and tar works congregated along the banks.[75]

In the Midlands and North, where canals had always been more successful and widespread than the London area, they also continued to attract industry throughout the railway age. The effect of their

70. Colin Clark, 'The Location of Industries and Population', *Town Planning Review*, 35 (1964–5), 195, 211 *et seq.*
71. Peter Fleming, *Map of the City of Glasgow* (1807 and 1821). George Martin, *Map of the City of Glasgow*, (1842). S.G. Checkland, 'The British Industrial City as History: the Glasgow Case', *Urban Studies*, I (1964), 45.
72. A.E. Smailes, *The Geography of Towns* (1964), 94–5, and Fig. 12. *Conurbation: A Survey of Birmingham and the Black Country*, (Birmingham, 1948), 18, 'Remote from natural communications it owes its creation to its mineral resources, but its structure to canals and railways.'
73. L. Wharfe, 'The Emergence of the Metropolis', *Rich Inheritance* (ed. N.J. Frangopulo, Manchester, 1962), 107–9.
74. Wilfred Smith, 'The Location of Industry', *A Scientific Survey of Merseyside* (Liverpool, 1953), 179. Jonathan Bennison, *Plan of the Town and Port of Liverpool* (1835).
75. Henry Rees, *The North Eastern Expansion of London since 1770* (London M.Sc. Econ. thesis, 1946), 52–63. See also J.E. Martin, 'Three Elements in the Industrial Geography of Greater London', *Greater London* (ed. J.T. Coppock and H.C. Prince, 1964), 258–61 and Fig. 53.

established location was cumulative. 'The canals have been in existence a great many years, and a great many mills and industries of various kinds have been carried on upon the banks of the canals, brought there by the facilities which the canals afforded from time to time, and the traffic to all those places could not be carried so conveniently by rail as it could by canal.'[76] They were far better suited for local, factory to factory traffic of single loads than main line railways; and the water they supplied was invaluable to industrial users. In fact several canals with urban stretches, such as the Regent's Canal in London, found themselves earning an appreciable proportion of their revenues from selling their water rather than from carrying traffic; and in general urban canals continued to provide exceptions to the general picture of decline in waterborne transport.[77] Birmingham still imported over a million tons of coal by canal in the late 1860s; and a correspondence of great vehemence conducted with the canal company was one of the major preoccupations of the Chamber of Commerce in 1870.[78] It was to the idea of enlarged, or 'ship', canals that the Corporations of Manchester and Birmingham naturally turned early in the following decade.[79] If we are looking for locational factors for industry, within the area of the three conurbations, Manchester, Birmingham and Glasgow, the railways must obviously share their role with the canals.

Two points of particular relevance to urban history emerge from studies of railways, canals, and the regional location of industry. The first is that nearly all goods, except those manufactured near the point of export, or those marketed locally, spent part of their journey as railway freight. Coastal shipping and canals were competitive for minerals, building materials, for industrial goods on very short distances, and for some categories of agricultural produce, but otherwise long distance transport virtually *was* railway transport. To this extent the possession of private sidings, or the seeking of locations adjacent to the line, was not the distinguishing mark it might at first appear. Indeed there were cases of firms which had local access to a branch line still finding it worth their while to cart

76. H.C., 1872, XIII, Q. 4182.
77. The Regent's Canal company sold 5,000,000 gallons of water per day, the greatest amount, in proportion to its length, of any canal. The Grand Junction company sold 4,000,000. For E.J. Lloyd's arguments on the subject of short distance competition by canals see H.C., 1872, XIII, QQ. 5060–78.
78. A differential urban rate was levied on canal traffic in Birmingham. Letter, 3 July 1870, Birmingham Reference Library (hereafter BRL), Chamber of Commerce Reports, 1865–87.
79. BRL, Council Proceedings, Committee appointed to investigate the possibility of enlarging the Birmingham and Worcester canal for 200-ton vessels, Report 20 March 1888. Charles Hadfield, *British Canals: an Illustrated History* (1959), 247–54.

their goods to a more central terminus.[80] On the whole, however, it is clear that the direct rail transport of goods from suburban sites was not open to the same objections as the transport of passengers. Although similar inconveniences tended to build up at peak hours, time was not so critical a factor; and, for all the complaints, the freight rates for merchandise goods were well within the means of manufacturers and their agents. Indeed the appeal was put forward, more than once, that 'Trains that would deal with men as you deal with the clothes they wear and the food they eat, passing them at the same rate of price (*i.e.* 14 workmen per ton) would enable you to give a greater amount of assistance to the labouring classes in London than by any other mode.'[81] Moreover the charge on goods, whether high or low, could be handed on ultimately to the consumer. The working man was not in an analogous position regarding his own transport costs. So although, when his works migrated from Bridge Street, Birmingham, to Bournville, Richard Cadbury regularly walked the distance, and his biographer describes him helping his workmen to clear the snow off the *tram lines* in the winter, at least the railway accommodation for his products and raw materials was far more adequate than that for his men.[82]

The second point, stemming from what has been said, is that to the extent to which the suburban dispersal of factories was associated with an increased supply of suburban workers' houses, the problem of urban congestion and overcrowding was being tackled in the most effective way possible. It was all very well to agitate for the provision of really cheap workmen's services as the means of enabling the working class to enjoy the low rents and low death rates of the suburbs, whilst working in the city, but the 'dormitory' ideal raised serious practical problems. A more logical solution was to disperse both industry and workers, and to do it in that sequence. 'At present it operates this way,' William Denton complained in 1884, 'the railway companies avoid the employers of labour, and they only remove the employed, and then you must have overcrowding; whereas if the employers of labour were removed – then their people would go with them.'[83] When the Metropolitan railway were building their extension from Aldersgate to Moorfields, for example, their route was selected so as to avoid Whitbread's Brewery. If they

80. Glasgow City Archives, *Petitions, Briefs and Minutes of Proceedings*, Glasgow Corporation Tramways, Bill II, 425. Turton also reports, in a recent survey, that only three firms out of 18 situated in the 'railway towns' of Swindon, Crewe, Eastleigh and Ashford, received or distributed more than 50 per cent of their freight by rail. B.J. Turton, *loc. cit.* 110.
81. H.C., 1846, XVII, QQ. 2829–31.
82. H.C. Alexander, *Richard Cadbury of Birmingham* (1906), 232.
83. H.C., 1884–5, XXX, Q. 10688.

had not, the consequence, Denton claimed, would have been that Whitbreads would simply have moved to the outskirts, taking the workpeople's traffic they generated with them. 'At the present moment most of the large brewers are occupying ground which they only occupied in the first instance because it was at a distance from London at that time; but London has come up to them.'[84] He saw more hope in moving industries outwards, where there was building room, so that the workmen might be able to live near their work, than in cheap fares. Yet although, in his evidence, Denton strongly enjoined this policy upon the Royal Commission on the Housing of the Working Classes, its implications were too drastic to gain acceptance. The railway companies would have had to be directed to pass, where possible, through expensive industrial property; a course which was impractical, belated, and certain to meet with the firmest resistance from the parties involved. Not merely were his views not taken up, but they were not even given passing mention in the Commissioners' Report. A glance at two cases where the compulsory purchase of factories was envisaged, is sufficient to show why the recommendation seemed hopelessly impracticable. At one stage of the M.S. & L.'s central station plans in Manchester, the scheduling of the Oxford St works of Messrs Sharp, Stewart & Co. fell under discussion. The Corporation of Manchester favoured the idea, but did they realize Mr Denison Q.C. asked, that the factory was valued at half-a-million?[85] Moreover, as the N.B. railway company's dealings with the Coatbridge Iron Works demonstrated, no factory premises could be partially taken. In view of the complex factors which might be involved in a change of layout, or the loss of part of their space, factory owners and their solicitors had the right to insist that the *whole* premises, or none at all, be scheduled. The subsequent legal discussions also led, on occasions, to troublesome concessions over future rates of carriage.[86]

Even without legislative encouragement, however, the migration of industry to sites on the outskirts or in the suburbs of the major cities gathered momentum in the last quarter of the century. But it must be recalled that the fastest growing employment sector in Britain's economy in the late nineteenth century was not in manufacture but in tertiary, white-collared services, and many of these were associated with the city's central districts.[87] So the

84. *Ibid*. Q. 10695–7.
85. BTHR PYB 1/383, 18 May 1866, QQ. 3302–5.
86. G.U. Coll. Sol. Papers. Box 3, N.B. railway company, Coatbridge branch.
87. The real problem was the transfer of the central business functions, as some observers realized by the end of the nineteenth century. 'Any transfer of work to the country will not do more than slightly reduce the rate at which the business population of London has been growing in recent years.' H.C., 1906, XLI, Q. 4743.

problem of urban housing remained, and to many it still seemed at the end of the century that the only solution lay in 'improved locomotion'. If rail services were cheapened and extended, 'the relief of pressure would be immediate', Charles Booth wrote in 1901. 'The action would be something like that of land drainage on stagnant, water-logged land; whereas the attempt to meet the evils of overcrowding by piling up great blocks of model dwellings is like an attempt to obviate a marshy foundation by putting in concrete, digging a hole and pumping out the water.'[88]

88. Charles Booth, *Improved Means of Locomotion as a first step towards the cure of the Housing Difficulties of London* (1901), 17.

Chapter 7

URBAN FAMINE OR URBAN CRISIS? TYPHUS IN THE VICTORIAN CITY

Anne Hardy

[from *Medical History*, **32** (1988): 401–25]

The central issue, was typhus less an indicator of urban food shortages and more a consequence of social dislocation, enables Hardy to explore not just the decline in epidemic typhus from 1870 but to fuse epidemiological explanations and medical factors with nineteenth-century social history. Social crises – overcrowding, housing clearances associated with railway building, Irish immigration, and cyclical unemployment – combined periodically to induce social distress which together with the inherent characteristics of the infectious organism produced epidemic outbreaks of typhus. These subsided under conditions of rising real wages, less disruptive housing conditions and modest cleansing programmes in the last third of the nineteenth century. The analysis exhibits a number of important characteristics: source evaluation and an eclectic interdisciplinary approach is evident; statistical underpinnings do not obscure the importance of the conclusions; twentieth-century interpretations and values are not imposed on those of contemporaries; issues of urban scale and density are accorded pivotal importance; metropolitan experience though central to the empirical evidence does not exclude that of other boroughs in the urban hierarchy; a sense of dynamic urban change is conveyed; and the attention to stress-related explanations of disease spotlights an approach to urban history which incorporates the psychological in what might be termed an urban version of mentalités.

There were four horsemen of the Apocalypse: War, Famine, Disease and Death, a historic association which has continued into modern times. For most of history, the disease most commonly linked with this awful partnership has been typhus, and typhus has become known as the archetypal famine fever. The aetiology of the disease

209

has, however, rarely been examined in its historical context; as a result, historians have often misinterpreted its significance. In one recent article, for example, the disease was treated as an indicator of urban famine, of the extent to which the nutritional status of the Lancashire textile operatives was reduced by the Cotton Famine of the 1860s.[1] In the nineteenth century, however, epidemics of typhus occurred in both times of stress and times of prosperity: unlike its cousin, relapsing fever, typhus is not a primary indicator of 'true, nutritional famine'.

Why did typhus disappear as a significant cause of death in the late nineteenth century? The disease was almost certainly endemic in pockets of cities across Britain in the eighteenth and early nineteenth centuries; from time to time there were epidemic outbreaks. What were the different factors that permitted the survival of the disease, stimulated epidemics, and finally led to its virtual disappearance in the 1870s? The commonly-assumed causal link between typhus and famine, or at least malnutrition, raises the question of dearth and living standards in the nineteenth century. The harvest-related subsistence crisis had vanished by the late eighteenth century; but do typhus epidemics indicate periods of dearth in nineteenth-century cities? Or was typhus's survival rather a question of hygiene? For the urban historian H.J. Dyos, typhus was an indicator of 'dirt and destitution'; for Thomas McKeown, of malnutrition and low levels of personal hygiene.[2] The answer is perhaps more complex: in a recent analysis of the European subsistence crisis of 1740 John Post has argued that the links between food shortages and disease are more social than nutritional, that typhus is not an indicator of famine *per se*, but the consequence of social dislocation produced by harvest failure and distress.[3] In such social crises, patterns of human behaviour alter; and increased mobility, domestic crowding and reduced personal hygiene result in epidemics. The behaviour of epidemic typhus in the nineteenth century supports this argument: the disease survived as long as social dislocation continued to be an

---

1. D. Oddy, 'Urban famine in nineteenth-century Britain', *Econ. Hist. Rev.*, second series. Feb. 1983, **37**: 83.
2. H.J. Dyos, 'Some historical reflections on the quality of urban life', in David Cannadine and David Reeder (eds). *Exploring the urban past. Essays in urban history by H.J. Dyos*, Cambridge University Press, 1982, p. 72; Thomas McKeown. *The modern rise of population*, London. Edward Arnold, 1976, pp. 126, 132, 141.
3. John D. Post, *Food shortage, climatic variability, and epidemic disease in preindustrial Europe; the mortality peak in the early 1740s*, Ithaca, Cornell University Press, 1985; see also, *idem*. 'Climatic variability and the European mortality wave of the early 1740s', *J. interdisciplinary Hist.*, summer 1984, **15**: 1–30.

intermittent feature of urban life, before rising and stabilizing real wages reduced the impact of economic upheavals on the lives of the working classes.

The language of urban crisis, of subsistence crisis, and of urban famine, generally appears in the historiography of the pre-industrial world,[4] and is rarely applied to the nineteenth century. Historical debates about dearth and disease in the later eighteenth and nineteenth centuries centre on long-term issues, especially that of the extent to which improving – or stationary, or regressing – nutritional status influenced long-term trends in mortality from a range of endemic and epidemic diseases.[5] In this debate, the mortality crises which continued to occur in individual cities, and the diseases which caused them, have received relatively little attention.[6] Yet local studies may help our understanding of the mechanics of mortality change. Recent American research shows a correlation between short-term variations in urban mortality and the business cycle. The relationship is said to hold for both major epidemics and other diseases, and to be closely related to the pattern of European immigration:[7] the epidemiological peaks illustrate the pattern of social and economic dislocation. Although this model is not entirely applicable to Britain, typhus is a disease of social dislocation, and its survival as an epidemic disease in England as late as the 1860s reflects not simply or necessarily hunger, but the complex social consequences of the inherent instability of an emergent industrial economy.[8]

4. Among a large literature, see for example, Peter Clark and Paul Slack, *English towns in transition*, Oxford University Press, 1976: Charles Phythian-Adams and Paul Slack, *Urban crisis or urban change?*, Milton Keynes, Open University, 1977; John D. Post, *The last great subsistence crisis in the Western world*, Johns Hopkins University Press, 1977; Paul Slack, *The impact of plague in Tudor and Stuart England*, London, Routledge & Kegan Paul, 1985, chapter 3.
5. The literature includes F.W. Notestein, 'Population – the long view', in T.W. Schultz (ed.), *Food for the world*, Chicago University Press, 1945, pp. 36–57; T. McKeown and R.G. Record, 'The decline of mortality in the 19th century', *Population Stud.*, November 1962, **16**: 98–122; McKeown, op. cit., note 2 above; A.B. Appleby, 'Nutrition and disease: the case of London. 1550–1750', *J. interdisciplinary Hist.*, summer 1975, **6**: 1–22; and the essays in the following Special Issues of *J. interdisciplinary Hist.*: 'Hunger and history', autumn 1983, **14**, no. 2, and 'Population and history', spring 1985, **15**, no. 4.
6. Of the diseases which caused such crises, only cholera has been examined in detail. Cholera incidence is unrelated to nutritional status, and the disease was, like plague before it, an 'invader': the term is used by Slack, op. cit., note 4 above, p. 14.
7. R. Higgs, 'Cycles and trends of mortality in 18 large American cities, 1871–1900', *Explor. Econ. Hist.*, 1979, **16**: 381–408.
8. L. D. Schwarz, 'The standard of living in the long run: London, 1700–1860', *Econ. Hist. Rev.*, second series, 1985, **38**: 32.

If 'urban crises' are seen as continuing into the nineteenth century, the circumstances in which typhus epidemics occurred may throw further light on mortality decline, and on the role of nutrition in this decline. This paper contends that typhus has a significance beyond nutritional levels. In terms of social history, Victorian typhus illustrates the social and economic insecurity of urban life up to the 1870s, and the way in which local economic conditions helped to determine outbreaks of disease; on the medical side, typhus's independence of nutritional status explains both its unpredictable appearances, and its disappearance from England at a time when the nutritional- and, probably, the hygienic level of the 'submerged tenth' remained relatively unchanged.[9]

I

By the nineteenth century, typhus had become an essentially urban disease of sporadic outbreaks, in England and elsewhere. Throughout the century, Liverpool in particular continued to provide 'a habitation and a name' for the disease.[10] Nevertheless, in the 1870s typhus mortality entered a decline which can now be seen to have been final. The social associations of typhus suggest reasons for its disappearance, but do not fully explain its epidemic pattern. In an attempt to understand why epidemic typhus disappeared in the later nineteenth century, circumstances in London, a city where the disease was almost endemic and repeatedly epidemic in the earlier part of the century, are here examined more closely. London experienced a major, but final, typhus epidemic in 1861–69. Of four previous epidemics during the century, three had been associated with economic depression, and the other with the potato famine of 1847–48.[11] The epidemic of 1861 began without any obvious trigger: indeed, it began in London in December 1861, but in Lancashire in October 1862. It is clear that in the 1860s London was a city under stress: this condition was not without parallel in other English cities, but it was unrelated to any wider, national economic crisis.

9. For brief recent surveys of standards of living in the later nineteenth century, and the survival of the 'submerged tenth', see E. H. Hunt, *British labour history 1815–1914*, London, Weidenfeld and Nicolson, 1981, pp. 73–129; Michael S. Teitelbaum, *The British fertility decline*. Princeton University Press, 1984, pp. 37–43.
10. *Lancet*, 1896, **ii**: 548.
11. See note 57 below.

Gareth Stedman Jones has shown that there was a continuing economic crisis in London's East End in the 1860s. It began with the final decline of the silk-weaving industry, was compounded by the collapse of the Poplar ship-building industry in 1866, and its social effects were aggravated by house demolitions making way for factory- and warehouse-building, improvement schemes, and railway construction.[12] The last was not limited to the East End, and in 1860 distress had been increasing generally among London's working population as a result of building trade strikes. At this time, the national economy had barely begun to recover from the effects of the Crimean War. Average real wages, which declined sharply during the war years, returned to normal in 1859–60, but were undermined by bad weather and poor harvests in 1860–62 and again in 1866–68.[13] National concern focused on the Lancashire textile districts suffering from the effects of the Cotton Famine; and the crisis in London went almost unremarked, except by the medical press, hospital workers and the recently appointed Medical Officers of Health, whose duties were intimately connected with the condition of the people.[14]

The London building trades strikes beginning in 1859 were among the first serious manifestations of the Nine Hours Movement which had emerged in Liverpool in 1846. In 1859, the London master builders resorted to a lock-out of those men who would not pledge themselves not to join a trade union. The strike, or lock-out, lasted from 21 July 1859 to March 1860. Twenty-four thousand men were said to have been locked out; by the end of September some 14,000 were receiving allowances from the conference of the trade societies.[15] The allowances were far from adequate, however, and as the means and credit of the men failed, the effects of the lock-out were felt more widely: small shopkeepers, for example, instead of taking £9–10 weekly from building-trades families, took no more than £2–3. As long as there was bread, the Registrar-General observed, the children had it, but weakened, cold and ill-clad, they died in unusual numbers towards the end of the year.[16]

In the spring of 1861, when the masters tried to introduce a system of payment by the hour, the workers struck again. This time, the strike lasted barely a month. The 1859 strike and the cold winter

12. G.S. Jones, *Outcast London*, Oxford, Clarendon Press, 1971, chapters 3–5.
13. B.R. Mitchell and P. Deane, *Abstract of British historical statistics*, Cambridge University Press, 1962, pp. 343, 498; Jones, op. cit., note 12 above, pp. 44–6.
14. *Lancet*, 1863, **i**: 422. The London Medical Officers of Health took up their duties in the city's civil parishes in 1856.
15. For the background to these strikes, see Richard Price, *Masters, unions and men: work control in building and the rise of labour 1830–1914*, Cambridge University Press, 1980, pp. 15–54.
16. *Twenty-Second Annual Report of the Registrar-General*. (PP, 1861, XVIII, p. 41).

of 1860–61 had lowered the resources of both men and unions: such masters as Lucas and Kelk, under contract for the Great Exhibition building for 1862, were anxious to avoid any protracted argument. By 20 April, the strike was at an end.[17] The cumulative effect of the strikes was probably to weaken the economy of working-class London generally. There was scarcely a district of the city in which, by 1861, these trades did not form a substantial proportion of the working population: between 7.5 and 11.5 per cent of the males over twenty years old.[18]

1861 also saw the beginning of clearances preparatory to three major railway projects, affecting central and east London. The Charing Cross Railway's new junction at Red Cross Street, with an extension to Cannon Street, displaced 557 persons; the North London Railway's extension from Kingsland to Broad Street displaced between four and five thousand; the Metropolitan Railway's extension from Smithfield to Finsbury Circus displaced 1,100.[19] In Southwark, South London, two major railway operations, in 1859–64 and 1860–64, forced over 7,700 persons to move.[20] In north London, the demolition of the Agar Town slum to make way for St Pancras Station in 1862–4, sent waves of dislocation through Marylebone, St Pancras and St Giles.[21] By 1862, London's major working-class areas, in the southern, central and eastern districts, were all subjected to large scale railway clearances. The slum-clearance and street-building operations of the Metropolitan Board of Works added to the problem.[22] Both developments were quick to take effect: as early as 1863, Medical Officers of Health were aware of increased overcrowding. In 1867, Dr Pearce of Bethnal Green estimated that in some cases rents had increased by as much as 50 per cent.[23]

The impact of overcrowding in London in the 1860s can be illuminated, to some extent, by modern research. Density in American cities has been found to have a uniformly positive and statistically significant effect on mortality. Household density is thought to aggravate such stresses as do exist in low-income populations, which in certain circumstances affect mental and

17. *The Times*, 23, 26, 28 March 1861; 20 April 1861.
18. The district percentage figures were: East, 7.5; Central, 7.6; South, 9.2; West, 10.6; and North, 11.5 per cent of males over 20.
19. H.J. Dyos, 'Some social costs of railway building in London', *J. transp. Hist.*, 1957, **3**: 21. See also *idem*, 'Railways and housing in Victorian London', *J. transp. Hist.*, 1955, **2**: 11–21.
20. Ibid.
21. *Medical Officer of Health Annual Report* (hereafter *MOAR*) St Pancras, 1862, 6; 1864, p. 8.
22. Dyos, 'Railways', op. cit., note 19 above; Jones, op. cit., note 12 above, pp. 162–3, 215–17.
23. *MOAR* St Giles, 1863, p. 16; *MOAR* Shoreditch, 1863, p. 11; *MOAR* Bethnal Green, 1867, p. 4.

physical health. In nineteenth-century cities, erratic employment, nutritional deficiencies, insecure living standards, high immigration levels of people with no previous experience of urban life, and overcrowding created 'optimal conditions for pervasive morbidity and high mortality'.[24] In the London of the late 1860s, these conditions existed in no mean degree, and were aggravated by ruthless slum-clearance and coincident depression in the working-class economy. Provincial immigration probably added to the problem. It has been estimated that immigration into London rose in 1861–71 to 331,000, over 286,000 in 1851–61. It rose again, to 498,000 in 1871–81, falling only to 402,000 in 1881–91.[25]

The year 1861–62 marked the beginning of an 'artificial' subsistence crisis, one not related to food shortages and excessively high prices. It was nonetheless real, and in the forms of social dislocation, increased overcrowding and rising rents, it lasted for several years, in fact until about 1870, when the initiation of new railway operations began to slacken in pace. Between 1867 and 1872, no major works were begun;[26] and it was during these years that the great typhus epidemic, which had afflicted the poorer districts of the city since the end of 1861, finally came to an end.

II

Typhus, the 'spotted fever' of sixteenth-century England, the 'gaol fever' of the eighteenth, the 'Irish fever' of the mid-nineteenth, has a long and distinguished history intimately associated with the social upheavals caused by war and famine.[27] Although long confused with typhoid, the two diseases have distinct behavioural patterns: typhoid is endemic, typhus epidemic. The eighteenth century, from *circa* 1708 to 1815, constituted the last 'great typhus period'. After 1815, the disease only once attained its former scale of diffusion in Europe, in 1846–7.[28] In the first half of the nineteenth century there were

24. R. Higgs and F.D. Booth, 'Mortality differentials within large American cities in 1890', *Hum. Ecol.*, 1979, **7**: 353–69.
25. H.A. Shannon, 'Migration and the growth of London, 1841–91. A statistical note', *Econ. Hist. Rev.*, April 1935, **5**: 84.
26. Dyos, 'Social costs', op. cit., note 19 above, p. 27.
27. See Hans Zinsser's classic. *Rats, lice and history*, London, George Routledge and Sons, 1935.
28. August Hirsch, *Handbook of geographical and historical pathology*, vol. 1, London, New Sydenham Society, 1883, pp. 554–5.

numerous localized outbreaks of the disease, but after 1850, except in particular circumstances (notably in Eastern Europe during World War I), epidemic frequency in Europe declined markedly.[29]

The universal decline of epidemic typhus makes the analysis of reasons for its disappearance problematic. Hans Zinsser, admitting the problem, pointed to the 'co-operative forces of modern civilized society'; to the development of intensive agriculture and rail transport, which prevented the prolonged isolation of famine districts; to the rise of modern diagnostic and preventive medicine; and especially to the fact that wars, in this period, were of short duration and affected relatively circumscribed areas.[30] Charles Creighton, referring to England only, argued for improved nutrition as a factor.[31] George Rosen favoured slum-clearance, the regulation of lodging-houses, provision of baths and washhouses, the increased use of cotton clothing which could be more frequently washed, as well as rising living standards, as the principal causes of decline.[32] McKeown and Record distinguished environmental improvements, especially improved water supplies, and better diet as salient features.[33] In a recent study, Bill Luckin largely dismisses these factors, and points to the pattern of Irish immigration into England.[34] Finally, John Post's important analysis suggests the reasons for the behaviour of the disease in Europe as a whole.

The infectious organism of typhus, *Rickettsia prowazeki*, appears to be invariably louse-borne among human beings. Like dysentery, typhus appears wherever poverty, crowding and insanitary conditions prevail, in times of social dislocation, and principally in the winter months. The incubation period of the disease in man is ten to fourteen days. Infected lice invariably die, usually within seven to twelve days; and although the infection is not transmitted to their eggs, it can survive in the dust of their faeces for months or even years.[35] The human louse is sensitive to temperature, preferring that of 29°C which it finds in the folds of clothing worn by a healthy person. Lice therefore tend to leave febrile patients, and

29. Zinsser, op. cit., note 27 above, pp. 290–301.
30. Ibid., p. 292.
31. C. Creighton, *A History of epidemics in Britain*, vol. 2, Cambridge University Press, 1894, p. 215.
32. G. Rosen, 'Disease, debility and death', in H.J. Dyos and M. Wolff (eds), *The Victorian city*, vol. 2, London, Routledge & Kegan Paul, 1973, pp. 633–4; *idem*, *A history of public health*, New York, M D Publications, 1958, pp. 339–40.
33. McKeown and Record, op. cit., note 5 above, p. 116.
34. Bill Luckin, 'Typhus and typhoid in London', in R. Woods and J. Woodward (eds), *Urban disease and mortality in 19th-century England*, London, Batsford Academic, 1984, pp. 111–116.
35. *British encyclopedia of medical practice*, second edition, vol. 12, London, Butterworth, 1952, p. 392.

corpses, in favour of those with normal temperatures, but die in a few hours if exposed to room temperature. They are easily killed by common antiseptics, and once a typhus patient has been deloused and bathed, he cannot transmit the infection by contact to others. Case-fatality in man varies from 10 to 40 per cent in untreated cases; nineteenth-century case-mortality is estimated to have been between 20 and 45 per cent. Typhus fatality rises sharply with age, but one attack confers immunity on survivors for many years.[36]

Throughout the nineteenth century, however, doctors and public health officials worked in total ignorance of the true nature and origins of typhus. Only in 1909 did Charles Nicolle and his colleagues at the Institut Pasteur in Tunis show that infection is spread by the body-louse ingesting the infected blood of the typhus patient.[37] After about a week, the *rickettsiae* have multiplied in the louse gut and are excreted in the faeces. Healthy persons are generally infected through the skin, by scratching, and sometimes by the inhalation of dust containing dried but still viable *rickettsiae*. Transmission may thus occur through either individual louse infestation, or the inhalation of infected dust. Modern treatment of the disease is with a broad spectrum of antibiotics; prevention by the control or elimination of the insect vector, by reducing louse infestation to a minimum and preventing overcrowding. In 1939–45, for example, such long-acting insecticides as DDT were impregnated into clothing, and sprayed over houses and potentially infected areas.[38]

In the 1860s no such certainty existed. The diagnostical distinction between typhoid and typhus, made by William Jenner in 1847–51, had become generally accepted. There was general agreement, too, over the circumstances of typhus transmission: in overcrowded localities and in times of destitution.[39] The disease was broadly recognized as contagious – hence the perceived dangers of over-crowding – but disagreement over the finer points of its behaviour continued. In particular, Charles Murchison, the greatest fever

---

36. Medical information on typhus has been drawn principally from William Topley and Graham Wilson, *Principles of bacteriology, virology and immunity*, vol. 3, 7th edn, ed. G.R. Smith, London, Edward Arnold, 1984, ch. 77; F.H. Top and P.H. Wherle, *Communicable and infectious diseases*, St Louis, MO, Mosby, 1981, ch. 57; F. L. Horsfall and I. Tamm, *Viral and rickettsial infections of man*, London, Pitman, 1965; P.D. Hoeprich (editor), *Infectious diseases*, Maryland, Harper and Row, 1977. The estimate of nineteenth-century case fatality was made by Bill Luckin, op. cit., note 34 above, p. 104.
37. Topley and Wilson, op. cit., note 36 above, p. 575. See also James Busvine, *Insects, hygiene and history*, London, Athlone Press, 1976, pp. 233–239.
38. Ibid., p. 578.
39. Margaret Pelling, *Cholera, fever and English medicine*. Oxford University Press, 1976, p. 283, notes that medical interest in typhus declined from the second quarter of the nineteenth century, as the disease waned in epidemic importance.

expert of the 1860s,[40] thought that typhus might be independently generated, *de novo*, in conditions of squalor and overcrowding.[41] This belief was disputed by colleagues, and gradually became discredited after Murchison's death: in many places, overcrowding and squalor were constant, whereas typhus was only occasional.[42] By the 1880s, medical men still concerned with typhus were almost certain that it was transmitted exclusively by contagion, but they had no positive means of proving their contention.[43]

The disagreement over spontaneous generation does not invalidate Murchison's observations on the behaviour of typhus. It was generally known that typhus frequently appeared without warning, and without the traceable contacts on which contagion should depend. Murchison chose to explain this phenomenon by a hypothesis of spontaneous generation; others assumed that the contagion was imported in a fashion that defied detection.[44] Observation similarly indicated the role of infected clothes, and suggested that of infected housing.[45] However, there could be no clear explanation until the role of the louse and its faeces as vector, and the dangers of infected dust, were understood. Following the distinction of typhoid and typhus, and in the absence of any bacteriological certainty, differing explanations of the observed behaviour of the disease were perhaps inevitable.

Observations, however, led to a fundamentally correct preventive approach to the disease, of which thorough disinfection was the basis. From its earliest days, the London Fever Hospital followed this policy with regard to typhus – 'the infectious malignant fever' of the metropolis – and besides removing infected individuals, attended to the disinfection of apartments, furniture and clothing in affected localities.[46] For the rest of the century this remained the accepted method of dealing with typhus, and was generally found effective, provided it was thoroughly carried out. In the district of St Olave in the 1860s, for example, houses were disinfected with

40. Charles Murchison (1830–79): Assistant Physician, London Fever Hospital, 1855: Physician, 1861–70; author of *A treatise on the continued fevers of Great Britain* (first edn 1862).
41. C. Murchison, *Continued fevers*, 3rd edn, W. Cayley (ed.), London. Longmans. Green & Co. 1884, pp. 99–104.
42. Ibid., p. 99.
43. See George Buchanan and J. Spear in the *Sixteenth Annual Report of the Medical Officer to the Local Government Board* (PP, 1887, XXXVIII, pp. 635, 959–62); Alex Collie, *On fevers*, London, H.K. Lewis, 1887, pp. 105–7.
44. Ibid.
45. *MOAR* St Olave, 1867–8, p. 23.
46. W. F. Bynum, 'Hospital, disease and community: the London Fever Hospital 1801–1850', in C. Rosenberg (ed.), *Healing and history*, New York, Dawson Science History Publications, 1979, p. 101.

Calvert's powder, carbolic acid and chlorine, and infected bedding (a recognized vehicle of typhus) was disinfected before being burnt.[47] This, with the isolation of patients as far as possible, was the standard preventive treatment. Even so, the remedy was flawed. Disinfection might be incomplete, and there were often difficulties with contacts: in practice it was not easy to secure the disinfection of persons, and clothes, exposed to typhus. Preventive authorities frequently, and generally fruitlessly, urged the necessity of establishing houses of refuge where personal purification could be carried out.[48] The London Fever Hospital early found fumigation and white-wash to be inadequate in certain areas.[49] In some cases, the final remedy was closure of affected houses. In Orange Street, St Saviour, where eleven typhus cases occurred in January 1887, disinfection proved ineffectual, and the series of cases only came to an end when all the inhabitants were removed to a temporary shelter, and all the houses in the street closed.[50]

The recognition of typhus as a separate entity from about 1850 makes it possible here to treat it as a unified disease. This approach may be criticized on the grounds that the Registrar-General did not distinguish the disease from typhoid and simple continued fever until 1869, and that statistics and diagnoses before that date, and to some extent after it, are unreliable. There is clear evidence, however, that even before William Jenner distinguished the different fevers in 1849, many physicians were aware of their differing natures, and of the different treatments they required.[51] After 1849 the distinction between these fevers was very commonly accepted and made. In his report for 1848, the physician of the London Fever Hospital outlined the clinical distinction between typhus and typhoid, and from then on, the two diseases were regularly separated in the Hospital's admissions- and mortality figures.[52] From the 1850s, writers and correspondents in the *Lancet* commonly used 'typhus' and 'typhoid' correctly, and although there were still those who claimed that the two were varieties of one fever, the argument had died away by the 1860s.[53] The diagnoses of the London Fever Hospital, in particular, are likely to be reliable: the Hospital's physicians were among the foremost experts in diagnosis of these diseases, and its admissions figures for the two diseases were regarded by the Registrar-General

47. *MOAR* St Olave, 1867–8, p. 23; *MOAR* St Saviour, 1871, p. 7.
48. Buchanan and Spear, op. cit., note 43 above, p. 960.
49. Bynum, op. cit., note 46 above p. 106.
50. *MOAR* St Saviour, 1887, pp. 28–9.
51. W. Jenner, *Lectures and essays on fevers and diptheria, 1849 to 1879*, London, Rivington, Percival & Co., 1893; Murchison, op. cit., note 41 above, pp. 31–51.
52. *London Fever Hospital annual report (LFHAR)* 1848, p. 9.
53. *Lancet*, 1855, i: 436; 1856, i: 159; 1857, i: 504.

as the best index of their relative presence in London.[54] In 1868, Carl Wunderlich's publication of the results of his temperature researches finally provided a reliable determinant for the diagnosis of typhoid, in distinction to typhus;[55] this was probably the basis on which the Registrar-General officially admitted the distinction between the two diseases in 1869. Errors in diagnosis, or terminology,

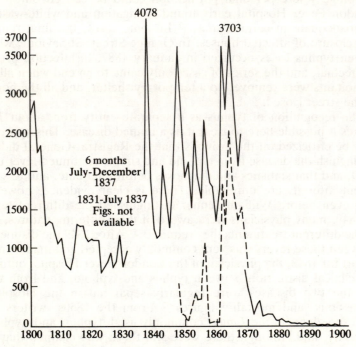

Fig. 1 Typhus in London, 1800–1900
– – – Typhus cases admitted to the London Fever Hospital, 1848–70
(*source: London Fever Hospital Annual Reports*)

1800–30: 'Typhus' (most fever) deaths (*source*: J. Marshall, *The mortality of London*, 1832); 1837–68: 'Typhus' (typhus and typhoid) deaths (*source: Annual Reports of the Registrar-General*); 1869–1900: Typhus deaths (*source: Annual Reports of the Registrar-General*).

54. *LFHAR* 1872, p. 5; *Lancet*, 1859, i: 337.
55. L. G. Stevenson, 'Exemplary disease: the typhoid pattern', *J. Hist. Med.*, 1982, 37: 168.

continued to occur during the 1870s,[56] and they demonstrate that aggregate mortality figures should be treated with caution.

The variety of factors involved in the epidemiology of typhus make unlikely any monocausal explanation of its virtual disappearance from England, indeed from Europe, in the nineteenth century. Epidemics occurred widely in Britain in between 1816 and 1819, following the end of the Napoleonic Wars, and in 1847–48, consequent on poor harvests and the potato famine. In London, there were additional epidemics in 1826, following the financial crisis of 1825; in 1836, again during major cyclical depression; in 1856, after the end of the Crimean War and coincident depression; and in the period 1862–70.[57] The 1860s also saw major typhus epidemics in Liverpool (1862–67) and Glasgow (1861–70); and various lesser outbreaks in Lancashire in the autumn of 1862, during the early, acute phase of the Cotton Famine, and in Aberdeen, Greenock and Dundee. Epidemics apart, however, the disease was never entirely absent; indeed deaths from typhus continued to be registered down to 1900 (Figure 1).[58] Similarly, the register of admissions to the London Fever Hospital show that even during non-epidemic years, the disease was active in the city (Figure 1). Although the epidemic conditions of the disease disappeared in the years after 1870, the *materies morbi*, ever diminishing, remained.

The distribution of typhus in London was, until the 1870s, linked to specific areas within the central, southern and eastern registration districts. Within these areas, certain localities, possibly never free from fever, were popularly designated 'fever nests' from at least the 1830s;[59] they were generally recognized by the public health

56. *Lancet*, 1878, **i**: 323; **ii**: 414.
57. In general, the pattern of typhus epidemics closely follows that of economic depression. Thus, in the last decade of the eighteenth century, the depressions of 1794–5 and 1797–1800 were accompanied by typhus: Creighton, op. cit., note 31 above, pp. 156–7, 159–62; Murchison, op. cit., note 41 above, pp. 38–9. Exceptionally, the severe depression of 1840–2 did not produce a typhus epidemic in England, only one of relapsing fever. This was perhaps because the great epidemic of 1836–8 had eliminated adult susceptibles.
58. Not all deaths from typhus were erroneously registered in the later period. In 1890 for example, there was an outbreak in St Olave, Southwark, and there were outbreaks in Cardiff (1892–93), Edinburgh (1898), Dundee (1900), and elsewhere.
59. This phenomenon is impossible to substantiate closely. By the time accurate statistical series for streets and houses become available, the disease was so far in retreat that the location of cases is almost meaningless. The spot maps published by the Metropolitan Asylums' Board from 1892 onwards thus show an annual scattering of generally isolated cases across London, from which no pattern of infection can be deduced. In St George, Southwark, small groups of cases suggest a possible lingering of some local source of infection, but in St Giles only one case of typhus was notified between 1892 and 1900. Total annual typhus notifications for the city were by this time in single figures. It should be noted

authorities as the particular haunts of typhus.[60] In the parish of St Giles, for example, the courts and alleys around Great Wild Street and Drury Lane were notorious.[61] In East London, Whitechapel was the 'nucleus of the metropolitan fever field', while among the southern districts, St Olave and St George Southwark were prominent.[62] In these districts and others like them, it was apparently true that particular houses constituted the foci of infection. William Rendle, for twenty-four years the Poor Law medical officer in St George Southwark, and subsequently, if briefly, its Medical Officer of Health, declared that there were comparatively few centres of infection for typhus, and that most typhus cases came from certain houses.[63]

One such house, 131 Drury Lane in St Giles, was described in detail in a *Lancet* report of 1865 as 'a capital illustration of the method of preserving typhus'. A large, three-storey building with a dirty plaster front, it housed a second-hand clothes shop in the basement. A notice advertised rooms to let, notwithstanding that the whole house was full of typhus. Every room contained two or three people. The disease had begun with a second-floor family whose daughter, living in nearby Drury Court, had caught the infection from a fellow lodger there. For two months the disease spread from family to family at 131 Drury Lane, but did not interrupt the various occupations pursued under that roof, including the manufacture of trinkets for ladies' heads and dresses.[64]

If such houses were not cleansed and disinfected once typhus cases had occurred, infected louse faeces shaken out of clothing and bedding might lie undisturbed for years, awaiting the arrival of further non-immune occupants, or the disturbance caused by increased crowding, to generate fresh cases. As late as 1879, Dr Lovett of St Giles could declare that every outbreak of typhus in the district had been traced to Lincoln Court and Orange Court, Drury Lane.[65] More than forty years earlier, Gerhard observed a similar phenomenon in Philadelphia.[66] Charles Murchison's belief

that the published figures are not corrected for the misdiagnoses which certainly occurred. For the earlier part of the century, however, Dickens's observation (in *Bleak House*, Harmondsworth, Penguin Books, 1971, p. 364) of 'fever houses' where 'for months and months' the inhabitants were carried out dead and dying by the dozens, should not be forgotten.

60. *MOAR* St George-the-Martyr, 1866–67, p. 6.
61. *Lancet*, 1865, **ii**: 522.
62. Ibid., pp. 267, 602, 657.
63. W. Rendle, *London vestries and their sanitary work*, London, John Churchill, 1865, pp. 11–12; *Lancet*, 1869, **i**: 737.
64. *Lancet*, 1865, **ii**: 522.
65. Ibid., 1879, **ii**: 793.
66. L. G. Wilson, 'Fevers and science in early nineteenth-century medicine', *J. Hist. Med.*, 1978, **33**: 401.

in the spontaneous generation of typhus, based on particular instances, also suggests that the houses themselves were implicated.[67] The role of housing in sustaining the disease was probably assisted by the rapid turnover of inhabitants in quarters such as St Giles. In 1861, for example, the London City Mission found that in one month half the families in Monmouth Court, St Giles, had been replaced.[68] Unrecognized cases, particularly among children, who are not seriously affected by the disease, undoubtedly also sustained typhus in particular districts and among a particular class.[69]

The persistence of typhus in particular localities, and its spread into new ones,[70] were determined by specific factors: the character of the population living there, their dirt and the filthy conditions of the houses in which they lived, and particularly overcrowding. Medical Officers repeatedly pointed out that overcrowding, lack of ventilation and want of cleanliness were the chief causes of the disease, and that these characterized the dwellings of the poorer classes.[71] The Medical Officer for Liverpool went further. In a survey of the disease in Liverpool over the years 1862–66, he discovered that 93 per cent of the city's typhus deaths occurred among the weekly-wage earning class, who inhabited courts and alleys 'where sanitary provisions are conspicuously absent'. Of the remaining typhus deaths, 5.4 per cent took place among the small shopkeeping class, and 1.3 per cent (some 100 individuals) among scripture readers, medical men, relieving officers, pawnbrokers and undertakers, who all risked contact with typhus patients in one way or another.[72]

In London, weekly-wage earners constituted a large proportion of the working class, and most were in occupations that experienced seasonal slackness, with under- or unemployment. Among this class, it was a common emergency economy for families and friends to double up in accommodation.[73] When a seasonal depression coincided with severe weather, the living conditions of this class deteriorated, leaving them more vulnerable to contagious disease.

---

67. Murchison, op. cit., note 41 above, pp. 99–104.
68. Lynn H. Lees, *Exiles of Erin*, Manchester University Press, 1979, p. 58.
69. Collie, op. cit., note 43 above, p. 107.
70. This was the case in Poplar. See below notes 80, 81.
71. *MOAR* Mile End Old Town, 1859, p. 6; *MOAR* Westminster, 1864–5, p. 14: *MOAR* Camberwell, 1864–65, p. 25. For the mechanics of typhus transmission in overcrowded conditions, see W. P. MacArthur, 'The medical history of the famine' in R.D. Edwards and T.D. Williams (eds). *The Great Famine*, Dublin, Browne and Nolan, 1956, pp. 271–2.
72. *Lancet*, 1867, ii: 608.
73. Jones, op. cit., note 12 above, pp. 117–18.

In the early 1860s, increased crowding in habitations infested with typhus exposed more people to infection.

To this background of overcrowding and dirt should be added a third factor. Charles Murchison thought that overcrowding, lack of ventilation, and destitution with starvation were the most important causes of typhus.[74] All writers on the subject agreed with him, including the eminent German epidemiologist, Rudolph Virchow.[75] Creighton, as mentioned above, thought that supplies of cheap food, fuel, and clothing were chiefly responsible for the virtual disappearance of the disease. Modern epidemiologists are less certain as to the relationship between nutritional standards and typhus susceptibility.[76] Again, the link between typhus and nutrition is only indirect. Hungry people – who need not be starving, or even malnourished – feel the cold more. Personal hygiene is affected: cold people do not like undressing. In such conditions, lice find congenial hosts.

The spread of typhus was determined more by these factors than by actual nutritional levels. Although the disease did not spread among the middle and upper classes, it had no trouble in developing in well-nourished hosts when offered the opportunity. This was made abundantly clear during the Irish epidemic of 1848–49,[77] and the 1860s epidemic also offers ample evidence. In April 1862 two Poor Law medical officers in St George-in-the-East died of typhus; in 1866 London society was shocked by the death of the distinguished Dr Henry Jeaffreson, of St Bartholomew's Hospital, from typhus; in 1868, the Reverend Henry Lance, who had served notably during the cholera epidemic, died of typhus caught while visiting the poor. In 1869 the *Lancet* observed, on the occasion of the deaths of two Rotherhithe doctors from typhus, that the disease was 'relentlessly' claiming many members of the profession. By 1872 typhus was 'that scourge of our profession'.[78] Middle-class victims were almost certainly infected by inhaling contaminated dust: they never contracted relapsing fever, for which contact with the body fluid of the louse is required.[79]

74. Murchison, op. cit., note 41 above, p. 52. In the final analysis. Murchison regarded overcrowding as the single most important element: ibid., pp. 340–1.
75. *Lancet*, 1867, ii: 701; 1868, i: 561, 572. This reference was to the second edition of Virchow's work. For the development of Virchow's ideas, see Paul Weinding, 'Was social medicine revolutionary?'. *Bull. Soc. Hist. Med.*, June 1984, 34: 13–18.
76. Post, *Food shortage*, op. cit., note 3 above, pp. 272–3; Luckin, op. cit., note 34 above, p. 113.
77. MacArthur, op. cit., note 71 above, p. 278–9.
78. *Lancet*, 1862, i: 448; 1866, ii: 680; 1868, i: 102; 1869, i: 306; 1872, i: 276.
79. MacArthur, op. cit., note 71 above, p. 280.

Poor nutrition was therefore not a primary determinant of typhus outbreaks, and typhus cannot be accepted as an unqualified indicator of urban famine. The disease continued to exist in household dust and among children in pockets where squalor maintained, and an adult population which was generally immune limited its activities. Unusual local population movements could activate the epidemic propensity of this residual infection. Thus social distress could start the typhus sequence where indigenous disease existed, or where it was imported. But hunger or distress were not the sole causes of social dislocation in Victorian cities.

The appearance of typhus in places experiencing good times confirms the importance of dislocation, as opposed to distress. The marked revival of the disease in the East London district of Poplar in the 1860s,[80] for example, was probably due to sudden, 'stress' over-crowding. Poplar enjoyed a surge of prosperity in the early 1860s, during which the numbers employed in the ship-building yards there increased from 13,000 in 1861, to 27,000 in 1865.[81] Greenock similarly experienced a typhus epidemic when overcrowding accompanied prosperity.[82] The typhus outbreaks in Whitechapel and St Olave in 1873 occurred during a 'period of unprecedented prosperity' and in mid-summer.[83] It seems likely that the dislocation caused by the Shoreditch improvement schemes in the East End, from 1872,[84] and by demolitions for Peabody Trust developments in Southwark in the early 1870s,[85] was responsible for these outbreaks which were, according to the *Lancet*, by no means on an epidemic scale.[86]

III

Typhus admissions to the London Fever Hospital increased considerably in the spring after the severe winter of 1860–61, but it was not until mid-December that the disease became epidemic. It then spread rapidly: in January 1862 the number of Fever Hospital admissions for typhus was 140, among the highest monthly totals in its history.[87]

80. Luckin, op. cit., note 34 above, p. 110.
81. Jones, op. cit., note 12 above, p. 102.
82. Collie, op. cit., note 43 above, p. 107.
83. *Lancet*, 1873, ii: 22.
84. See Percy J. Edwards, *History of metropolitan street improvements 1855–1897*, London County Council, 1898, pp. 45–51. It was admitted that 2,920 persons had been displaced by these operations.
85. J.N. Tarn, *Five per cent philanthropy*, Cambridge University Press, 1973, pp. 49–50.
86. *Lancet*, 1873, ii: 212.
87. Ibid., 1862, i: 207–8.

From 1862 until 1870 the number of typhus admissions to the Hospital, and the number of 'fever' deaths registered in London, remained at epidemic level (Figure 1). The epidemic of 1862–70 was almost certainly self-generated, not introduced to the city from elsewhere. The disease had been introduced from Ireland in 1847–48, and it was widely assumed by the 1860s that typhus was generally the result of Irish importation.[88] In 1856, however, there was no typhus epidemic in Ireland; the London outbreak was an isolated one.[89] Similarly, in 1862 there was no evidence to support a suggestion of Irish origin. The disease did not become epidemic in Ireland until 1863,[90] of 992 typhus cases admitted to the London Fever Hospital in the first six months of 1862, only forty-four were Irish, and of these, all but five had lived in London for more than three months and none had recently arrived from Ireland.[91] Almost all the first cases admitted were unemployed male tramps with no fixed address, who had suffered from want for many weeks. Many of them had been only a few weeks in London,[92] but the ten-day incubation period of typhus indicates that they contracted it in London itself. The Irish were not responsible for introducing epidemic typhus in 1856 and 1861, nor can the decline in typhus be linked to any reduction in Irish immigration. Although the proportion of Irish-born persons living in London fell steadily after 1851, the actual numbers arriving from Ireland increased in the 1870s and 1880s. The Irish contributed 14,000 immigrants to London in the decade 1851–61; 7,000 in 1861–71; 19,000 in 1871–81; and 20,000 in 1881–91.[93]

Charles Murchison argued that, while the Irish did not import typhus to London in all instances of epidemics, they contributed substantially in another way. It was well known, he wrote, that by the 'immigration of the lower classes of Irish, pauperism and habits of overcrowding and personal uncleanliness – the main causes of the prevalence of typhus – have been greatly augmented in the large towns of Britain'.[94] In the twelve years 1855–1867, 4.9 per cent of London Fever Hospital admissions were Irish-born, against the 75 per cent who were natives of London. A high proportion of the latter were, however, children of Irish parents or of Irish

---

88. Luckin, op. cit., note 34 above, pp. 106–7.
89. Murchison, op. cit., note 41 above, p. 57; Hirsch, op. cit., note 28 above, p. 556; *Lancet*, 1863, i: 422. Although typhus was certainly introduced by the Irish in 1846, the situation in English cities was such that the disease would probably have appeared within a relatively short time in any case: Creighton, op. cit., note 31 above, p. 205.
90. Murchison, op. cit., note 41 above, p. 52.
91. Ibid., p. 55.
92. Ibid., pp. 58, 54.
93. Lees, op. cit., note 68 above, p. 58; Shannon, op. cit., note 25 above, p. 84.
94. Murchison, op. cit., note 41 above, pp. 58–9.

extraction.[95] Murchison's views were based on his experience at the Hospital. The second Medical Officer of Health for St Giles, Dr Ross, shared Murchison's view of Irish domestic habits. The Irish were, he wrote, 'destitute of any notion of the proper use of the domestic appliances instituted for cleanliness and decency in towns'. Ross's experience was firsthand: in the Great Wild Street – Church Street area, within the St Giles fever nest, was an Irish colony with a fairly constant number of changing individuals.[96] Modern historians confirm the squalor and destitution of the Irish slums: there can be little doubt that they were ideal habitats for typhus.[97]

From the spring of 1862 to November 1863, the typhus epidemic was confined to the poorest and most densely populated parts of the city.[98] In 1862, 53 per cent of the cases admitted to the London Fever Hospital came from eight districts, with St George-in-the-East contributing 179 cases, St Pancras (where the Agar Town slum had just been razed) 162, and the City 157.[99] In 1863 nearly all the cases received by the Hospital were reported as having come, to date, from the most crowded areas, from Bermondsey, Lambeth, St George-in-the-East, Rotherhithe and the City.[100] At the end of October 1863 it was observed that several parishes had experienced marked fluctuations in the incidence of the disease, but St George-in-the-East and St Pancras furnished the 'most constant and equable supply' of patients. A month later patients were still being received mainly from the south and east (from Rotherhithe, Bermondsey, Lambeth, St Saviour, and St George-in-the-East), but there were indications that the disease was spreading. More cases were arriving from Shoreditch and the City, and others were being brought in from Hackney and Kensington, which had not furnished cases for months previously.[101] By 1864, the epidemic was more generally diffused through the city, although its focus remained the poorest areas.[102] In 1865, it was prevalent in the southern and central districts, but from 1866 on, the focus shifted to the east, where it remained until the epidemic began to wane. In 1868, for example, typhus cases were coming to the Hospital principally from Stepney, Whitechapel, Shoreditch and other East End districts.[103]

The London Fever Hospital's records do not provide a straightforward picture of the epidemic's distribution. Not only were milder

95. Ibid., p. 57.
96. *MOAR* ST Giles. 1870, p. 13. See also Lees, op. cit., note 68 above, p. 66–7.
97. Lees, op. cit., note 68 above, pp. 71–87; M.O. Tuathaigh. 'The Irish in nineteenth-century Britain', *Trans. Royal Hist Soc.*, 5th series, 1981, 31: 154.
98. *Lancet*, 1863, ii: 422.
99. *LFHAR*, 1862, p. 6.
100. Ibid., 1863, p. 7.
101. *Lancet*, 1863, ii: 603.
102. *LFHAR*, 1864, pp. 6–7
103. Ibid., 1868, p. 189; Luckin, op. cit., note 34 above, Table 5.1, pp. 108–9.

cases generally treated at home, but although the Hospital was the only metropolitan institution for typhus victims before October 1871, cases were not automatically sent to the Hospital from all the districts in the metropolis. Some parishes preferred to save the expense of treatment and deal with cases in their own workhouse infirmaries. Significantly, Whitechapel and St Giles were both in this class.[104] Whitechapel provided perhaps the most notorious example of the practice. As its Medical Officer of Health observed in 1868, it was probably inhabited by the poorer classes to a greater extent than any other district in London;[105] it was said to be the centre of the metropolitan fever field.[106] In the decade 1851–60, the district contributed the largest number of metropolitan fever deaths, and the *Lancet* suspected it of playing a 'too prominent' part in fostering the great 1861–70 epidemic.[107]

In 1865 it was estimated that of Whitechapel's 9,000 houses, 5,000 were let out as lodging-houses, each containing an average of three families. The parish's population in 1861 was 79,000; a density of 195 persons per acre. In the Poor Law year (Lady Day, i.e. 25 March, to Lady Day) 1864–65, 37 per cent of this population received indoor or outdoor relief.[108] Until 1866, the Whitechapel authorities made no use of the London Fever Hospital, and typhus victims were treated either in the workhouse or at home.[109] Both practices contributed to the spread of infection. The *Lancet*'s own investigations had clearly shown that the treatment of typhus victims in workhouse infirmaries resulted only too frequently in extensive 'in-house' epidemics;[110] home treatment was equally recognized as only multiplying the foci of infection. Vestry policy on the treatment of typhus cases was only one element in the epidemic spread of the disease, and it was clearly not the most important.[111] Nevertheless, in the context of the

104. *L. HAR*, 1866, p. 13. Three other districts also avoided the LFH charges: Mile End, Lewisham and Poplar. St Giles began sending cases to the LFH on 1 April 1865; Whitechapel on 1 December 1865. Poor Law cases were charged by the LFH at the rate of 1s a day until 1868. Thus the cost to, for example, St George-in-the-East and St Pancras of typhus cases in 1862 came to approximately £161 and £145 8s 0d. respectively.
105. *MOAR* Whitechapel, vol. 2, 1868, p. 12.
106. *Lancet*, 1865, ii: 656.
107. Ib d.
108. Ib d.
109. *MOAR* Whitechapel, 1865, p. 5
110. *Lancet*, 1865, ii: 656.
111. Nevertheless, vestry policy was probably important in sustaining the endemic level of the disease. The London Fever Hospital's inability to eliminate typhus from certain courts may have been due to repeated importation from uncontrolled areas of the city, or to inefficiencies of disinfection. See Bynum, op. cit., note 46 above, p. 106.

social dislocation occurring among London's working class during the 1860s, the failure of vestries to ensure the effective isolation of cases at the London Fever Hospital contributed to the epidemic impetus.[112]

The waning of the epidemic in the later 1860s was not due to any change in the virulence of the disease. In a recent essay analysing the decline of typhus, Bill Luckin examined and convincingly dismissed the possibility of autonomous change in the nature of the disease.[113] Explanation lies elsewhere, and in this respect the current analysis differs from the Luckin interpretation. The ending of the London typhus epidemic in 1870–1 was sudden, but no more so than in 1848 or in 1857. In both those years, contemporary observers attributed the disappearance of the epidemic to the restoration of normal market conditions.[114] In 1870–1, the situation was not so simple and Murchison, for example, had no retrospective explanation to offer.[115] Bread prices stabilized in the early 1870s, but they did not fall dramatically.[116] It is possible that, having affected some 190,000 persons in the inner city in the years 1862–69, typhus had diminished the pool of accessible, non-immune potential victims;[117] but the conclusion of the major railway works was probably critical. While general levels of overcrowding did not diminish, during the 1870s London experienced a period of comparative quiet and prosperity,[118] which probably reduced the incidence of short-term, expediency overcrowding.

Urban crises did not disappear after 1870. Cyclical depression,

112. This element should not be exaggerated. Many typhus cases undoubtedly remained unknown to the authorities. In 1869, the first year for which such a calculation is possible, admissions to the London Fever Hospital constituted 17 per cent of estimated London cases; in 1870, 13 per cent. This calculation is based on the contemporary assumption of a case-fatality rate of 1 in 10. The London form of the disease was less virulent than that in Lancashire, where mortality was *circa* 23 per cent: *Fifth Annual Report of the Medical Officer to the Privy Council* (PP. 1863, XV, Appendix 2, pp. 229, 304).
113. Luckin, op. cit., note 34 above, pp. 113–14.
114. Murchison, op. cit., note 41 above, pp. 51–3; Creighton, op. cit., note 31 above, p. 205.
115. Murchison, op. cit., note 41 above, p. 54.
116. Mitchell and Deane, op. cit., note 13 above, p. 498.
117. The figure of 190,000 has been arrived at by taking the total typhus admissions to the LFH in the years 1862–9 and assuming, on the basis of note 112 above, that these represented 15 per cent of the total number of cases. The importance of provincial immigration in replenishing the non-immune pool was perhaps limited: such immigrants tended to settle in the outer suburbs of the city. Jones. op. cit., note 12 above, p. 130. In 1870, Murchison observed that the marked decline in typhus was 'to some extent' due to the elimination of susceptibles (*LFHAR* 1870, p. 8), but he did not offer any retrospective confirmation of this observation.
118. Jones, op. cit., note 12 above, pp. 276–7.

unemployment and distress, aggravated by the exceptionally severe winter, returned in 1878–9.[119] During the 1880s the city experienced a particularly prolonged period of social crisis, at its worst between 1884 and 1887.[120] Throughout this period, overcrowding in the working class areas of the city scarcely abated. Average real wages, however, began to rise steadily,[121] and the post-1870 London crises differed from those earlier: there were no bread riots or semi-violent distress, and there were no typhus epidemics. The disease continued to decline steadily (Figure 1).

Yet typhus had declined substantially before. In the years 1803–15 it was markedly absent in England.[122] Between 1858 and 1860, it was so rare in London that there were serious plans to convert the London Fever Hospital into a general hospital.[123] The decline of typhus in the 1870s was not so sudden or dramatic that it was regarded by contemporaries as anything more than a temporary respite. After all, even the seventy odd deaths registered in London in 1879 and 1880 represented, in terms of contemporary calculation, some 700 cases.[124] Indeed the distress in London in these years caused the *Lancet* to warn against the outbreak of epidemics.[125] The final decline of typhus in London dates not from the early 1870s, but from the late 1870s and early 1880s. The role of the nutritional factor is indirect; but important developments in the sanitation of housing, water supplies, and hospital treatment,[126] and changes in the nature of urban social dislocation, both occurring in the years around 1870, were probably critical to the subsequent history of typhus.

Very little improvement occurred in the housing conditions of the poorest of the London working classes in the later nineteenth century,[127] but developments in the later 1860s and 1870s may

119. Ibid., pp. 46, 277.
120. Ibid., pp. 281–2.
121. Mitchell and Deane, op. cit., note 13 above, pp. 345–6. See also the recent assessments by Hunt, op. cit., note 9 above, and Teitelbaum, op. cit., note 9 above.
122. Creighton, op. cit., note 31 above, pp. 162–7.
123. *LFHAR*, 1861, p. 6; Murchison, op. cit., note 41 above, p. 53.
124. In 1878 the *Lancet* calculated on the basis of 25 per cent mortality, among 179 completed cases at the Metropolitan Asylums Board hospitals, that there were 636 cases of typhus in London in 1877, *Lancet*, 1878, i: 324. There were 151 registered typhus deaths in London in 1877, giving, on this basis 604 cases.
125. *Lancet*, 1879, i: 63, 385–6.
126. Given modern assessment of the aetiology of the disease, I cannot agree with Luckin (op. cit., note 34 above, p. 113) that sewerage was a necessary condition for the eradication of epidemic typhus. Human urine and faeces can only transmit typhus if they contain blood: this method of transmission is not considered important by any of the authorities cited in note 36 above.
127. Jones, op. cit., note 12 above, pp. 174–8; A.S. Wohl, *The eternal slum*, London, Edward Arnold, 1977, chapter 2.

have been significant to typhus. In the first place, there were the demolitions for railways and street improvement, and after the passing of the Artisan Dwellings Act of 1875 these were supplemented by vestry- or Medical Officer of Health-sponsored clearance schemes specifically aimed at fever nests. In St Giles, for instance, the old fever dens of Great Wild Street and Little Coram Street were swept away by 1883, and the clearance of two more (Shelton Street, Drury Lane, and the Colonnade) was contemplated.[128] In 1887, the *Lancet* went so far as to remark that the St Giles clearances had cleared typhus from London.[129]

Meanwhile, although the provisions for the regulation of common lodging houses in the Sanitary Act of 1866 had proved almost unworkable, sanitary departments were taking steps under existing legislation to remedy the worst of the superficial conditions as far as possible. Specific sanitary defects were rectified under the Nuisance Removal Acts; more generally, houses were cleaned and lime-washed. In St Martin-in-the-Fields, Dr Beale 'nearly succeeded' in having every tenement house cleansed and whitewashed at least once a year during the late 1860s. Conditions in some courts, he admitted, continued to be 'disgraceful', but he stated that he found the cleaning and repairing of tenement houses less difficult every year. In 1867, notices to cleanse had been attended to with 'tolerable exactness', and in no instance had it been necessary to call on the magistrates for aid.[130] In St Giles, 12,573 improvement orders were issued between 1875 and 1883, and 7,770 houses cleansed – an average of 971 per annum.[131] Since this district had only 3,968 inhabited houses in 1881, apparently some 24.5 per cent of its housing stock was cleansed every year.

The combination of fever-nest demolition and regular cleaning may have gone some way to removing the old typhus habitats. If low-level non-epidemic typhus was sustained between epidemics by the survival of *Rickettsia prowazeki* in dried louse faeces, and by the continuous flow of newcomers into (and out of) poor lodgings, the regular cleaning of this type of housing would break the cycle of transmission. In Liverpool, for example, it was said that regular cleaning and supervision had eliminated typhus from the city's common lodging houses between 1848 and 1863.[132] It may also be relevant that in the years 1868–79, the London Medical Officers

---

128. *MOAR* St Giles, 1883, p. 73. Shelton Street went in 1889: ibid., 1889, p. 21.
129. *Lancet*, 1887, i: 632.
130. *MOAR* St Martin, 1867, p. 19. Beale found that these houses rapidly became dirty again: ibid., 1868. p. 18.
131. *MOAR* St Giles, 1883, p. 73.
132. *Seventh Annual Report of the Medical Officer to the Privy Council* (PP, 1865, XXVI, appendix 8, p. 478).

of Health had to contend with three successive major outbreaks of contagious diseases recognized as epidemic: scarlet fever, in 1868–70; and smallpox, in 1870–73 and 1876–78. The direct results of these epidemics were widespread house-to-house visitations in search of contacts and unvaccinated children; and equally widespread disinfection of the homes, bedding and clothing of victims throughout London, both on a scale never experienced before. The implementation of these preventive measures was undoubtedly particularly thorough in the poorest areas which were the most vulnerable to sanitary supervision.

In these years, increased provision was also made to enable the poor to cleanse their bodies, clothes and homes themselves. Bill Luckin has argued that, although per capita water consumption in the eastern and northern districts rose from twenty to twenty-four gallons a day by the mid-1870s, it was not until the 1890s that more than 50 per cent of this population had access to company water, or were provided with a more than intermittent supply.[133] In fact, company-supplied constant service was widely provided in the east, although less so in the northern districts, by 1880.[134] The East London Water Company was a pioneer in this respect. As early as 1868, Dr Liddle recorded that the poorest parts of Whitechapel were probably better provided with water than 'any other district in London'.[135] In 1869, the East London Company resolved to extend constant supply throughout its district, and had achieved this object within its metropolitan area by 1883.

Although in the poorest courts water was often supplied by standpipes, not laid on to houses, the convenience of a constant supply and the alteration in patterns of water usage which this entailed became widespread in East London in the 1870s. It is

133. Luckin, op. cit., note 34 above, p. 112. It is possible to disagree with the last part of this statement, since the sources on which it is based stem from the London County Council (LCC) – a body notoriously involved in the politics of the water question. Aggregate water supply figures given in the 1890s generally refer to 'Water London', an area considerably larger than Registration London: *Nineteenth Annual Report of the Local Government Board* (PP, 1890, XXXIII, Appendix B no. 2, p. 237). The LCC commonly seems to have used the statistics of Water London as if they referred to the smaller area of Metropolitan London. The wider issues of the politics of London water in the 1890s have not as yet been satisfactorily analysed. But see A. Shadwell, *The London water supply*, London, Longmans Green and Co., 1899, especially chapter 1; and A. K. Mukhopadhyay, 'The politics of London water', *London J.*, 1975, 2: 207–12; *idem.*, The politics of London water supply 1871–1971, unpublished Ph.D. dissertation, London University, 1972.

134. Anne Hardy, 'Parish pump to private pipes: London's water supply in the nineteenth century', in W.F. Bynum (ed.), *Living and dying in London 1700–1900*, London, Routledge, 1991.

135. *Lancet*, 1868, i: 273.

difficult to assess how far the availability of a constant supply improved personal cleanliness.[136] While it is clear from evidence presented before the 1884 Royal Commission on Housing, for example[137] that an inadequate water supply continued to be a difficulty in some of the poorer districts of the city, the extension of constant water supplies may have contributed to household cleanliness, and thus to the typhus ecology.

Hospital provision was the third area in which significant developments occurred. Although the pressure which the 1860s epidemic brought to bear on workhouse services caused many districts to resort early to London Fever Hospital treatment for their typhus cases, this was an expensive proceeding for economy-minded Guardians to sanction. The situation altered with the passing of the Metropolitan Poor Act of 1867, which introduced rate equalization as a means of spreading the financial burden of London's poor more evenly. Money spent on the hospitalization of infectious-disease victims could be reclaimed from the Common Poor Fund, thus removing inhibitions about excess spending.[138] The number of admissions to the London Fever Hospital certainly rose sharply in 1868 (typhus admissions increased to 449, from 254 in the previous year, in the three months June–August), but as the numbers of typhoid admissions and of registered fever deaths also rose, the impact of the new legislation in this area cannot be quantitatively assessed. Given the aetiology of the disease, however, increased hospitalization was likely a more effective preventive measure for typhus than for such genuinely infectious diseases as scarlet fever and smallpox. During the 1870s, moreover, hospital provision for fever patients was extended with the opening of the Metropolitan Asylums Board hospitals.[139]

Finally, during the 1870s, the rate of railway demolitions eased. Although railway displacements continued to be made in the 1870s, these were not on as large a scale, or quickly effected, as those which took place in the central and eastern districts in the early to mid-1860s. Between 1867 and 1885, some 19,000 persons were displaced

136. Martin Daunton, *House and home in the Victorian city*, London, Edward Arnold, 1983, p. 42, notes that one bath and one clothes' wash a week were still customary in working-class households well into the twentieth century.
137. *Report of the Royal Commission on the Housing of the Working Classes* (PP. 1884–5, XXX, p. 13). It should be noted that local authorities had no power to compel the supply of water for domestic purposes, only for sanitation. Domestic water provision thus remained a frequent difficulty in small houses whose owners were reluctant to pay 3d a week for it: ibid., q. 9632; in any case the supply was generally of cold water only.
138. Metropolitan Poor Act 1867, 30 & 31 Vict. c. 60, ss. 61–69.
139. G.M. Ayers, *England's first state hospitals and the Metropolitan Asylums Board*, London, Wellcome Institute of the History of Medicine, 1971, part I.

by railway schemes, compared with 37,000 between 1859 and 1867.[140] Pressure on housing in the centre did not ease, because railways, street improvements, slum demolition and warehouse construction continued relentlessly,[141] but the impact of these operations was more diffused and the degree of social dislocation less acute than in the previous decade.

In this sense, and with the temporary stabilization of the metropolitan working class economy, London's crisis of the 1860s, and with it the essential conditions for the continuance of epidemic typhus, passed in the 1870s. During that decade crucial environmental improvements eventually, although perhaps not finally until the 1880s, dislodged the disease from its seats of residual survival. Rising real wages meanwhile took the edge off urban distress in the later years of the century, and prevented large-scale 'stress' overcrowding. Poverty and misery did not disappear in London, but bread riots and semi-violent distress did.[142]

IV

The importance of local conditions, and of social dislocation in particular, in creating an environment favourable to epidemic typhus is confirmed by what can be ascertained of the behaviour of the disease in towns and cities other than London. Edinburgh's non-manufacturing population was vulnerable to typhus in seasons of general distress, but social dislocation generated by specific factors was rare. Nevertheless, when in 1826 the city experienced failures in building speculations which disturbed its internal economy, typhus became seriously epidemic.[143] In the early 1850s, Dr James Brown, practising his newly acquired skills in the diagnostic distinction of fevers, searched diligently in Rochester, Chatham and Strood for cases of typhus and relapsing fever. The towns were in constant contact with London, and were on the tramp routes. Typhoid was endemic, but neither of the 'famine fevers' occurred, because, Brown concluded, there was very little overcrowding or destitution.[144] When typhus appeared at Preston in July 1862, it had been absent from the town for fifteen years; contemporaries traced the origin of the first

140. Dyos, 'Railways', op. cit., note 19 above, p. 14.
141. Jones, op. cit., note 12 above, chapter 8: Wohl, op. cit., note 127 above, chapter 2.
142. Jones, op. cit., note 12 above, pp. 45, 54.
143. Murchison, op. cit., note 41 above, pp. 45, 54.
144. *Lancet*, 1855, i: 436.

cases to 'overcrowding',[145] which was probably caused by stress. The disappearance of the disease, from January 1863, probably indicates the extent to which the charitable relief which poured into the area succeeded in ameliorating the textile operatives' distress: this was also the opinion of contemporary experts.[146]

During the 1860s typhus was seriously epidemic in Liverpool and Glasgow, as well as in London. Unlike London, however, both cities had direct connections with Ireland, and both suffered continuously from typhus. Once again, however, it is clear that the initial epidemic impetus could not have come from Ireland, as the epidemic only developed there subsequently. The circumstances of Glasgow are obscure, although as late as 1886 the city's Medical Officer of Health wrote that it was never free of typhus.[147] Contemporary opinion differed as to the cause of the Liverpool epidemic: the Medical Officer of Health thought it due to stress, following the Cotton Famine, which went largely unrelieved because the city was outside the central Lancashire textile district.[148] George Buchanan, investigating for the Privy Council disagreed but was unable to reach any firm conclusion as to the epidemic's causes.[149] There seems to have been no extraordinary distress in Liverpool in the later 1860s,[150] but it may be significant that this decade saw railway operations advance into the heart of the city.[151] The parish of Liverpool lost 2,717 inhabited houses and 31,389 inhabitants in the years 1860–71, and its excess of deaths over births stood at 2,660 per annum.[152] Typhus was already endemic in the city, and local circumstances are likely to have been responsible for its epidemic escalation in these years.

Typhus continued to exist in the centres of most large towns until the 1880s,[153] but showed little inclination to escalate in these years of general prosperity, except briefly in 1874. The return of less settled conditions in the early 1880s brought some indications of a resurgence. Various small outbreaks of the disease in the northern

---

145. Murchison, op. cit., note 41 above, p. 54; *Fifth Report of the Medical Officer to the Privy Council* (PP. 1863, XXV, p. 18).

146. George Buchanan, 'Recent typhus in Lancashire', *Trans. epidem. Soc.*, 1862, 2: 23.

147. *Lancet*, 1886, ii: 620. The current argument's relevance to conditions in Glasgow is not illuminated by Olive Checkland and Margaret Lamb (eds), *Health care as social history: the Glasgow case*, Aberdeen University Press, 1982.

148. *Lancet*, 1867, ii: 608.

149. *Seventh Annual Report of the Medical Officer to the Privy Council* (PP. 1865, XXVI, appendix 8, pp. 481–51).

150. Ibid., p. 481.

151. J.R. Kellett, *The Impact of Railways on Victorian Cities*, London, Routledge & Kegan Paul, 1969, p. 201.

152. *Lancet*, 1875, i: 96–7.

153. Ibid., 1878, i: 323.

towns came incidentally to the Local Government Board's notice in these years, causing anxiety in the Medical Department. Finally, George Buchanan, then Medical Officer to the Local Government Board, mindful of 'the conditions of so many industrial communities', arranged for these outbreaks to be studied more closely in 1885–86. The investigation proved revealing. In five of the seventeen towns investigated, the disease was shown 'with strong probability' to have been imported.[154] None of the importations were from Ireland, although in five cases outbreaks were in north-eastern seaports where Irish communication was a reality. At Carlisle, Gateshead and Oldham, tramps were the vehicle of infection; at Quarry Bank, hop-pickers returning from Herefordshire; at Middlesbrough, a discharged prisoner. Importation was also suspected in Sunderland.[155] In Leeds, West Derby, and Hartlepool, it proved impossible to trace the origins of the outbreaks. All three occurred in very poor areas (in Leeds and Middlesbrough, the localities were Irish), and spread by recognized channels, among relatives, friends and neighbours. At Hartlepool, it was noted that poverty amounting to distress had been present in the winter of 1885–86, because of the depressed state of the shipping industry: at Quarry Bank, a town dependent on the chain-making industry, trade had also been much depressed, and a strike had further reduced wages, when typhus appeared in a particularly insanitary district.[156]

In Maryport and Liverpool, eastern seaports with histories of typhus where free communication with Ireland might have been found to have been a crucial factor, the Board's Inspector Spear was not convinced of its significance. In Maryport, most of the frequent and 'somewhat mysterious' reappearances of typhus could not be so explained. The Maryport outbreaks recurred in one poor quarter of the town where the lodging houses, the resort of sailors and dock labourers, were found. Nelson Street, in particular, saw repeated cases. In Liverpool, the Medical Officer of Health's inquiries only occasionally revealed importations from Ireland or elsewhere. Liverpool typhus, whether in its endemic or epidemic form, appeared within certain well-defined limits, in the older and generally low-lying districts towards the river, in South Toxteth ward and neighbouring localities. Here were long narrow streets, confined courts and cellar dwellings occupied by the poorest of the poor, mainly Irish unskilled labourers, who found a precarious livelihood

154. The seventeen were Accrington, Carlisle, Flint, Gateshead, Hartlepool, Jarrow, Leeds, Liverpool, Maryport, Middlesbrough, Newcastle-upon-Tyne, Oldham, Quarry Bank, Salford, Sunderland, West Derby, and Warrington. See Fig. 2.
155. Spear, op. cit., note 43 above, p. 957.
156. Ibid., pp. 947, 950.

in the docks, and their families. In these localities, Spear observed, typhus appeared to be indigenous, and most frequently an outbreak would appear to be linked with an earlier one, 'or antecedent cases before unrecognised are found to have occurred amongst the children of the resident population (if the constantly shifting seething mass of squalid humanity may be so designated), and there all further trace is lost'.[157]

Typhus thus continued endemic, if generally submerged, in Liverpool until the later 1890s at least, with occasional epidemic outbreaks to testify to its survival. In London, the chance discovery of a typhus-nest in the district of St Olave, in 1890, suggests the possibility of a similarly submerged existence.[158] The experience of Nelson Street, Maryport, is yet more instructive. Here Spear found reason to attribute the outbreak to 'the revivification of long dormant household contagion'. He discovered that Nelson Street contained a marine store dealer, whose proprietress admitted that she had often taken rags from fever-stricken houses. Her business had probably been the source of the many cases in the district over the years, and the culminating outbreak occurred when she moved house, and her contaminated rag-store was disturbed.[159] In Carlisle and Salford, furthermore, difficulty had been experienced in avoiding recurring outbreaks in rooms supposed to have been disinfected; Spear warned particularly against the premature withdrawal of surveillance from infected localities.[160]

The conclusions which Spear drew from his inquiries in 1886–87 illustrate the extent to which different factors operated in different areas, even within a limited period. He emphasized the difficulty of identifying the origin of most outbreaks, and noted that early cases were frequently so mild as to pass unrecognized, and that the habit of the disease was to 'creep steadily on' for some time until multiple cases in different households combined to exert an 'explosive force'. Cases appeared amid destitution and squalor; he attributed the current relative inactivity of typhus to the comparative absence of distress. Spear himself seems to have favoured migration as the trigger for outbreaks,[161] but the evidence of Maryport, Carlisle and Salford clearly suggests the importance of residual or dormant

---

157. Ibid., p. 956.
158. This outbreak, of between thirty and fifty cases, occurred in Sard's Rents, a blind alley with a population of 211 and thirty houses which were mostly offensive from dirt and poor ventilation, old, and partly dilapidated. The first victims slept on bare floorboards which may have harboured infected dust. The *Lancet* spoke of Sard's Rents explicitly as 'one more of the spots in London where typhus can maintain itself'. *Lancet*, 1890, ii: 406; see also MOAR St Olave, 1889–90, pp. 76–80.
159. Spear, op. cit., note 43 above, pp. 953, 960.
160. Ibid., p. 959.
161. Ibid.

infection in some areas. The mildness of early cases also suggests continuing, submerged infection among child populations in some towns. This may have activated outbreaks among adults when the 'ecological' balance of housing for the poor was disturbed in times of stress, as it was, for example, in Hartlepool and Quarry Bank in 1885–86. By this date, the degree to which outbreaks escalated often depended on the vigilance of the local health authorities: at Leeds, Hartlepool, Carlisle, Middlesbrough, Oldham, Newcastle, Flint and

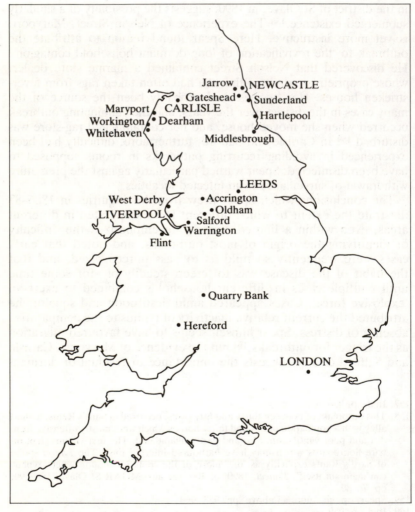

Fig. 2 Map of towns involved in typhus outbreaks 1885–87

repeatedly in Liverpool, the disease became established through the neglect of unrecognized cases; but in Accrington, Warrington. Gateshead, Sheffield and Jarrow, and in Chelsea, Southwark and Camberwell where there were also episodes at this time, initial cases were promptly recognized and dealt with, so forestalling any considerable outbreak.[162]

Spear's inquiry, while it provides no evidence of serious Irish links, suggests that migration, household dust infection, and residual endemic typhus all contributed at times to epidemic outbreaks, but that the critical factor in epidemic escalation was often extraordinary distress caused by local economic factors and accompanied by social dislocation.[163] In Liverpool, the disease was maintained among a poor population which, within certain geographical limits, was constantly mobile in squalid and overcrowded living conditions. In Maryport, similarly, the disease occurred principally in an area of the town with a poor and highly mobile population. The predominance of ports among the towns studied in 1887 (see Figure 2) may be explained by their greater vulnerability to imports, but also by their social structure. By their very nature, ports could not avoid the growth of quarters of cheap housing and a transitory and often disreputable population. Sanitary supervision was difficult in such quarters, and it was here that typhus stood its best chance of residual survival. Given its endemic survival in places such as Maryport and Liverpool, coastal traffic and ordinary population movements would ensure occasional outbreaks elsewhere, especially in other seaboard towns attracting a similar traffic and population. The origin of the 1887 outbreak at Carlisle, for example, was traced to Maryport, via a man who had travelled through Cumberland in search of work, while a prolonged outbreak at Workington in 1884 had spread by demonstrable links to Dearham, Maryport and Whitehaven.[164]

V

The disappearance of epidemic typhus from Victorian cities constituted a significant improvement in the living conditions of adult urban populations, and marks something of a watershed in urban health history. Rural immigrants to these cities had been especially vulnerable; now a major cause of their mortality was removed.

162. Ibid., p. 960.
163. Ibid., p. 961.
164. Ibid., pp. 943, 947.

In epidemic terms, life became considerably more secure for the urban poor and for the middle classes directly involved with them. For social and medical historians, the survival of epidemic typhus until the 1870s suggests the continuation of urban crises of the pre-industrial type, in which social dislocation was associated with epidemic disease, long after the towns had been released from harvest-related supply problems; as well as the significance of local economic conditions in determining disease behaviour. The disappearance of typhus represents, on the one hand, the arrival of structural, as well as economic and social, stability; on the other, the effectiveness of local public health programmes after 1870.

Detailed analysis of the nineteenth-century typhus experiences of individual towns can alone confirm the hypothesis that social dislocation was the principal determinant of epidemic outbreaks. According to Murchison, the disease was not endemic on the Continent between epidemics as it was in Britain and, to an even greater extent, in Ireland.[165] In England, industrial development and rapid urbanization from the later eighteenth century undoubtedly resulted in widespread stress among increasing urban populations, to an extent which may have paralleled the stress produced by warfare on the Continent. The conditions which sustained epidemic and endemic typhus in Ireland are still not elucidated fully, but urban stress and the low expectations of Irish urban immigrants may have been critical. To Murchison, Ireland's whole social and economic structure lay at the root of her typhus endemicity.[166] Nevertheless, Irish importation of epidemic typhus into England was not crucial in determining explosions of the disease there. It was rather the social condition of individual cities that allowed the epidemic escalation of imported or residual endemic typhus; and the steady disappearance of typhus after 1880 reflects both the vigilance of health authorities, and the degree to which serious social and economic dislocation was modified in English cities in the closing decades of the nineteenth century.

165. Murchison, op. cit., note 41 above, p. 57.
166. Ibid., pp. 137–8.

Part Three

THE SOCIAL FABRIC OF THE CITY

Chapter 8

CLASS CONSCIOUSNESS IN OLDHAM AND OTHER NORTH–WEST INDUSTRIAL TOWNS, 1830–50

D.S. Gadian

[from *The Historical Journal*, **21** (1978): 161–72]

Urban history has always made a contribution to the wider debate on the nature of class formation in Britain, a social process long associated with conflict and with industrial towns. Gadian makes a careful critique and analysis of local sources and continues the tradition of explaining the nature of class formation in a locality in terms of the specific urban economic structure and political experience of that locality. As elsewhere, Oldham showed that politics and elections were dominated by local issues. Often, such issues were reflected in the politics of a major local figure, in Oldham, the radical paternalistic millowner, John Fielden, who directed attention to factory labour conditions. In this period, national politics was a mosaic of such local figures and issues. Although this article has sometimes been read as dismissive of the part played by class conflict, what Gadian in fact did was to add depth and subtlety to class analysis. First he showed that conflict in Oldham was based upon an alliance of radical middle-class and working-class leaders, and need not always be identified with the labour–capital relationship. Secondly, he related that conflict to the relatively small size of units of production in Oldham, but in this and later work, he retained class formation as an important outcome and an explanatory variable in the urban social process, but one which operated more effectively in large mill communities such as Preston.

Recently considerable interest has been shown in the growth of a radical political consciousness in Oldham during the first half of the nineteenth century.[1] This development also attracted much attention

---

1. J. Foster, *Class struggle and the industrial revolution* (1974). Also A.E. Musson, 'Class struggle and the labour aristocracy 1830–1860', and J. Foster, 'Some comments on "Class struggle and the labour aristocracy"', *Social History*, III (Oct. 1976), 335–66.

from contemporary observers, the people of Oldham then being well known for the radicalism of their politics. Samuel Bamford, describing the period following Peterloo, wrote that 'amongst the best and truest supporters of persecuted radicals and the radical cause were a small but firm band of patriots at Oldham. Their like never, to my recollection, existed previously in Lancashire, nor has it ever since.'[2] The local journalist Edwin Butterworth also spoke of this 'small but firm band of radical reformers at Oldham, who proved themselves the truest supporters of the cause of radical reform of any party in the country'. Discussing the way in which radical political sympathies later spread through a large part of the local population, Butterworth wrote that the peculiarities marking the inhabitants of Oldham were in no way more clearly manifested than in the manner 'by which a powerful party have acquired an apparently deep seated ascendancy over the minds of the local population'.[3] More recently John Foster has explained in detail how control of the local vestry and police commission gave Oldham's radicals a decisive influence over such critical aspects of life as law and order, Poor-Law relief and church expenditure. Moreover, during this period radical strength in Oldham was sufficient to secure the election to parliament of John Fielden and William Cobbett, both staunch supporters of universal suffrage.[4]

In his first writings John Foster described Oldham's radical leaders as a 'coherent and stable group of social revolutionaries . . . working for the overthrow of the existing pattern of ownership and production'.[5] In a subsequent article, though, Foster has denied that he aimed to prove that working-class radicalism in Oldham was 'some early variant of revolutionary class consciousness' and instead has asserted that he was simply trying to investigate what sort of consciousness did emerge.[6] Despite this change of emphasis, the concept of the working class achieving power within the local community remains central to Foster's analysis of the class struggle in Oldham. For example, in the introduction to *Class struggle and the industrial revolution* Foster clearly states that 'throughout the second quarter of the century the town was more or less permanently under the control of the organised working class'. This situation apparently did not change much until the end of the 1840s when 'the town moved remarkably quickly towards class collaboration and a "labour aristocracy" type of social structure'.[7] This article will not question

---

2. S. Bamford, *Passages in the life of a radical* (1843 Cass reprint 1967), p. 196.
3. E. Butterworth, *Historical sketches of Oldham* (Oldham, 1856), pp. 172, 251.
4. Foster, *Class struggle*, pp. 51, 64.
5. J. Foster, 'Nineteenth-century towns: a class dimension', *The study of urban history*, ed. H.J. Dyos (1968), p. 285.
6. Foster, 'Some comments', p. 357.
7. Foster, *Class struggle*, pp. 1–2.

the extensive power and mass support won by radical politicians in Oldham. But it will show that class collaboration, rather than class war, between working and middle-class groups was the key to radical success in the town. Indeed, the growth of an independent working-class consciousness, expressed through the Chartist movement both regionally and nationally, eventually helped to undermine, rather than to advance, the unity and thus the strength of radicalism in Oldham.

Foster has argued that coercion and exclusive dealing were used by Oldham's working-class radical group to dominate elections in which the vote was confined to the more wealthy property owners.[8] In fact, there is little evidence to suggest that violence or intimidation played an unusually prominent part in Oldham's political life. For example, the 1832 general election campaign elsewhere in Lancashire produced many of the expected popular disturbances; but in Oldham, where the ultra-radicals gained one of their few successes with the election of Cobbett and Fielden, the election proceeded in an unusually peaceful manner. Following his defeat the Whig candidate, Bright, congratulated the people of Oldham on their peaceful conduct of the election. Butterworth noted that no election could have passed off more quietly.[9] Perhaps the only really violent incident was an attack upon a Whig bill-poster but, even in this case, the Oldham Political Union intervened to settle the matter amicably.[10] It is true that exclusive dealing, involving the boycott of those tradesmen who failed to vote as required, was a declared policy of the Oldham radical movement. But neither was this electoral tactic confined to Oldham, nor was it generally particularly effective. The *Poor Man's Guardian*, while praising the efforts of the operatives of Blackburn, Bolton, Sabden, Stockport and various other towns to promote exclusive dealing during the 1832 election campaign, was forced to admit that these exertions were not attended 'with the success we could have desired'.[11] There were no peculiar local circumstances that made Oldham's tradesmen particularly vulnerable to such methods of persuasion. Moreover, radical successes in Oldham did not reflect the more extensive use of the tactic of exclusive dealing in that town. Butterworth, no supporter of Cobbett and Fielden, recorded that exclusive dealing lasted only a few weeks after the 1832 election and that the electoral position of the radicals would have been secure without its use. A comment made by local publican Jonathan Nield at a workingmen's Conservative Association dinner held in August 1836 also helps place

8. Ibid. pp. 1–2, 53, 59.
9. Butterworth diary, Dec. 1832, Oldham Local History Library.
10. *Manchester and Salford Advertiser*, 12 Jan. 1833.
11. *Poor Man's Guardian*, 5 Jan. 1833.

245

the significance of exclusive dealing in a proper perspective. Nield's assertion that many radicals were his customers but 'they cared as much for his politics as he cared for those of their party' hardly points to the tradesmen electors being terrorized into political submission, as Foster suggests.[12]

The most obvious indication of the breadth of support obtained by Oldham's ultra-radical movement lies in the composition of its leadership, in which the middle class was consistently well represented. At least half of the town's leading radicals possessed the £10 suffrage qualification.[13] Prominent among them were James Halliday, John Halliwell, Joshua Milne, William Knott and Alex Taylor. Taylor, a shopkeeper, was described by one contemporary writer as the 'major domo' of Oldham radicalism between 1832 and 1852.[14] Millowners James Halliday and John Halliwell regularly chaired radical meetings during this period. Another local millowner, Joshua Milne, who nominated Fielden for parliament in 1832, turned down the offer of following William Cobbett as one of Oldham's radical parliamentary candidates in 1835. A future Oldham lord mayor, the hat manufacturer William Knott, played perhaps the key role in the establishment of radical control of local government during the 1830s.[15] The presence of significant numbers of the middle class in Oldham's radical leadership is recognized by Foster, but he sees them as 'largely abandoning any independent line of their own and being forced (for a time) into a one-sided alliance with the working-class radicals'.[16]

In fact these men involved themselves in radical politics because they considered that middle-class interests were best served by a programme of radical political change. Alex Taylor always insisted that reform was vital for both the working and the middle classes, explaining to one meeting that 'he for his own part could say that though he did business to the amount of £150 a week yet he could get no more than he used to get by hand labour'.[17] Taylor was later accused of making a fortune out of the custom of his radical followers but, during the early 1830s, at the height of radical strength in Oldham, his claims concerning the impoverishment of the middle classes were echoed by other local businessmen.[18] Joshua

---

12. Butterworth diary, Dec. 1832, Aug. 1836.
13. The diary kept by Edwin Butterworth serves as the best source of information about Oldham's radical leaders: see also 1832 Oldham pollbook, Oldham, L.H.L.
14. B. Grime, *Memory sketches: history of Oldham parliamentary elections* (Oldham, 1887), p. 100.
15. Butterworth diary, *passim*, also for Milne, June 1835.
16. Foster, *Class struggle*, p. 137.
17. Butterworth diary, May 1832.
18. For the accusation against Taylor see Grime, *Memory sketches*, p. 59.

Milne, a cotton spinner and manufacturer employing 700 hands in four factories, told the 1833 select committee on manufactures, commerce and shipping that without drastic reforms trade would become increasingly unprofitable for the employer. Although 1832 had been a profitable year, overall profits were generally going down, Milne argued. Asked about possible remedies, Milne proposed the abolition of the corn law, tithes, unjust monopolies, malt and hop duties and the assessed taxes. He urged that they should be replaced by property and income taxes with total taxation reduced by a half. He also suggested that interest on the national debt be reduced and that more paper money should be issued.[19] A report in the *Herald of the Rights of Industry* on the evidence of Milne and other witnesses to the committee concluded that 'all are sinking, all are suffering who are in any way connected with useful employment . . . nothing is prospering in the country but the money changers, the Jews and robbers'.[20]

In fact such hostility towards bankers and fundholders was a constant theme of radical propaganda in Oldham, and resolutions condemning banking monopolies and the like provided a firm basis for the unity of the town's working and middle-class reformers.[21] Popular feeling on the issue was expressed by one Oldham audience, which jeered one of the candidates for a Lancashire county seat who refused to countenance the breaking of the nation's obligation to pay interest on the national debt.[22] Oldham's MP, John Fielden, himself regularly expressed the grievances of the industrious classes against bankers and money-lenders. William Cobbett recalled in his *Political Register* one speech of Fielden's which 'could not fail to stir the gall of the paper-money tribe, particularly those of Manchester, who are still preying upon the distress of the manufacturer and taking part of the miserable meal from the working people'.[23] Like Cobbett, Fielden blamed bankers as well as aristocrats for the fact that although 'the people of this country are superior in skill, industry and science to any people in the world . . . the productive classes are in a state of the most unparalleled distress'. Generally Oldham's radicals regarded their own struggle as that of the productive classes against the parasitical fundholders and landed aristocrats. None of the pledges drawn up by them during 1832 to submit to potential parliamentary candidates excluded the industrial middle classes from

---

19. *Select committee on manufacturers, commerce and shipping* (Parl. Papers, 1833, VI), pp. 655–7.
20. *Herald of the Rights of Industry*, 1 Mar. 1834.
21. For examples of resolutions passed on this subject see Butterworth diary, July 1832.
22. For a description of Wood's reception see Butterworth diary, Dec. 1832.
23. *Cobbett's Political Register*, 29 Sept. 1832.

the ranks of the popular cause. At public discussions of these pledges, resolutions welcoming the downfall of the aristocracy, attacking banking monopolies and urging the reduction of national debt were passed, but none followed the lead of the *Poor Man's Guardian* in condemning the profits of the industrialist. One such gathering was concluded with thanks to 'the employers who had liberated their workpeople for the purpose of attending the meeting'.[24]

Cobbett's determination that the nation should not 'pay any fundholder any single farthing' and his comparisons of moneylenders with 'those vermin which fatten upon the diseased bodies of animals' were undoubtedly consistent with the pledges demanded by his radical constituents in Oldham.[25] Nevertheless Cobbett's sponsors in Oldham's first parliamentary election were keen to resist any suggestion that their man threatened the stability of society. In proposing him as their candidate, James Halliday declared Cobbett to be a staunch supporter of the due rights of property. William Fitton, who appeared on the hustings in place of the absent Cobbett, denied that their future representative wished to spoliate public and private property. Fitton, a leading local radical, argued that Cobbett wished to 'prevent revolution' by devising means to secure the 'stability and safety of all', thus hardly appearing as a spokesman of a movement with any conscious revolutionary tendencies. Halliday's contribution was reported as being cheered by all parties and the cautious tone of the speeches of these radical leaders both reflects and helps explain the exceptional degree of unity achieved between middle- and working-class reformers in Oldham at this time.[26]

Such unity had enabled a vigorous campaign in favour of the Reform Bill to be mounted in Oldham, although in nearby Manchester and Bolton divisions between working- and middle-class reformers were to make this impossible. For example, on 6 October 1831, in response to the Lord's rejection of the Bill, leading ultra-radicals joined with other prominent local citizens in addressing a public meeting, which was judged by Butterworth to be 'probably the largest assemblage that ever took place here'. An address to the king in support of the Reform Bill was carried by a vast majority.[27] At a meeting in nearby Royton held during 1832 Fitton summed up the position of Oldham radicals on this issue when urging that they should support Lord Grey but at the same time press for further measures of reform. The continuing resistance of the Lords towards reform led to a further mass meeting being held in Oldham on

24. Butterworth diary, Oct. 1832, July 1832.
25. *Cobbett's Political Register*, 2 June 1832, 29 Sept. 1832.
26. Butterworth diary, Dec. 1832.
27. Butterworth, *Historical sketches*, p. 247.

14 May 1832. Senior constable John Jackson took the chair and radical leader Alex Taylor echoed other speakers in stressing the need for united action. Arguing that it appeared plain that the greedy and avaricious aristocracy of the country were determined to stick fast to their pensions, Taylor emphasized that the Reform Bill was vital for both middle and working classes. A resolution demanding the withholding of supplies was passed and a petition for reform quickly gained 8,000 signatures.[28]

Following the passing of the Reform Bill and their success in the 1832 general election, Oldham radicals continued to put forward a programme that could appeal to both working- and middle-class reformers. For example, at a well-attended public meeting held in the town during February 1833, William Knott proposed the first motion that the people's distress and misery were the result of heavy taxation. Subsequently sinecures, pensions, the interest paid on the national debt, the standing army, tithes and church lands, were all condemned as infringing the rights of the industrious classes. Later Oldham radicals were able to achieve great success in uniting all the local community against the introduction of the Poor Law Amendment Act into the town. General Johnson, who in 1837 became one of the town's two radical MPs, on one of his first visits to Oldham noted the unison of feeling among all classes in the area upon this issue. In fact, so united was Oldham opinion against the attempt to operate the new law that, at first, no one even could be persuaded to nominate the guardians needed to serve under the new system.[29] The campaign against the new law there was led by the Radical Association and in March 1837 it was only in Oldham that a sufficiently disciplined unity existed for a totally successful boycott of the proposed elections to take place. Lasting several years, this boycott was achieved in Oldham not by violence but by co-operation between different social groups.[30] Great efforts were made to ensure the continuing support of respectable people, and typically James Mills, a leading local trade unionist and future Chartist delegate, warned one meeting of the state of insecurity for both persons and property that would result from this unjust law.[31]

Whereas the Poor Law question naturally encouraged local unity in the face of outside interference, other matters of public concern brought forward by Oldham radicals tended to lay bare antagonisms between the town's industrialists and industrial workers. During the

28. Butterworth diary, Apr. 1832, May 1832.
29. Ibid., Feb. 1833, March 1837.
30. For a good account of the achievements of Oldham radicals on this issue see N. C. Edsall, *The anti-Poor Law movement 1834–1844* (Manchester, 1971), pp. 80–3.
31. *Manchester and Salford Advertiser*, 27 Jan. 1838.

course of the campaign for factory hours legislation in Oldham, as elsewhere, orators like Oastler eloquently predicted that the 'race of millowners is plunging forward in the broadway to perdition'. The veteran local radical champion John Knight still spoke in traditional terms when asserting that the factory system involved the imposition of the 'idle upon the industrious portion of the population', but now he clearly included employers among those who lived off the labour of others. However, at the same meeting in March 1833 William Knott, himself a hat manufacturer, probably was trying to avert any general expression of hostility towards business interests when he spoke of how small businessmen as well as the workers were being crushed by the large capitalists. Moreover, radical millowner James Halliday went on to minimize the importance of factory-hours legislation by stressing that 'this bill might be passed but we should still be pressed down to earth by taxes'.[32] A few years later, William Fitton fully accepted that without shorter hours the factory system would become a bitter curse and proceeded to deny strenuously that 'England owes its greatness to the modern discoveries of steam and machinery.'[33] Indeed, there is no doubt that the struggles for better wages and shorter hours which accompanied the rise of industrial capitalism increasingly threatened the political unity of Oldham's industrious classes, which men like Fitton had so carefully built up. John Knight was cheered by one audience when he bemoaned the fact that 'whereas formerly masters and men were quite familiar, now there were high and mighty distinctions betwixt them – in fact the whole thing was pregnant with evil and nothing else'. In similar vein William Knott looked back to the golden age of labour when 'persons worked in their own houses and not in destructive factories'. Speaking at a meeting held in Oldham during 1837 to protest at the attacks made upon the Glasgow cotton spinners' union, master joiner Abraham Sutcliffe disclosed a real concern about the possibility of preserving the class harmony upon which Oldham's radicals depended for their success. Sutcliffe himself insisted that as the working classes produced all that was valuable and were the largest consumers of articles of necessity, it was advantageous to all ranks to render their situation comfortable.[34]

Understandably, then, the importance of developing new policies which could maintain the unity of the productive classes in the face of the realities of the advancing factory system had been a major preoccupation of a number of leading radical figures in Oldham earlier in the 1830s. The establishment of the National Regeneration

32. Butterworth diary, Mar. 1835, Mar. 1833.
33. *Manchester and Salford Advertiser*, 23 July 1836.
34. Butterworth diary, Mar. 1833, Nov. 1837.

Society in Manchester during the autumn of 1833, for the purpose of instituting an eight-hour day throughout industry, was largely inspired by a group of radical millowners from the Oldham area. The scheme originated with John Fielden, the society's chairman was Joshua Milne and two other Oldham manufacturers, John Travis and William Taylor, sat on its committee.[35] In reply to criticisms made by William Fitton about the scheme's practicality, Fielden proclaimed that the general selfishness of the people would be gratified 'by the general adoption of this plan among the productive classes'. He went on to assert that the eight-hour day would be 'advantageous to the productive classes both masters and workmen' as the lessening of production would overcome the problems of over-production and consequently increase both prices and profits. The scheme won little support from employers in the region as a whole, but James Mills did report from Oldham that 'many masters were favourable and he did not doubt that most of them would concur in the measure when put into execution'.[36]

Such new conceptions of the common interests of the working and middle classes had helped to maintain the united strength of Oldham's radicals and thus, at the advent of Chartism, Oldham played its expected prominent part in that movement. For example, at the north-west's first great Chartist gathering held at Kersal Moor near Manchester during September 1838, not only was John Fielden in the chair but two Oldham radical leaders, William Fitton and James Halliday, also were among the illustrious cast of speakers. During May 1839 a membership of around 1,700 was reported from Oldham association, a number which far exceeded that reported to the regional delegate meeting by any other local Chartist organization.[37] However, before long Oldham's traditional radical leadership began to detach itself from the mainstream of the region's Chartist agitation, in which there was increasing talk of physical violence and ever more forthright condemnations of the middle classes. As early as September 1838 one articulate Oldham reformer had written to the *Northern Star* opposing the attacks made by Bronterre O'Brien upon the middle classes. Speaking as a tradesman and using the name 'Observatus', he asserted that 'it is the undoubted interest of all the middle classes to support the interest of and promote the prosperity of the working class. My experience goes to prove that the more the working classes receive in wages, the more I receive in the way of business and that my profits are in

---

35. *Cobbett's Political Register*, 7 Dec. 1833; *Herald of the Rights of Industry*, 8 Feb. 1834.
36. *Herald*, 26 Apr. 1834.
37. *Northern Star*, 29 Sept. 1838, 27 Apr. 1839.

ratio to their remuneration of labour'.[38] For 25 May 1839, the day of the second great Kersal Moor Chartist gathering, a rival universal suffrage meeting was organized in Oldham with the firm request that no firearms or weapons should be exhibited. On the eve of the 25th bills, signed by Feargus O'Connor and urging the 'brave men of Oldham to attend at Kersal Moor and not at any local meeting got up by frightened politicians and landlords to keep the people of Oldham from Kersal Moor', were posted in the town. O'Connor himself visited the town early on 25 May to lead the Oldham Chartists to Kersal Moor, but Butterworth reported that few had gone with him. Despite O'Connor's claim in his Kersal Moor speech that half of Oldham had followed him there, it does seem that many of Oldham's radical supporters attended the meeting organized by their own leaders.[39] At this latter meeting James Mills, Oldham's delegate to the Chartist National Convention, reiterated one of the main themes of most of the speeches when urging that peace be preserved in the town.[40] Mills, who had always advised caution to the Convention, actually withdrew from its proceedings during the summer of 1839.[41] Although subsequently new working-class leaders rose to the fore in Oldham, the town's Chartist movement was never to regain its earlier pre-eminence. Ironically the very success of Oldham's radicals in securing the effective co-operation of working- and middle-class groups had been sufficiently unique for its achievement to have become an awkward irrelevance for the radical reform movement as a whole. Indeed, the industrial suburb of Royton, previously the strongest centre of radicalism in Oldham, was one of the last communities in the area to embrace the new outlook of the National Charter Association. When a NCA branch was eventually formed there in December 1841, an outside organizer had to be drafted in to 'arouse the good and true of the working classes of Royton'.[42]

John Foster originally explained class consciousness in Oldham at this time within the context of an advanced capitalist industrial structure with '12,000 worker families selling their labour to 70 capitalist families', although admittedly less emphasis is placed on this point in his major work on the subject.[43] In fact a large proportion of the adult males in the town were employed in such workshop industries as shoemaking and tailoring in which small-scale

---

38. Ibid., 13 Oct. 1838.
39. Butterworth diary, May 1839. For O'Connor's version of events see *Northern Star*, 1 June 1839.
40. Butterworth diary, May 1839.
41. *Northern Star*, 27 Apr. 1839, 11 May 1839 for Mills' convention speeches; 21 Sept. 1839 for a report of his resignation.
42. Ibid, 24 Dec. 1841.
43. Foster, '19th-century towns', p. 284. Foster, *Class Struggle*, ch. IV.

productive units were the norm. Just over one third of the adult males were engaged in cotton textiles, the town's dominant industry.[44] Oldham's cotton industry, though, was exceptional within the factory districts for the prevalence of commission spinning, the small size of its industrial enterprises and for the limited concentration of its millownership. The average size of the workforce in Oldham mills in 1838 was the smallest in the north-west, less than eighty compared to a figure of over 200 for Stockport, Blackburn and Manchester (see Table 1). Moreover, though it was common practice in the industry

TABLE 1   The average size of the workforce in cotton mills in north-west towns, 1838

Town	No. of mills	No. of workers	Workers per mill
Stockport	86	23,772	276.4
Blackburn	44	10,460	237.7
Manchester	182	39,363	216.3
Middleton	12	2,537	211.5
Wigan	37	6,137	165.9
Ashton	82	12,143	148.1
Bolton	69	9,918	143.7
Bury	114	13,652	119.8
Rochdale	117	10,520	89.9
Whalley (includes Burnley)	113	9,960	88.1
Oldham	220	15,291	76.5

Source   Figures taken from *Report of the Inspectors of Factories* (Parl. Papers, 1839, XLII).

generally for one firm to operate several factories, in Oldham it was also reported that 'contrary to the general practice in the cotton districts it is here common for several masters to rent the same mill – each having his portion and each paying his proportion towards the steam engine which serves them all'.[45] Consequently the 1841 figures concerning the average size of the workforce employed by each firm reveal an even greater disparity between Oldham and the rest of the cotton towns than do the 1838 figures dealing with the capacity of mill buildings. They show that the average size of cotton textile firms in Oldham was less than a third of that for Blackburn, Manchester

44. *Census occupational abstracts 1841* (Parl. Papers, 1844, XXXIII); *Number of men employed by different types of employer 1851* (Parl. Papers, 1852–3, LXXXVIII), part 2, pp. 654–6.
45. *The cotton metropolis.* First published in the *Morning Chronicle*, 1849–50, subsequently as a tract by W.R. Chambers (republished 1972 by Shipperbottom, Manchester), pp. 28–9.

and Ashton (see Table 2). Three-quarters of Oldham's cotton textile firms employed less than a hundred workers compared to a figure of less than a quarter in Manchester and less than 40 per cent in Bolton and Blackburn. Three out of 201 firms in Oldham did employ more than 500 workers but this must be compared to figures of eleven out of 115 in Manchester, fourteen out of 93 in Ashton and eight out of forty-nine in Blackburn. No cotton textile firms in Oldham employed over 1,000 workers (see Table 3).

TABLE 2   The average size of the workforce employed by cotton textile firms in Lancashire towns, 1841

Town	No. of firms	No. of workers	Workers per firm
Blackburn	49	13,829	281.4
Manchester	115	30,316	263.6
Ashton (parish)	93	22,476	241.4
Bolton	55	11,965	217.5
Bury	87	14,113	162.2
Whalley	127	14,683	115.6
Rochdale	77	8,084	105.0
Oldham	201	15,947	79.3

Source   Figures taken from *Report of the Inspectors of Factories* (Parl. Papers, 1842, XXII).

TABLE 3   Size distribution of Lancashire cotton firms – by workforce employed, 1841

Town	Total firms	Firms employing the following labour force (full capacity)						
		0–	20–	50–	100–	200–	500–	1000+
Blackburn	49	1	3	15	13	9	5	3
Manchester	115	3	13	10	35	43	6	5
Ashton (parish)	93	2	13	23	29	12	8	6
Bolton	55	1	7	13	11	19	2	2
Bury	87	15	17	14	19	16	5	1
Whalley	127	25	31	23	27	16	5	0
Rochdale	77	10	17	20	16	14	0	0
Oldham	201	67	50	31	33	17	3	0

Sources   Figures taken from *Report of the Inspectors of Factories* (Parl. Papers, 1842, XXII).

Note   The differences between the total numbers of workers employed in Tables 1 and in 2 and 3 are largely due to the use of different geographical boundaries.

Political relationships are not determined merely by economic situations. Nonetheless the predominance of petty capitalists in Oldham's major factory industry could be expected to have had an impact upon social relationships there. The contemporary journalist A.B. Reach set out to find out about this for the *Morning Chronicle*. He discovered that some Oldham folk considered the larger capitalists, who had not themselves previously been operatives, to be most generally and continuously popular with the workpeople on account of their establishments being the best regulated. Indeed, Joshua Milne and John Travis of the National Regeneration Society were partners in one of Oldham's largest cotton firms. However, Reach also reported that many regarded the small capitalist, the operative employer as the most popular with the millhands. It was said that 'these masters are just the same as if they were the fellow workmen of those they employ. They dress much in the same way, they live much in the same way, their habits and language are almost identical and when they get on the spree they go and drink and sing in low taverns with their own working hands'.[46] In fact, *evidence* from pollbooks does suggest that the less wealthy employers were more radical politically than their more prosperous competitors and more likely to support candidates favoured by the working people. Of those whose occupations are listed in the pollbook for the 1832 Oldham borough election all eight master tailors, all twelve master cloggers and all nine master shoemakers voted for Fielden and Cobbett, the radical candidates who won overwhelming support at the public hustings. Of the fifty-three cotton spinners and manufacturers who were listed as radical voters in the 1832 Oldham borough election only eleven possessed an additional voting qualification for the county election, but thirteen of the thirty-one cotton spinners and manufacturers who voted Whig and Tory were qualified to vote in county elections.[47]

That the prevalence of small-scale industry in Oldham did much to enable masters and men to 'harmonize and unite in some common remedy', as was possible in Birmingham,[48] is further suggested by the fact that a significant level of political co-operation between middle- and working-class reformers also was achieved in Rochdale, the north-west industrial town whose economic structure most resembled Oldham's. In 1841 the average number of workers in Rochdale's cotton firms, though some 20 per cent higher than in Oldham, still was lower than that for any of the other major centres and

---

46. A.B. Reach, *Manchester and the textile districts in 1849*, ed. C. Aspin (reprinted Helmshore 1972), p. 80.
47. Oldham pollbook 1832, Oldham L.H.L. and County electoral register 1832, Lancashire CRO.
48. For a discussion of this relationship in Manchester, Birmingham and Leeds see A. Briggs, 'The background of the parliamentary reform in three English cities 1830–1832', *Cambridge Historical Journal*, x, 302, for this quotation.

only just above a third of that for Blackburn (see Table 2). In addition, no cotton textile firm in Rochdale employed more than 500 workers (see Table 3). Moreover in 1841, 2,600 adult males were employed in Rochdale's woollen textile industry in which units of production were smaller than in the cotton industry, which employed some 2,000 of Rochdale's male adults.[49] In Rochdale the unity that was forged between middle- and working-class reformers made possible the success, in the 1841 parliamentary election, of Sharman Crawford, a wealthy Irish landowner who supported both universal suffrage and the repeal of the Corn Laws and was able to unite both working-class radicals and middle-class liberals behind his electoral banner. Despite the jeers of Tory opponents that local radical leader Thomas Livsey would have 'the honour of introducing Chartism and a Chartist member into this borough' and that 'John Bright has very happily consented to play second fiddle', Crawford won by 399 to 335 votes in 1841 and in 1847 was returned to parliament unopposed.[50]

Though being urged in the *Northern Star* to follow this example,[51] Chartists elsewhere in the north-east could not repeat the electoral successes achieved in Rochdale and Oldham. In such communities as Stockport, Blackburn, Manchester, Bolton and Ashton-under-Lyne, where large-scale factory industry had developed furthest, working- and middle-class reformers were unable or unwilling to achieve the effective level of class collaboration that was managed in Oldham and Rochdale. Independent working-class political organization in Ashton, for example, did make great strides forward during 1838 and 1839 but generally, where the economy of a community was dominated by a few wealthy employers, working-class radicals in this period found great difficulty in accomplishing even short-lived successes. For instance, Chartists in Openshaw near Manchester claimed that as 'the few cotton lords who employ the generality of the slaves in the neighbourhood belong to the liberal reforming Anti-Corn Law League', they themselves had been 'labouring under many disadvantages, it being the risk of being turned into the street to avow themselves Chartists'. In Blackburn, a centre of large cotton firms, popular agitators became exasperated at the submissiveness of the town's working people. At one Chartist meeting, held in Blackburn in July 1839, William Beesley attacked the working men there for fawning on their rich tyrants. 'Like dogs, they licked their shoes', he proclaimed.[52] On the other hand, the Tory *Blackburn*

49. *Census* (P.P., 1844, XXXIII).
50. A scrapbook of Rochdale elections, Rochdale L.H.L. For a good description of Crawford's election see W. Robertson, *The social and political history of Rochdale* (Rochdale, 1889), pp. 321–8.
51. *Northern Star*, 17 July 1841.
52. Ibid., 27 Nov. 1841, 13 July 1839.

Standard reported proudly during July 1839 that 'in few towns of its size and importance in the manufacturing districts are to be found in a greater degree the elements of pacific organization of which the quiet spirit of industry – the co-operative discharge of the social duties – are more strongly valued'.[53] In Stockport also, another centre of large textile mills, the Chartists, at first, struggled to gain a foothold, with threats of dismissal from the millowners being the explanation of the poor turnout at the first great Kersal Moor meeting which was reported in the *Northern Star*.[54]

In all of the north-west industrial communities the growth of the factory system involved the emergence of two major social classes whose relationship was the central factor in the development of political agitation. Where the working and middle classes were not yet deeply divided economically their fruitful co-operation in reform movements was a real possibility. Where economic divisions had advanced further, workers had to rely upon their own strength if they were not to submit to the wealth, influence and power of their employers. Although this might have been their way forward in the future, it must be remembered that during the second quarter of the nineteenth century only a small minority of the population of the country as a whole was engaged in large-scale industrial production. Thus the experience of independent working-class political action itself tended to indicate that working-class movements needed to win support from other sections of the community if they were to be successful. Even Ernest Jones, a close friend of Marx and Engels, came to realize the crucial importance of working alongside middle-class radical reformers and actively sought to establish common ground with them.[55] One of Lancashire's most sophisticated Chartist thinkers, James Leach, by 1842 had fully realized the importance of winning allies for their struggle, offering the right hand of fellowship on the part of the working classes to the middle classes. Leach declared that he would 'unite with the devil himself if he would give the people universal justice'.[56] Support for alliances with middle-class reformers should not be regarded, necessarily, as evidence of the retarded growth of working-class consciousness. As in Oldham, alliances based around the realization of the divergence as well as the interdependence of separate class interests might well reflect the advanced political consciousness of those who participated in them.[57]

53. *Blackburn Standard*, 10 July 1839.
54. *Northern Star*, 16 Oct. 1838.
55. *Ernest Jones, Chartist* (ed. J. Saville 1952), p. 36.
56. *Northern Star*, 3 Mar. 1842.
57. For a more detailed discussion of this whole subject see D.S. Gadian, 'A comparative study of popular movements in north west industrial towns 1830–1850', unpublished Ph.D. thesis, University of Lancaster, 1976, *passim*, but particularly ch. 3.

Chapter 9
MUNICIPAL SOCIALISM AND SOCIAL POLICY

Hamish Fraser

[unpublished paper]

In recent years theorists have increasingly realized that urban growth with its resulting density and complexity of human interaction has generated a need for a variety of non-market interventions in economic and social matters, even in a society like nineteenth-century Britain where the market was such a dominant force. The goods and services involved ranged from fire-fighting and regular supplies of clean water to public baths, parks and library books. This widely circulated but unpublished account of 'municipal socialism' shows that extensive and innovative interventions by local government were a major response to this need during the nineteenth century. Glasgow became a showpiece of municipal enterprise by 1900, visited by policy-makers from all over the world. The article shows how extensive intervention had become despite periodic ratepayers' revolts. These activities were more properly called municipal trading. They were sponsored by a political class of tradesmen and middle-class professionals. Only at the end of the period did labour movement politicians from the Fabians and ILP begin to see local government as the basis for more fundamental changes. Late nineteenth-century local authorities were very different from those of the 1990s heavily dependent on centralized government and politics.

In an article in the *Political Quarterly* in 1933, W. A. Robson pointed out the way in which the Labour Party had, by 1933, abandoned the idea of an important route to the socialist commonwealth being by way of local government. Twenty years later, in the same journal, he was to repeat his warning of the steady encroachment of central government upon the activities formerly undertaken by the local authorities.[1] The Labour Party was as responsible as any for this trend, largely, he argued, because of the 'extreme emphasis' that it placed upon equality. By 1933 variations in service between different areas were regarded as quite indefensible and the ironing out of these differences could be achieved by 'nationalization' of industry and services, not by 'municipalization'. One of the things that this paper will seek to show is that, even before 1914, there were some doubts about whether municipal effort could attain as much as was hoped without commensurate national effort. Nonetheless, up until 1914 there were few who doubted that municipal socialism had a major part to play in the process of social change.

It was the Fabians who raised municipal socialism to an important part of socialist thinking. The Webbs, in their *Constitution for the Socialist Commonwealth of Great Britain* (1920), still saw the municipality as central to their new society:

> The case for a local administration of industries and services rests primarily on the consciousness among the inhabitants of a given area, of neighbourhood and of common needs, differing from those of other localities, and on the facility with which neighbours can take council together in order to determine for themselves what shall be their mental and physical environment and how it can be improved. . . . This sense of solidarity among neighbours, living in the same environment and using the same complex of local services, is a valuable social asset which Socialism aims at preserving and intensifying. . . . The very differences among localities, with the different local administrations that they involve provide an increase in the scope for individual choice, a widening of personal freedom, and a safeguard against a monotonous uniformity and a centralised tyranny over the individual.[2]

Ironically, in their defence of freedom through variety, in the suggestion that 'those who did not like the arrangements of Hampstead would always be able to move to Highgate and live under a different local government',[3] the Webbs were identifying themselves with a long-established theme in the history of British administration: local over national control.

The great battles of the 1850s, of Toulmin Smith and his associates, against the 'alien' centralization of Edwin Chadwick had been won by the anti-centralizers, with the result that much of the social legislation of the 1860s and even later was permissive. It was up

1. W.A. Robson, 'The Central Domination of Local Government', *Political Quarterly* IV (1), 1933; 'Labour and Local Government', Ibid., XXIV (1) (1953).
2. S. and B. Webb, *A Constitution for the Socialist Commonwealth of Great Britain* (1920), pp. 213–4.
3. S. Webb's Preface to 1920 ed of *Fabian Essays*, Asa Briggs (ed.) (1962), p. 274.

to specific local authorities to decide whether to adopt workshops acts or appoint public analysts or have free public libraries or deal with the problems of public health. The result was an extraordinary variety and variation in the nature and quality of municipal activities. How much was done depended upon the influence of individuals and groups in particular towns.

The City of Glasgow was a pioneer among those towns who sought to use municipal powers for social improvement. As in Manchester, Leeds, Liverpool and other places, it was over the water-supply that the first major step in municipal activity was taken.[4] The inadequacies of the two private water companies in the city, particularly their failure to keep their pipes full at night for the benefit of the fire engines,[5] persuaded a majority of the Town Council to support municipal purchase on very generous terms.[6] The problem of supply was solved by the new Loch Katrine water scheme opened in 1860. It was probably the sheer size of the social problems that Glasgow faced, that was the crucial factor in causing the Corporation to look beyond the water supply to other areas of social concern. A local committee recommended in 1859 that additional powers be obtained under the local Police Acts to deal with overcrowding and insanitary housing, to prevent factory discharge into common drains, to make all ashes and night-soil the property of the city. Such powers among others were granted in 1862 for an experimental period of five years and in 1866 were made permanent.[7] The best-remembered result of this was the less than successful attempt to get to grips with overcrowding by means of ticketing houses with less than 2,000 cubic feet of space. The inspectors had access to such houses at any time and the midnight knock of the inspector was to be the experience for some of Glasgow's population up until the 1930s.

Another recommendation of the 1859 Committee was to obtain powers to acquire property by compulsory purchase for the sake of sanitary improvement. This was implemented in the City's Improvement Trust Act of 1866, which was later to prove a model for the Cross Acts. Property was bought, new streets laid and the most insanitary buildings abolished. Although the moving spirit behind the scheme, Lord Provost Blackie, was ousted by a ratepayers' revolt, the work of the City Improvement Trust proceeded with considerable vigour between 1869 and 1878. No municipal building was undertaken at this stage since private builders were, especially

4. On the debates on water-supply see D. Fraser, *Urban Politics in Victorian England* (Leicester 1976), Chapter 7.
5. *Forward*, 9 Oct. 1909.
6. Ibid., 20 April 1907.
7. Albert Shaw, *Municipal Government in Great Britain* (1895), p. 100.

in the booming days of the early 1870s, ready to build on the cleared sites.

In spite of the ratepayers' rebellion against the Improvement rate, there was little sign of a dampened municipal spirit, and in September 1867 the unanimous decision was made to take over the gasworks. This, in fact, ended a decade of battles with the gas companies. Indeed, there was active parliamentary encouragement to deal with the problem of monopoly gas companies, (since competition had to all intents ceased), by municipalization. Legislative attempts to restrict dividends in order to bring down prices had failed.[8] The typhus outbreak of 1869 resulted in the city's first municipal fever hospital at Belvidere, with facilities for disinfecting the clothes of fever victims.

The homeless poor, 'the dregs of the population' who 'probably belonged to the criminal class' and who 'were more or less familiar with vice', as the author of the *Red Flag* described them[9] were given an alternative to the private and notorious common lodging houses of the slums with the building by the Improvement Trust, in 1870, of its first two model lodging houses. Another five followed in 1874, 1878 and 1879, but even with seven houses the city was providing only a third of the total lodging-house accommodation in the 1880s: nearly 2,000 beds out of a total of 6,273 reported by the lodging houses' inspector.[10] Although the authority to build baths and wash-houses was included in the local Police Acts of the 1860s, it was not until 1878 that the first was opened. Another four followed by 1884, providing swimming baths, bathrooms and wash-houses at lower than cost price, as well as running a general laundry business 'drawing its patronage from all classes of society'.[11]

The manner in which a municipal social policy developed in the two decades of the 1860s and 1870s in Glasgow is remarkable, in a sense, when one remembers that there was no lack of ratepayers' pressure. A 'hostile shop-keeping element' proved very successful in defeating all attempts to get the Free Libraries' Act adopted. Also, the vote in Town Council elections was confined to those who had paid their rates in full before the election, thus excluding a substantial number of the working class. It was believed that by the 1890s about 50,000 were kept off the municipal roll because of this. This restricted franchise, by which 'the whole body of men who are ignorant, vicious, and irresponsible is practically outside the pale of politics',[12] was something that most American commentators were to admire, as freeing the city rulers from the pressures of the mob.

8. H. Finer, *Municipal Trading. A Study in Public Administration* (1941), pp. 45–9.
9. J. Connell, *Glasgow Municipal Enterprise* (1898), p. 52.
10. Shaw, op. cit., p. 106.
11. Ibid., p. 110.
12. Ibid., p. 42.

The motive force behind this early exercise in municipal socialism was a middle-class concern at the dangers which the slums held for them: dangers of disease, dangers of crime and disorder. Housing improvement, ticketed houses, inspected lodging houses were all ways in which the municipal authorities could exercise control over the patterns of life of the slum-dwellers. Municipal water was necessary to protect property from fire and the population from illness. It was essential that the populace be encouraged to wash to eradicate the contamination of the slums, and Glasgow made much of the fact that per capita consumption of water was twice that of any English city.[13] Municipal gas, too, was about social control; it was to light the gloomy stairways and closes as well as to provide cooking and lighting in the home. In Glasgow no distinction was made between water and gas, as a later Lord Provost declared: 'We regard the lighting of the streets of the city and courts, and stairs, and providing a cheap supply of light for the citizens as just about as essential as the supply of clean water.'[14] Municipal gas and water were about cheapness and this was to be a fundamental difference in approach between Scotland and England. Municipal enterprises in Scotland were not expected to make a profit and under no circumstances was any surplus to be used to subsidize rates. Instead the price had to be reduced as rapidly as possible. As a result, when the Corporation took over gas it was 4s 7d per 1,000 cubic feet; within a few years it was less than half that,[15] and soon no city in the world had so many of its households supplied by gas as Glasgow.

The Birmingham approach was, of course, in marked contrast to the Scottish one, though Chamberlain was familiar with what had been done in Glasgow. The municipalization of Birmingham's gasworks was for the purpose of making a profit. Birmingham had no property of its own and all expenditure had to come from the rates. 'It is with the object of diminishing the direct taxation of Birmingham that we are promoting this Bill', Chamberlain told the Select Committee on the Birmingham Gas Bill.[16] The two gas companies were bought out in 1873, the water company in the following year, and new supplies were found in the Welsh mountains. The profits contributed to Chamberlain's 'crowning achievement', the Improvement scheme, when, under the Artisans' Dwellings Act of 1875, much of central Birmingham was cleared to make way for the commercial elegance of Corporation Street. In addition, a comprehensive sewerage scheme with treatment and the use of

13. Ibid., p. 115.
14. *Select Committee on Municipal Trading*, P.P. 1900, VII, Q.2668.
15. Ibid., Q.2677.
16. Ibid., Q.1894.

sewage farms, as an alternative to the pollution of the River Tame, was carried out.

There was little that was new in the individual measures undertaken between 1873 and 1876 but the totality was impressive, and Joe Chamberlain revealed all his skills at self-advertisement in the way in which the activities were publicized. It was Birmingham that awakened the nation to the possibilities of municipal enterprise as the main hope of improving the condition of large towns. As E.P. Hennock has said, Birmingham's municipal reform was 'more than a successful attempt to provide a rather backward borough with necessary municipal services. The crucial innovation was a new vision of the function and nature of the corporation.'[17] The Birmingham example gave a momentum that continued for decades, helping to improve the quality of local government throughout the land.

Collectivism through municipal socialism seemed to offer an acceptable alternative to state action. Chamberlain's translation to Westminster brought the language of Birmingham's Town Hall into national politics. As he was telling an audience in 1885,

> For my part I am convinced that the most fruitful field before the reformers at the present time is to be found in an extension of the functions and authority of local government. Local government is near the people. Local government will bring you into contact with the masses. By its means you will be able to increase their comforts, to secure their health, to multiply the luxuries which they may enjoy in common, to carry out a vast co-operative system for mutual aid and support, to lessen the inequalities of our social system, and to raise the standard of all classes in the community. I believe that in this way you may help to equalise to a great extent the condition of men, and to limit the extremes which now form so great a blot on our social system.[18]

At the Board of Trade, he gave active encouragement to municipal effort, particularly in the realm of electric lighting. His 1882 Electric Light Act granted companies a mere twenty-one years' lease before they could be purchased by local authorities. Although this was eventually extended to forty-two years in 1888, the electricity interests were certainly to believe that the officials of the Board of Trade gave active encouragement to municipalities to apply for provisional orders to supply the new light themselves. Once having blocked private enterprise, it was claimed, little was done, especially since these municipalities that owned gasworks were not enthusiastic about

17. E.P. Hennock, *Fit and Proper Persons* (1973), p. 172.
18. 'State Socialism and the Moderate Liberals, 28 April 1885' quoted in Hennock, op. cit., pp. 174–5.

encouraging a competitor.[19] Only Bradford had municipal electric lighting by the end of the 1880s. In his brief tenure at the Local Government Board Chamberlain had time to issue his Circular of 1886 which authorized municipal schemes of public work to relieve unemployment.

The pattern of municipal activities in the 1880s was largely a question of pushing forward from foundations that had already been laid. In Glasgow, there were in the depressed conditions of the early 1880s few innovations but a steady expansion of existing activities. A regular system of emptying ash-bins was introduced, with a refuse despatch works that burned what could be burned and sold the ash as fertilizer. There was, however, a renewed interest in the matter of housing. John Bright in his rectorial speech at Glasgow University in 1884 had dwelt on the horrors of Glasgow's slums and that, plus the publications and talks of J.B. Russell, the city's MOH, stimulated concern.

Since 1878 the Improvement Trust had been largely inactive. General industrial depression and the financial disaster of the collapse of the City of Glasgow Bank in 1878 had left the city with a large quantity of unwanted property and land. For a decade little was spent on the properties owned by the Corporation, repairs were kept to a minimum and the Trustees had in their hands some of the worst and most insanitary property in the city.[20] Private developers showed no interest. A few 'model' houses were built by the Trust in the hope of stimulating private enterprise. It was badly needed to revive areas where the Trust held rentable property. From 1888 a more ambitious scheme of demolition and municipal building was embarked upon. There was no attempt to provide housing for the poorest class or for those displaced. The tenements built in Saltmarket Street and elsewhere were for the 'better-class of working people', yet there is further evidence that the principal concern was to promote a market for the nearby property. Rents ranged from £4 10s p.a. for single apartment houses to £17 for three apartments.[21] All in all 1,362 houses were eventually built by the Trust over the next decade.[22] At this stage, then, Glasgow's involvement in housing was an attempt to solve a business problem not a social one.

The next landmark in the development of municipal socialism came on the issue of tramways, and, again, Glasgow was at the

---

19. *S.C. on Municipal Trading*, Q.794.
20. *Souvenir Handbook of Glasgow issued by the Corporation on the Occasion of the Twenty-Second Congress of the Sanitary Institute held in Glasgow from 25th till 30th July, 1904*, p. 40.
21. H.W. Bull, *Working-Class Housing in Glasgow 1862–1902*, unpublished M. Litt. thesis, University of Strathclyde (1973).
22. *Souvenir Handbook*, op. cit., p. 41.

centre of it. George F. Train who had built the first British tramways in London and Birkenhead had arrived in Glasgow in the 1860s at the height of the period of municipal consciousness, but found his attempts to get parliamentary authority to begin operation in Glasgow blocked by the Corporation, who insisted that only it could have control over the city streets. The city was granted powers to lay the tramlines and lease them to a company to operate. Nothing was done by Train, but eventually a locally backed company was given a lease of twenty-three years to operate cars on the corporation-owned lines. The General Tramways Act of 1870 gave blanket approval to local authorities to own the lines, but not to own or operate the trams.

The possible social significance of the tramways was recognized by the spokesman for the Scottish municipal authorities before the Parliamentary Committee on the 1870 Tramways Bill, when he stressed the part that tramways could play in relieving overcrowding in the city centres:

> . . . if the tramways were in the hands of the corporation, they could be carried to such a distance as to bring the poorer people to their work at low fares, or they would stipulate with the contractor (lessee in the case of the tramways being leased) to run certain carriages, at certain hours of the day, at low rates.[23]

In fact, much of this was wishful thinking since, as in the case of most cities, Glasgow had difficulties in operating beyond its inadequate boundaries. Also, again as with other cities, it had no wish to encourage a massive exodus of population.

There was a number of issues that turned Glasgow towards municipal operating. The possibility of this had been pinpointed in 1882 when Huddersfield was granted permission to actually run its own trams, because no private company showed any interest in operating in its steep streets, and Plymouth and Blackpool were later to get 'Huddersfield clauses'. It was, however, projected plans by the Glasgow Tramway Company to expand into the provision of cabs and carriages in 1887 that brought up the issue initially. The Corporation was opposed to these plans and, although they were withdrawn, it was decided that the matter of renewal of the Company's lease would be discussed in 1889, five years before the lease was due to expire.[24] As this date approached there were increasing numbers of complaints publicly voiced against the Company: cars were dirty, irregular and lacked a standardized colour; the drivers and conductors were given

23. Quoted in Hugo R. Meyer, *Municipal Ownership in Great Britain* (New York 1906) p. 98.
24. Glasgow Town Council, Minutes, 10, 17 March 1887, Tramway Committee.

no uniforms and were generally unkempt; unsightly advertisements carried by the cars defaced the city. There were running battles between the tramway committee and the Company on who should be responsible for line repairs. It was as discussions on the future of the lease were getting underway that the Glasgow Trades Council entered the scene. The Trades Council had become involved when they had been asked to assist in forming a tramwaymen's union in May 1889 to campaign against excessive hours, low wages and a harsh fining system. Those tramwaymen most active in organizing found themselves sacked within days.[25] The Trades Council now began to campaign for the Corporation to manage and work the service themselves.[26]

Debate became centred on the conditions of the tramway workers. The Company's refusal to discuss these matters merely succeeded in producing a more hostile Tramway Committee, who laid down fairly harsh conditions for the renewal of the lease, forbidding the Company to move into new areas of enterprise and insisting on no more than a sixty-hour week, proper uniforms and adequate lavatories for the drivers and conductors.[27] Meanwhile, amid wide public discussion, the Trades Council continued to campaign for municipalization and the municipal elections of November 1890 were largely on this issue. By the next election, the decision had been taken to take over the undertaking. The fact that Glasgow's Tramways legislation preceded the 1870 General Act made this possible without fresh legislation.

It was, then, the condition of the workers in the industry, together with a fear that the local authority would lose out if the Company turned to other forms of transport that had brought about municipalization. There was really no attempt to justify the acquisition in terms of either principle or social policy. However, just as had been the case with gas, no attempt was made to make profit from the enterprise to aid the rates. The fares were reduced in the new service which opened in July 1894, partly as a policy decision, but partly in response to the old tramway company's last-ditch stand with halfpenny omnibuses. Corporation tramcar fares were reduced to a halfpenny for four stages, just over half a mile, and a penny for nearly 1¾ miles, and they remained at this level until 1914. For many the halfpenny fare was seen as revolutionizing working-class travel, but there was no attempt to use the tramways as a means of encouraging the working class to move out of their traditional areas. Indeed, there were frequent complaints from labour organizations that it was the middle class of Pollokshields who gained most from

25. *North British Daily Mail*, 13, 16 May 1889.
26. Glasgow United Trades Council, *Annual Report 1888–89*.
27. Glasgow Town Council, Minutes, 22 October 1891, Tramway Committee.

the trams with their penny fares and there were many unsuccessful attempts to get the halfpenny distances extended.[28]

During the 1890s other towns were to follow the Glasgow example of municipalizing the tramways, in most cases south of the border, seeing it as a further source of municipal revenue. In all the Scottish legislation, however, it was spelled out that any surplus had to be applied to a reduction in price. There was no serious effort to assess the social value of the tramways other than in the vaguest of terms. Who exactly was encouraged to 'move from their squalid inner city dwellings to better houses in the suburbs' was never analysed. Sir Thomas Hughes of Liverpool did suggest one possible social effect: men could now go home for lunch thus avoiding the need to spend 10d in a 'cook shop', while at the same time keeping an eye upon the wife, who if left all day 'feeling that she was loose for the day, very often fell into bad and drunken habits'.[29]

It was mainly the issue of municipal tramways that brought working-class organizations into the campaign for municipal socialism. Up until that time municipal authorities were regarded with as much suspicion as any other public body. The most frequent form of communication between a trades council and a town council was a protest against increases in the salaries of municipal officials or against some corporation extravagance. There was certainly rarely positive encouragement for municipal initiative. During the depressed months of 1885, the Glasgow Trades Council objected to the Corporation using the Water Committee plumbers to repair Corporation property[30] and even had doubts about a motion that the Town Council should provide work for the unemployed on the grounds that this would assist non-unionists.[31] It also protested at the taking over of the Partick, Maryhill and Hillhead gasworks by Glasgow on the grounds of cost.[32] Edinburgh was something of an exception among trades councils in that it did actively petition for municipalization of the gasworks on a number of occasions in the 1880s, though when this did in fact take place it protested at the high level of compensation paid.[33] Influenced by an analysis of industrial depression which blamed the system of landownership, the Trades Council, after considerable discussion, unanimously supported a motion expressing 'the desirability of placing in the hands of the municipal authorities the power to acquire land in and contiguous

28. Glasgow Trades Council, *Annual Report 1900–1901*.
29. *S.C. on Municipal Trading*, Q.2125.
30. Glasgow Trades Council, Minutes, 18 Feb., 1885.
31. Ibid., 25 Nov. 1885.
32. Ibid., 17 Oct. 1888.
33. Edinburgh Trades Council, *Annual Report 1886–87*.

to their towns for the purpose of being leased for building sites, or put to such other use as might be advantageous to urban problems'.[34]

No other trades councils appeared to show much interest until the tramways became an issue. The London Trades Council supported the moves on the LCC, in 1891, to introduce a municipal service.[35] Other towns followed later in 1890s, the timing depending on when the lease of the private company expired.[36] In all cases there were usually two reasons given: firstly, the poor quality of the service; secondly, the treatment of the tramwaymen. In the era of new unionism, rallying to the tramwaymen provided a relatively easy way of expressing solidarity with the unskilled, without the danger of giving offence to any craft vested interests. As with the agricultural workers in the 1870s all unionists could agree that their cause was just.

The protection of other groups of non-organized workers, especially those in the sweated trades, encouraged further trade union pressure for the extension of municipal power. London unionists had succeeded in persuading the School Board to adopt a fair-contracts resolution at the end of the 1880s and 'fair contracts' became part of the election programme of most trades councils. By 1894 about 150 local councils and boards had adopted such resolutions, but, even when these were passed, trades councils had their work cut out to ensure that they were enforced. They also pressed to have such resolutions extended and tightened up in such a way as to close loopholes. The demand for municipal workshops to undertake tailoring contracts was a logical extension of this campaign. London, Glasgow, Birmingham and Bradford Trades Councils all passed resolutions asking for the establishment of municipal workshops in the 1890s.[37] The Glasgow Trades Council welcomed the new municipal tramway in July 1894, 'as a further step towards municipal socialism', and urged the Corporation 'as a further step towards the humanitarian ideal, to take the making of all official clothing into their own hands, and so remove the stigma of being parties to the sweating of tailors and tailoresses of the city'.[38]

It was this same concern with the condition of the workers that largely motivated the first Fabian involvement in the campaign for municipalization, as part of their programme for the LCC. During

34. *Scottish Leader*, 2 March 1887.
35. London Trades Council, *Annual Report 1891*.
36. Nottingham Trades Council, Minutes, 2 Sept., 1896; Sheffield Federated Trades Council, *Annual Report 1895–96*.
37. *Glasgow Echo*, 7 Feb. 1895; Edinburgh TC, *Annual Report 1897–98*; *Cotton Factory Times*, 10 Jan. 1896; Bradford TC, Minutes, 11 Sept., 1896; Alliance Cabinet Makers' *Annual Report*, Feb. 1895.
38. *Glasgow Echo*, 5 July 1894.

1891 the Society published four tracts on Municipalization of the Gas Supply (No. 32), the Tramways (No. 33), the Water Supply (No. 35) and the London Docks (No. 35), together with one on 'A Labour Policy for Public Authorities' (No. 37). Any profit to be made from taking over the gasworks, they declared, was less important than the control which ownership would give over the conditions of the gasworkers. Municipalization would ensure 'fair wages, proper hours of work, and adequate protection against accidents'.[39] To take over the tramways would ensure an improvement in the conditions of the 5,000 tramway workers, who were 'among the hardest worked, most cruelly treated, and worst paid of London's wage slaves'.[40] The municipal control of the docks would be the first step in dealing with the problems of casual labour, 'the spreading social ulcer of the East End'.[41] Their municipal policy in 1891 was largely concerned with the proper treatment of labour: eight-hour days, trade union rates, the right of combination, weekly rest days and the prohibition of overtime. The direct employment of labour by the local authority would ensure this and, by extending its activities, the subcontracting that led to sweated labour could be eliminated.[42]

In most areas the issue of municipalization of the tramways gave a boost to the pressure for an independent labour movement. It was an issue which could attract votes beyond the narrower labour matters. The momentum of the tramways' campaign carried ten labour members on to the Glasgow Corporation by 1897. These 'Stalwarts', as they were known, came to symbolize the demands for municipalization in the city, though their main concern remained largely the improvement of working conditions for the existing municipal workers. They successfully achieved a minimum wage of 21s a week for municipal employees in October 1898.[43] It was hoped that through the Labour bureau, set up in 1896, that preference in the matter of employment by the municipality would be given to local ratepayers (though this was never the case). The demand for a maximum working week of forty-eight hours, with trade union wages remained at the forefront of the programme of the Glasgow Workers' Municipal Election Committee, which co-ordinated the political activities of the Trades Council, local trade unions, the co-operative societies, the United Irish League, the ILP and the SDF in the city, for more than a decade.[44] Any wider vision of the role of municipal socialism was remarkably limited, and when the one witness to the Select Committee on Municipal Trading who

39. *Fabian Tract No. 32*.
40. *Fabian Tract No. 33*.
41. *Fabian Tract No. 35*.
42. *Fabian Tract No. 37*.
43. Connell, op. cit., p. 76.
44. *The Times*, 6 Oct. 1902.

came nearest to being a working-class spokesman, William Maxwell, the president of the SCWS, was asked how he would like to see the municipal system further developed, he replied, 'Cemeteries take the first place with me', though he did make a case for municipal insurance.[45]

Yet, little labour pressure was required. The success of municipal tramways rekindled the civic spirit and there were few dissenting voices among Glasgow Corporation. New ventures were embarked upon willingly. Two corporation 'family homes' were established where widowers with children could obtain accommodation, together with day-nursery supervision for the children.[46] The principle of municipal insurance was adopted in 1896, though only for the Corporation's own property at first. A motion in support of municipal banking was carried unanimously by the Town Council in 1896 and, in October 1899, a committee of the Council reported in favour of applying to Parliament to issue Corporation notes and to establish deposit and lending banks.[47] There was talk of municipal pawnshops and municipal bakeries, though on the latter there was some difficulty for the Labour Party, since the largest part of the baking trade was in the hands of co-operative societies. Dr James Erskine, an ILP member of the Corporation, campaigned for municipal sanatoria, and a municipal home for inebriates was in fact established. The aim of the Corporation, a Glasgow councillor was reputed to have claimed 'was to provide everything the population required in its passage from the cradle to the grave'.[48] Elsewhere municipalities seemed bent on similar comprehensiveness. In Huddersfield there was talk of the Council owning coal mines because the price of coal affected the supply of gas.[49] Other councils were seeking power to manufacture and sell gas-fittings.[50] In St Helens the problem of a notoriously high infant death rate was tackled by a municipal milk depot where nursing mothers could receive a daily supply of sterilized milk feeding bottles.[51]

This new emphasis was reflected in Fabian publications. From the end of 1897 until the end of 1900 a stream of tracts was issued with a longer list of areas for municipalization: the Drink Traffic (No. 86), the Milk Supply (No. 90), Pawnshops (No. 91), Slaughterhouses (No. 92), Bakeries (No. 94), Hospitals (No. 95), Fire Insurance

45. *S.C. on Municipal Trading*, Q.4231.
46. Shaw, op. cit., pp. 107–8.
47. Connell, op. cit., p. 76.
48. *The Times*, 30 Sept. 1902.
49. *S.C. on Municipal Trading*, Q.823.
50. Ibid., Q.49.
51. Ibid., Q.3203.

(No. 96), Steamboats (No. 97). The emphasis was much more on the municipal contribution to social policy. The municipal pub-manager would discourage customers from drinking to excess and would eliminate bad liquor, as well as eradicating the political power of the public house and the brewers. Only municipalization of the milk supply, establishing municipal farms and milk stores could deal with the most frequently adulterated and contaminated of all foodstuffs. The growing concern about the spread of tuberculosis was the justification for municipal control of slaughterhouses, where no obstacle would be put in the way of regular inspection of cattle. There was a distinct switch of emphasis from the municipality as an 'Association of Producers' to the municipality as an 'Association of Consumers' with a responsibility for 'the collective provision for the citizens, as consumers, of whatever services they, as consumers required';[52] and so, municipal bakeries: 'Bread is as much an article of universal consumption as water. A municipality, after all, is but a corporate association of bread consumers. Why should it not produce what it consumes?'[53]

These new areas of municipal enterprise stimulated a debate, really for the first time, on the values and dangers of municipal socialism. Municipal corporations were forced to justify their actions in a way that had never before been required. The defence adopted by different spokesmen varied. Sir Thomas Hughes of Liverpool stressed advantages which a local authority had in borrowing at lower interest rates than private concerns. He talked of the popular support that municipal enterprises had and of their ability to attract men who were devoted to the public service and who would prefer not to 'ally themselves with private undertakings'. Local authorities had a duty to provide services for the poorest class, baths, wash-houses and homes which private enterprise could never provide:

> We rightly think, just as in the case of baths, when you are dealing with what might be called, or what would otherwise become a class dangerous to the public health, it is better even to spread a little through the rates to give an advantage to the other parts of the community in preventing infectious disease and bad results of that sort, which naturally flow from people not being properly housed.[54]

Glasgow's Lord Provost, Samuel Chisholm, laid down what he saw as three prerequisites which justified municipalization: 'that it was more or less practically a necessity'; 'that it is practically a monopoly'; 'that

---

52. Webb, Preface to 1920 ed *Fabian Essays*, loc. cit., p. 273.
53. *Fabian Tract* No. 94.
54. *S.C. on Municipal Trading*, QQ.2085–2297.

it requires the use of the streets'. He believed that where any two of these conditions existed the municipality ought to take over.[55]

The Town Clerk of Birmingham, Edward Orford Smith, took a more complex position. Municipal ownership was about making profit to finance urban needs. The working class, he argued, had been educated to expect certain things 'which might have been called luxuries' but were now treated 'as rather prime necessaries of urban life'. They will demand these 'luxuries' and 'so long as you provide these things out of profits with generally a reduction in the cost of the article sold, nobody is hurt, but directly you begin to deprive the people of those luxuries that they have been accustomed to, they will vote them out of the rates. Once upon a time a restricted franchise would have protected the large ratepayer, but that is now gone.'[56]

Like the Fabians, many of the other defenders of municipal socialism saw it as a means of 'national efficiency'. The often limited significance of 'party' in local politics attracted Liberal Imperialists like Rosebery, with his experience of the LCC, who regarded 'party' as an evil. Admiration for German efficiency included envy of the 'expertise' of German local government with its particularly effective control over city and surrounding land.[57] The success of officials like Young and Dalrymple in Glasgow encouraged the view that there existed in British towns an 'expertise' that waited to be tapped.[58]

The critics came from a number of directions. Few of them had much to say against municipally-owned water. It was, after all, as Sydney Morse of the London Chamber of Commerce pointed out, 'to a man's interest that his neighbour should wash, whereas with regard to the tramway it is not to his interest that his neighbour should travel by tramway'. Similarly with gas, 'it makes no difference to householder A whether householder B has any light at all'. Morse's principle was that 'any matter for which the capital may be properly raised from every ratepayer is probably a matter that may properly be undertaken by the municipality'.[59] Some saw the main pressure for the extension of municipal power coming, not from social needs, but from the local officials: 'the larger the business and the greater the ramifications of the business that is carried on by a municipality the larger the salaries the permanent officials naturally can ask for'.[60] There was much concern about the possible role of municipal

---

55. Ibid., Q.2758.
56. Ibid., Q.1949.
57. See, for example, T. C. Horsfall, *The Improvement of the Dwellings and Surroundings of the People. The Example of Germany* (Manchester 1904).
58. For a discussion of some of these issues, see G.R. Searle, *The Quest for National Efficiency* (1971) and Bernard Aspinwall, 'Glasgow Trams and American Politics 1894–1914', *Scottish Historical Review* LVI (1) (1977).
59. *S.C. on Municipal Trading*. QQ. 835, 852, 926.
60. Ibid., Q.1321.

employees with the vote, who might use it to exert pressure on councillors for their own advantage. John Wilson Southern of the Manchester City Council saw representatives of the ILP, 'which does not care for any other interests than those of labour', as especially liable to succumb to the pressure of employees.[61] Birmingham's Town Clerk favoured the disenfranchisement of corporation workers.[62]

The main arguments against municipal trading were summarized by the ubiquitous Lord Avebury, the former Sir John Lubbock, in evidence, speeches and books. He talked of the growing mountain of municipal debt, the risk of ultimate loss that municipalities faced, the lack of innovation on the part of municipal owners that would inevitably lead to a check on industrial progress, the overburdening of councillors, the interference with natural laws and the general undesirability of involving governments and municipalities in labour questions.[63] At least some of the attacks on municipal socialism were inspired by vested interests such as electrical supply and electric traction companies, who were behind the Industrial Freedom League, but there was genuine concern.[64]

The most contentious area came to be municipal involvement in housing. The main legislation under which municipalities could undertake housing was the Housing of the Working Classes Act of 1890, which consolidated the earlier Torrens's and Cross's Acts. Under Part I of that Act unhealthy areas could be cleared and dwellings provided for those displaced as part of an improvement scheme. Part II of the Act gave similar power for small improvements and individual closure and replacement of unhealthy houses. Part II of the Act had no reference to unhealthy areas or unhealthy dwellings, but enabled a local authority 'to provide dwellings, if they think fit to do so, for the working classes'.[65] It was to Part II that a number of councils were turning.

In London, although the need for municipal intervention had been widely accepted since at least the Royal Commission on the Housing of the Working Classes in 1884–85, the LCC was slow to embark on a massive task. However, with a slow beginning in 1892, the LCC by March 1900 had accommodated over 10,000 persons in forty-eight blocks and in its first municipal lodging house for 324.[66] Most of the flats provided were three or four bedrooms and there was a

61. Ibid., Q.2477.
62. Ibid., Q.1947.
63. Ibid., Q.1548; Lord Avebury, *On Municipal and National Trading* (1906).
64. Major Leonard Darwin, *Municipal Trade* (1903); Hugo Meyer, *Municipal Ownership in Great Britain* (1906); R. R. Porter, *The Dangers of Municipal Trading* (1907). The well-known *Times* articles on 'Municipal Socialism' were from August to November 1902.
65. *S.C. on Municipal Trading*, Q.975.
66. Ibid., Q.3340.

specific rejection of one-roomed tenements, with the result that the poorest section was as always excluded.[67] Alongside building under Part II of the Act, slum clearance continued until the Moderates got control in 1907. Here too the rents, together with the fact that the keeping of lodgers was forbidden, excluded most of the displaced, and subsidized housing was specifically rejected by Progressives and Moderates on the LCC.

Liverpool Corporation, in contrast, seems to have seen its function as being to deal with the poorest. By 1900 it had cleared 5,000 of its back-to-back houses, but faced the recurring problem of finding accommodation for the displaced. The Local Government Board laid down a duty that provision had to be made for at least half of those dispossessed, but few of the private speculators or builders showed any interest in providing dwellings for the class displaced. Therefore, the Corporation found itself forced to build tenements in Victoria Square with rooms at 1s to 1s 3d per week. There was the added difficulty that improved areas had only space for one-third replacement on the spot, but the LGB laid down, as a condition of loan, that people should not be driven more than two miles from where they were dispossessed.[68] Even at rents of 1s, however, the corporation found that they were still not catering for the poorest section of the population, because the insistence on a regular payment or eviction deterred those who preferred to keep moving rather than to pay rent.

It was the problem of the poorest section of the population that troubled Glasgow also, but the issue became caught up in a general reaction against municipalization which appeared in 1898 in the form of the Citizens' Union, a body that included such a former enthusiast for municipal enterprise as William Smart, professor of political economy at Glasgow. By 1901 the Citizens' Union had succeeded in ousting most of the Labour 'Stalwarts' from the Corporation. It was not, argued Smart and others, the task of the Corporation to provide houses for the 'decent' poor, but for 'the improvident and destructive, but not criminal class':

> The construction of such houses should be based on the well-known destructive habits of this class. They should be houses which the tenants cannot spoil – four bare walls, say, of concrete, with an indestructible set in fire place, and an indestructible bed-frame. So far as possible, no wood to hack or burn; no plaster to fall down; no paper to tear away; no fittings to carry off by the light of the moon; well-lit,

67. A.S. Wohl, *The Eternal Slum* (1977), p. 258.
68. *S.C. on Municipal Trading*, Q.2267.

that there be no concealment of evil-doing; with, of course, a sufficency of air-space and sanitary appliances.[69]

In fact the City Improvement Trust had not, apart from the model lodging houses, concerned itself with the poorest. Under the new Improvement Act of 1897 the Corporation had successfully petitioned the Secretary of State to be relieved of the duty of making provision for the displaced, on the ground that there was ample existing accommodation in the immediate neighbourhood. A few £5 single apartment and £8 room and kitchens were provided, but most were for those earning 22s to 26s per week and were expected to go mainly to municipal employees at the new gasworks.

About the same time, the chief sanitary inspector launched a campaign to draw attention to housing conditions and asked that 2,000 small workmen's houses be provided by the Corporation so that he might be in a position to enforce the city's by-laws on overcrowding.[70] It was to start on this project that the Corporation proposed to borrow £750,000 for the provision of workmen's houses. The Provost Samuel Chisholm was the prime mover and it was on Chisholm that the hostility to municipal house-building focused. He had already antagonized the 'Trade' by blocking attempts to have public houses on municipal property. He had antagonized powerful vested interests by his campaign for a municipal telephone system in competition with the National Telephone Company. Now he took on the Glasgow Landlords' Association. At the election of November 1902 Chisholm was unseated, and this was taken by the loan commissioners as a sign that the citizens of Glasgow were not in favour of the municipality building workmen's houses and the loan granted was only £150,000, to finish schemes in hand.[71]

The Scottish municipalities laboured under a particular disability when it came to municipal housing. By amendments to the 1890 Act, local authorities in England had obtained the power to go outside the borough boundaries for the purchase of land for municipal house-building and, secondly, had succeeded in getting the time for repayment of loans extended to eighty years (though, in practice, the LGB allowed eighty years on money spent on land, but no more than sixty years for repayment of other expenditure). These amendments did not apply in Scotland and, under Scots Law, the maximum period of repayment was thirty years, which, of course, added substantially to the price.[72]

69. William Smart, *The Housing Problem and the Municipality* (Glasgow 1902) p. 24.
70. Mabel Atkinson, *Local Government in Scotland* (Edinburgh 1904), p. 193.
71. *Forward*, 20 Oct. 1906.
72. *Forward*, 15 June 1907.

There were a variety of other approaches to particular housing problems in different localities. Stafford seems to have been one of the few boroughs that decided to use the rates to keep down the rent of any house they built to 4s per week, while Sheffield Town Council attempted some social engineering by reputedly choosing the site of their workmen's dwellings to 'gie a turn', as one councillor put it, to the wealthy residents of Ranmoor.[73]

Housing was obviously an area of particular working-class interest and, like other trades councils, Glasgow Trades Council campaigned for municipal housing. They wanted the Town Council 'to erect people's dwellings beyond the city boundaries, to be let at such rentals as will meet the cost of erection and maintenance' and organized various demonstrations and conferences on the issue, which resulted in the formation of a Housing Reform Council for the West of Scotland.[74] It failed to convince the electors.

Other labour demands in Glasgow did not change much in the years before 1914. There was still the concentration on the condition of municipal employees with the call for a forty-eight-hour week. Some wanted to ensure that gas-workers would have security of employment and not be faced with dismissal in the summer months. This was in line with Shaw's argument in *The Commonsense of Municipal Trading* (1908) when he assumed that the ratepayer had a responsibility for his labourers 'from the cradle to the grave'.[75] Tom Drife of the ILP took a similar position in a series of articles in *Forward*. Municipal socialism could help 'abolish poverty within the city'. It would help steady the labour market. Men would not be dismissed in times of bad trade, wages would not be reduced in municipal enterprises. 'This would ensure a steady demand for goods of all kind. And this, again, would almost abolish depression.' Men would no longer have to 'struggle for a living'. 'Men will cease to expend all their energies in the getting of bread. They will strive to excel in other ways.'[76] From time to time municipalizing the drink traffic, taxing land values, acquiring and working coal mines to supply coal to householders and municipal banks came to the fore, but to little effect.

A disillusion and disenchantment appears to have affected Glasgow municipal life after 1902. It proved extremely difficult to stir any enthusiasm for further municipalization. As an editorial in *Forward* admitted in 1908, once the initial éclat derived from the municipalization of the tramways had run its course, there was not

---

73. *Times*, 21 Oct. 1902.
74. Glasgow Trades Council, *Annual Reports* 1899–1900, 1900–01; *Glasgow Herald*, 12 March 1900, 22 Sept. 1902.
75. G.B. Shaw, *The Commonsense of Municipal Trading* (1908), p. 20.
76. *Forward*, 28 Aug., 18 Sept., 25 Sept. 1909.

much left to sustain it. In spite of all the talk of municipalization, little had emerged since the 1890s and, therefore, a reaction had set in.[77] This period, 1907–08, coinciding as it did with the victory of the Moderates in London, marked a turning point in attitudes to municipal socialism, with a growing doubt about its efficacy. As the *Forward* editorial went on: 'Our municipalities do not have the power of German, French and Italian municipalities of promoting many schemes for the public advantage on their own initiative.' Municipal development had outrun national development and, therefore, it was necessary to win more power in Parliament.

Various factors had led to this conclusion. The blocking of the Corporation's house-building schemes in 1902 by the refusal to grant a provisional order was a major setback. The failure of the Education (Provision of Meals) Act to apply to Scotland meant the subsequent blocking of municipal effort in that direction. Then there were doubts about the success of what was already municipalized. There were questions even about the much-lauded tramways. Wages on them did not compare favourably with other areas. There were too many officials, 'all of them better treated in every way than the rank and file', and loss of the 'opportunities for making a bit on the side that there had been under the old regime'.[78] Attempts to raise the minimum wage of municipal employees to 25s were defeated.[79] The varieties of treatment under the Unemployed Workmen's Act during the distress of 1907–08 had revealed how inadequate local effort could be and highlighted the need for more national aid for the unemployed.[80]

The final blow, as far as Glasgow was concerned, came at the end of 1908 when the proposal was put forward by the Lord Provost, backed by the *Glasgow Herald*, that the profits of municipal enterprises should go to relieve the burden of the rates. This of course had been normal practice south of the border, and some of the Glasgow ratepayers had no doubt looked enviously at places like Bolton, Burnley, Leicester, Nottingham, Salford and others where 1s in the pound was saved from the tramway and gas profits. But the tradition in Scotland had always been that there should be no relief of the rates.

The threat to the principle of low prices that this entailed helped rouse some defence. Tom Drife's articles were part of this, others wrote on the need for new projects like municipal coal and municipal bread.[81] George Barnes contributed an article on 'Where Germany

---

77. Ibid., 14 Nov. 1908.
78. Ibid., 16 March 1907.
79. Ibid., 29 June 1907.
80. Glasgow T.C., *Annual Report 1908–9*.
81. *Forward* 9, 23 April 1910.

Wins' in which he enthused on the familiar theme of the strength and independence of German local government, particularly on the powers of town planning.[82] However, the disenchantment continued. Joseph Burgess wrote of the 'inherent capitalism' of the Glasgow Corporation. By reducing rates the Corporation had shown themselves to be no different from English authorities, and even the earlier policy was suspect:

> The real reason why Glasgow Capitalists have not followed the example of their English brethren is to be found in the different conditions affecting ratepayers in the respective countries. In England, virtually all working class rates are compounded. In Scotland, it is only in the case of £5 rentals that rates are compounded. In England all rates fall directly on the owners. In Scotland, some rates are paid by the owner, some by the occupier, and some are shared between occupiers and owners.

In England, therefore, the concern of the *rentier* and capitalist was to reduce rates. In Scotland the policy was full rates, but cheap services, from which the big customer gained most.[83]

Sacred cows were toppled in Burgess's scathing indictment. The Labour Bureau was 'never anything more than a servants' registry'; the milk depot set up in 1904 was 'simply a department of the Medical Officer's Department'.

> The tramways undertaking is the only instance of Glasgow municipalization to which the capitalistic majority of the Town Council was opposed on principle, and what really turned the edge of their opposition was not, as the Labour Party assumed, the force of public opinion aroused by the agitation in the early 'nineties, but the gradual perception that a municipal tramway service could be turned to capitalistic account.[84]

Yet, he had little to offer in the way of an alternative. A municipal works department was still he felt the only means 'pending the collapse of Capitalism to remove large bodies of workers from the sphere of competition'. A municipal note issue and a municipal bank were the only ways to free municipal enterprises from the tutelage of being mortgaged to capitalism.

The tramwaymen's strike for a forty-eight-hour week in August 1911 was yet another blow to the image of Glasgow's municipal enterprise, causing a damage which all the self-publicity of Lord Provosts could not repair. Municipal socialism became less significant

82. Ibid., 30 July 1910.
83. Ibid., 8 Oct. 1910.
84. Ibid., 15 Oct. 1910.

in the thinking of groups such as the ILP. Only central legislation could make a fundamental difference and it was on this that future concentration was to be. Keir Hardie did seek to give some encouragement with his Local Authorities (Enabling) Bill of 1910, which would have allowed municipalities to embark on trading without Government departments being able to put obstacles in their way. Two or more councils were to be permitted to combine 'to take over coal mines or wheat fields', and 'to supply themselves with the things they require'. The surpluses from such trading were to go into a common-good fund for unspecified social projects. There was still much of a vague faith that 'the city which served its citizens with bread, water, houses, clothing, and fuel would be already in a fair way to solving many of the most ghastly problems of our modern civilization'.[85] It was the common-good fund that, in Glasgow, was likely to have an annual income of £200,000–300,000 from 1915, once the tramway debts had been paid off, which John Wheatley suggested, in 1913, should be the means of financing a programme of house-building. Wheatley's scheme was for 10,000 four-roomed cottages to be rented at £8 a year.[86] It came to nothing, and Wheatley too was to come to see that some measure of national intervention was to be essential.

Few of those who were behind the extension of municipal ownership up to 1914 saw the process as a move towards municipal socialism. It was the opponents of such developments who sought to block them by branding them as socialist. The motivation for the take-over of gasworks, water-works, and tramways generally came from the experience of years of inefficiency of private enterprise. The local authority, it was believed, would maintain more acceptable standards. Obviously, an element of civic pride was also a factor and comparisons with other towns could be the means of stimulating municipal enterprise. Rarely was there any wider vision of the municipality as the vehicle of social change. Birmingham in the early 1870s was an exception, but few other towns linked municipal ownership and improvement schemes, and the attraction of low rates tended to be too great. Municipal hospitals, municipal baths and wash-houses were obvious extensions of the public health role that local authorities had, with varying degrees of enthusiasm, taken up since at least the 1840s. The emphasis in Scotland on cheap services rather than low rates did mean that such services were available to a wider section of the population than elsewhere, but it is difficult to assess how much effect this had. Suggestions for municipal bakeries and municipal workshops made only slight

85. J. Keir Hardie, *The Common Good. An Essay in Municipal Government* (Manchester n.d.) pp. 6–8.
86. John Wheatley, *Eight-Pound Cottages for Glasgow Citizens* (Glasgow 1913).

progress. When there were not sound arguments in terms of business efficiency local authorities were not particularly enthusiastic about extending their role.

The working class had learned to be suspicious of authorities run by shopkeepers and businessmen. They had no reason to believe that the municipality would necessarily be a better employer than the private company. On the other hand, the working-class electorate could exert some pressure on the town council to improve conditions. It was, however, Liberals and Progressives, not the working class, that had any real faith that municipal enterprise could be a kind of socialism. It seemed often to stem from an optimism that social problems could be solved relatively easily and cheaply by municipal activities, with the minimum interference with individual rights. The working-class organizations had, on the whole, a further grasp of the immensity of the social problems and the need for a perspective that went beyond the town hall.

280

Chapter 10

THE POLICEMAN AS DOMESTIC MISSIONARY: URBAN DISCIPLINE AND POPULAR CULTURE IN NORTHERN ENGLAND, 1850–80

Robert D. Storch

[from *Journal of Social History*, **9** (1976): 481–509][1]

The creation of the 'new' disciplined police forces of the 1830s and 1840s was firmly identified with the needs of the growing towns. These forces are often discussed in the context of improvement and administrative reform. Storch places emphasis on the gradual assertion of control over the day-to-day activities of working people, such as drinking, trading and gambling. This article was written at a time when the concept of 'social control' and a concern for class relationships were central to historians' analytical concerns. Storch showed that class bargaining was more characteristic of relationships than 'control', for he identified considerable independence and resistance on the part of working people. The urban place was the stage for a series of interlocking endeavours by middle-class élites to influence popular culture. The ratepayer-elected governments were one base for these activities, but such actions were not limited to urban environments and spread by way of the county police forces to small towns and rural areas.

Historians of the police, public order, and the criminal law have understandably concentrated on the role of the police in the repression of crime, public disorder, and popular political movements or have studied the police from the point of view of social ad-

---

1. An earlier version of this article was presented at the Shelby Cullom Davis Center, Princeton University, in January 1975. The criticisms of the Davis seminar were invaluable, especially those of Professor Wilbur Miller. The author also wishes to thank Professors Stephen Haliczer and Richard Price of Northern Illinois University and Professor David Stafford of the University of Victoria, British Columbia, whose critical instincts he has often relied upon.

281

ministration.[2] The police had a broader mission in the nineteenth century, however – to act as an all-purpose lever of urban discipline. The imposition of the police brought the arm of municipal and state authority directly to bear upon key institutions of daily life in working-class neighborhoods, touching off a running battle with local custom and popular culture which lasted at least until the end of the century. Riots and strikes are by definition ephemeral episodes, but the monitoring and control of the streets, pubs, racecourses, wakes, and popular fêtes was a daily function of the 'new police'. It was in some part on this terrain that the quality of police–community relations in the second half of the nineteenth century was determined. In northern industrial towns of England these police functions must be viewed as a direct complement to the attempts of urban middle-class elites – by means of sabbath, educational, temperance, and recreational reform[3] – to mold a labouring class amenable to new disciplines of both work and leisure. The other side of the coin of middle-class voluntaristic moral and social reform (even when sheathed) was the policeman's truncheon. In this respect the policeman was perhaps every bit as important a 'domestic missionary' as the earnest and often sympathetic men high-minded Unitarians dispatched into darkest Leeds or Manchester in the 1830s and 1840s.

Engels observed that 'every week in Manchester policemen are beaten',[4] a fact of Victorian social life by no means restricted

---

2. J.M. Hart, 'Reform of the Borough Police 1835–1856', *English Historical Review* 70 (1955); F.C. Mather, *Public Order in the Age of the Chartists* (London, 1959); E.C. Midwinter, *Social Administration in Lancashire 1830–1860* (Manchester, 1969) and *Law and Order in Early Victorian Lancashire*, Borthwick Institute Paper No. 34 (York, 1968); H. Parris, 'The Home Office and the Provincial Police', *Public Law* 6 (1961); L. Radzinowicz, *A History of the English Criminal Law* 4 (London, 1968); C. Reith, *The British Police and the Democratic Ideal* (London, 1943); and *A New Study of Police History* (London, 1956); J.J. Tobias, *Crime and Industrial Society in the 19th Century* (London, 1967).
3. E.P. Thompson, 'Time, Work Discipline and Industrial Capitalism', *Past and Present* 38 (1967); B. Harrison, 'Religion and Recreation in Nineteenth Century England', *Past and Present* 38 (1967) and *Drink and the Victorians* (London, 1971); B. Harrison and B. Trinder, *Drink and Sobriety in an Early Victorian Town: Banbury 1830–1860*, *English Historical Review* Supplement No. 4 (London, 1969); B. Harrison, 'Animals and the State in Nineteenth Century England', *English Historical Review* 87 (1973); R. Johnson, 'Educational Policy and Social Control in Early Victorian England', *Past and Present* 49 (1970); R. Price, 'The Working Men's Club Movement', *Victorian Studies* 15 (1971); R. D. Storch, 'Middle Class Moral Reform Movements and the Problem of Working Class Leisure' (Unpublished paper presented to Edinburgh University Symposium on 'Aspects of Class Relations in 19th-Century Britain', May 1967).
4. F. Engels, 'The Condition of the Working Class in England', in *Marx and Engels on Britain*, 2nd. edition (Moscow, 1964), p. 263.

to either Manchester or to the 1840s. Why were they beaten? What accounts for the suspicion and enmity the police seemed to engender? In what ways did they represent an unwelcome intrusion in working-class neighborhoods? One need not go far to discover numerous instances of police–community conflict in connection with strikes or great public disturbances.[5] Far from being sporadic, however, conflict was endemic and chronic, and it stemmed from the interventions of the police in the daily lives and recreational activities of the working classes, from their insertion into the heart of the working-class neighborhood.

At the time of their introduction in England fear of a modern, efficient police had several roots: the traditional English apprehension of a standing army, with which the police were initially identified in many quarters, fear of administrative centralization, fear of the political uses to which they might be put,[6] objections to their cost,[7] and fear of their being used as an auxiliary to the new Poor Law.[8] However, fully to assess the impact of the police after the period in which they were installed, one must go beyond these factors to an examination of their role and activities on the city streets and in those aspects of their mission which lay beyond the narrow repression of serious crime.

Some initial insight is gained when one gauges the effect of the 'new police' upon unpoliced or insufficiently policed communities. Upon their introduction in the West Riding of Yorkshire in 1857, county police instantly made themselves obnoxious by imposing a more efficient supervision of pubs and beerhouses. Their firm insistence that pubs close during hours of divine service on Sunday

---

5. For example, the *Leeds Mercury*, 20 December 1859, reported the severe beating of a West Riding policeman near Barnsley. The latter had been assigned the unenviable task of escorting blacklegs to the Wharncliffe–Silkstone colliery; Cf. for the Black Country, D. Phillips, 'Riots and Public Order in the Black Country, 1835–1860', in J. Stevenson and R. Quinault, eds., *Popular Protest and Public Order* (London, 1974), p. 161; R. Roberts, *The Classic Slum. Salford Life in the First Quarter of the Century* (Manchester, 1971), p. 71; H. Hendrick, 'The Leeds Gas Strike 1890', *Thoresby Society Miscellany* 16 Part I (1974), p. 87. For a much later period see N. Branson and M. Heinemann, *Britain in the Nineteen Thirties* (London, 1971), pp. 95–6, 105, 108; and W. Gallacher, *The Rolling of the Thunder* (London, 1947), pp. 117–19, 130–1.
6. E.P. Thompson, *The Making of the English Working Class* (London, 1963), p. 82; Radzinowicz, *English Criminal Law*, pp. 261–6; *Poor Man's Guardian*, 5 November 1831; *Destructive and Poor Man's Conservative*, 2 November 1833.
7. E.C. Midwinter, *Social Administration in Lancashire*, pp. 160–1; I. Prothero, 'Chartism in London', *Past and Present* 44 (1969); *Northern Star*, 12 September 1840; *Northern Star*, February 20, 1841; *Lancaster Gazette*, 1 August 1840.
8. Radzinowicz, *English Criminal Law*, p. 78; *Report From His Majesty's Commissioners For Inquiring Into The Poor Laws*, Parliamentary Papers 1834 (44) XXVIII. Reports of Assistant Commissioners, Appendix A, pp. 197, 331; *Northern Star*, 16 March 1839.

created great bitterness among working men in the out-townships of Leeds and Huddersfield. At West Ardsley the police cracked down on footracing; at Wibsey near Bradford on cockfighting; and near Wakefield on Middlestown feast, a hitherto unpoliced affair.[9] In the wake of these novel interventions assaults on the West Riding police began: at Deighton and Lindley near Huddersfield; at Wibsey, Clayton Heights, and Halifax.[10] The appearance of the police at Middlestown feast resulted in a massive confrontation with local colliers and a considerable riot. Another random example: at Skelmanthorpe near Barnsley two constables were on duty at 1.30 a.m. when suddenly a large crowd materialized and attacked them with stones.[11]

The very look of the new police seemed to give offense. They were described near Coventry in 1840 as 'well clothed and shod, with a pair of white glove . . . and a great coat for bad weather. They go strutting about . . . armed with a bludgeon . . . with 18s per week . . . while the labourer toils from morning till night for 10s.'[12] The police were at first resented in working-class districts because they were felt to be parasites. A Halifax publican remarked that 'they were too idle to work, and such, as he had to keep them'.[13] Many of the terms used to describe the police in the popular press – 'blue plagues', 'blue drones', 'blue idlers', 'blue locusts' – were synonyms for persons who do not really work for a living. Most obnoxious to the policed perhaps was the imposition of the 'move-on system'. The practice of breaking up congregations of men on the streets and in front of pubs was considered novel and humiliating. Part of the background of a near anti-police riot at Ashton Under Lyne in May 1839 was to be found in working-class outrage at being moved on;[14] similarly, it fed directly into the massive Colne anti-police riots of the spring/summer of 1840,[15] and into a large disturbance at Lees during the cotton famine.[16] The coming of the police produced what was perceived as an attack upon a traditionally sanctioned freedom

9. *Leeds Mercury*, 20, 24 January, 10 February, 20 June 1857; *Leeds Times*, 27 December 1856, 6 June 1857; cf. Philips, 'Riots and Public Order', p. 167.
10. *Leeds Mercury*, 10 March, 2 May, 6 June, 20 June, 2 July 1857.
11. *Leeds Mercury*, 13 June, 1857. Perhaps the provocation was given in the previous weeks.
12. *Northern Star*, 6 June 1840.
13. *Leeds Mercury*, 18 June 1857. The theme of the 'blue locust' or 'idle drone' was still alive in the 1880s; cf. F. Thompson, *Lark Rise to Candleford* (Oxford, 1954), p. 554.
14. *Northern Star*, 18 May 1839.
15. R.D. Storch, 'The Plague of Blue Locusts: Police Reform and Popular Resistance in Northern England, 1840–1857', *International Review of Social History* 20 (1975): 1: pp. 79–83.
16. *Ibid.*, pp. 87–8.

– freedom of assembly in the streets – and a keenly felt sense of humiliation. Popular reaction to the policeman's refrain, 'move on there!'[17] must be considered in assessing the sources of working-class resentment and resistance.

The degree to which the police were considered a daily pest no doubt varied from group to group and trade to trade, but between the police and street traders open warfare was the usual condition. Among these elements one finds a concern with the police which understandably bordered upon obsession. 'Can you wonder at it sir', a coster told Henry Mayhew, 'that I hate the police? They drive us about, we must move on, we can't stand here, and we can't pitch there.'[18] In street trades the consciousness of being hounded was reflected in political feelings. Mayhew's coster-Chartists conceived of the struggle for the People's Charter in terms of an Armageddon-like war between them and the police, and were unable to understand why they were exhorted to moral force 'when they might as well fight it out with the police at once'.[19] The first appearance of county police in the Rochdale area was marked by increased pressure on pedlars, match-sellers, and street vendors of all types.[20] There can be little doubt that the police were viewed with hostility and suspicion by such persons and by the unskilled generally throughout the last half of the nineteenth century. Evidence is relatively scarce regarding the attitudes of skilled workers. Thomas Wright, describing the lives of skilled London artisans in the mid-1860s, referred specifically to the elaborate precautions which had to be taken to evade police surveillance while drinking during hours of divine service on Sunday.[21] Being a skilled worker did not necessarily purchase immunity from the pressure of surveillance it seems, and this was perhaps reflected in these workers' attitudes toward the police.

The initiatives of the police authorities in these areas of course cannot be viewed apart from the attitudes, prejudices, and momentary reformist enthusiasms of the municipalities, magistrates, and local élites who employed them. This was especially the case outside

17. The 'move-on system' was duly noted in the broadside literature. See 'Manchester's An Altered Town', in Charles Hindley ed., *Curiosities of Street Literature* (London, 1871), no pagination; J. Lawson, *Letters to the Young on Progress in Pudsey* (Stanningley, 1887), p. 133.
18. H. Mayhew, *London Labour and the London Poor* vol. 1 (London, 1851), p. 22. On Guy Fawkes Day 1876 in London the costers of Somers Town and Holborn came out with giant effigies of those police inspectors who strictly enforced the Sunday Observance Acts (*Annual Register*, 1876).
19. Mayhew, *London Labour*, p. 16.
20. *Northern Star*, 6 June 1840. For France cf. R. Cobb, *The Police and the People* (Oxford, 1970), passim.
21. T. Wright, 'A Journeyman Engineer,' *Some Habits and Customs of the Working Classes* (London, 1867), pp. 225–26.

of London where the police were much less independent of local control than in the metropolis. For this reason police actions must be considered as forming the cutting edge of a wider and larger effort in northern industrial towns to impose new standards of urban discipline. It was the boroughs after all who charged the police with the monitoring and suppression of popular activities and recreations considered conducive to immorality, disorder, or crime; it was the police who had to discharge that mandate as best they could or at least convince those to whom they were responsible that they were doing so. In 1843 the Manchester council formally prohibited dogfighting, cockfighting, and bull- and badger-baiting;[22] instructions to the new Leeds police by the watch committee included specific directives to suppress cruelty to animals.[23] In February 1836, the Leeds council requested the mayor to direct the police to give information 'as shall lead to the conviction of all . . . persons as shall continue to prophane the Lord's day',[24] to pay particular attention to drinking places on Saturday nights, to strictly enforce proper closing times, and to 'observe those who resort to the public house or use sports in time of divine service'.[25] A series of local acts over the next three decades closed chinks in the law which inhibited the functioning of the police in these areas: the Leeds Improvement Act of 1842 gave them power to enter unlicensed theaters and arrest those within, to prosecute publicans who managed houses where cocks, dogs, or other animals were fought, and to fine hawkers of indecent songs or ballads and those who performed them in the streets; and the Improvement Act of 1866 brought music and dancing saloons attached to public houses under much closer control and supervision.

In Bradford before police reform a parish vestry committee reported in December 1831 that 'moral and municipal discipline is on the decline . . . and without an entire reform in the police . . . it may become questionable whether even property itself will not become deteriorated'.[26] Complaints appeared frequently in the press lamenting the large numbers of 'men and women [reeling] about the streets . . . but no policeman to take them into custody'.[27] Fair days were nightmares for respectable townsmen when disorder and

22. A. Redford, *The History of Local Government in Manchester*, vol. 3 (London, 1940), p. 212.
23. Manuscript Minutes of Leeds Watch Committee, 22 April 1836.
24. Manuscript Minutes of Leeds Town Council, vol. 4, 5 February 1836.
25. *Ibid.*, 25 August 1836; *Yorkshire Evening Post*, 3 June 1936.
26. G. H. Smith, 'The Law Enforcement Agencies in Bradford in the Early Nineteenth Century' (Unpublished paper, part 5, pp. 5–6); W. Cudworth, *Historical Notes on the Bradford Corporation* (Bradford, 1882), pp. 68–69.
27. *Bradford Observer*, 9 December 1836.

popular revelry ran unchecked. The *Bradford Observer* reported in 1845 that on the last fair day 'the town was left absolutely without any police whatever', the entire force of constables having been off attending Quarter Session at Wakefield.[28] By contrast at Leeds, at the first fair held after the new borough police came into operation, the watch committee assigned a detachment of *extra* police to monitor it.[29]

It must not be supposed that this municipal assault upon traditional working-class leisure activities met with either immediate or, for that matter, even long-term success. It was one thing to direct the police to monitor assemblies in the streets, drinking places, feasts, and fairs, or to suppress brutal sports or gambling; it was another to succeed at the task. Huddersfield at mid-century provides an interesting case study of the results of unusually intensive police attacks. Superintendent Tom Heaton, heading a group of semi-reformed parish constables, made a strenuous effort not only to monitor and control but to smash the locales of working-class recreational life by direct intervention at every opportunity. The 'Huddersfield Crusade', as one Leeds newspaper called it, revealed the limits of this type of program of indiscriminate intervention. During its course an average of four to five publicans a week were prosecuted for permitting Sunday drinking, gambling, or illegal sports.[30] Heaton was able to sustain what amounted to a perpetual beerhouse sweep by providing his constables with shilling witness fees and a percentage of the fines paid on conviction. Heaton ransacked the statutes for obsolete, disused laws to enforce, attempting for example to obtain the conviction of three men for watching a cricket game on Sunday and not attending church when bidden – though here the magistrates refused to convict.[31] He brought charges against pubs which, following local custom, ignored the usual closing hours on the Feast Sunday. The magistrates convicted in this case. Heaton was an avid reader of *Sporting Life*, by means of which he kept himself abreast of all projected local activities, using this intelligence to break up numerous prizefights and other events in the area.[32] He cracked down on the widespread practice of holding sweeps or St Leger clubs in the pubs. In short, he made himself a neighborhood pest. But what concrete results did the 'Huddersfield Crusade' produce in the end? Illegal Sunday drinking did not diminish; when the new West Riding police took over in 1857 they found the offense very

28. *Ibid.*, 6 March 1845.
29. Manuscript Minutes of Leeds Watch Committee, 22 July 1836.
30. See *Leeds Times*, 5 August 1848, for a typical week's proceedings at Huddersfield during this period.
31. *Ibid.*, 28 April 1849.
32. *Ibid.*, 1 February 1851.

widespread.[33] Cockfighting, dogfighting, and gambling in the pubs and lanes probably diminished in the long run but were still reported with great frequency by the West Riding police, who launched their own crusade in the months immediately following their installation.

Quite generally, working-class recreational locales proved much less amenable to change by any means – whether through the instrumentality of educational, temperance, or sabbatarian reform movements or the policeman's truncheon – than middle-class élites of northern towns had originally hoped. The characteristic working-class response to both approaches to moral reform was evasion or resistance rather than immediate capitulation. It could not have been otherwise, for the police were unleashed upon many of the most vital popular habits and institutions – repulsive, immoral, harmful, or frightening though they may have appeared to others. In the discharge of their 'domestic mission', then, the police were placed at the point of a larger attempt to transform popular culture. Let us examine this further.

Police authorities themselves often drew a direct parallel between popular leisure and crime and believed a close surveillance of key neighborhood recreation centers was essential to both the preservation of good order and the prevention of crime. 'I have no doubt', wrote a Leeds Chief Constable,

> that an extended closing of public houses on Sunday would lead to the promotion of good order. . . . I should not object to see *Beer Houses* entirely closed on that day as [they] harbour the lowest class of company . . . dog fanciers and the race running fraternity. . . . I am sure that so long as the working classes imbibe the . . . decoctions of Beer sellers there will not only be drunkenness and poverty but crimes of open violence amongst us.[34]

For the police as well as for many Victorian moral reformers the public house was bad and the beershop infinitely worse. Chief Constable Wetherell of Leeds was positive that 'so long as the present system of licensing continues many of them will remain . . . pests of society and the resort of dogfighters and racers, prizefighters and others taking part in demoralizing games'.[35] The monitoring of working-class drinking places and the suppression of many of the activities attached to them was taken quite seriously by the police; even a cursory examination of raw police records

33. *Leeds Mercury*, 10 February 1857.
34. Chief Constable's Manuscript Letter Book (Leeds Police Headquarters). Letter to Edward Baines, April 10, 1868; *Borough of Leeds. Report of the Efficiency of the Police Force* . . . (Leeds, 1869), pp. 4–5, 18.
35. Chief Constable's Manuscript Letter Book. Letter to Leeds Watch Committee, 17 December 1868.

shows an enormous number of man-hours expended on public-house surveillance as well as a great concern with petty gambling in the streets by juveniles.[36] Leeds chief constables saw themselves as natural allies of the temperance movement, with whose local leaders they corresponded,[37] and the SPCA Wetherell actively encouraged the monitoring of popular amusements on Woodhouse Moor by the local SPCA agent and even made him a constable 'to give him additional support'.[38]

It must not be supposed, however, that the locales of working-class recreational life were under direct assault all the time; to attack all the activities attached to the pub would have placed absurd demands upon the resources of the police. Especially in the largest cities the police authorities quickly became quite realistic about the chances of actually suppressing public-house gambling, brutal sports, and illegal drinking. Campaigns of overt repression – as distinguished from normal surveillance – were often employed when the police were under pressure from the magistrates or from powerful individuals or groups concerned for the moment about some specific abuse, or immediately after a significant change in the law. At such times there might be a brief but intense flurry of beerhouse sweeps – the week or two before the annual Brewster Sessions was a favorite time – prostitute round-ups, penny-gaff closings, and charges of permitting gambling or illegal sports. Local policy of course varied, but in general the police were almost never either willing or able to follow strict municipal rules in these matters; Heaton's efforts in Huddersfield were thus atypical.

Sir Richard Mayne, one of the commissioners of the Metropolitan Police, perfectly illustrates the more common posture. Mayne professed that ideally all places of public entertainment should be duly licensed and under police control so that cockfights, dogfights, and so forth could be observed and stopped if necessary. In fact, however, as far as music halls and dancing saloons were concerned, the duties of the police were primarily to see that licenses of some sort were possessed and order preserved. Even if the material presented were immoral Mayne did not think the police 'would consider it their duty to notice it' unless 'it was very grossly immoral'. Nor would he strike against the penny gaffs: 'Many persons consider them . . . objectionable inasmuch as they induce boys and girls to steal the entrance money; if that be so that is beyond the knowledge of

---

36. Manuscript Occurrence Books (1869–1884), Headingly and Beeston Police Stations (Leeds Police Headquarters), passim; cf. Roberts, *Classic Slum*, p. 129.
37. Chief Constable's Manuscript Letter Book. Letter to W. Hind Smith, 23 January 1872.
38. *Ibid.*, Letter to Secretary of SPCA, undated but written in October 1868.

the police.' He refused to engage the time of his men in attempts to suppress dancing in pubs licensed only for music: At 'many of these places . . . they dance. . . . The women are not very correctly dressed, but I think it would be oversqueamish looking at the class of persons who frequent these places to find fault with them.'[39] Even if known prostitutes were present he would not necessarily press for removal of a license if their behavior were 'decorous'. Mayne sometimes felt obliged to proceed against houses putting on unlicensed dramatic entertainments. In 1838 the Metropolitan Police carried out an extensive penny-gaff sweep in the East End,[40] and again in 1859 a number of them were raided and suppressed.[41] But where, asked Mayne, does one draw the line? Some pubs had a piano and singing 'which is very near being a private entertainment', and in most cases he refused to interfere.[42] Out of sheer realism, Mayne pointed out that quashing the penny gaffs paid no permanent dividends; many would quickly reopen, offering a crude pantomime or dumb show in order to remain within the strict letter of the law. Mayne acquired a pragmatic awareness of the resiliency of these popular institutions and became quite hesitant to dissipate the energies of his force in constant open warfare with them. Licensing and decorum became the keynotes of Richard Mayne's bureaucratic style of policing in these areas.

Major J.J. Grieg, the Chief Constable of Liverpool in the mid-1860s, adopted a similar course regarding public houses sponsoring music and dancing. He was unsure whether he even possessed the legal authority to attack them, but in any case the problem was simply too overwhelming: 'The tonnage of Liverpool brings in so many sailors, those dancing houses are principally where the sailors' boarding houses are; they go there, and you cannot find anything that will carry a conviction.'[43] In other towns, however, where these abuses were apparently less highly concentrated the police might feel emboldened to adopt a much more repressive stance. In the mid-1860s, Sheffield seemed to have had only two dancing rooms attached to pubs. Both were shut down by the police, not on the grounds that unlicensed dancing was carried on – this was perfectly legal outside of London – but because they harbored prostitutes.[44] At

39. *House of Commons Select Committee on Theatrical Licenses and Regulations*, Parliamentary Papers 1866 (373) XVI.1. Evidence Sir R. Mayne, qq. 969–1144.
40. James Grant, *Sketches in London* (London, 1840), p. 192.
41. Mayhew, *London Labour*, pp. 42–43; G. Godwin, *Town Swamps and Social Bridges* (London, 1859), p. 95.
42. *House of Commons Select Committee on Theatrical Licenses*, Evidence Sir R. Mayne, q. 991.
43. *Ibid.*, Evidence J.J. Grieg, qq. 6698–99, 7012.
44. *Ibid.*, Evidence J. Jackson, q. 7236.

Bolton the magistrates tried to drive the popular singing and dancing saloons out of business in the early 1850s by forbidding entrance to those under eighteen. No doubt both they and the police knew that dancing saloons were important components of the working-class marriage market and vital to courting, so that excluding those under eighteen was tantamount to a death sentence on these places. They were also aware that they had no real legal power to enforce this stricture, but threatened publicans with redoubled police surveillance if they refused to comply.[45]

In the early 1850s Leeds police authorities professed themselves reluctant to move against known rendezvous of prostitutes, because, as they put it, 'the sons and daughters of vice *would* find a resting place [in] respectable neighbourhoods where their proximity would be deeply deplored'.[46] Seventeen years later the Leeds police were willing to pursue a more active course under a new chief constable, but found themselves hampered by the courts, which had ruled that evidence had to be shown that prostitutes had assembled to practice their trade and not merely to eat or drink.[47] This question in fact created a great deal of confusion among both police and magistrates. At Preston the police thought that they were authorized to forbid prostitutes from sitting in beershops, and the local magistrates convicted; at Blackburn at the same time the magistrates were unwilling to convict and the police stopped intervening.[48] In this matter an overall policy of vacillation and hesitation resulted, varying during the tenure of one chief constable and perhaps changing entirely during the administration of the next. This particular problem was inherently so intractable, whatever changes in administration or law occurred, that no policy could have resulted in significant suppression of the target abuses. In actually making decisions to mobilize police resources for an all-out assault on prostitution and many other lower-class activities, police authorities of necessity had to engage in a cost-effectiveness calculus, based upon disposable manpower, size of the district, and the extent of the pressure being exerted by moral-reform interest groups, magistrates, or watch committees. In large sprawling port cities like Liverpool or London, the policy employed by Sir Richard Mayne was not only calculated to preserve his own sanity, but was really the only one which could have been adopted.

45. *House of Commons Select Committee on Public Houses*, Parliamentary Papers 1852–53 (855) XXXVII.1. Evidence G. Wolstenholme, qq. 4437–43, 4475.
46. *Criminal and Miscellaneous Statistical Returns of the Leeds Police Force for the Year 1852* (Leeds, 1852), p. 4.
47. Chief Constable's Manuscript Letter Book, Letter to G. Tatham, 2 January 1869.
48. *House of Commons Select Committee on Public Houses*, Evidence Rev. J. Clay, q. 6176.

Hence despite some dramatic confrontations, the police carried out their mission as 'domestic missionary' in the largest cities not by pursuing a policy of overt suppression at every opportunity, but rather through the pressure of a constant surveillance of all the key institutions of working-class neighborhood and recreational life. It was no doubt hoped by the police and by those to whom they were responsible that ultimately after-hours drinking, low theaters, brutal sports, public-house gambling, and the like would dwindle under unremitting monitoring; but if they did not it would at least be a gain if a modicum of decorum resulted and a better flow of intelligence as to what was transpiring in the lanes and courts of Leeds or Manchester was secured. It was precisely the pressure of an unceasing surveillance and not the intense but sporadic episodes of active intervention and suppression which ultimately produced the main impact on working-class neighborhood life. The technique was thus well chosen, for it recognized that many popular recreational phenomena were not amenable to quick and easy suppression by any conceivable strategy. The pressure of surveillance cannot be calculated by precisely measuring police manpower per capita or per acre, interesting though it might be and however useful for answering other types of questions. As far as the policed were concerned the impression of being watched or hounded was not directly dependent on the presence of a constable on every streetcorner and at all times. What produced this effect was the knowledge that the police were always near and likely to appear at any time. This it seems was – and still is – the main function of the pressure of surveillance.

This approach of course did not eradicate the target abuses, but drove them into more covert channels. The Huddersfield example examined earlier, had hosts of parallels elsewhere. The dogfights or cockfights, once quite public affairs, were pushed behind the doors of the pub or out into the fields or moors of the surrounding countryside,[49] that is, to locales outside the normal range of the force and/or to times of the day – such as change of shift – when the vigilance of the police might be relaxed. This was duly noted even in the dialect literature:

> *Jack* Well, oud lad, its all up we yer fancy dog-feighting nah; there's a act passed for preventing cruelty to animals. Wot thinks ta abaht that, my buck, eh?
> *Savage* O they shant hinder us, an we'll feit em it spoit o ther teeth; *we can gooa intot woods whoile they're it Chetch.*[50]

49. W. Rose. *Good Neighbours* (New York, 1942), p. 135; J. Batty, *The History of Rothwell* (Rothwell, 1877), p. 227.
50. A. Bywater, *The Sheffield Dialect*, 2nd edition (London, 1854), p. 163. (My emphasis.)

In the mid-1870s James Greenwood was told in a Potteries beer-shop that it had become 'as difficult . . . to "pull off" a dog-fight all right and regular, and without any hole and corner business . . . as it was to bring off a man-fight under the same open conditions.'[51] Nonetheless, Greenwood ascertained that dogfighting had by no means been eliminated in the district; though well hidden, it survived in a very healthy state. Greenwood incidentally got a bit more than he had bargained for during his visit to the Potteries: an opportunity to witness an extremely brutal contest between a man and a dog. A Liverpool observer reported in the mid-1850s that though dogfighting had been driven underground by the 'efforts that have from time to time been made by the police to put an end to this "manly and elevating" British pastime', it continued to employ 'the leisure hours of great numbers of the working population in this as well as other towns. . . . Not a week elapses . . . in which several dogfights do not take place, some more or less openly, many, particularly those involving large sums of money, strictly private.'[52] The same writer provided an excellent account of the evasive tactics engaged in to practice this sport. Before a match they

> talk in the coolest manner of fighting their dogs, but there is one thing you never hear them name publicly, 'the trysting place'. You never hear them state the hour . . . at which the fight will take place. This is learned in a quiet way. . . . In Liverpool the risk that landlords run in holding dogfights . . . is said to be very great, therefore the landlords . . . undertake the risk in turns. . . . The time chosen is generally early in the morning, when the police are going off duty, and we were told that Sunday was a very good time.[53]

The forcing of many of these activities into covert channels perhaps had certain virtues as far as the police were concerned. They might still gain the congratulations of local businessmen or clergy who could be allowed to believe that such abuses had been caused to vanish, a 'fact' which some occasionally even reported to parliament.[54] In reality the police learned that popular recreations had remarkable resiliency – hence the general avoidance of frontal assault – and in addition, that the repression of one barbarous practice often resulted in its replacement by another objectionable one. When the Bradford police moved to shut down the beerhouse-attached brothels in Southgate in 1858, the beerhouse keepers immediately converted them into 'low concert rooms'.[55] The police could then have chosen

51. J. Greenwood, *Low Life Deeps* (London, 1876), p. 19.
52. H. Shimmin, *Liverpool Life* (Liverpool, 1856), pp. 76–77.
53. *Ibid.*, pp. 78–79.
54. D. Philips, 'Riots and Public Order', note 184 on p. 180.
55. Bradford Temperance Society, *Annual Report*, 1858.

to attack the concert rooms, but chose to let matters rest. In London by mid-century, public-house cockfighting and dogfighting had declined to be replaced by the craze – classically described by Mayhew – for rat killing. A few decades later an observer reported rat matches very rare, but described the current mania for the turf and the efforts of the police to stop ready money betting.[56]

From within the pub or beerhouse nexus a wide variety of evasive tactics could be resorted to in order to baffle the authorities and convince them not to spend too much time hunting down illegal or objectionable recreations. The chief constable of Wolverhampton recounted his frustration in trying to deal with the problem of illegal drinking:

> The house door is shut, and to all appearance everything is quiet; at the same time parties are card-playing and drinking . . . in the back premises. . . . You knock at the door. . . . You are kept perhaps five minutes, the cards are removed . . . and the ale is got off the table . . . then you come in and find a very quiet and orderly company, and you are informed that these parties are lodgers.[57]

It was equally difficult to deal with gambling. The courts had ruled that if play was not for money or moneysworth there was no offense. The police discovered many individuals who did not even attempt to remove the cards from sight; the only way to get a case was to plant a plainclothesman. Gambling for moneysworth was especially difficult to prove since what was being wagered for was not put out on the tables.[58] Sometimes the expedients resorted to were outrageously comical: at an Idle (Bradford) pub located near the River Aire patrons drinking during illegal hours were loaded onto a boat and rowed downriver when lookouts reported the police on their way;[59] occasionally a constable could be bribed to overlook irregularities;[60] and near Huddersfield beerhouse keepers figured out the police Sunday visitation schedule and closed for a short time when they were due to appear.[61]

---

56. G.R. Sims, *How the Poor Live and Horrible London* (London, 1889), pp. 79–81. Changes in popular recreational patterns, though often greatly affected by police attitudes, were, we should remember, conditioned as well by changes in cultural fashion.
57. *House of Commons Select Committee on Public Houses*, Evidence G. Hogg, q. 6617.
58. *Ibid.*, qq. 6617–20. In some places the magistrates were not so scrupulous about the law and convicted even when it could not be proven that play was for money or moneysworth. See *Leeds Mercury*, 31 January 1860.
59. *Leeds Mercury*, 1 November 1856.
60. T. Wright, 'A Journeyman Engineer', *Some Habits and Customs of the Working Classes*, pp. 225–26.
61. *Leeds Times*, 1 November 1851.

In the case of activities which had either traditionally been centered on the pub or had been forced to migrate behind its doors, the police operated at something of a disadvantage; with little trouble gambling, illegal drinking, brutal sports, and prizefighting could be shielded from their eyes and often from their knowledge, or gradually transformed into other, still objectionable forms.[62] In the case of the traditional popular fête however, the terms of the situation were reversed, and by the same token surveillance could be shunned in favor of direct action. By definition popular celebrations were public affairs and had to occur in the open. Here the police were both willing and able to intervene actively, confident of achieving a great measure of success. In fact they had to intervene; in this area, both they and the magistrates were politically very much on the spot. Respectable citizens might have heard rumors of dogfights or other such activities, but were rarely in a position to witness them. It was easier to convince such people that the police were vigorous with regard to such matters and that the situation was under control. It was quite otherwise in the case of football through the town, stang-riding, Guy Fawkes celebrations, or other highly-visible lower-class fêtes. Either the police acted to suppress them or they faced severe loss of face and were open to the charge that they were failing in one of their primary missions, the preservation of municipal order and decorum. The willingness of the police not merely to monitor these activities[63] but to attack them produced violent confrontations and, in some cases, left a legacy of bitterness long after the point of successful suppression. The police proved to be a weapon well-tuned to the task of terminating the popular fête with all its connotations of disorder, drunkenness, sexual license, and property damage. However, although the popular fête had nowhere to migrate or to hide once the authorities felt confident enough to act, the history of its suppression was often marked by riotous protest, for the popular culture involved was as deep-rooted as that expressed in activities that could be moved about.

The custom of stang-riding was particularly distasteful to Victorian respectables. It was first of all an open public affair always accompanied by disorder: marching, chanting, and shouting. In the West Riding the new county police attacked it as a breach of the peace.[64]

62. 'A Modern Professor', *British Boxing* (London, n.d.), reported that rule 21 of the sport read, 'In the event of . . . interference it shall be the duty of the umpires and referees to name the time and place for the next meeting, if possible, on the same day.'

63. Popular fêtes such as feasts and fairs which, by and large, were not earmarked for total or immediate suppression were nevertheless subjected to intense monitoring after police reform.

64. See *Leeds Mercury*, 28 May 1857, for one such incident at Oxspring near Barnsley.

At first some efforts were made by the participants either to compromise with the police or evade their intervention. At Honley near Huddersfield the arrival of the county police in 1857 forced local residents to resort to the novel expedient of asking police permission to ride the stang for an adulterer. In some places in the West Riding it came to be believed that if the performance were conducted within three townships before being officially noticed it acquired 'legality' and the police were bound to stand aside. At Grassington in Wharfedale it was thought that marching three times around the parish church would legally protect stang-riders.[65]

Some of the traditional uses of this custom go far to explain why the authorities seemed so determined to put it down. It had been used around Newcastle against blacklegs in labor disputes, and in Sunderland against those who informed on striking keelmen and those who were instrumental in the kidnapping and impressment of sailors.[66] The Welsh wooden horse or 'Ceffyl Pren', an analogous practice, greatly disturbed the Cardigan magistrates: a figure of a horse was carried

> to the door of any person whose domestic conduct may have exposed him to the censure of his neighbours or who may have rendered himself unpopular by . . . contributing to enforce the law. . . . The right . . . thus arrogated of . . . publicly animadverting on . . . another man's domestic conduct, is certainly characteristic of a rude state of society; but when the same measures are applied to . . . thwarting the operation of the laws of the land, they become of much more serious import.[67]

Because stang-riding and similar customs represented survivals of old forms of popular justice or self-policing or else were used as vehicles for social protest, because they symbolically short-circuited all modern agencies and bureaucracies of established authority, the police and magistrates were ruthless in their attempts to put them down.

Superintendent Heaton of Huddersfield achieved one notable and permanent success in his efforts to make the police a leading edge of moral reform. During his tenure the traditional Huddersfield Guy Fawkes celebration was quelled. At least since the 1820s local

65. Revd A. Easther, *A Glossary of the Dialect of Almondbury and Huddersfield* (London, 1883), p. 129; F. Cobley, *On Foot Through Wharfedale* (Otley, n.d.), p. 262.
66. *Monthly Chronicle of North Country Lore and Legend*, May 1887; also see E.P. Thompson's interesting article on stang-riding and related phenomena, 'Rough Music: Le Charivari Anglais', *Annales* 27 (1972).
67. *Report From His Majesty's Commissioners For Inquiring Into the Poor Laws*, p. 44.

authorities had made sporadic efforts to prevent the customary bonfire from being lit in the town center. The reorganization of the local constables under an Improvement Act and the advent of Heaton led to a frontal assault on Guy Fawkes in 1848. A redoubled 'move-on' policy was put into effect, and when that failed to stop the usual crowd of shopmen and apprentices from assembling Heaton ordered water hoses turned on them. The result of course was a serious riot in the course of which Heaton himself was felled, kicked about, and rolled in the mud. The police were put to rout and the crowd returned to its business of milling about and discharging fireworks.[68] The Huddersfield police lost the battle of 1848, but in so doing won the war over the perpetuation of Guy Fawkes. Neither in 1849 nor 1850 were attempts made to hold the traditional revels in the marketplace; in 1851 Guy Fawkes activities were reported being held on the far outskirts of town, the transfer signalling their disappearance in the customary form.[69] Popular resistance to the determination of the Huddersfield police to end the affair in 1848 was violent, but ultimately quite brittle. Displaced from its customary locale in the center of the town, Guy Fawkes reappeared in the suburbs and then died away, eventually becoming what it is today in most places – a begging occasion for small children.

At Richmond and Malton, towns located in the agricultural districts of Yorkshire, riotous resistance was more prolonged, lasting at least through the 1870s.[70] At Wakefield, Guildford (Surrey), and Lewes (Sussex), Guy Fawkes in the mid- and late nineteenth century became a ritual occasion used by working-class youths to stand up for local custom and tradition while having a 'legitimate' go at the police. Especially in Guildford the Fifth of November bore the character of a semi-institutionalized anti-police riot, an occasion on which one might square a whole year's debts with the police and other local authorities. As for the authorities themselves, as one Yorkshire magistrate put it, 'the celebration of the 5th of November was a most degrading practice . . . and all intelligent and thinking persons had ceased to be connected with it. To Lord Macauley we were indebted for getting rid of such things as services for the 5th of November. . . . The law and the public had agreed to let such days be forgotten, but at Ossett they must forsooth keep them up.'[71] The bulk of society was expected to follow the new policies of the upper classes quickly and

68. An account appears in *Leeds Times*, 11 November 1848.
69. *Ibid.*, 8 November 1851.
70. *York Herald and General Advertiser*, 7 November 1863, 9 November 1867, 8 November 1877.
71. Speech from the bench by J.B. Greenwood, a Dewsbury magistrate, before fining a Guy Fawkes celebrator £23 for assaulting the police, *(Leeds Mercury*, November 24, 1859).

if it did not the police could be employed to speed the process. By this time both the magistrates and the police authorities were often being put under intense pressure by local merchants and shopkeepers who were forced to close early, suffer the desertion of their shop assistants, lose an evening's custom, and bear the galling expense of boarding up their premises.[72] There was one other reason for the concern of the authorities: in some places in the last half of the nineteenth century, Guy Fawkes had been transmuted into a popular celebration with strong overtones of political and social protest.[73]

At Lewes – where Guy Fawkes survives even to this day – the celebrations were arranged by two societies of 'Bonfire Boys'. Each group presided over the building of its own bonfire, decked out a member in bishop's garb, and burned its guys. The 'bishop' of each society habitually gave an oration of a quasi-political nature, always alluding to 'the evils of the day'.[74] At Ludlow (Shropshire) it was reported: 'If any well known person in the place should happen to have excited the enmity of the populace, his effigy is substituted for or added to that of Guy Fawkes' and burnt.[75] At Guildford the proceedings were also organized by a semi-secret society called 'the Guys'. The latter appeared in the town center dressed in grotesque disguises and armed with bludgeons to defend themselves against the police. Guildford celebrations were distinguished by systematic and 'deliberate attacks on the property of selected citizens, who were usually members of the corporation or of the police'.[76] At

72. See [M.A. Lower] 'An Old Inhabitant', *Observations on The Doings in Lewes on the Evening of the Fifth of November 1846* (Lewes, 1847). Lower argued (p. 9) that Guy Fawkes created an unhealthy climate for business; cf. a petition of thirty Lewes householders to the magistrates, undated but marked September 1847, complaining of the insufficient police establishment and demanding that Guy Fawkes be put down. My thanks to Ms C. Connelly of the Lewes Area Library for providing me with this document.

73. In Wakefield Guy Fawkes was shielded for a short time by local Tories, who courted the lower classes in the interest of preventing municipal incorporation. The Tories organized a pro-Guy Fawkes anti-incorporation demonstration, paid a band, and provided fireworks. During the ensuing riot of 1849, Tory councillors cheered the crowds in their battles with the police and showered coins on them from the balcony of a local inn. All this represented a dying echo of a time when marked links (often manipulative) between urban crowds and their 'betters' were a regular feature of the social and political landscape. For an account see *Leeds Times*, 10, 17 November 1849.

74. A.R. Wright, *British Calendar Customs*, vol. 3 (London, 1940), p. 156.

75. C.S. Burne (ed.), G.F. Jackson, *Shropshire Folklore*, vol. 3 (London, 1886), p. 390.

76. J.K. Green, *Fireworks, Bonfires, Illuminations and the Guy Riots* (Guildford, 1952), p. 3; cf. Professor Hobsbawm's remark that the 'mob's activities, whatever their ostensible object, ideology or lack of theory, were always directed against the rich and powerful . . .' (*Primitive Rebels*, New York, 1959), p. 111.

Guildford 'the Guys' and their constituents were so formidable that in the 1850s the local police despaired of coping with them. They were often barricaded inside their station houses by the chief constable and plied with bread, cheese, and beer while 'the Guys' went about their business.[77] Interestingly, 'the Guys' might appear on other days beside November fifth; in 1865 they appeared on an election day. After the great riot of 1865 Guy Fawkes at Guildford was suppressed by a resort to the military. In 1867, though the usual crowd materialized and waited for 'the Guys' to come out, they did not appear.[78] The Guildford fête, though more organized and centered more clearly upon themes of social protest than at Huddersfield, proved equally fragile once the authorities made a determined and concerted effort to mobilize the force needed to quell it.[79]

An examination of the suppression of other types of popular fêtes by the magistrates and police reveals similar patterns.[80] At Leicester a number of traditional Shrovetide practices were ended in 1847 to the accompaniment of strong popular resistance. On Shrove Tuesday the 'Whipping Toms', another society of disguised young men, would appear in the Newark carrying large cart whips and preceded by a bellman whose ringing was presumed to give them 'legality'. After 1.00 p.m. anyone of any social station was liable to be whipped below the knees unless a fee was paid to the Toms. In 1846 a clause of a Leicester Improvement Act specifically declared the 'Whipping Toms' and the rough game of folk football which usually followed their performance to be illegal and punishable by a £5 fine. At Leicester the frequent warnings of the authorities in the weeks previous to Shrove Tuesday, 1847 were enough to discourage the Toms from appearing; but their constituents, a large crowd, did come out and milled about under the eyes of the borough police and a group of special constables sworn in for the occasion. At 2.00 p.m. the crowd, cheated of the 'Whipping Toms', proceeded to the customary game of football; the police attempted to stop it

---

77. In the riot of 1864 four of the 'Guys' were captured: two painters, a cooper, and a coachbuilder's laborer (Green, *Fireworks*, p. 5).

78. *Ibid.*, p. 5; G.C. Williamson, *Guildford in the Olden Time* (Guildford, 1904), p. 187.

79. For some connections between popular fêtes and social protest see N.Z. Davis, 'The Reasons of Misrule: Youth Groups and Charivaris in Sixteenth Century France', *Past and Present* 50 (1971); A.W. Smith, 'Some Folklore Elements in Movements of Popular Protest', *Folklore* 77 (1967); E.P. Thompson, '"Rough Music"': D. Williams, *The Rebecca Riots. A Study in Agrarian Discontent* (Cardiff, 1955), passim.

80. For bull-running and football see R. Malcolmson, *Popular Recreations in England, 1700–1850* (Cambridge, 1973), passim; M. Marples, *A History of Football* (London, 1954), pp. 98–100; Harrison and Trinder, *Drink and Sobriety*, p. 47.

and a serious riot ensued. Eventually the Newark was cleared and the crowd dispersed. On Shrove Tuesday of both 1848 and 1849 all was quiet; neither the 'Whipping Toms' nor the usual crowds made an appearance and the task of suppression was complete.[81]

The police were forceful in attempting to end other customary days of popular license, occasions on which the social order was symbolically inverted and the usual lines of authority and deference unilaterally suspended by the lower classes. At Chetwynd (Shropshire) the populace had traditionally enjoyed the right to pelt anyone with crab apples during the wakes celebration: nobody from the lowest to the highest was exempt from the 'rules' governing the fête. In 1862 the aged rector of Newport was attacked by an apple-throwing crowd; the police were sent for and the custom was suppressed.[82]

It should be noted that in the past many of these customs and celebrations had not only been tacitly sanctioned by the upper classes but openly and sometimes even officially patronized by them. Once the latter decided to dissociate themselves from their old roles, however, it was usually not long before the police were unleashed and the fete in question placed under assault. In eighteenth-century Liverpool for example, the burgesses officially sponsored a bear-baiting through the town each October tenth to mark the annual election of a mayor.[83] At Ludlow (Shropshire) the rope for the traditional tug of war through the town was customarily purchased out of corporation funds and thrown out by the mayor himself. In 1851 official participation was suddenly ended amidst talk of possible 'dangerous accidents' and 'disorderly scenes'.[84] The affair was then quickly suppressed by those who had once presided over it.

Most obviously with regard to popular fêtes, but eventually even with more private recreation, police action ultimately had profound effects. Many nineteenth-century contemporaries specifically linked the coming of the police to the decline of traditional customs and amusements. A Batley (Yorkshire) observer writing in the 1880s spoke of the time when

> the first policeman came into our midst, to plant the thin edge of the wedge, which was . . . to revolutionise our manners and customs. Since he came . . . we have lost all trace of mumming: all trace of Lee Fair, . . . most of our mischief night; as nearly all the peace eggers; for what are left of the latter are of another mould to those of my own

81. W. Kelly, *Notices of Leicester Relative to the Drama* (London, 1865), pp. 177–79; *Leicester Journal*, 19 February 1847. Note the resemblance of the Leicester 'Toms' to the Guildford 'Guys'.

82. G. Burne (ed.) *Shropshire Folklore*, p. 390.

83. T.F.T. Dyer, *British Popular Customs Present and Past* (London, 1876), p. 385.

84. G. Burne (ed.), *Shropshire Folklore*, p. 390.

childhood days. . . . If mummers were to be seen upon the street now, the police would interfere . . . I put a deal of this severance from ourselves of old customs down to the advent of the policeman in uniform.

Walter Rose, describing a rural district, spoke of the process by which the old mummer's play was hounded out of public by the local police towards the end of the nineteenth century: 'The police made it their duty to hover on the heels of the players, keeping a watch on their conduct; so that they became fearful of making an unannounced entry to a private house. Thus it was that . . . the public house became almost the only place where the play could be rendered correctly.' Alfred Williams attributed at least part of the decline of the folksong to the interventions of the police, who drove it even from the pubs: the 'police looked upon song-singing as a species of rowdyism. Their frequent complaints and threats to the landlords filled them with misgivings; the result was that they were forced, as a means of self protection, to request their customers not to sing on the premises.'[85] It would be absurd to advance any single explanation for nineteenth-century transformations of popular culture, but there is no question that interventions of the police and of those who directed them played a considerable role.

Yet while almost all aspects of popular culture changed, the differential between festival and other recreations remains vital, and this affected police–community relations. Ironically, while suppression of festivals often caused a riot, it was usually relatively clear-cut; lingering bitterness is hard to discern. Not so with the pub-centered recreational nexus, where the police perforce relied on ongoing surveillance. It was the pressure of surveillance on institutions and activities that long eluded direct attack that maintained the police in the role the workers of Lancashire and Yorkshire had understood at the moment of their installation: an alien element in the community and a daily source of both major and petty annoyance. Policemen continued to be beaten all through the nineteenth century, for such reasons as interfering too closely in family or neighborhood affairs or public-house proceedings, providing escort for strike-breakers, engaging in brutality, or moving people on too forcefully, especially

85. J. Binns, *From Village to Town* (Batley, 1882), pp. 95–96; W. Rose, *Good Neighbours*, p. 135; A. Williams, *Folksongs of the Upper Thames* (London, 1923), p. 24; S. Walker, *Cuffs and Handcuffs. The Story of Rochdale Police . . .* (Rochdale, 1957), p. 44; Harrison and Trinder, *Drink and Sobriety*, p. 47. The decline in the violence of the annual Guy Fawkes town-versus-gown rows at Oxford apparently began with the police reforms of the early 1870s. The change was hastened by the appearance of strong themes of economic protest on the town side during the great riot of 1867 (T.F. Plowman, *In the Days of Victoria. Some Memories of Men and Things* (London, 1918), p. 87).

in times of high unemployment. Vignettes such as the following were not atypical at least up to the 1890s. In confrontation in the mid-1860s over preparations for Guy Fawkes at Dunnington in the East Riding of Yorkshire, William Nicholls was charged with an assault on a policeman. In court the defense argued that the accused was engaged in gathering thorns for making a November fifth bonfire and that the policeman said that Nicholls told him: 'Thou b[ugge]r, thou hindered us having a fire last year; thou shan't this.' When they reached Nicholls' house his mother came out and egged the men on, one of the others exclaiming 'We'll shoot the b[ugge]r before the winter's over.' The policeman followed the group of men to the common where they began unloading. At that point he was knocked unconscious with a pitchfork. All present swore that the policeman used his stick first, though this was not believed by the magistrate.[86] In the winter of 1864 a group of young men beat up two constables outside the Black Bull Inn at Pudsey near Leeds. The magistrates observed 'Pudsey is well known for this sort of thing.' Near Wakefield a prizefight in Lupset Pastures was interfered with by a Sgt Coop and a PC Houlton of the West Riding force. Both were 'frightfully beaten' and Houlton almost died. A Leeds policeman was assaulted for no apparent reason by a William Hezlenden. When asked why he did it he replied he just 'wanted to have a tussle with a policeman'.[87]

An informant told Stephen Reynolds that the 'first thing a policeman ought to know is when to let well alone'.[88] Reynolds discovered as much resentment against the police in the early twentieth century as this writer found in Lancashire in 1840 or Yorkshire in 1857.[89] George Sturt wrote convincingly of his turn-of-the-century Surrey folk that they were

> aware of the constraint imposed upon them by laws and prejudices which are none too friendly to people of their kind. One divines it in their treatment of the . . . policeman. There is probably no lonelier man in the parish . . . One hears him mentioned in those same accents of grudging caution which the villagers use in speaking of unfriendly

---

86. *York Herald and General Advertiser*, 7 November 1863; cf. a similar incident near Dewsbury: the police tried to stop the lighting of a bonfire and were stoned and beaten by a crowd (*Leeds Mercury*, 17 November 1859).
87. *Leeds Mercury*, 12 June 1860, 7 July 1863, 23 February, 1864.
88. S. Reynolds et al., *Seems So!* (London, 1911), p. 91; in the 1840s Exeter constables were popularly referred to as 'the busy Bs of the police' (R. Newton, *Victorian Exeter* (Leicester, 1968), p. 69).
89. R.D. Storch, 'The Plague of Blue Locusts', pp. 70–87; see also T.H.S. Escott, *England: Its People, Polity and Pursuits*, vol. 1 (London, 1880), p. 421, and Charles Rowley's remark that the inefficiency of the Manchester police in the 1880s was linked to 'public distrust of the force' (*50 Years of Work Without Wages* (London, n.d.), p. 58).

property owners, as though he belonged to that alien caste. The cottagers feel that they themselves are the people whom he is stationed in the valley to watch. . . . In theory, the policeman represents the general public; in practice; he stands for middle-class decorum and the rights of property.[90]

The police, Reynolds wrote 'are charged . . . with a whole mass of petty enactments, which are little more than social regulations bearing almost entirely on working class life. . . . Nor can it . . . be otherwise since the duties of the police have been made to tally with upper class . . . notions of right and wrong, so that a working man may easily render himself liable to arrest . . . without in the least doing what is wrong in his own eyes or in the opinion of his neighbours.'[91] Writing about the same period in Salford, Robert Roberts reported strikingly similar attitudes: 'Nobody in our Northern slum . . . ever spoke in fond regard . . . of the policeman as a "social worker" and "handyman of the streets". Like their children, delinquent or not, the poor in general looked upon him with fear and dislike. When one arrived on a "social" visit they watched his passing with suspicion and his disappearance with relief.'[92]

If there were disputes to be settled within working-class communities, the instinctive reaction of the poor was not to call upon a 'handyman of the streets' but to settle things among themselves. A mid-century magistrate reported that 'great scenes of outrage take place [in pubs] and violent conduct frequently occurs; when they come out the police interfere, and endeavour to stop it; and then they all set upon the police; this frequently occurs'.[93] A wealth of contemporary evidence confirms Henry Pelling's observation that the English working class has always put a high premium on being left alone by the state and its agents.[94] It is difficult to get a firm line on the question of relations between the police and the working class from Victorian official sources alone. The truth was often left unsaid by magistrates and police authorities in testimony before parliamentary committees and royal commissions; the amount of sheer cant under which discussion of this issue was camouflaged

---

90. 'George Bourne' [George Sturt], *Change in the Village* (London, 1955), pp. 117–18; cf. Engels' remark that the 'English bourgeois finds himself reproduced in his law as he does in his God.' For that reason 'the policeman's truncheon has for him a wonderfully soothing power. But for the working-man quite otherwise!' (*Marx and Engels on Britain*, p. 263).

91. S. Reynolds, *Seems So!*, pp. 86–87.

92. R. Roberts, *The Classic Slum*, pp. 76–77.

93. *Select Committee of House of Lords on the Sale of Beer*, Parliamentary Papers 1850 (25) XXIV, 265. Evidence W. Harris, p. 59.

94. H. Pelling, *Popular Politics and Society in Late Victorian Britain* (London, 1968), pp. 1–6, 16–18, 62–71; cf. W.A. Williams, *Gosforth: The Sociology of an English Village* (Glencoe, Ill., 1956), pp. 171–2.

was perhaps an index of its sensitivity. One is compelled to resort to the local press, to an examination of working-class epithets – 'blue locusts', 'rozzers', 'crushers', 'busy Bs', 'raw lobsters' – music-hall songs, or to the analyses of sensitive contemporary observers such as Sturt or Reynolds.[95] Yet occasionally the wall of official silence lifts and a candid voice confirms what we know from other sources to be accurate. When asked by the 1908 Royal Commission what the feeling toward the police in his area was, the Chief Constable of Glasgow replied that it depended on the locality: 'The feeling towards the police is decidedly good in the better class localities, and among the shopkeeping class. In the rougher localities the feeling is hostile and always in favour of the arrested person.'[96] The issue was not only suspicion of the agencies of law enforcement but what E.P. Thompson has called 'alienation from the law' itself. These were facts of nineteenth-century social life to which not enough attention has been directed, and they suggest in turn that the English working class was not as easily reconciled to the advent of a policed society and to newer standards of public order as official sources have led many to think.

It is known that the initial implantation of the police was often accompanied by episodes of violent resistance. After that period mass rioting against the police became more rare, but other forms of anti-police outbreaks occurred frequently throughout the nineteenth century in defense of popular recreations and customs in reaction to instances of police brutality, in protest against police interference in strikes, and in a multitude of other daily-life situations.[97]

The charge of the new police with a 'domestic missionary' function and the monitoring of many important facets of everyday life in working-class neighborhoods reflected a profound social change as well as a deep rupture in class relations in nineteenth-century Britain. One consequence of the creation of what political economists called 'free labor' was the appearance of its concomitant, 'free leisure', and of a working class by and large left to itself once it passed out through the factory gate or workshop door in the evening. By the middle of the nineteenth century – if not earlier – a profound interruption of communications had occurred between the classes: both the 'language' and the objectives of urban masses were, if intelligible at all, deeply frightening. The upper classes saw 'themselves threatened by agglomerations of the . . . rapidly multiplying poor of cities whose size had no precedent in Western

---

95. See discussion in W. Miller, 'Police Authority in London and New York City, 1830–1870', *Journal of Social History*, 8 (1975), pp. 92–3.
96. *Royal Commission on the Duties of the Metropolitan Police*, Parliamentary Papers 1908 (Cd. 4261), LI.I., vol. 3, q. 40246; Roberts, *Classic Slum*, p. 77.
97. R.D. Storch, 'Blue Locusts', pp. 87–88.

history'.[98] The older understanding that movements of the lower orders had rational, legitimate, or at least comprehensible ends was replaced in the first half of the nineteenth century by the feeling that they aimed at the utter unravelling of society. To some extent these fears were reflected in a concern that the lower classes had escaped from all social control except the discipline of work. The activities of workers after their release from the salubrious discipline of the workshop or factory therefore became a matter of both profound interest and apprehension. Dogfights, cockfights, gambling, popular fêtes – always described in contemporary sources as both 'sensual' and 'barbarous' – were symbolic of the fear of social anarchy which always lay beneath the surface of early Victorian professions of optimism. It is probably true that after mid-century the English upper classes became both more discriminating and less fearful, and began to identify 'dangerous classes' with casual labor or the residuum and not with the working classes as a whole. Yet we know that in the last half of the nineteenth century the pace of middle-class cultural missionizing did not slacken but rather gathered momentum. The history of the temperance movement and the annual accounts of Social Science Association gatherings in the 1870s or 1880s display ongoing concern over the demoralization and ignorance of the lower orders and the dangers to the social fabric such reformers thought this posed.[99]

In the new industrial cities whatever connections had subsisted between social classes in terms of common enjoyment had been decisively severed. This was tacitly recognized by the Dewsbury magistrate who stressed that 'all intelligent and thinking persons' had divorced themselves from the celebration of the Fifth of November. The chaplain of Preston jail made a similar point:[100]

Have you any doubt that these were very common sports at Preston?
– In former times I believe they were.
Before the Beer Act came into operation? – Yes.
They must have been in some place? – They were in the . . . Cockpit. I recollect persons being present at these cockfights, who are the highest in the land now.
The upper classes used to encourage it at one time, now the beerhouses do? – That is precisely the fact.

98. A. Silver, 'The Demand for Order in Civil Society', in D.J. Bordua, ed., *The Police. Six Sociological Essays* (New York, 1967), p. 31. This is by far the best theoretical piece to date on these matters.
99. B. Harrison, *Drink and the Victorians*, passim, and 'Animals and the State in Nineteenth-Century England', passim.
100. *House of Commons Select Committee on Public Houses*. Evidence Revd. J. Clay, qq. 6270–6281.

Flora Thompson pointed out that in her area the local gentry had by the 1870s long since left the local feast celebration entirely to the lower classes; in the 1820s Miss Lister of Shibden Hall in the Halifax area locked up both herself and her horse when fairtime came.[101]

The disintegration of a common sphere of enjoyment was of course paralleled by a physical separation of the classes – classically described by Engels – unprecedented in western history. The Victorian bourgeoisie which set the moral tone of cities like Manchester and Leeds were not likely to patronize the cockpit as the Preston gentry of the late eighteenth century had done, nor to shower coins on a Guy Fawkes crowd as Wakefield Tories still felt at liberty to do at mid-century. Such gentlemen were much more inclined to either mind their own business and businesses or else to patronize temperance or rational recreation societies or mechanics' institutes. It was also they who supported the moral-reform mission assigned to the police and added to it in the language of numerous local improvement acts. The new demands for civil order in nineteenth-century England produced a novel type of surrogate to replace older and perhaps more personal lines of authority and deference which were now conceived to be moribund. The police, a 'bureaucracy of official morality',[102] were produced to try to fill this vacuum and to act as a lever of moral reform on the mysterious terrain of the industrial city's inner core.

The police, as we have observed, once successfully installed confronted a number of serious problems in the discharge of their moral-reform mission. Many problems proved utterly intractable, leading some police authorities to quickly gauge the real limits of their effectiveness in these areas. Though the full measure of the charge to the police by the Victorian municipality and the state could never be fully lived up to, the nineteenth century saw the forging of a modern and generally effective technique of order-keeping: the installation of the eyes and ears of ruling élites at the very centers of working-class daily life. The free leisure activities of the urban lower classes proved much less amenable to the interventions of both middle-class reform movements and the pressure of the police than had been originally hoped; however, the basic technique of daily surveillance of the streets and recreational centres of working-class districts proved a lasting one, and would ultimately be applied not only to nineteenth-century Leeds or Manchester but – in highly sophisticated variants – to twentieth-century police work as well.

101. F. Thompson, *Lark Rise To Candleford*, p. 505; Manuscript Diary of Miss Lister of Shibden Hall (Halifax Reference Library), 22 June 1822.
102. The phrase is Jack Douglas's. See his discussion of the historical development of the concept of policing in modern society in *American Social Order. Social Rules in a Pluralistic Society* (New York, 1971), p. 49ff.

Chapter 11

THE BUTCHER, THE BAKER, THE CANDLESTICKMAKER: THE SHOP AND FAMILY IN THE INDUSTRIAL REVOLUTION

Catherine Hall

[from Liz Whitelegge et al., *The Changing Experience of Women* (London 1982)]

This study shows the interaction of two of the major social and spatial processes operating in urban Britain. The renegotiation of gender relationships in the first forty years of the nineteenth century involved a separation of spheres entailing the withdrawal of 'respectable' women from workplace environments and the consequent separation of home and work. This was closely linked with the reorganization of urban space, notably the creation of the residential suburbs described in Chapter 5 and the expansion and specialization of central business districts. This chapter shows the value of a carefully chosen case study – here, the Cadbury family of Birmingham – in illuminating general patterns of change. Despite the centrality given to gender, this is not a one-factor explanation. Changes in the organization of shopping were related to growing town size. The removal of markets from main streets related to the need for improved urban circulation. Increased understanding of the considerable influence which changing gender relationships had on the creation and use of urban space remains a major challenge for urban historians.

In Mrs Gaskell's famous novel *Cranford*, Miss Matty, the kind-hearted and genteel friend of the narrator, loses all her money in the collapse of a country bank. Faced with surviving on a tiny income, it is proposed to her that she could add to it by selling tea. She is assured that she could maintain her gentility and that only small alterations would need to be made to her home: 'The small dining-parlour was to be converted into a shop, without any of its degrading characteristics; a table was to be the counter; one window was to be retained unaltered, and the other changed into a

307

glass door.'[1] Mrs Gaskell published *Cranford* in 1853, but she was describing the culture of a small country town in her childhood – looking back to those days before the face of England had been significantly altered by the growth of industrial towns and cities, of factory production and of new transport systems. A less obvious feature of that transformation, and one which Mrs Gaskell may have had in mind when she described the simple alterations needed to turn Miss Matty's dining parlour into a shop, were the changes which had taken place in the organization of shopping. Between 1780–1850, developments in the pattern of production, of distribution and of consumption combined to alter some of the physical characteristics of shops and the ways in which people acquired their food and clothing. These changes provided the necessary preconditions for the 'retailing revolution' of the second half of the nineteenth century – when consumer goods started to be mass-produced and shops both increased in size and amalgamated into chains.[2]

It is the shopkeepers themselves that we are primarily concerned with in this chapter – the butchers, bakers and candlestickmakers of the late eighteenth and early nineteenth century – and the changes which took place in the organization of the shop and the family. Furthermore, it is a substantial middle-class sector – those with their specialized shops on the high streets of the rapidly growing towns – whose custom came mainly from the local middle class. Their counterparts were the small shopkeepers running general stores who serviced the working-class population. Such small shops for the working classes were rapidly on the increase in the early nineteenth century. Rural immigrants, who had been able to grow a good deal of their own produce in the country, mainly had to rely on buying food in the towns and came to rely on local general shops. Markets and itinerant traders also continued to play an important part in retailing; they were the hawkers and sellers so powerfully portrayed by the journalist and commentator Mayhew in his series on London life in the 1850s.[3] Small shopkeepers and traders were certainly not a part of the middle class. Their links were far more with both the 'respectable' and the 'rough' working class who provided their clientèle and their neighbours.

High street traders, however, were a different matter. Their customers might range from the local gentry coming into town

1. Gaskell, Mrs E. (1853) *Cranford*.
2. For an account of this process see Adburgham, A. (1964) *Shops and Shopping 1800–1914*, London; Davis, D. (1966) *A History of Shopping*, London; Alexander, D. (1970) *Retailing in England during the Industrial Revolution*, London.
3. Thompson, E.P. and Yeo, E. (1973) *The Unknown Mayhew. Selections from the Morning Chronicle 1849–50*, Harmondsworth.

for business and services, to the best paid of the skilled artisans. They would primarily have relied, however, on the urban middle class – those merchants, manufacturers and professionals whose numbers were growing in an economy which was rapidly being industrialized – and on farmers. Such traders were running good-sized businesses, with none of the 'degrading characteristics' referred to by Miss Matty, and were themselves living the life of the middle class. The men were becoming the backbone of their churches and philanthropic and voluntary societies, they were mixing with professionals and small manufacturers and they were regarded as respected members of the community. Such small traders with their established tradition of retailing respectability, are nicely evoked in a memoir of a distinguished Birmingham Unitarian minister whose father was a draper. Though such men stood behind counters they had a 'quiet, gentlemanly dignity of bearing' which challenged the old adage that a tradesman could not be a gentleman.[4] Arnold Bennett placed a draper's establishment at the heart of his most popular novel *The Old Wives' Tale*. The shop was in St Luke's Square, the centre of Bursley's retail trade. The Square,

> . . . contained five public-houses, a bank, a barber's, a confectioner's, three grocers', two chemists', an ironmonger's, a clothier's, and five drapers'. These were all the catalogue, St Luke's Square had no room for minor establishments. The aristocracy of the Square undoubtedly consisted of the drapers (for the bank was impersonal); and among the five the shop of Baines stood supreme. No business establishment could possibly be more respected than that of Mr Baines was respected. And though John Baines had been bedridden for a dozen years, he still lived on the lips of admiring, ceremonious burgesses as 'our honoured fellow-townsman'.[5]

Businesses such as Baines the drapers were family affairs. Mrs Baines helped in the shop at busy times, but reserved Friday for pastry-making and early Saturday morning for her own shopping. After her husband's illness, the shop was basically managed by one of the young men who had been apprenticed there and she continued to help when necessary.

But this sexual division of labour within the shopkeeping family, associated with a physical environment which combined work and home, was gradually changing in our period. From the late seventeenth century the wives of wealthy London tradesmen had been castigated by commentators such as Defoe for their attempts to be genteel.[6] The most prosperous were furnishing their living apart-

4. Kenrick, J. (1854) *Memoir of the Rev. John Kentish*, Birmingham, p. 9.
5. Bennett, A. (1908) *The Old Wives Tale*, Pan edn (1964) London, p. 30.
6. See Davis, D. *op. cit.*

ments elegantly, putting their servants into livery, and refusing to be seen in the shop themselves, as it was not considered ladylike. As the businesses of provincial tradesmen expanded in the late eighteenth and early nineteenth century, so their aspirations also grew. They increasingly wanted their homes to be separated from their workplace and their wives and daughters to be dependent on them; these had become powerful symbols of belonging to the middle class. By 1851 the numbers of lock-up shops in town centres, with their proprietors living elsewhere, were on the increase.[7] This separation between work and home had important effects on the organization of work within the family and the marking out of male and female spheres.[8] Men were increasingly associated with business and public activities which were physically and socially separated from the home; women with the home and with children.

For working-class families the separation between work and home was rooted in the changes in the organization of production. A family producing woollen cloth at home in the late eighteenth century, for example, with the wife spinning and the husband weaving, would by the mid-nineteenth century have been forced into factory production because they would not have been able to compete with the cheaper cloth produced by mechanized processes in the factory.[9] This separation between work and home, between the production of things and the reproduction of people, which has had such far-reaching effects on industrial capitalist societies, did of course take place at significantly different times in different trades. Some trades were mechanical much later than others, and at mid-century many working-class men and women were still working inside the home. Industrial capitalism did not only mean factory production – it also brought with it a vast expansion of the sweated trades and of outwork.[10]

Within the middle class also the separation between production and reproduction was also a long, drawn-out and uneven process, depending in part on the particular kinds of work which people were doing. Clergymen, for example, have never quite lived in their workplaces though they have often lived next door to them. Doctors and dentists, on the other hand, until the recent advent of

7. Alexander, D. *op. cit.*
8. This separation between the shop and the home was confined to the most prosperous tradesmen, while many shops still remain combined workplace and home in the late nineteenth century. See Vigne, T. and Howkins, A. 'The small shopkeeper in industrial and market towns', in G. Crossick (ed.) (1977) *The Lower Middle Class in Britain 1870–1914*, London.
9. See Hall, C. 'The home turned upside down? The working-class family in cotton textiles in the early nineteenth century', Whitelegge et al., (1982) *The Changing Experience of Women*; London.
10. See Samuel, R. (1977) 'Workshop of the world: steam power and hand technology in mid-Victorian Britain', *History Workshop* No. 3, Spring.

health centres, were still likely in the twentieth century to combine home and workplace. Large-scale manufacturers often lived next door to their factories so that they could easily oversee them – as did Mr Thornton in Mrs Gaskell's novel *North and South*, or indeed the first generation of the Greg family in Styal on whom it is thought Mrs Gaskell may have based her picture of the hard-nosed industrial capitalist.[11] For those small manufacturers who relied on workshop production, it was most convenient to combine home and workplace and many merchants had their warehouse at the back of their living quarters. Technological advances which revolutionized the labour process rarely forced those in middle-class occupations to establish a home away from work, yet by the mid-nineteenth century this separation was becoming increasingly popular.

Take a town like Birmingham. Birmingham had grown from a population of around 35,000 in 1780 to a quarter of a million in 1850, its expansion being based on the metal trades for which it was famous. It had always been the pattern for the most prosperous members of the middle class to move to the small versions of the gentleman's country house which ringed the town when they could afford it. Joseph Priestly for example, the well-known scientist, theologian and minister of one of the Unitarian congregations in Birmingham, was living at Fair Hill about two miles from the town centre in the 1780s, and Dr William Withering, another member of the famous Birmingham Lunar Society, and an eminent physician in the town, was living at Edgbaston Hall – a charming rural retreat away from the hustle and bustle of the town centre. By the 1820s and 1830s they were being followed by families who were considerably less wealthy, but were looking for a modest version of country living in houses which were close enough to the town for the men to walk daily to their places of work. By the mid-1840s Edgbaston, the leafy suburb of Birmingham, carefully planned with restrictive leases that prevented the building of workshops in gardens or the opening of shops on the premises, was growing apace and the most popular domestic retreat of the growing Birmingham middle class.[12]

The domestic ideal which underpinned such a development was premissed on the notion of a male head of household who supported his dependent wife and children. The women and children were able to be sheltered from the anxieties of the competitive public world by living in their 'haven' or home – away from the political

11. Gaskell, Mrs E. (1854) *North and South*, Harmondsworth (1970); Rose, M.B. (1978) *The Gregs of Styal*, London.
12. Davidoff, L. and Hall, C. 'The architecture of public and private life: English middle-class society in a provincial town 1780–1850', in Fraser, D. and Sutcliffe, A. (eds) (1983) *The Pursuit of Urban History*, London. For a more extensive discussion of the development and management of Edgbaston, see Chapter 4, p. 135 *et seq*. (Eds).

dangers associated with such movements as Chartism, and the business worries of the town. This ideal was popularized from the late eighteenth century particularly by evangelical Christians who believed that a proper religious household must form the basis of a reformed society.[13] The pulpit, the tract and the manual of behaviour provided some of the main vehicles for the promulgation of such ideas. The ideas were institutionalized in the new organizations formed by the middle classes – the self-improvement societies and the philanthropic societies, for example – in their business practices and in the new schools which they established for their sons, and eventually for their daughters.[14] Well-to-do shopkeepers were not slow to attach themselves to such ideas – ideas which called for significant changes in their established way of life 'above the shop'.

What was this established way of life? The records of the Cadbury family in Birmingham provide a valuable insight into the changing patterns of moderately successful shopkeepers over three generations.[15] Richard Tapper Cadbury, the originator of the Birmingham dynasty, arrived in the town in 1794, and having done his apprenticeship in Gloucester and served as a journeyman in London, he set up in business in Bull Street – a major Birmingham shopping street – as a silk mercer and draper. In 1800 he moved in with his wife and rapidly growing family above the shop. Elizabeth Cadbury was clearly actively engaged in the business, though she had not of course had access to the kind of training her husband had acquired. She helped in the shop when it was necessary, she looked after affairs when her husband was away and she organized the large household which included apprentices and female shop assistants as well as her own immediate family. That immediate family consisted of ten children – eight of whom survived, and her own mother who lived with them in her old age. In addition there were at least two women servants who helped with the organization of the household.

The provision of meals and linen for such a household, at a time when there were no mechanical aids and not even piped water, must have been an enormously time-consuming activity. It also has to be remembered that Elizabeth Cadbury had a baby every one to two years for the first fifteen years of her married life. Yet at the same time she was taking an active part in the business and living above

---

13. Hall, C. (1979) 'The early formation of Victorian domestic ideology' in S. Burman (ed.) *Fit Work for Women*, London.

14. Davidoff, L. and Hall, C. (1987) *Family Fortunes. Men and Women of the English Middle Class, 1780–1850*, London, Ch. 10.

15. The material on the Cadburys which forms most of the rest of the paper is drawn from the Cadbury Collection. The Collection, which is housed in Birmingham Reference Library, comprises a rich series of manuscripts plus drawings and illustrations.

the shop at a time when virtually no limitations existed on shop hours. This meant that household affairs had to be organized to fit in with those hours. In 1815, for example, when Richard was away in London buying fabrics for the shop, one of his letters to his wife included not only family news and inquiries about the children but also information about his commercial activities. He had already sent 'some coloured and scarlet whittles and scarves', some with the car men and others to go in the coach the next day. 'Bombazines I have been after', he told her, 'but I find it difficult to get all my colours. Such as I have met with are very nice and tomorrow I am to look out my black ones.' He was anxious to know whether she had had any news from Ireland about the linens; meanwhile he had ordered a bonnet for his daughter Sarah and assured his wife that the fresh eggs from Birmingham which she had sent had arrived safely.

In 1812 business was going sufficiently well for Richard Tapper Cadbury to take a modest second house in Islington Row, on the outskirts of the town and virtually in the country. The younger children went there to live with their nurse whilst their parents got away from the business as often as they could to visit them. The family kept pigeons, rabbits, a dog and a cat at the country house and since the garden was small, a second plot of land was rented nearby where strawberries and other fruit and vegetables were grown. Mrs Cadbury was now supervising two households and with her own older daughters she moved constantly between them. In 1827 she was unwell and soon after, Richard was glad to be able to report to his youngest daughter Emma that he had been gratified to find her well enough, 'to see her walk to town, and to bustle about all day without apparent fatigue'. The sons followed in their father's footsteps and were apprenticed – the eldest, Benjamin, to a draper in London in training to take over the family business. The second son, John, was apprenticed to a tea and coffee dealer in Leeds and in 1824, after a spell in London to gain more experience, he came back to Birmingham and set up in business next door to his father and brother.

The daughters, again like their mother, had no formal apprenticeship. Indeed there were very few trades where it was possible for girls to be apprenticed, since craft rules had always been concerned with the guarding of skills for men. But the Cadbury girls had informal domestic apprenticeships. They learnt to help their mother from a very early age and Maria and Ann would often assist their father in the shop. They were clearly brought up to see this as in no way reflecting on their femininity or gentility. Like their mother, they were no doubt just as much at home cooking, preserving, or preparing the house for winter by putting old extra carpets down. The business was a part of the life of every member of the family; as Elizabeth Cadbury wrote when, in 1828, the Bull Street premises were being altered and they were worried as to the effect this would have on the light in the parlour, '. . . I suppose we must not complain as it is for the business'.

Richard Tapper Cadbury's business was clearly doing quite well in the 1820s and he was publicly regarded as one of the substantial Birmingham tradesmen. But he could not afford to let matters drift, for around him the patterns of retailing were changing and this offered considerable opportunities. Despite the absence of a technological revolution in the retail trade, its organization was soon marked by the changes associated with the early development of industrial capitalism. Population growth and urbanization meant that there were large concentrations of people needing to buy. Factory production meant that some consumer items became much more easily and cheaply available – the Staffordshire pots for which the region was famous are examples of such items. In time the transport revolution meant that distribution networks could be established and transport speeded up. The traditional fairs and markets which had been central to eighteenth-century consumer patterns were not specialized enough to supply the new demands. Sometimes consumers themselves tried to organize adequate supplies of what they saw as important items. A public subscription was established in Birmingham in 1791 to try to get a good fish shop set up in the town. This effort, together with other consumer-oriented activities, was lauded by James Bisset in his *Poetic Survey around Birmingham* of 1800.

> And Epicureans, then, may have their wish,
> And tho' an inland place, find good fresh fish,
> For many schemes suggested have been tried,
> To have our markets constantly supplied
> With ev'ry thing that's good, and cheap in reason,
> Fruit, fish or fowl, and rarities in season . . .[16]

Weekly markets remained very important for the sale of food-stuffs; in fact there was no national marketing system for food until after 1850, but gradually the markets became more organized. In the late eighteenth century a cattle market would often occupy the main street of a town one day a week, and this interfered considerably with other kinds of business and trading. Mrs Lucy Benton recalled New Street, which became one of Birmingham's main shopping streets, in the year 1817; there was an inn, the 'Old Crown' where the pig market was held: '. . . all respectable females who traversed the street on market days had to turn into the middle

16. Bisset, J. (1800) *A Poetic Survey around Birmingham*, Birmingham.

of it to preserve their cleanliness, the footpaths being reserved for the special accommodation of the superior animal to whom the spot was devoted.'[17]

Such an arrangement would hardly do for a town which depended economically on attracting buyers and selling its products to the rest of the country. The Birmingham markets were first centralized into the Bull Ring, and then construction of a market hall began in 1833, authorized by one of the town improvement acts and with a market committee responsible for its good order.[18]

Meanwhile shopkeepers were beginning to think about changing their practices. Larger towns meant the decline of custom based on kinship and on friendship – customers now had to be attracted from the streets and into the shops. This meant that the display of wares assumed a new importance and changes had to be made in the appearance of shops. John Cadbury was the first retailer in Birmingham to introduce plate glass windows which allowed for a much more attractive display. His friend Thomas Southall, who had a chemist's shop opposite, also had the new windows installed and the two of them would chat whilst they carefully polished them up in the mornings. A guide book to Birmingham in 1825 referred to the town as in 'the high tide of retail trade'. 'The shops', it continued, 'of the higher degrees are very handsomely fitted up; the form and sweep of the windows, and the style of the decorations, emulating those of the Metropolis.'[19] Superior shopkeepers began to advertise in the local press as another way of attracting trade, though some of the old-established families were shocked at this 'puffing', as it was called. Richard Tapper Cadbury made a regular practice of advertising in *Aris' Birmingham Gazette* and, like many other drapers, he would make a particular point of advertising when he had just brought in his new stock from London.

Contemporaries who commented on improvements in the organization of shopping tended to refer to the drapery business for it was the first branch of the trade to exhibit the characteristics of modern retailing systematically. Many traders in the eighteenth and early nineteenth century combined production and distribution; the butcher killed and cut his meat, the baker baked and sold his bread, the candlestickmaker produced his metal goods as well as retailing them. This combination of production and distribution, based on a large household which utilized the labour of all family members, was in decline at least in the large town by the mid-

17. Benton, Mrs Lucy (1877) *Recollections of New Street in the Year 1817*, Birmingham.
18. On the municipal history of Birmingham see Gill, C. (1952) *History of Birmingham* vol. 1, Oxford.
19. Drake, J. (1825) *The Picture of Birmingham*, Birmingham, p. 69.

nineteenth century. Town butchers were increasingly specializing between killing and cutting on the one hand and retailing on the other. Candlestickmakers no longer existed as such; the production of hardware in workshops and small factories had become the staple trade of the Black Country and ironmongers would then sell these products. Baking, however, was still dominated by the independent master who baked and sold – the big change there had been from the home baking. The draper had the advantage of being relatively free from production functions; the only item which required preparing for sale was thread. Developments in textile production, particularly cotton, meant that there was an expanding mass market for cloth and by the 1820s the drapery shops in towns and cities were bigger than any other shops. Drapers were able to concentrate their capital on shop improvements. They were frequently the first to introduce plate glass windows, window displays and gas lighting, and they also led the field in price ticketing and cash trading which were two of the next developments.[20]

Despite the advantages of his trade, however, Benjamin Head Cadbury, who took over the drapery business from his father, does not seem to have been such a good businessman as his brother, John. John not only introduced the latest retailing improvements in his tea and coffee shop but he also decided to branch out into the manufacture of cocoa as soon as he had the capital available. This production was not based on the household, however, rather he established a completely separate factory and ran the two sides of the business simultaneously for as long as he could. In 1826 he married his first wife Priscilla, but she died in 1828. Around 1830 the introduction of cocoa powder made possible an instant chocolate drink, and this led John in 1831 to set up a small factory around the corner from the shop. In 1832 he married for the second time. His wife Candia Barrow was the daughter of a Quaker shipping merchant. Initially the couple lived over the shop, but after the birth of their first son John they moved to Edgbaston and soon found the house which became the family home for nearly forty years. It was not a large house but they gradually altered and extended it. Their daughter Maria, in her recollections of her childhood, commented on the fact that her mother lived on the business premises initially; by the time that Maria was writing it was obviously something that had to be explained, and her account was that Candia liked to be beside her husband all the day in the early part of their marriage. There was no mention of the importance of her contribution to the work which had to be done. The profits from the shop and the factory were sufficient to warrant setting up a suburban home, but there

20. Alexander, D. *op. cit.*

was no money to spare. Candia could cook and she supervised the home wash once a fortnight in the back kitchen. But she was used to country living and it was these standards which they sought in their Edgbaston home, as Maria described it:

> . . . it was almost cottage like in appearance and too small without many alterations, but its countrylike surroundings decided our parents to take it, make more rooms, and lay out the gardens to their own taste . . . our Mother was exceedingly fond of gardening, but our Father was greatly occupied with business and town affairs and other interests and he had very little time during the week for his garden.

The house soon had a playroom, which was later turned into a schoolroom, and a nursery upstairs for the little ones. Such a differentiation between rooms had not been possible in the combined home/workplace in Bull Street. Suburban housing allowed for a different notion of childhood as well as a different role for women, and this differentiation of role was mirrored in the new definitions of physical space. Candia and her children's lives were focused on home and school, whilst her husband used the Edgbaston home as a happy family base for his business and public activities. 'Our dear Father was a very steady industrious man, noted for punctuality, and took great pride in his business, everything being arranged in beautiful order', wrote Maria. In 1847 John Cadbury opened larger premises for his cocoa production, some way from the shop but nearer to home. His time was increasingly spent at the factory whilst his brother Benjamin, who had recently come into partnership with him, managed the commercial side. Cocoa production provided a popular drink for temperance advocates in this period, and John and Candia were amongst the earliest supporters of the temperance movement. Indeed family habits clearly involved some small-scale advertising in themselves; when Maria was sent away to school her father sent some cocoa to the Misses Dymond who ran the school. Maria reported in one of her regular letters home that: 'Miriam Dymond told me that they liked Father's cocoas so much that they have persuaded their grocer to supply them regularly with it, and we have it regularly every 5th day morning for breakfast.'

Meanwhile Richard Tapper Cadbury had decided to retire. At sixty-four he left the business in the hands of his eldest son Benjamin and bought a house in Edgbaston, where he lived with his wife and two remaining unmarried daughters on a 'modest competency'. He still went into town a great deal, however, in connection either with his public activities or his business interests. For his wife and daughters it was a very different matter. Once they had physically moved from the workplace it became marginal to their lives – the business was simply where the money came from, rather than something which occupied many of their working hours. It was Elizabeth's daughter-in-law, another Candia – Candia Wadkin, who now took over the responsibilities in the shop. The Bull Street house had been smartened up before Benjamin and Candia moved in and an effort was made to make it more comfortable as a home. Candia was impressed to find it so

> . . . completely metamorphosed that it was almost difficult to recognize it as the old family mansion, the difference of furniture and the addition of window curtains have given the parlour quite another character, it now appears a much squarer room and more comfortable and had been dressed out with flowers . . . some hyacinths on the chimney piece are in full bloom in addition to this there are several plants in full blossom so that we have quite a country appearance. . . .

Obviously every effort was being made to downplay the urban features of Bull Street life. The yard had been whitewashed and the upstairs sitting room and bedrooms comfortably fitted up. Candia was kept extremely busy with a growing family: she soon had six daughters and a son, and the same kind of business responsibilities that her mother-in-law had assumed. In the 1830s, for example, she gave Benjamin news of the shop when he was away: 'Customers have been flowing in very satisfactorily today and all has, I believe, gone on comfortably, all appear attentive, equally so or more anxious to be so than if thou wast at home. . . .'

Candia was closely involved in the education of her children, as were her sisters-in-law. The girls' education was started at home and then they went to a Birmingham day school before going to the same Quaker boarding school as their cousin Maria. They were given an early training in domesticity; dolls, prams, pincushions and workboxes figure prominently as presents, and they were taught to knit and to sew, to make their own clothes and to repair them. The family stayed in the Bull Street house until 1844 and then they too moved into the outskirts of Edgbaston; the last clear links were cut between the women and the family businesses. In 1846 Benjamin gave up the drapery business and went into partnership with John, presumably having decided that with the new, larger factory about to open there would be plenty of work and enough profits for the two of them.

The separation between home and work made substantial differences to the daily lives of both men and women in middle-class families. The Cadbury men still went to work every day and then came home to their families. This meant that there was a much clearer distinction between work-time and leisure-time and there was also much clearer distinction between public and private life. As long as home and workplace were combined it must often have been difficult to categorize whether activities which went on there were 'public' or 'private' and indeed it would probably have been a pretty irrelevant question. Was feeding an apprentice, for example, who would usually have been the son of a friend and who would have generally been treated as one of the family, a business or domestic matter? The point is, of course, that they were one and the same thing, and one clear demonstration of this is that shopkeepers such as the Cadburys started to keep separate household accounts only when the separation had taken place between work and home. The physical separation of the two was the culmination of a long process during which time middle-class men's activities had become increasingly differentiated from those of middle-class women. Women's participation in family businesses had always tended to be an informal affair; the fact that married women had no property rights meant that the business was always legally owned by the husband as long as he lived. Only widows and spinsters could run their own businesses in their own names. Furthermore the training and skills had always been tied to masculinity – women were not apprenticed to drapers or to tea and coffee dealers. But the increasing complexity of the commercial world and its increasing formalization in this period meant that it was becoming more difficult for women to participate even informally. Furthermore, as new retailing skills became important, the training which encouraged these skills was not available for women. The informal 'picking up' of the business which was what women relied on was no longer necessarily enough.

But in addition to the increasing difficulty of women learning how to do business, there were the aspirations for a separate domestic sphere and the positive desire to move away from the shop if this were financially possible. Initially efforts were often made to make the shop more like a 'home' – as, for example when the Bull Street parlour was made more comfortable with curtains for Benjamin and Candia, and an attempt was made to make it look more countrylike by putting in flowers and plants. But in the end the only way to have a fully private home, where family time would not be interrupted by the apprentices, late customers or visiting business contacts, was by geographically dividing the home from the workplace. The most crucial effect of this in terms of sexual divisions was that it meant wives and daughters were no longer there to be called upon for help. Daughters were educated to be wives and mothers and to expect to be financially dependent on their husbands. This did not mean that women no longer had any financial relation to the business. Their money, acquired through marriage settlements, remained a vital source of capital. In fact John Cadbury's sons saved the family cocoa business, which went through a bad patch in the 1850s, by investing some money left to them by their mother. But the *direct*

319

working relation of women to the business had gone and 'work' was now what their husbands did when they left the house in the morning.

Women were furthermore increasingly cut off from the variety of other *public* activities which their menfolk engaged in. 1780–1850 was the age of societies, when societies were formed in aid of every possible cause. These societies ranged from ones with a primarily political orientation to those concerned with commercial activities, self-education in its broadest sense and philanthropic works. It was exceedingly difficult for women to be involved in any of these except the philanthropic, and even there they were encouraged to participate privately and informally rather than being engaged in the public activities – the meetings and the dinners.[21] A typical day for John Cadbury might have involved an early rise, a walk with some of the children and the dogs, back home for breakfast, a walk into town to work, a morning in the shop or factory, a 12 o'clock meeting at the Public Office of the Street Commissioners (the oligarchic élite which was responsible for some aspects of town government up to 1851 and of which he was a member for many years), followed by something to eat in the respectable hostelry next door where street commissioners often gathered, an afternoon back at the business with a 5 o'clock philanthropic meeting of one of the many committees of which he was an active member, after which he would have returned home for what was left of the day. Candia, by contrast, would have spent her day in Edgbaston caring for the children both physically and educationally and supervising the household. In 1851, when they had six children, she had two female servants in the house and this was certainly not a generous number for a middle-class household, given the amount of domestic labour required in a pre-mechanical age.

If she had a little spare time she might have visited one or two poor families in whom she took a special interest, but as her daughter Maria recalled, she rarely left home: 'Our precious Mother had a very busy home life with her five boys and one girl, living amongst them as much as possible; she was a lovingly watchful and affectionate wife and mother seldom visiting from home.'

Candia's social life centred on her extended family and the Quaker network of Friends. Candia was indeed an essentially 'private person' whilst her husband was well known as a 'public man'. Such a social demarcation of male as 'public' and female as 'private' was both reinforced and encouraged by the physical separation between work and home.

21. Davidoff, L. and Hall, C. *op. cit.*; Prochaska, F.K. (1980) *Women and Philanthropy in Nineteenth-Century England*, Oxford.

ACKNOWLEDGEMENTS

This chapter is part of a larger research project, financed by the Social Science Research Council, and done jointly with Leonnore Davidoff, with whom all aspects of this article have been discussed. Thanks also to Veronica Beechey, Stuart Hall and Susan Meikle for their comments.

Chapter 12

THE ROLE OF RELIGION IN THE CULTURAL STRUCTURE OF THE LATER VICTORIAN CITY

J.H.S. Kent

[from *Transactions of the Royal Historical Society*, **23**, 5th series (1973): 153–173]

Religion has always been important in debates about British cities since the clerics of the 1820s started complaining about loss of faith in the growing towns, and the turn of century sociologists identified towns with rational patterns of thought, and rationality with secularization. On the other hand, theory also suggested that the alienating and disorientating effect of urban life might increase the attractions and power of religion, and recent historical studies suggested that religious provision and observance may have increased up to the 1900s. Kent's article sets the scene for these debates in a balanced and perceptive way by reminding us that religious influence was not just a matter of buildings and attenders. He identifies social processes both urban and more general which weakened the influence of religion. Class divisions, suburbanization and the decline of key urban voluntary institutions play a part in a debate which is by no means over. Note that recent work by Stedman Jones and Ellen Ross allows historians to set aside Kent's doubts about the existence of a working-class community. Still, he serves a useful reminder that the Church provided common cultural elements across the class as well as being a source of conflict.

One obviously cannot make generalizations covering all the towns and cities of late nineteenth-century England. London was a case by itself; Liverpool a very different port from Bristol; an industrial town like Rochdale seems very remote from Dorchester. Nor is it possible to give a single brief definition of a city, though many have tried. 'Just as there is no single form of the pre-industrial city', wrote R.E. Pahl, 'urbanization as concentration of population does not lead to any single pattern of class action and conflict.'[1] Attempts to provide a definition of a city culminate in David Riesman's comment that the city is what we choose to make it for the purposes of analysis. One has to accept that Bristol, Dorchester, Rochdale and Liverpool were towns without exaggerating what they had in common.

Most Victorian towns prospered and their population increased. Religious institutions multiplied at the same time. In Liverpool, for example, in 1800 there were twelve Nonconformist chapels in a population of 77,000; in 1840 sixty chapels in a population of 223,000; in 1900, 325 chapels in a city of 716,000. This does not mean that religious institutions expanded at the same pace as urban society in general: in the case of Liverpool itself, the increase in chapels had been erratic and unplanned, so that the *Daily Post's* religious census of 1908 showed that there was a total morning attendance in the Free Church chapels of 20,000 and an evening attendance of 47,000, which meant an average attendance per chapel of sixty-two and 145 respectively.[2] Robert Currie argues that, looked at in terms of a membership–population ratio, Wesleyan Methodist membership declined continuously from 1841 to 1921; the second largest Methodist body, Primitive Methodism, declined from 1881 to 1931; the smaller Methodist Free Church, in its various guises, declined in Currie's absolute sense from 1871.[3] As for the Anglican Church, the comparison that stands out is between the two attempts in our period to calculate the size of religious groups in London: the *British Weekly* survey of 1886 and the *Daily News* census of 1902–3. It was claimed that for a comparable 'London' the estimated total attendance at all kinds of religious institutions fell from a *British Weekly* total of 1,167,312 to a *Daily News* total of 1,003,361, while the population of the area had risen by about 700,000. Within these figures, which no one at the time challenged very seriously, Anglican attendances had decreased from about 535,000 in 1886 to 396,000 in 1902–3.[4] At the time it seemed very important that during the same years Free Church attendances in 'London' had hardly fallen at all, but this was misleading: the Baptist and Congregationalist groups had just come to a peak from which they were to decline continuously.[5] It is fair for Professor Owen Chadwick to remind us that for many at the time what seemed most evident was the increase in the number of churches and chapels and of the number

1. R.E. Pahl, *Readings in Urban Sociology* (London, 1968), p. 4.
2. I. Sellers, 'Nonconformist Attitudes in later 19th-Century Liverpool', *Trans. Hist. Soc. Lancashire and Cheshire*, cxiv (1962), pp. 216–17.
3. R. Currie, *Methodism Divided* (London, 1968), pp. 85–103.
4. R. Mudie-Smith, *The Religious Life of London* (London, 1904), p. 281.
5. Peak year for the Baptists, for example, was 1906, when the United Kingdom membership was 434,741; in 1967 the equivalent figure was 290,313.

of people using them,[6] but the period of substantial growth had lain between 1800 and about 1860. There is no question of any second evangelical awakening in England in 1859,[7] and from 1870 at the latest the leaders of the religious institutions were aware that development was at least slowing down – and they did not need E.R. Wickham's *Church and People in an Industrial City* (1957) to tell them that the urban working classes had largely withdrawn from contact with them.[8]

In any case, it may be regarded as axiomatic that the strength of religious institutions depends, not on the number of people who are existentially committed to a particular theological outlook, Christian, Buddhist or Islamic, but on the social roles which are available to the institutions as such. Apart from the increase in population, social conflicts, not a sudden change in the number of people prepared to accept Christian beliefs, or, more generally, a 'religious' outlook, explain the expansion which can be seen taking place in some cities. A good example of what this could mean can be found in Bristol. The principal Victorian middle-class expansion of Bristol was on to the higher ground overlooking the medieval city on the western side. Here the main road ran fairly straight for about a mile, culminating in Blackboy Hill. Along this road, which came to divide Clifton, on the left, from Cotham and Redland on the right, a number of churches and chapels were built during the Victorian period. On the Clifton side the parish churches were St John's (1841, morning attendance 1881,[9] 520, evening attendance, 380) and St Paul's (built in 1853, given a parish in 1859, burned in 1867, replaced with a second church 1868, a.m. in 1881, 920, p.m., 726); further into Clifton were Christ Church (1841, a.m. 923, p.m. 920), Emmanuel (1865–69, a.m. 740, p.m., 537) and All Saints, which replaced an older building in 1868 and was designed by G.E. Street (a.m. 652, p.m. 820): this was the only High Church parish in the area. On the other side of the Whiteladies Road there were St Mary the Virgin, Tyndall's Park (1874, a.m. 715, p.m. 664), and St Nathanael's, Cotham (1875, a.m. 241, p.m. 301).

The Wesleyan Methodist chapels were Victoria, at the start of the Whiteladies Road (1862/63, a.m. 320, p.m. 312); Trinity (1866/67, a.m. 347, p.m. 405), about half the way to the Blackboy Hill; and at

6. O. Chadwick, 'The Established Church under Attack', in *The Victorian Crisis of Faith*, ed. A. Symondson (London, 1970), pp. 91–107.
7. *Cf.* J.E. Orr, *The Second Evangelical Awakening in Britain* (London, 1949).
8. Wickham's city was Sheffield.
9. J.F. Nicholls and J. Taylor, *Bristol Past and Present* (Bristol, 1881), pp. 305–8. For another view of D. Carter, 'Social and Political Influences of the Bristol Churches' (M. Litt. thesis, Univ. of Bristol, 1970). Bristol population 1881, 211, 659.

the top of the hill the Methodist Free Church opened a chapel called The Mount of Olives in 1855, six years after the Wesleyan schism of 1849, (a.m. sixty, p.m. 110), but this chapel passed into the hands of the Wesleyan Methodists in 1892. A second and more successful Methodist Free Church chapel was built in Redland in 1876 (a.m. 242, p.m. 219), before the Redland Court estate was finally broken up and built over. In Cotham (1878, a.m. 273, p.m. 304) was a third Wesleyan chapel. Wesleyan Methodism suffered badly from the 1849 schism in Bristol: the communicant roll fell from 3,849 in 1850 to 1,453 in 1854, and it was 1891 before the higher figure was reached again.

There were three Baptist chapels: Tyndale (1867/68, a.m. 372, p.m. 320), started with thirty-eight members from older Baptist chapels in the city; Cotham Grove (1872, a.m. 267, p.m. 192), also founded with forty-five members from older Baptist chapels; and Buckingham chapel, on the Clifton side, built in 1847 (a.m. 273, p.m. 193). The first Congregational chapel in the district was Highbury in Cotham (1841, a.m. 621, p.m. 426), the first major commission of the High Church architect, William Butterfield: members from this church established Redland Park (1861, a.m. 552, p.m. 486), on the Redland side of Whiteladies Road, where Tyndale Baptist, Trinity Wesleyan and Redland Congregational appeared, close together, in rapid succession. In Clifton there was a Unitarian chapel, Oakfield Road (1864, a.m. eighty-five, p.m. seventy-six), and a meeting of the Christian Brethren, Bethesda (a.m. 312, p.m. 133. The absence of Bible Christian, Primitive Methodist or Salvation Army groups helps to characterize the area.

For Anglicanism the seven new parish churches mentioned were part of the nineteenth-century drive to extend the small-parish system which was the bane of Victorian Anglican planning: between 1823 and 1903 forty-one new parish churches were built in Bristol, which, with mission chapels, provided about 36,000 sittings. The predominantly middle-class nature of the area is shown by the fact that here Anglican gross attendances in the religious census of 1881 exceeded Free Church attendances by about nine to seven, whereas in Bristol as a whole Free Church attendances exceeded Anglican by about 61,000 to about 45,000.[10] It was significant of the social prestige of the area and of the price of having a bishop that when the Bristol see was restored in 1897 (having been combined with that of Gloucester since 1836), the new palace, costing £14,000, was placed on one side of Redland Green, and built 'in the style of the simple old manor houses in districts where stone is the local building material'.[11]

10. J.F. Nicholls and J. Taylor, *Bristol Past and Present* (Bristol, 1881), pp. 305–8.
11. C.S. Taylor, *Bristol. Illustrated Guide to the Church Congress* (London, 1903), p. 115.

For the Bristol Free Churches, however, the establishment of this series of strong chapels meant the formation of a new middle-class social and political leadership which carried more weight than did the leadership of the older chapels in the central part of the city, or of the new Victorian chapels standing on the southern side of the river Avon in the poorer districts of Bedminster and Totterdown. A hard-core membership of 300–400 was good for any of these chapels, but larger numbers passed through them – for example, between 1868 and 1894 Richard Glover, pastor at Tyndale Baptist, made about 800 members, but in 1901 the three Baptist chapels had total memberships of Buckingham, 117; Cotham Grove, 259; and Tyndale, 321.[12]

The strength of these Free Church chapels lay not in numbers but in their ability to organize and lead a pressure-group whose urban programme they legitimized on religious grounds, and pressed on the amorphous Liberal Party of the late nineteenth century. Standish Meacham has suggested that Nonconformity accepted the development of the industrial city in a sense that Anglicanism did not. The social groups from which Anglican leadership came clung to the feeling that the city was vulgar and *for* the vulgar.[13] What Meacham said about Anglicanism was probably true, but although Nonconformists accepted the city as an arena of conflict they also rejected it, because the city made them conscious of their lack of social power. Their social programme, which demanded the abolition of Anglican and Roman Catholic day-schools, the stamping out of prostitution, the closure of public-houses, the prohibition of gambling and in general a kind of frozen Sunday, reflected this dislike of the city as it was, part 'Anglican' and 'upper-class', part 'working-class'. Nevertheless, Meacham is right in so far as one must distinguish between anti-urbanism of an Anglican kind, its roots in the English governing class's arcadian attitudes and low view of commerce and industry, and a Nonconformist anti-urbanism, its sources to be found in social and political frustration. Where one differs from both Meacham and Asa Briggs, who advanced similar views of the urban role of Nonconformity in terms of Birmingham, is in doubting that one can distinguish between a negative Anglican and a positive Nonconformist attitude to the changing urban situation.[14]

In any case, one must be cautious about generalization. In Bristol the Free Churches retained through the second half of the nineteenth century the leadership and support of a number of local businessmen of various kinds, but if one took Liverpool, much the more successful

---

12. *The Baptist Handbook for 1901* (London, 1900), p. 256.
13. S. Meacham, 'The Church in the Victorian City', *Victorian Studies*, xi (1968), Summer Supplement (on Victorian urban history).
14. *Ibid*.

port of the two in the Victorian period, as an example one would find a different picture. Ian Sellers writes:

> Nor can it be said that in the later years of the century Liverpool Nonconformity contained within its ranks the numbers of successful, self-made businessmen who elsewhere financed Nonconformity and also provided it with vigorous lay leadership. Throughout this period most denominations in Liverpool complained of impoverishment or the lack of wealthy adherents, and their complaints are borne out by the testimony of independent witnesses. Thus, when the Baptists closed down Comus Street chapel in 1877, a most pathetic letter was sent round the churches', begging them to allow the proceeds of the sale to be used as a nucleus for the support of their many impoverished churches. 'The number of rich Baptists in Liverpool', the circular concludes, 'is diminishing; we now have very few.' The only two really prosperous congregations which, if the figures for Hospital Sunday collections are an accurate guide, far outstripped the rest in material source – Sefton Park Presbyterian and Ullet Road Unitarian – were curiously isolated from the rest of Liverpool Nonconformity, and pursued singular patterns of political behaviour.[15]

Sefton Park (1880), was dominated from its foundation to 1905 by the Reverend John Watson, whose original Jacobitism became in Liverpool a sanctimonious vision of England as a peasant utopia presided over by a benevolent Tory government; he backed the Boer War as a cure for national debility and loved to appear in full-dress uniform in the streets of Liverpool as chaplain of the Liverpool Scottish.[16] The social role of urban Presbyterianism, however, like that of urban Roman Catholicism, was very much a racial question.

These expanding religious institutions took a place in a new urban structure. How far one can speak of a Victorian urban civilization is another question; one could hardly compare the cities that I have mentioned with Florence, Venice, Amsterdam or Paris. Culture, however, is a term subject to definition, and the following may serve as headings here. An urban culture will combine elements of government, economic patterns, education, recreation and religion. In the late Victorian period institutionalized religion (as distinct from more diffuse 'religious' behaviour of all kinds) came so frequently into conflict with other institutions in matters which affected the other elements in the urban culture (as I have already suggested in referring to the social programme of the Nonconformists) that not only is the idea of cultural conflict an important qualification of the urban role of institutionalized religion, but it also becomes

15. I. Sellers, *op. cit.*, p. 217.
16. See the life of Watson by W.R. Nicholl (1908), entitled *Ian McLaren* (Watson's pseudonym as an author).

necessary to ignore denominational differences to some extent and think instead in terms of a religious sub-culture which was slowly separating itself, institutionally, from the dominant, largely secular culture. This was an urban phenomenon, partially concealed at the time by special circumstances. In the case of Anglicanism, this shift towards a common identity with other religious institutions was modified psychologically by persistent memories of having been part of the dominant culture in the past, and this explains why it was especially Anglican dignitaries who felt it their role to insist on the essential unity of society. Thus in 1876, for example, Canon, later Bishop, Westcott told the Peterborough Volunteers of the vital unity of the nation:

> I do not forget [he told them] that there are forces at work among us which tend to separate class from class, and to set one against another in fratricidal rivalry, I do not forget that some would represent loyal homage to rank and blood as derogatory to the generous spirit which it purifies. But I am sure that the great heart of England is sound still. I am sure that the unity of which I speak is real, if often concealed, and that reverence is as yet powerful among us if often dissembled. . . . There is a living circulation between our many ranks which makes mutual understanding easy. On the other hand, there is an age-long tradition round each one which preserves its distinctions intact. We do not yet think that we have made or that we can unmake the dignity of the throne. . . . We believe – the whole framework of our life helps, nay forces, us to believe – that our manhood is one, and at the same time, in order that the whole may be one, differentiated in countless fragments of which each fulfils its proper office.[17]

In the case of the Free Churches the complicating factor was that between about 1890 and 1914 the clerical leaders went through a period of intense and disastrous exaltation, when they believed that their denominations were about to inherit the place of Anglicanism (which they accepted as still being part of the dominant culture) and even to impose their own patterns of behaviour upon British society as a whole. Despite this inner conflict, and the suspicion with which many in both groups viewed Roman Catholicism, urban religious institutions were beginning to approximate to one another in social composition and ethos in the late Victorian period, and it is this process which explains the movement towards institutional unity (which also began before the end of the nineteenth century), and not, as has been suggested by Bryan Wilson and Robert Currie, falling membership figures combined with a clerical conspiracy.[18]

17. B.F. Westcott, *Peterborough Sermons* (London, 1904), pp. 364–65.
18. For these ideas, see B. Wilson, *Religion in Secular Society* (London, 1969), pp. 151–205; and R. Currie, *op. cit.*, especially pp. 293–316.

Looked at from the point of view of institutional religion, therefore, one cannot describe Victorian urban culture as a unity: the religious sub-culture was not simply the religious expression of the dominant cultural pattern. Conflict emerged at the level of local government, for although religious institutions sympathized with the general middle-class Victorian desire for order, they also tried, especially in the 1890s, to use local authorities to enforce their own moral aims. The Reverend Charles F. Aked, left-wing pastor of the Pembroke Baptist chapel in Liverpool from 1890 to 1906 (when he left for the Fifth Avenue chapel in New York), told the first National Council of the Evangelical Free Churches in 1896:

> Law is one thing, but the enforcement of it is another. The experience of Liverpool by this time is well known. . . . The civic authorities protected vice . . . the policy of concentration was the one followed. Two districts were given up to the trade in vice. If the evil-doers opened business in other neighbourhoods they were prosecuted, but so long as they kept within the infected areas they were safe. . . . When we were exploring I was accosted by women at ten different houses in one street, and at five houses out of six standing together . . . I counted one night forty-four fallen women coming out of one liquor place in ten minutes, and sixty-six at closing-time. But at last the conscience of Liverpool was touched. The Churches put on strength. The people arose. Then a political party inscribed 'social reform' upon its banners, won seats at elections. . . . The old gang was broken up. The Watch Committee had a new chairman and a new policy. The law was set in motion. . . .[19]

Setting the existing laws on prostitution, drink and gambling in motion and campaigning for new laws as well dramatized the cultural conflict between strongly opposed views as to how the industrial city should be organized. At the economic level, however, the intensive but selective exploitation of urban space which characterized the nineteenth century tended to be taken for granted by the religious institutions precisely because their most sophisticated and influential leadership came from the protected areas. As H.J. Dyos has written: 'the middle-class Victorian suburb was both an invention for accentuating social distinctions and a means of putting off for a generation or two the full realization of what was entailed by living in a slum.'[20] There was never any real question of there being an organic whole, 'the city'. In Bristol, for example, the nineteenth-century city expanded from the medieval, low-lying port up steep escarpments into Clifton, Cotham and Redland, while at the same

19. *Proceedings of the First National Council of the Evangelical Free Churches* (London, 1896), pp. 199–200.
20. H.J. Dyos, 'The slums of Victorian London', *Victorian Studies*, 11 (1967), p. 27.

time forming new industrial areas at a distance from this middle-class citadel. The city moved both westward (bourgeois) and south and east (industrial). The role of religion could not be described as the same in both directions, nor were the two areas at all profoundly related, still less united, in the consciousness of most individuals. But a city like Bristol did not only exist as a kind of class system – as was very obvious in other new towns like Swindon, where the poor and the better-off crept towards one another's proximity for most of the century: the city also existed less as economic structure than as the momentary product of many economic stresses. From one point of view everything in a Victorian town was constantly in decline, moving away from being new, fashionable, solid. Railway building ripped into the core of many large cities destroying housing and worsening the lives of the poor. There was often more stress than structure. The older forms of the western religious tradition had been able to rationalize what seemed, down to the eighteenth century, to be an almost changeless economic structure; they were not so well adapted to rationalize rapid and unpredictable economic change and growth. This did not seem to matter very much in the eyes of the institutional leaders themselves until, towards the end of the century, it emerged that industrial workers were capable of organizing themselves: a further cultural clash became inevitable at this stage as it became clear that what the pamphleteer had meant by 'the bitter cry of outcast London' – a Macedonian call for help in his religious vocabulary – had only existed in his own clerical imagination.[21] Even so, the response of the religious institution could expose the cultural conflict in bizarre forms. In 1894 the Baptist popular preacher, F.B. Meyer, pastor of Christ Church in Westminster Bridge Road, instituted a 'People's Drawing Room' for working women, to balance the 'Pleasant Sunday Afternoon' which he already provided for the men. 'I have a number of palms for decoration', he said,

> and shall try to procure one or two canaries to make the surroundings as comfortable and homelike as possible. Babies will have to be given up at the door, and for them we have our crêche, where feeding-bottles, rattles and other toys will be provided, and our kind amateur nurses will set the mothers free for an hour of quiet self-culture and social intercourse. I hope to read them selections from Tennyson and Longfellow. . . .[22]

21. *The Bitter Cry of Outcast London* (London, 1883) has been attributed to several authors, but A. Mearns and W.C. Preston, the probable co-authors, were both Congregationalist ministers.
22. F.B. Meyer, 'The People's Drawing Room', *Bristol Christian Leader* (1894), p. 132.

This recipe for social reconciliation was repeated with breathless admiration by the *Bristol Christian Leader* (April 1894), the monthly organ of Bristol's Nonconformist institutions in the 1890s. The conflict really sharpened when organized labour challenged the political role of the Free Churches by breaking with the Liberal Party, to which Nonconformity had seen itself offering the labour vote; but the independence of the new labour movement, and of the trade unions, was equally a cultural split from the Anglican and Roman Catholic institutions.

The bulk of the urban middle class absorbed nineteenth-century economic change without excessive physical or psychological suffering; those among them who identified with religious groups did not regard economic development as threatening the significance of their religious institutions; the liberal, non-dogmatic theology which many of them favoured in the last quarter of the century approved of 'progress'. This meant that the middle-class leaders of religious institutions concentrated their moral attention on leisure, not work. Paradoxically, industrial workers, and even more those who lived in urban poverty, also concentrated their vitality on leisure, but did so because they could not accept the consequences of economic change, and especially the Victorian industrial town, as moral. There was a mutual, but incompatible, repudiation of the town as it was. Over leisure and recreation the conflict between the articulate leadership of religious institutions and the poorer groups of society (together with the small group of the aristocracy proper, a favourite target of the popular preacher), became absolute towards the end of the century, even if the absoluteness was sometimes the absoluteness of unreality, as when the Free Church Congress of 1896 demanded legislation to close public-houses on Sunday. For example, in Middlesbrough (population at the turn of the century 97,000) a local census recorded that on a given Sunday 22,000 people attended sixty different chapels, churches, etc.; about 90,000 were seen to enter 100 public-houses and thirty-six off-licences during the same day.[23]

But the vigour with which religious institutions denounced public-houses, 'blood-tubs' and music-halls, bookmakers and betting in general, prostitution (though this was partly because of the attraction to middle-class boys), professional football (though not cricket, which remained part of the wealthier classes' cultural scene), also reflected a confidence born of an awareness that the cultural structure of a Victorian city was so deeply divided that religious institutions could expect outside support as long as they were seen to be criticizing working-class (or aristocratic) conventions of behaviour.

23. Lady Bell, *At the Works* (London, 1911), pp. 33, 187.

Here an Anglican comment on football may balance the references made to Nonconformity. *Commonwealth*, started in 1896 as a journal which believed itself to be Christian Socialist, said, during the South African War:

> War rages, great social changes are toward, disasters intervene, there are discussions on bread and education, but the adult male population of England and Scotland is watching its football matches. The sight is a portent, a hundred thousand young adult males, all in black roundhats, small moustaches and short pipes, gazing with painful intensity at the twenty-two combatants they have hired to compete before them. So long as the Saturday afternoon is preserved, and the sixpence for the match secure, England need never fear revolution.[24]

No doubt Scott Holland,[25] who was a parson, wrote this, but the distancing of the young men in their bowler hats with their short pipes, and their intensity which is painful, not to them, but to the journalist, is significant of the cultural conflict. It was, after all, a parson who was supposed to have gnawed through the handle of his umbrella while watching Spofforth, the Australian fast bowler, wreck the English batting in 1882, but *his* intensity was thought to be a proper reaction to an epic situation. One finds a similar attitude in the *Bristol Christian Leader* in November, 1893, during a local mining strike, when trade union leaders had criticized Bristol religious institutions for alleged indifference. 'It seems to be the toilers' grievance that employers form the bulk of the ruling element in the Churches, and the Churches, they reason, are therefore against them. We cannot agree with this.' The *Leader* said that it would support 'any safe course to take towards bringing in a happier temporal state for the toilers'.[26] Of the whole way of life to which both secular and religious institutions wanted to bind the industrious poor, Alexander Paterson wrote: 'How low are the civic standards of England, how fallen the ideals and beauties of Christianity. No man that has dreams can rest content because the English worker has reached this high level of regular work and rare intoxication.'[27]

What had happened was that the bringing together of masses of working-class people – the steelworkers of Middlesbrough and the Great Western Railway factory workers at Swindon, for example – in similar streets, factories and workshops produced a psychological situation different from that produced by the traditional presence

24. *Commonwealth* (1902), p. 146.
25. H.S. Holland (1847–1918) was Regius professor of divinity at Oxford from 1910 to his death, a comment on Anglicanism rather than on Holland.
26. *Bristol Christian Leader* (1893), p. 324.
27. Alexander Paterson, *Across the Bridges* (London, 1914), p. 146.

in the countryside of agricultural labourers, always thinly scattered on the ground, often living in detached groups of cottages, and isolated from one another much of the time by the jobs they were doing. In the late Victorian town a middle-class, or suburban consciousness of the working-class was quite as real, if not a more real, phenomenon, than a proletarian class-consciousness. Despite the sentimentality of a writer like Richard Hoggart, one doubts the existence of a significant working-class culture as such, to be identified, for example, as '*for* life'.[28] The state of mind of the majority of the poorer people living in places like Bristol, Liverpool or Swindon seems to have been more a consciousness of not belonging fully to the dominant, though sub-divided culture.[29] Given that these were positive and negative forms of the same culture, the difference between them was partly imposed by the controlling groups. Suburban society in general believed, and may have needed to believe for the sake of its own identity, that the poor had a different way of life which suited their limited capacities: the poor were not supposed to present a reflection, however inadequate, of suburban culture. Popular education, which in Victorian times was meant to act as a limiting factor on the development of the poor, and which was deliberately remoulded in a more élitist direction by the 1902 Education Act, was the secular means of imposing cultural forms: Robert Roberts, for instance, in his fascinating description of Salford at the opening of the century, emphasizes how the slum school which he attended indoctrinated its pupils with the cult of empire.[30] The role of the major religious institutions, one which they seemed to accept, was that of legitimizing suburban attitudes while rejecting as incompatible with religious behaviour the normal leisure activities of the working classes (and the aristocracy).

This steady criticism of secular leisure had a financial basis as well. Victorian chapels were built on debt, and in the course of the century two and even three buildings were put up by the same local group; the Anglican equivalent was usually the 'iron church' which preceded a hardback building. The cost of paying for buildings, ministers, and also for overseas missions had to be found by a comparatively small group on an annual basis. The feeling that the religious society should separate itself from the secular society, a feeling powerful in the Catholic, Protestant and small-sect groups,

---

28. As supporting evidence here, cf. H.J. Gans, 'Culture and Class in the Study of Poverty', in *People and Plans* (London, 1972), pp. 298–330.
29. Since it seems usually to be held that an articulate working-man is not typical it is difficult to justify this statement from such writers as Alfred Williams (see below, p. 169) or Thomas Wright; the journals of city missioners suggest the same conclusion.
30. R. Roberts, *The Classic Slum* (London, 1971), pp. 101–15.

was now reinforced by financial pressures. The survival of all these groups depended upon their absorbing the time and money of their adherents, and secular leisure ate away at both. And if working-class men and women patronized public-houses, bet on horses (the typical form of gambling of the period) and went to football matches they were unlikely to support financially the parish churches and mission-chapels which middle-class religious institutions erected in working-class areas.

The education of the children of the poor, the final element which I suggested as part of an urban culture, had been a constant source of conflict. In the 1840s, as one sees clearly, for example, in the reports on the mining areas in Staffordshire and the north-east,[31] the ministers of all religious institutions saw the working-classes as ignorant, easily led astray by agitators (Chartists, of course, at that time), unaware of their best interests (and therefore tempted to strike, which, as middle-class commentators were already willing to tell them, was never in their best interests). The ministers saw themselves, and wanted government to see them, as the agents of civilization in a society which was falling apart, and therefore they favoured more schools of an elementary kind as long as they themselves controlled them, and as long as some variety of Christianity was taught in them. For a brief period in the 1840s government was sufficiently alarmed to welcome this support, but between the 1840s and the 1880s the situation changed and religious institutions ceased to play a vital part in the strategy of the English ruling groups. Thus Bishop Westcott's 'Christian Socialism' was not a move to obtain concessions from the state by threatening to support urban revolutionary societies, but expressed the hope that by showing sympathy for trade unionism and preaching industrial conciliation (not strikes) institutionalized religion might still put in a claim to be playing an important role in the structure of the state. In education, the act of 1870 did not finally decide the future, but wrote off the past, that is, the hope of the leaders of the religious bodies that their fundamental role in the new urban structure might be in providing education, especially at the level of the poor. The Board School system pointed towards new secular institutions in which the schoolmaster would finally replace the priest: the decline in the number of ordination candidates began then and has gone on ever since.

From this point of view Forster gave his Nonconformist friends a last chance: if, out of fear of Anglicanism, and especially of Anglicanism in the villages, where they did not believe in the

---

31. See the report on the South Staffordshire mining area by T. Tancred in 1843, and *The Report of the Commissioner into the State of the Mining Districts* (1846) by H.S. Tremenheere.

possibility of a conscience clause, they abandoned denominational schools, for which in any case they could not pay, the system of local, and especially urban, Board Schools might give them the chance, at least in some cities – Bristol, for instance, where the non-Anglicans held a majority most of the time, or Swindon, but not Salisbury, where an Anglican local majority prevented competition from non-Anglican schools in the name of the theory that cathedral towns were now the last fortresses of the Church of England proper – to destroy or at least greatly weaken the Anglican and Roman Catholic denominational schools, without surrendering all religious content in education at the same time. And if they could break the hold of the Anglican/Roman Catholic groups on elementary education in the towns they would have changed their own urban role profoundly. In other words, the struggle between religious institutions in the towns over the education of the children of the poor was not primarily about education, but about social power: it was a contest for a social role in late Victorian cities between two groups for whom educational policy was a convenient and natural way of expressing conflict. While they fought one another for social and cultural control, however, the dominant culture slipped further and further out of the reach of both of them. In urban terms, between 1870 and 1902 Nonconformity certainly succeeded in weakening Anglicanism, but the conflict only damaged the religious sub-culture of which both were part.

Two quotations from the Anglican journal, *Commonwealth*, may help to fix the conclusion here. C.F.G. Masterman, writing in 1902 against the background of renewed education controversy, still romantically defended the ideal of total religious education which was rapidly disappearing: he longed for a religious school in which a lesson in arithmetic would somehow be different from a mathematics lesson in a secular school. The London School Board had made 'religious instruction' a brief subject among subjects. He continued:

> we have the one damning fact of the religious position of South London today after thirty years of this admirable instruction: a population practically heathen, with little knots of worshippers in a great ocean of indifference. . . . The children learn of a book or a creed . . . the knowledge remains with no relation to the real world of their daily existence; and it sloughs off as the benefit of three quarters of school life sloughs off in the two or three years succeeding school. . . .[32]

This was romantic because Masterman was writing as though the 'religious school' was still a credible alternative in what was no

32. C.F.G. Masterman, 'The Fight for the Schools', *Commonwealth*, vii (1902), p. 164.

longer simply a state system for the teaching of poor children. As middle-class children began to enter what was becoming a national education system it was no longer possible to impose the form of the 'religious school' on what were ceasing to be really local schools. What Scott Holland called 'the religious half-hour in the secular school' spread through the surviving denominational network: it was an open secret by 1902 that at the level of the urban day school the religious teaching of many denominational schools hardly differed from that in the Board Schools.

My second quotation is from Scott Holland, writing as editor of *Commonwealth* in November 1902. 'The melancholy lesson is forced upon us by the present education controversy that Dissenters do really hate the Church' – by which he meant Anglicanism – 'so that their opposition to it is the one thing that rouses them to special enthusiasm'.[33]

Holland was correct in implying, on this particular occasion, that education was not the point, and correct in stressing the intensity of feeling; but he was mistaken in putting the issue in clerical terms, as between Anglicanism and Dissent. This was how the clerical leaders of the religious institutions wanted to have the controversy understood. But there were at least four parties involved: the religious sub-culture split into two parties by an urban conflict between middle-class groups; a secular Conservative political party, prepared to rescue the Anglican – Roman Catholic alliance from defeat but not interested in imposing the 'religious school' in the state system on an urban level; and the working-class, whose representatives on education commissions normally objected to what they called dogmatic teaching and supported the Board School tradition. In 1902 Nonconformity finally discovered that it had lost its power-base in the cities, while the other major religious institutions averted similar catastrophe.

At the urban level all these cultural conflicts can be consolidated in a single example, the differing time-structures to be found in the city. There was a superficial unity, because, in theory, if not in practice, every one was subject to traditional clerical time, modified in England by a Protestant willingness at the Reformation to sanction the disappearance of many religious holidays. During the nineteenth century there had been a renewed campaign to impose a complete Sunday shut-down, and this had largely succeeded, partly because this was an issue on which the religious sub-culture remained united, and partly because the campaign fitted into a middle-class desire for the establishment of urban public order.

33. *Commonwealth*, vii (1902), p. 339.

Thus Sunday became the urban working-man's day of leisure, given him by tradition, sabbatarianism and public convenience. Theoretically, the time-structure of his life was similar to everyone else's: a working-week rhythmically interrupted by a silent Sunday on which, after all, the religious institutions were theoretically open to him. Leisure or no leisure, however, he was not to be entertained, though innovations like the Pleasant Sunday Afternoon revealed a clerical awareness that this denial of the demand for entertainment could not be maintained indefinitely. During the nineteenth century liberal pressure from outside the religious sub-culture mounted in favour of at least intellectual concessions, and one finds *Commonwealth*, in its initial liberal mood of 1896, welcoming the vote of the House of Commons in favour of the Sunday opening of museums and art galleries: only small amounts of labour would be required and Jews, who allegedly operated the Birmingham public library on Sundays, could always be employed. In Bristol, however, the religious institutions remained broadly against a proposal made in 1892 to open municipal library and museum on Sunday. It was a step towards the secularization of the Sabbath, said the *Bristol Christian Leader*: 'The working-classes neither demand nor appreciate the opportunities which are claimed for them' – while to see the neighbourhood of the Suspension Bridge on a Sunday evening 'is enough to make a Christian's heart sink within him'[34] Out of 107 Free Church ministers in the city (fifty-five Methodist, thirty-five Congregational, fifteen Baptist, One Moravian and one Presbyterian), only one replied in favour of Sunday opening when sent a questionnaire in 1893, and the local council finally rejected the proposal by a vote of about two to one.

Nor was this simply the conservatism of the south-west: in Lady Bell's Middlesbrough about 1907 the theatres, the working-men's clubs and the museum all had to close on Sunday and only the newspaper rooms at the Free Library opened its doors.[35] And although a Joint Committee of Convocation had reported in favour of the change in 1893, in 1902 one finds Scott Holland in *Common-wealth*, no longer so liberal, pointing out that Anglican liberals had only meant to make Sunday joyfully religious, not to introduce a secular Sunday. Which again suggested a misunderstanding on his part of the role of the religious sector, for the movement to alter the tone of Sunday had been a response to the secularizing tendency of the dominant culture: to preserve a role in the urban structure religious institutions were expected to legitimize changes of this kind. Now, however, Holland wanted to fight for Sunday

34. *Bristol Christian Leader* (1893), p. 62.
35. Lady Bell, *op. cit.*, pp. 186–87.

– 'its social value as enforced relief – its religious value as spiritual necessity' – quite forgetful of the working-classes against whom he was really fighting.[36]

The first article in the series which he commissioned on the issue touches directly on the underlying problem of time-structures. Armitage Robinson, as a canon of Westminster, was perhaps not the best person to write it. Special services on a Sunday afternoon – no doubt he was thinking of his neighbour F.B. Meyer among others – drew in some working-class people, but their neglect – so, he worded it, somehow supposing them to be Christians in any case – their neglect of the first half of Sunday must be remedied. It emerges at one stage of his argument that he knew that working-class people in London did not only stay up late on Saturday night in order to enjoy themselves, but that people waited as late as possible before buying meat which had cheapened as the night wore on, but nevertheless he felt that 'we' must teach the working-man how to spend his Saturday night better. 'He now sleeps late because he has supped so late', the Canon concluded.[37]

It should be added here that in discussions of working-class behaviour at this time religious writers were still obsessed with the concept of conversion as a rapid change of life-direction. This, after all, was the revivalist period *par excellence*, of Moody and Sankey, Torrey and Alexander, and 'converting' preachers like H.P. Hughes. Thus Armitage Robinson really thought that the working-man had only to will a difference in his own behaviour, and largely ignored the extent to which individual conduct is enmeshed in an economic and social structure.

As the problem of food prices implies, there was a distinct working-class time-structure, and this is most easily illustrated by a particular example. This comes from Alfred Williams' description of *Life in a Railway Factory*, an account of the Great Western Railway works at Swindon in the last year of the nineteenth century. Williams was born in 1877 and worked there for more than twenty years.

Williams said that the factory-year was divided into three general periods, *i.e.* from Christmas till Easter, Easter until the 'Trip', which took place in July, and from 'Trip' until Christmas. It will emerge incidentally, however, that it was only partly Christmas which marked the second turning-point. All three were breaks in the factory routine, but there was little travelling at Easter; instead men put their gardens and allotments in order. Despite the prominence of ecclesiastical names, the factory revolved around the July 'Trip': over 20,000 people left the town, many going to London, many to Weymouth. About half the total came back the same night,

---

36. *Commonwealth*, vii (1902), p. 226.
37. *Ibid.*, p. 227.

but the remainder usually stayed for the eight days of the unpaid holiday. The Trip trains were free. By the time they came back most of the men had little or no money at all. They saved up for months beforehand, and whatever new clothes were bought for the summer were first worn on this occasion. From Christmas until Easter, Williams said, was a time of rising spirits; from Easter to the July Trip one of comparative ease and satisfaction; 'from August till December the feeling is one almost of despair. Day after day the black army files in and out of the entrances with the regularity of clockwork'.[38] The popularity of the Saturday football match (rather than the canon's morning service at Westminster) explains itself in the existential context. It is not surprising that Williams noted that 'many a workman boasts that he has denied himself a Sunday dinner in order to find the money . . . to attend Saturday's match'.[39] The stress involved is clearer when it is realised that the time until Christmas, the first half of the football season, was also the time when whatever money was to be saved had to be saved.

As for the week, there was a lethargic Monday, a productive Tuesday, and then a series of variable days ending in a wasted Saturday half-day which was still worked at the end of the century.

> Sunday is the day of complete inactivity with most of the workmen, and it is possibly the weakest and least enjoyed of all. If the day is dull and wet a great number stay in bed till dinner-time, and sometimes they remain there all day and night till Monday morning comes. This will not have done them much harm.[40]

The mention of despair in the weeks between August and December is interesting because Williams, without being quite conscious of it, goes on to describe a kind of New Year Festival. He wrote:

> New Year's Eve was always suitably observed and celebrated by those on the night-shift . . . [The work came gradually to a halt.] The steam-hammers were silenced, the fires were damped and the tools were thrown on one side. All that could be heard was the continual 'chu-chu' of the engine outside forcing the hydraulic pumps, and the exhaust of the donkey engine whirling the fan. Then an inventive and musical-minded workman stretched a rope across from the principals, and came forwards with two sets of steel rods, of varying lengths and thicknesses, capable of emitting almost any note in the scale . . . Some one fetched a big brass dome from a worn-out boiler, while several others had brought old buffers from the scrap waggons.

38. A. Williams, *Life in a Railway Factory* (London, 1915), p. 250.
39. *Ibid.*, p. 287.
40. *Ibid.* p. 254.

> Shortly before midnight, when the bells in the town and the far-off villages began to peal out, the workmen commenced their carnival. Bells were perfectly imitated by striking the bars of steel . . . the buffers contributed their sharp notes, and the brass dome sounded deeply and richly. When the noise had been continued for a sufficient length of time food was brought out . . .
>
> They ate, drank and slept. . . . they seldom started work any more that morning. The foremen and the watchmen were usually missing on New Year's Eve . . . . All this happened some twenty years ago and would not be permitted today. . . .[41]

The whole pattern, the year, the week, the Sunday, the New Year Celebration, with music and feasting, the annual Trip with its spend-out atmosphere, produced a time structure subtly different from that which contained the lives of those who served in religious institutions and sometimes took up their pens to write about the English Sunday – now, as the vicar of St John the Divine, Kennington, told *Commonwealth* readers, 'lost, and it can never be restored'.[42] I don't want to conclude this section by making exaggerated claims for the existence of a Victorian working-class 'religious attitude', which, though it was sometimes parasitic on institutionalized religion, as in the use of Christian passage rites, was, nevertheless, not essentially Christian at all. But there are parallels for this enthusiasm for the New Year festival, while the Harvest Festival, for a few years towards the end of the century, seems to have filled many urban chapels and churches with working-class people for one service only. The role of religion in the working-class world proper still waits for full investigation.

In earlier periods of European history, religion, while not necessarily directly inspiring outbursts of aesthetic achievement, had at any rate offered symbols and ideas through which painters especially could express themselves. If one goes to the cathedral in Antwerp, for example, one can see in Rubens's three great paintings, *The Planting of the Cross* and *The Descent from the Cross* which flank the altar-piece, *The Assumption*, the extent to which the western religious tradition still offered symbolic clothing to the vitality of an urban culture. The situation had changed by the nineteenth century but Victorian religious institutions still hoped to reverse what had become a firmly secularizing trend. Such hopes had to be realized in the new urban society and comment is necessary because we are discussing urban civilization. At the level represented by Rubens little was achieved. The claim that the Catholic revival inspired a movement of artistic renewal in England was not supported by

41. *Ibid.*, pp. 271–73.
42. *Commonwealth*, vii (1902), p. 229.

the meagreness and derivativeness of much of what was collected for the Victoria and Albert Museum's 1971 exhibition of 'Victorian Church Art'.[43] There were efforts, nevertheless, and one of them is the chapel of Keble College in Oxford. In his recent biography of the architect of the college, William Butterfield, Paul Thompson says of the chapel:

> It is the mosaics which dominate the interior . . . and make it at
> first sight one of the least attractive of Butterfield's later displays of
> polychrome. Yet it is well worth a longer look. The chapel is treated
> as a single, vast space, the whole effect concentrated on the outer
> surfaces. All the furniture is kept deliberately low: only dark long
> lines of seats, and a light open wrought metal pulpit and altar rails.
> The choir seats are pushed back to form a great open floorspace
> at the east end, paved in white and grey stone, with encaustic tile
> patterns in yellow, plum, emerald green and seagreen. These colours
> are taken up in the walls. The lowest stage is a bold wall-arcade,
> the surface behind of glazed plum-coloured brick, with thin seagreen
> strips and broader bands of formalized mastic patterning set in
> stone-flowers, suns and tendrils. Next come the mosaics, rather softer
> in colour: green, pink, pale blue, a limp yellow, red and white. The
> colours seem in fact too soft for the strong archaic lines of the figures
> and their powerful architectural setting. Surely the white ground
> is especially mistaken? Above the mosaics, however, the colouring
> reaches a superb climax.[44]

Here a modern enthusiasm for polychrome in the abstract unduly distracts Dr Thompson from the archaic lines of the mosaics which, though they present deliberately impersonal images of the Christian past, were meant to seize and hold the attention of the observer by their restless activity, to persuade him that the empty chapel was filled with an invisible but overwhelming presence. I doubt if the white is a mistake: it is the whiteness of the ground that finally rules out the possibility of any kind of naturalism; the whiteness is also essential to the restlessness of the whole. Inflexible, unecstatic, appealing to dogma, not reason, and to authority, not emotion, the chapel as Butterfield conceived it perfectly translates John Keble into architecture. Whether Keble of all men had anything to say to urban society is questionable, but the almost unanimous rejection of the chapel in Oxford for nearly a hundred years – the mosaics were finished in 1876 – shows how much more vibrantly Butterfield made his point than Keble made his own in the long-forgotten, mediocre verse of *The Christian Year*. If there had been no more to the

---

43. The exhibition catalogue, *Victorian Church Art* (London, 1971), was excellent.
44. Paul Thompson, *William Butterfield* (London, 1971), pp. 246–47.

chapel than Keble it would, like Balliol Chapel, which Butterfield also designed, have been forgotten long ago.

For Butterfield's intention was to reassert the centrality of the western religious tradition to urban as well as rural culture. He described the 1870s as 'an age terribly subjective and sensational'; he deplored the point at which medieval painters' versions of Christ became 'anatomical and aimed at affecting the emotions';[45] the primitive atemporality of the chapel mosaics was intended as an affront to the 'modern mind'. The irony was that those whom he had thought were his own supporters were quite ready to use his chapel as a backcloth for *The Light of the World*, which Holman Hunt had painted in 1854, which reeked of the subjective, the sensational and the democratic and which might be described as Sankey and Moody in oils. 'Being a sentimental picture', Butterfield wrote, 'it is much more appropriate in my judgment to some other room, such as the library.'[46] *The Light of the World* duly hung in the library until Butterfield was safely out of the way, when it was transferred to a shrine specially added to the south wall of the chapel. But the College was right and Butterfield's only a superb failure, for when people visit the chapel they do so to see *The Light of the World*. And that is the measure of the failure of the religious sub-culture to maintain its ancient status in the urban world of the twentieth century.

45. *Ibid.*, p. 33.
46. *Ibid.*, p. 304.

Chapter 13

ST GILES'S FAIR, 1830–1914

Sally Alexander

[from History Workshop Pamphlet, no. 2 (Oxford 1970)]

Like many 'traditional' social forms the modern fair was a product of the urban industrial period. The history of St Giles's Fair was part of the history of leisure and urban space. It was part of the increasing density of urban life with the consequent need for control and regulation, although in this case the control was not as complete or tidy as the public park or the pay-at-the-gate football game. The town became the focus of increased commercialization and the use of the new technologies. The growth of the fair, as with so many other urban developments involved the railway, here making the town a central place for consumption, entertainment and information. This history with its rich texture of detail (which has had to be reduced because of confines of space in this volume) was the result of the careful use of oral evidence and local press and local government records.

THE 'NEW' FAIR

Fairs are often thought to have died out – or at least to have been reduced to a shadow of their former selves – through the coming of modern industry with its new forms of transport and distribution. Fairs, so the argument runs, had once provided, in medieval and early modern England, a vital market for the exchange of goods. But with the improvements in road transport after 1750, and the advent of canals and later railways, these economic functions disappeared. Moreover in the nineteenth century even their residual character as pleasure fairs came under attack. They were left to fight a losing battle, so historians have implied, against the mounting tide of

Victorian respectability and evangelically inspired disapproval of what came to be considered a superfluous and 'degrading' indulgence. Further research into the subject may well indicate that the decline of the fair in the nineteenth century was by no means universal.

In the meantime, if no general statement can be made until historians have directed their attention to the social history of the fairground, it can certainly be confidently said of St Giles's Fair, that so far from being the victim of nineteenth-century social and economic change, it was their offspring.

The parish of St Giles's in the early nineteenth-century was a large and mainly rural suburb, which included both Summertown and the low-lying tract of land later to be built up into Jericho within the parish boundaries.[1] It was still very much a place apart from Oxford. It had stayed outside the 'Oxford Incorporation' when the first city Improvement Act was passed in 1771,[2] and still thought it 'more expedient' to have a 'distinct and separate' administration during the cholera epidemic in 1832, when it was the only one of the eleven local parishes to refuse to place itself under the Oxford Board of Health.[3]

At the beginning of the nineteenth-century St Giles's Street was an open road on the outskirts of Oxford. A contemporary print depicts sheep being driven down the middle to the fields beyond. The Paving Commissioners' Minute Books record complaints in 1819 and 1822 of nuisances caused by pigsties in yards alongside the street.[4] A Minute for 2 September 1818 helps to support this impression of a definitely country aspect:

> The Mayor and Dr Wall represented that it had been found essential to the comfort of the Inhabitants that the street in St Giles's should be watered and that a subscription had been entered into amongst some of the Inhabitants and a Pump erected and Water Cart furnished, but as the dust was so great there owing to the street not being pitched like other parts of the Town it was thought the commissioners should take the matter into consideration and provide for the watering of the street at proper seasons.[5]

The street was fringed on the west side by shabby single- and double-fronted cottages interspersed with the occasional small shop. Behind

1. Ruth Fasnacht, *A History of the City of Oxford*, Oxford, 1954, pp. 189–90.
2. *Ibid*. p. 162.
3. Rev. Vaughan Thomas, *Memorials of the Malignant Cholera in Oxford*, Oxford, 1835, p. 6.
4. Oxford Town Hall Muniments, hereafter T.H.M., Paving Commissioners' Minute books, 5.5.1819, 4.8.1819, 15.5.1822.
5. *Ibid*, 2.9.1818.

these tenements lay a maze of little inns and courts, the remnants of which can still be seen today in the older buildings between Magdalen Street and Gloucester Green.

St Giles today has been altered beyond recognition. What was once a shabby plebeian area – the little working-class suburb of the Northgate Hundred straggling off into countryside – has been transformed into a 'handsome, leafy, boulevard'. Its working-class population, and the simple cottages which housed them, have disappeared and been replaced by such imposing buildings as Elliston's, a genteel department store, the Randolph Hotel, Pusey House and Blackfriars. The little working-class cafe on the west side is the last remnant of the old St Giles. The process was a slow one. It began with the building of two handsome terraces of town houses – Beaumont Street, 'the new Road to St Giles',[6] and St John Street, both of which were completed in the 1830s.[7] The appearance of wealth and elegance at the south end of St Giles was endorsed by the building of the Taylorian Institute at the corner of Beaumont Street and St Giles in 1844, and the opulent establishment of the Randolph Hotel on the other side of the street twenty years later.

At the other end of St Giles, to the north, the open fields and scrubland were swallowed up by imposing avenues and streets. After the end of university celibacy, North Oxford quickly established itself as a favourite residence for Dons' households and establishments, and by the end of the century was a fully built-up area.

Sandwiched between the encroachments of respectability to its north and to its south, the social character of St Giles itself slowly began to alter. This change was foreshadowed in the first half of the century by the demolition of the notorious Robin Hood tavern and its subsequent replacement by the Macros' Memorial – a monument put up by the anti-Catholic evangelical party in the town and university in 1841. The real change however took place in the last years of the century. A photo taken from above the Martyrs' Memorial in 1885 showed St Giles still dusty and unpaved. But by the end of the century its character had markedly altered and by 1912 the last row of houses and shops had been swept away to make room for Pusey House Chapel and Blackfriars. This quiet rise in status and pretension was to contrast more markedly with the swelling dimensions of Oxford's greatest and most plebeian fair.

St Giles's Fair is comparatively speaking a 'new' fair. Of Oxford's three annual fairs in the nineteenth century – St Giles's, St Clement's, and Gloucester Green – the last was almost certainly the oldest, while in earlier centuries the two great Oxford fairs had been

6. Paving Commissioners' Minute Book, 7.11.1821, 5.6.1822, 4.8.1824.
7. Beaumont Street and St John's Street were completed between 1827 and 1837. Fasnacht, *op. cit.*, p. 189.

St Frideswide's, and the May or Austin Fair.[8] St Giles's is not an ancient chartered fair, like the Nottingham Goose Fair, and little is known about it before the nineteenth century. Muncey claims that its origins may be traced to 1622, but neither Wood nor Hearne, the seventeenth-eighteenth-century Oxford antiquaries, mention the fair, 'which may be regarded as an indication of its insignificance in their day'.[9]

St Giles's was not in origin a fair at all, but a wake, a local parish feast, the annual dedication of the parish church of St Giles. Even in the early nineteenth century St Giles's was overshadowed in importance by the rival attractions of the Port Meadow Races and other Oxfordshire Fairs, in particular St Clement's and Wychwood Forest Fair, all of which occurred within a few weeks of St Giles's[10] in late August and early September. It was remembered at this time as a pleasure fair 'of the smallest possible extent, being confined to the space from St John's College to the Lamb and Flag on the east side; gypsies with their snuff-boxes and drinking booths occupying the west side of the street'.[11] As far as St Giles's had any distinctive character, it was that of a children's fair. A writer in the 1830s recalled that at the beginning of the century, the fair had scarcely 'extended half way up one side of St Giles's', and had 'consisted of two or three fruit and gingerbread stalls and a display of toys'. He went on to evoke the great changes that had occurred in the ensuing thirty years: 'persons of riper age are invited by shows of various kinds, theatre, horsemanship, bazaars, etc., and to these have of late been added, drinking and dancing booths, and much of the worst kinds of gambling, almost driving from their homes by these disgraceful annoyances, families residing in St Giles'.[12] By the 1830s St Giles's was already well on the way to becoming the great annual holiday of the working people, and in the course of the nineteenth century the physiognomy of the fair changed so dramatically that it

8. Fasnacht, *op. cit.* pp. 37–8 *Oxford Times* (hereafter *O.T.*), 3 Sept. 1898; Bodleian Lib., G.A. Oxon, b. 5, Henry Hughes Scrap Book.
9. Oxford City Ref. Lib., p. 294.6 'Note for the Town Clerk. St Giles's Fair'. This is a brief account which unfortunately gives a wrong reference for the interesting statement that in 1834 St Giles's was referred to as 'the modern fair'.
10. The feast of St Giles is celebrated on the first Sunday after the first of September, and the fair takes place on the following Monday and Tuesday. I have discovered only two references to the fair lasting more than two days: in 1816, 'When owing to the continuous rain of the two fair days the civic authorities arranged an extra day', *Jackson's Oxford Journal* (hereafter *J.O.J.*), 14 Sept. 1895; and in 1877, when the fair continued till midday Wednesday, *O.T.*, 8 Sept. 1877.
11. Henry Hughes Scrap Book, art. of 7.9.1889.
12. 'From a correspondent', *Oxford University, City and Country Herald*, 8 Sept. 1838.

is permissible to regard it as an authentic creation of the Victorian era.

The popularity and importance of the fair had been brought sharply to the attention of the authorities by the riot of 1830,[13] when troops were attacked at the corner of Beaumont Street, and the Otmoor prisoners were released by the crowd as they were being driven through the fair on the way to Oxford Castle. St Giles's was again a cause of anxiety to the authorities in 1832, during the cholera, when a strenuous handbill was issued by the Board of Health warning people of the dangers of the fair in time of epidemic. But it was not until 1838 that the civic authorities first attempted to bring the fair under control. A detailed set of regulations was issued concerning the 'arrangements to be observed at the commencement, during the progress, and at the conclusion of the fair', all of which, according to a newspaper account, were put into 'good effect by the police without the slightest degree of harshness or compulsion'. Two important prohibitions were attempted, one against drinking booths, the other against the 'snuff-box gypsies'.

As for the drinking booths, they were still very much in evidence at the fair, at least into the 1840s, according to the police reports. St Giles's Fair remained a great occasion for drinking throughout the century. In the 1870s,[14] public houses were granted permission to erect drinking saloons outside their premises during the fair, though at the same time the local Temperance Society was very active in the fair – running a refreshment tent for the sale of tea and coffee, distributing tracts on the evils of alcohol, and discreetly providing a ladies' cloakroom in front of St John's College.

If the city authorities were indecisive about their attitude towards drinking, they did increasingly control the general organization of the fair. 1851 was the last year that the showmen were allowed to enter St Giles at midnight on the Sunday before the fair. From 1852 until 1904 the hour of entry was 4 a.m.

The letting of the ground excited some controversy. As the fair expanded, the question of who was responsible for the allocation of the ground, and the collection of the tolls, became the subject of many disputes. Originally the rights to hold the fair belonged to the Manor of Walton, which has belonged to St John's College since 1573. However, the Manor of Walton only extends along the east side of St Giles Street, the west side falls beyond its boundaries. As the fair expanded to cover the whole of the thoroughfare, the Council's Markets and Fairs Committee, on their own initiative, took

13. For a full discussion of the 1830 riot at St Giles's Fair, see Bernard Reaney *The Struggle for Land on Otmoor*, History Workshop Pamphlet, 1970.
14. *Oxford Chronicle* (hereafter *O.C.*), 9 Sept. 1871.

CITY OF OXFORD

ST. GILES'S FAIR.

NOTICE IS HEREBY GIVEN,

That no Caravan or other Carriage, nor any Materials for erecting Stands or Stalls in Saint Giles's, shall be left to stand in any of the Streets, Lanes, or Public Highways, before the hour of Four o'clock on Monday Morning next, or after the hour of Nine o'clock on the Morning of the following Wednesday.

INFORMATIONS WILL BE LAID AGAINST ALL PERSONS offending against the above order, **AND THEY WILL BE LIABLE TO A PENALTY OF TEN SHILLINGS.**

INFORMATIONS will also be laid, and the Penalties strictly enforced, against all PUBLICANS AND KEEPERS OF BEER HOUSES, who shall permit or suffer any kind of Gambling therein, or keep their Houses open for the sale of Beer or other Exciseable Liquors. contrary to the tenor of their Licenses.

NOTICE IS HEREBY ALSO GIVEN

That NO BOOTHS or STANDS for the SALE of BEER, or other Exciseable Liquors, will be permitted to be erected within the Northgate Hundred, during St. Giles's Fair; nor shall any STAND or STALL for any other purpose be erected within the said Hundred of Northgate, unless previous permission is obtained from GEORGE MILLS, Town Hall.

JOSEPH ROUND,
MAYOR.

OXFORD, 2ND SEPTEMBER, 1875.

THE POLICE HAVE DIRECTIONS TO ENFORCE THE ORDERS NOTIFIED ABOVE.

BY ORDER OF THE OXFORD POLICE COMMITTEE,

ROBERT S. HAWKINS,

J. OLIVER, PRINTER, 49, GEORGE STREET, OXFORD.

CLERK TO THE COMMITTEE.

348

the responsibility of collecting the tolls on the west side of St Giles, and also of allocating the ground on that side. The two sides became known to the showmen as the 'college' side and the 'city' side. Each side had its distinctive character. Jack Hatwell told me that the small stall owners set up on the city side, and the large national shows on the college side.

A report to the Watch Committee in 1893, by Mr Beckwith, the Markets and Fairs official, confirms this: 'There are no shows only stalls on the Corporation ground',[15] he told them.

To some extent, the allocation of the ground was determined by custom. Jack Hatwell, who remembers Mr Beckwith, told me,

> We've had practically always the same site right through as far as I can remember . . . we were shifted once off Alfred St during Taylor's time . . . trees were allotted us . . . they're forty feet apart, now they're allotted to different showmen from tree to tree . . . the caravan we've got in Cassington, still got it as a family heirloom, the trees were no bigger than the caravan in the photograph. . . . The council was the ruling faction you see. If the council said to my father, 'Mr Hatwell, we're going to shift you off here, and put you down here', well, he'd have no say in the matter . . . they could reject you from the sites if they thought you was an unsuitable tenant . . . they could say you can't come here next year.[16]

The police later joined in the already uncertain arrangements between the city and the college authorities. In 1890 the Markets and Fairs Committee had asked for a policeman to accompany their official, Mr Beckwith, when he allotted the stands and collected the tolls.[17] In 1894 the police themselves requested control of the entire proceedings, although when the request was put to the committee it was rejected.[18] Although the police had no direct control over the lay-out of the fair, the city corporation co-operated with them. In 1893, at the height of the campaign to abolish the fair, Mr Beckwith told the Watch Committee, that 'There have been no peep-shows on the City ground during the 10 last years in which I have acted'.[19] Peep-shows had a rather unsavoury reputation, so it was considered safest to avoid them. Whenever there was a show hinting at indecency, or a pile of immoral photographs was discovered under an otherwise innocent stall, both the show, and its proprietor, were removed. The Mayors also ordered the prohibition of the successive

15. T.H.M. HH 1/6 Watch Committee Minute Book, 14 Dec. 1893.
16. S. Alexander, B. Reaney, Interview with the Hatwell brothers, Wolvercote August. 1969.
17. T.H.M. FF 2/5, Markets and Fairs Committee Minute Book, 6 Sept. 1890.
18. T.H.M. FF 2/6, Markets and Fairs Committee Minute Book, 10 Sept. 1894.
19. *Ibid.*, HH/1/6 Watch Committee Minute Book, 14 Dec. 1983.

'instruments of torture' (joke-toys) that appeared on the fair-ground each year, and attempted to curb the spread of the stalls beyond the limits of St Giles's.

In their efforts against the rogues, vagabonds and thieves that attended the fair the Oxford City Police sometimes had to make demands on other police forces. Throughout the 1890s until 1914, the Oxford Police were assisted by constables or plain-clothes police officers from London, Northampton and elsewhere.[20] The extra police were either employed to keep watch on the side streets, and entrances to the fair, in case of any indecencies, or house-breakings, or else as Jack Hatwell remembers:

> They used to have detectives from Birmingham, detectives from London, and detectives from any place Known to send crooks here. They used to 'ave 'em stationed on the railway station. Well, the detectives from Birmingham would know the crook which was comin' from that direction you see, and they used to pack 'em back on the train and send 'em back, they wouldn't let 'em leave the station . . . Oh, yes . . . pickpockets, that sort of thing, rogues and that.[21]

Police concern with the fair, and the demands made by it on their resources, nevertheless remained surprisingly small, considering its prodigious growth. Within a century, the few tawdry stalls which had registered its existence in 1800 had become quarter of a mile of brilliantly lit arcades. Scarcely known outside the confines of the parish at the end of the eighteenth century, St Giles's had become the great annual holiday centre for the working people of Oxfordshire at the end of the nineteenth.

MARKET ASPECTS OF THE FAIR

Historians argue that the economic function of fairs, as a market place for goods, was made obsolete by the coming of the railways, the development of canals, and improvement in road transport. This may have been true of the marketing of certain classes of goods, but not of those sold at St Giles's. St Giles's, as we have seen, flourished during the nineteenth century, and the opportunity that it provided for trade was an integral part of its character as a working-class festival. Fair time in Oxford was also market time, and even today stalls can be found at St Giles's for the sale of dress

20. See for example THM, HH 1/11 Aug. 30, 1906.
21. S. Alexander, Interview with the Hatwell brothers at Cassington, Sept. 1969.

and light furnishing material, china, crockery and other household items. In the nineteenth century, itinerant hawkers and vendors came to St Giles's with goods of all descriptions. They were certain of finding a profitable market. St Giles's fell at harvest time, when the country labourer had more money in his pocket than at any time in the year; the end of the summer was also a time when employment for the town labourer was brisk. Despite the attempts of such worthy institutions as the National Thrift Society to convert the working class to the value of savings, extra money, when it was available, was still spent on small luxuries and entertainments. St Giles's Fair provided a feast of them.

The newspaper accounts of the fair are comparatively brief in the earlier years, and we can glean little more about the market aspects of the fair in the mid-nineteenth century than that the stalls were numerous, and 'extended the whole length of the fair on each side',[22] that they were often laden with 'glittering ware', and that, as in 1842, they appealed especially to 'the younger portion of the fair folks, who delight in the more substantial things of this life', because they 'had every facility afforded them by the immense number of cake stalls; while the well-decked toy stalls presented attractions such as few of them could resist'.[23] The lack of information about the content of the stalls in these earlier accounts of the fair does not mean that the hawkers confined their activities to the sale of sweets and toys, but that the enumeration of commonplace items was less 'newsworthy' than descriptions of the more spectacular or novel exhibitions. But an account in 1875[24] leaves us in no doubt about the importance of fairground trade:

> The distinctive character of St Giles's fair annually becomes less that of a place of pleasure and more a mart for cheap basket ware, crockery, and fancy articles, a tendency not regretted by those of our more elderly readers who remember the days when it was thronged by so-called gipsies, who, aided by the riff-raff of the district, and fortified by the vile liquids dispensed at innumerable drinking booths, rendering it unsafe for a respectable person to pass through St Giles's at night.

The would-be abolitionists attempted to argue their case against St Giles's on the grounds that the economic function of fair was no longer relevant. They were resolutely silenced, and one of the chief arguments of local supporters of the fair was that, 'the fair attracts a great influx of visitors, and gives an impetus to the trade of the corn-dealer, the butcher, the grocer, the draper, the baker,

---

22. *J.O.J.*, 14 Sept. 1861.
23. *Ibid.*, 10 Sept. 1842.
24. *O.T.*, 11 Sept. 1875.

the confectioner, the tailor, the mechanic and the labourer, as well as the tavern-keeper'.[25]

The stalls for the sale of miscellaneous goods were so numerous that they constantly threatened to invade the adjacent streets. The side streets leading into St Giles were filled with 'fancy stalls, refreshment tents, and sweet meat and ginger bread stalls'. The sale of miscellaneous goods, then was an integral part of the fair, as important an aspect of the working-class holiday as the shows. Some of the stalls were laden with toys, others were more practical: 'baskets, glass and china ornaments, cheap tools, sweets, gingerbreads, cakes etc.', while there were scores of barrows on which were fruit, mostly apparently of a wholesome description: 'cocoa nuts, hedge nuts, cheap jewellery, photographs, ices, canaries and other cage birds, braces, gilding fluid, potato peelers, name stamps, and other things too numerous to mention. . . .'[26] Some of the articles that the itinerants sold were not only useful but attractive and of particular value because they were made by skilled craftsmen. A local Oxford man praised the 'gipsy productions of wickerwork, some especially very well and quaintly made, brooms, mats, etc.'[27] Or again, according to another account in 1883, 'There was almost everything to be bought except silence. You could be photographed, like one clergyman, by electric light in an attitude of protest. Then you could get a "tawdry lace and a pair of sweet gloves", not to speak of "ribands, inkles, cambrics, and lawns".'[28] Material and clothing were always to be found at St Giles's, although by 1896 apparently, the days had gone by 'when a tradesman could be furnished with a complete outfit for a few shillings'.[29] Nevertheless, in 1905 'Long curtains appeared to be selling briskly by a Nottingham firm, and E. Gillam, of Little Clarendon street, had a good show of stockings and other knitted garments.'[30] Household goods, domestic appliances and simple workmen's tools lay beside the 'cheap luxuries' that were 'calculated to please the eye, gratify the appetite, and extract money from the pocket'.[31]

Stalls for the sale of glassware and crockery, both useful and ornamental' seem at all times to have been a staple of the fair and their vendors. With household items and workmen's tools so much in evidence at the fair it is not surprising that sewing machines

25. *O.T.*, 4 Sept. 1880.
26. *J.O.J.*, 10 Sept. 1887.
27. *O.T.*, 22 Sept. 1894.
28. *The Oxford Magazine*, 17 Oct. 1883, p. 307.
29. *J.O.J.*, 12 Sept. 1896.
30. *O.T.*, 9 Sept. 1905.
31. *J.O.J.*, 9 Sept. 1854.

would eventually appear. In 1892, there was 'a very fine display of the celebrated "Singer" sewing machines'.[32]

The newspaper men always made much of local tradesmen. There was one in particular, Mr Arnatt, a well-known local confectioner, who maintained an elaborate refreshment booth at St Giles for fifty-two years, setting off his sweetmeats with brilliant displays of lighting. Mrs Buckland, who began her married life with a stall at St Giles seventy-five years ago, used to buy her 'swag' from a local firm called Delamere.[33] The swag was china, cups and saucers, necklaces, 'and all sorts of little things to put on the stalls to sell; dolls, little engines, drums, anything for little children'. They also sold rock. Home-made sweets, brandy snaps and Banbury Cakes were the staple diet of the food stalls at St Giles.

Most of the novelties were the business of the 'cheap jacks'. They were a class of industrious and hardworking men who travelled the roads selling goods to the working and lower middle classes, who would otherwise have been unable to obtain them.[34]

The finer nuances between what distinguishes the showman proper from the itinerant hawkers and cheap jacks sometimes appear to escape careful categorization. Perhaps the most easily comprehensible distinction is the one made by the *Oxford Times* in 1887 between the ordinary stall-holders and those who resorted to 'patter', though the latter, as in the following description from 1887, were so diverse as to cause some confusion to the historian.

> One pretended to be an ex-lifeguardsman, whose 'lay' was to sell penny cakes of 'Cyprus bark from the banks of the Ganges'; a second sold 'English-made dolls, big as a baby and light as a feather', of the intrinsic value of two shillings, for eightpence. The third, however, was more pretentious. Dressed in a scholar's stuff gown in longitude 'sorely scanty', which he averred he was under an obligation to wear in virtue of having been elected a Town Councillor of Newcastle-on-Tyne, and whose medical education, he said, had cost him more than the four chief physicians of Oxford 'rolled into one', gave advice gratis how to cure consumption in 'the first, or even second stages', and talked long and eloquently about the herb celandine as a specific for all diseases of the eye, but his speciality was the 'infallible cure' of deafness, provided always 'the drum of the ear is not broken'.[35]

Again in 1903, there was a curious collection, all of which the *Journal* labelled 'cheap jacks':

32. *J.O.J.*, 10 Sept. 1892.
33. S. Alexander. Interview with the Bucklands at Wallingford, Sept. 1969.
34. Charles Hindley, *The Life and Adventure of a Cheap Jack, by one of the Fraternity*, London 1881, p. 329.
35. *Oxford Times*, 10 Sept. 1887.

Magdalen-street, as far as George-street, was occupied by cheap jacks, who were as numerous and as deceptive as ever. Prominent amongst these were 'Prof. Duval and Madame Idaho', both of whom were 'gifted by nature' as character delineators, and would for a penny supply a delicately-tinted slip of paper upon which one's future was indicated. The 'cheap-watch' man, the 'needle-threader', the retailer of slabs of almond noyeau, and last, but not least, our visitor the 'five! furr! free! tuppence! all sahnd!' grape-merchant, were all here, yelling in strenuous discord.[36]

It seems they excelled in the sale of cheap novelties to which they adapted their selling techniques. The great point of the buying and selling that went on at the fair was the promise of a bargain. For street-traders and hawkers, as for showmen, St Giles's Fair disbursed the proceeds of summer prosperity.

THE INDUSTRIAL REVOLUTION AND ST GILES'S FAIR

Fairs are normally regarded as essentially pre-industrial in character, perpetuating a medieval or even pagan culture. St Giles's, on the contrary, was largely a creation of the nineteenth century. Not only did its growth coincide with the coming of the machine; it may be said to have been transformed and rejuvenated by the later stages of the Industrial Revolution and the application of mid- and late Victorian technology.

In the first place, the coming of the railways had a radical effect on the fair. The police view expressed in the Watch Committee's report of 1893, was that 'The Fair . . . was chiefly of local importance' until the introduction of railways, 'but owing to the increased facilities of travelling, and the larger population of Oxford and the neighbourhood, it attracts a greater concourse of visitors.'[37] A writer on the 'abolitionist' side, in the controversy of 1894, blamed the railways for transforming 'small-scale' evils into large ones, and making St Giles's a 'monster' ('much like Greenwich Fair, Bartelmy Fair, Portsdown Fair and many others').[38]

St Giles's came of age with the introduction of the excursion ticket. The first excursion run specially for the fair was the Great

36. *J.O.J.*, 12 Sept. 1903.
37. T.H.M., HH1/6, Watch Committee, Report of Sub-committee on St Giles's Fair, 1893.
38. Letter of 'Abolitionists', in *O.T.*, 2 June 1894.

Western Railway Company's, which ran from Banbury to Oxford in 1850, and took up passengers at the intermediate stations. The trains brought in 900 by excursion trips that first year.[39] They were soon a regularly established feature of St Giles's, and the catchment area from which people could visit the fair on a cheap day ticket extended as far as Cardiff, London, Birmingham, Gloucester and other major towns.

St Giles's Fair could be said to have served as the local 'Great Exhibition'. Each year it could boast of its scientific, industrial and mechanical curiosities, and their popularity was enduring. In 1856, for example there was 'a mechanical exhibition, where the whole process of riband making was very cleverly shown, by the aid of a miniature steam engine'. It included 'a glass of artificial humming birds, which, by means of certain delicate clock-work, were put in motion in various ways'.[40] Thirty years later, the *Oxford Times* described a similar exhibition of silk and riband making, 'the tiny bird that sprang from a piece of mechanism, certainly not more than three inches by one, sang its song, flapped its wings, and looked so natural all the time', and concluded that it was well worth 'six times the charge for admission'.[41]

More elaborate exhibits of the same genre included 'Clapton's Exhibition of Scenic and Mechanical Art', and 'Norton's Patent Incubator, or Egg-hatching Machine' both of which appeared in 1858. In the former there were

> some well-executed views of Florence and Verona, with the Monastery Church of St Francis, and the introduction of moving figures, and especially of a solemn procession at the funeral of Juliet, celebrated in Shakespeare, which had a very striking and imposing effect. A clever painting of Cawnpore, a representation of a ship on fire at sea, and a case of mechanical humming birds, that chirped and flew from branch to branch with all the appearance of animation and reality, combined to make one of the most pleasing and intellectual exhibitions that has attended this or any other fair.

Norton's Patent Incubator, an apparatus for hatching and rearing poultry, game 'and even serpents' by steam, was 'almost as attractive, and as well patronized'.[42]

The Great Exhibition was a landmark of industrial progress, but it had, as even the name suggests, a certain fairground flavour. Indeed, as Asa Briggs says in *The Age of Improvement*, 'The

39. *J.O.J.*, 14 Sept. 1850.
40. *Ibid.*, 13 Sept. 1856.
41. *O.T.*, 11 Sept. 1886.
42. *J.O.J.*, 11 Sept. 1858.

Exhibition, with its 13,000 exhibitors and its six million visitors, not only brought the facts to life, but invested them with a new romance'.[43] Fascination with scientific and industrial progress was one of the hall-marks of the Victorian working-man's aspirations towards self-help. However, these aspirations as reflected in the fairground were devoid of the prosaic utilitarianism that middle-class social reformers attempted to impose upon the lower orders. The showmen's devices were intended to arouse the imagination of their audience, as the preceding examples illustrate. Hence the arresting name given to some of the quasi-scientific shows – the 'glyptotheca', or 'hall of scientific amusements', for example, which appeared in 1879, and 'contained models of cities, towns, seaports, rivers, forts, valleys, and mountains'.[44]

Zoological and botanical gardens are taken for granted by the sophisticated children of the twentieth century. Wild animals are categorized and specified in their early books of ABC, and almost every child has experienced a trip to the zoo, or has watched television films of wild life. Rockets and trips to the moon seem much more interesting and relevant in 1970 than tales of Tarzan or Jungle Jim. However, zoos and travelling menageries were first popularized during the nineteenth century. Victorian curiosity in the unfamiliar and developing 'sciences' extended to include the natural sciences. The great travelling menageries became the 'aristocrats' of the road. Wombwell's the greatest of them all, termed themselves 'the wandering teachers of Natural History'.[45]

The original Wombwell started in 1805. He was 'engaged in business in Soho', and on a visit to the London Docks he bought two boa constrictors for seventy-five pounds. Within three weeks he had received more than his money back, and he continued from strength to strength, bringing his family into the profession. By the 1830s Wombwell's was a regular visitor to St Giles's, and in 1838, according to the Journal, 'The chief attraction . . . was Wombwells celebrated Menagerie and his no less celebrated band, which played most of our leading overtures, marches, and popular melodies in a most enchanting style.'[46] The exhibition was crowded throughout the two days of the fair.

All the famous menageries visited St Giles's during the course of the century, sometimes appearing side by side in the same year. Manders' was a frequent visitor during the middle years of the century. The *Oxford Times* gratefully acknowledged that 'as probably not half a dozen towns in the kingdom possess . . .

43. Asa Briggs, *The Age of Improvement*, London, 1960, p. 398.
44. *J.O.J.*, 13 Sept. 1879.
45. E.H. Bostock, *Menageries, Circuses, and Theatres*, London, 1927, p. 7.
46. *J.O.J.*, 8 Sept. 1838.

Zoological Gardens', the general public were 'much indebted to those who like Mr Mander bring to their doors so fine a collection of rare and wonderful animals. . . .'[47] The publication of Darwin's researches heightened the public interest in 'wild beasts'. The black ourang-outang was described with respect as 'This peculiar animal from Central Africa (which) bears the nearest resemblance to human nature of any tribe that has hitherto been discovered, and is so docile and intelligent, as well as friendly with strangers, that every one was struck with astonishment.'[48]

A fair without bright lights and noisy music seems inconceivable today. The first glimpse one catches of a fairground at night is of the flickering, coloured lights on the Big Wheel – and as one draws nearer the laughter of the crowds and the music from the mechanical organs combine to make the fairground almost irresistible. But the lights and the music were not always so vivid, at least not by night. Until the 1850s candles were the only lighting equipment available to the showmen. Every booth and joint was lit by candles set up either in candlesticks or in bottlenecks, which was generally inadequate, and also very expensive for the smaller showmen. Naphtha lamps were then a major discovery. They came into use on the fairground around the middle of the century. Lord George Sanger claims that he was the first to bring naphtha lamps to London in 1851. But the naptha flares were fraught with difficulties. Although they have a bright and attractive light, they were unsafe and a fire hazard, particularly in a menagerie. Bostock and Wombwell's had tin boxes in wooden cases especially supplied to them from Newcastle upon Tyne, as the liquid was difficult to obtain. Paraffin flares replaced the naptha six or seven years later at Bostock and Wombwell's. Although they did not give such effective light, they were safer and easier to work. Naptha remained in use until the end of the century – atmosphere that the dripping naptha lamps produced was sufficient incentive to ignore the safety hazards. The arrival of electric light at the fair was a sensation in itself. In 1882, there were three electric lights at the fair, their power being supplied by traction engines.

Mechanical organs are as closely identified with the fairground as galloping horses and the coconut shies. But like the horses and coconuts they only arrived in the fairground in the 1870s. A visitor to St Giles's in the middle of the century remembered that the showmen, 'worked hard and banged drums and gongs, and blew trumpets, and turned the handles of barrel-organs from eleven in the morning until eleven at night, and made much noise'.[49] Another recalls that 'every show had its drum, organ, brass-band,

47. *O.T.*, 14 Sept. 1869.
48. *J.O.J.*, 10 Sept. 1859.
49. W.E. Sherwood, *Oxford Yesterday*, Oxford, 1927, p. 59.

gong, or instrument of some sort to bray forth its whereabouts'.[50] Then of course there was the patterer who accompanied every show, not to mention the cheap-jacks, all of whom added to the cacophony of sounds. Mechanical organs replaced some of these sounds. Manufactured by Marenghi and Gavioli, and 'aided by the electrician' they seemed 'capable of anything'.[51] Their decor, 'in a style consistent with the highest French art'[52] was as much admired as their music; the marionettes that waltzed, danced or conducted on the fronts drew an appreciative audience around them.

Popular taste in music was extremely diverse in the nineteenth century. The 'pop' industry and mass media had not yet been invented, and the greater variety of tastes was reflected in the early mechanical organ music, as the following report of 1890 shows.

> One organ with automatic figure in front . . . giving forth the 'Halle-lujah Chorus', but its tone is harsh and unsympathetic; another, in softer cadence, and in slower measure, is playing 'Call me back again', while a third in a more subdued strain is piping 'The Pilgrim of Love'. . . . [on] the switchbacks . . . you had a short ride for twopence and a tune – 'Annie Rooney' or 'Two Lovely Black Eyes' – into the bargain.[53]

The showman's use of electricity was by no means exhausted by lights and mechanical music. Apart from living pictures, the showmen devised a number of somewhat bizarre entertainments. Electric shocks were a feature of St Giles's from the 1870s, and fairgoers were offered 'as large a dose as their nervous system could stand for a penny'.[54] Edison's Phonograph was also there, although no description of it at St Giles's has yet come to light. One of the more sensational shows involving the use of electricity appeared in 1908 entitled, 'Ouida: Dead yet Living', in which could be seen, for the price of twopence, 'some conjuring tricks and an agreeable looking young woman in Egyptian dress with a Yasmak, mesmerized and then electrocuted – or at least the man said the current would have killed half a dozen ordinary men who were not mesmerized'.[55] The Hatwell brothers remember the amazement caused by the arrival of an early wireless show at St Giles's when they were children, more than sixty years ago.

The most dramatic and vivid effect of the industrial revolution on St Giles's Fair, however, was the mechanization of the traditional

50. Bee, Bee, *op. cit*, p. 85.
51. *J.O.J.*, 9 Sept. 1905.
52. *Ibid.*, 10 Sept. 1904.
53. *O.T.*, 13 Sept. 1890.
54. *Ibid.*, 10 Sept. 1887.
55. 'Notes from an Oxford Lady' *Ibid*, Sept. 1908.

fairground entertainments. In the 1860s and 1870s the roundabouts were transformed from their hand-pushed or pony-drawn originals into four-abreast galloping horses, ostriches, and giraffes, steam yachts, and swirling motor cars, which, 'to be up to date', were 'resplendent with carved and gilded ornamentation and the electric light, driven by steam to the accompaniment of an orchestrion',[56] and which, moreover, cost two or three thousand pounds to purchase. The joy-ride thus became the 'pivot' of the fairground.[57] Twenty years later, however, their premier position was challenged by yet another technical invention, the 'Wonder of the Age' – 'Living Pictures'. From the 1890s until the First World War, the joy-ride and living picture shows vied with each other for supremacy and popularity.

By the second half of the nineteenth century, the traditional forms of entertainment were in decline, or undergoing a transformation. Strolling players seem to have disappeared from the fairground by the 1880s, and the wax-work and marionette shows, which used to present 'dramatic varieties', were also missing. This decline in the number of performing shows, for it was not a total absence, continued until the 1890s, when living pictures not only reintroduced 'drama' to the fairground, but also restored the 'parade' outside the booths. Dancing girls, acrobats and masters of ceremonies entertained the prospective audience in the front, while the pictures were showing inside.

The harnessing of steam to the roundabout created a minor sensation, but the real breakthrough came with the evolution of the centre-truck which was, and still is, the essential component of the travelling roundabout. 'Larger roundabouts could now be built, a faster ride achieved, and later complex mechanisms, compounding vertical and horizontal motion could be introduced.'[58]

As the joy-rides became more decoratively elaborate, so did their accompanying music. The centre-piece of the most extravagant rides was the mechanical organ 'a miracle of mechanical ingenuity crowned with an ornate proscenium'[59] as David Braithwaite puts it. The perfect marriage of the mechanical organ and the mechanical joy-ride was the cake-walk, which first appeared at St Giles's in 1909. It consisted of a series of hinged bridges, or gangways, which rose and fell by mechanical waves, causing the public to be swayed and gyrated as they walked or danced along it. In 1911,

---

56. 'Passing Notes' *O.T.*, 12 Sept. 1896. For an attractive discussion of the technical development of the joy ride, see David Braithwaite, *Fairground Architecture*, London, 1968.
57. Braithwaite, *op. cit.*, p. 65.
58. Braithwaite, *op. cit.*, pp. 40–3.
59. Braithwaite, *op. cit.*, p. 55.

There were 14 types of roundabouts at the fair, ranging from Thurston's diminutive Gordon-Bennett motor-cars and aeroplanes for children to the huge switchback railways, with their lavish gilding and decoration. These switchbacks were especially well patronized. There were Barker and Thurston's gondolas, Thurston's switchback, where 'Fall in and follow me' was occasionally given as a cornet-solo to supplement the organ, Studt's Daimler cars, Collins' scenic railway, T. Clarke's switchback, and Wilson's 'royal touring and racing motors', with their equipment of elephants, swans, dragons, and teddy bears. There were no 'Dreadnoughts' – huge swinging boats worked by steam power.[60]

The supremacy of the joy-ride at St Giles's was unchallenged until the end of the century when living pictures arrived. The newspapers do not tell us who first brought them to the fair – we learn only that Mr Gladstone's funeral was the chief attraction. In the following year 'Professor' Alf Ball brought his 'bioscope and dyograph' exhibition, and Barker and Thurston came with their 'electric veriscope'.[61] The bioscope soon created a large and admiring audience; visitors flocked to St Giles's to visit their favourite shows, and by 1909 one booth alone – Taylor's 'Royal Coliseum de Luxe', 'with its extensive front resplendent with gilt and electric light', occupied the 'greater part of the thorough-fare at the north end of the fair . . . In this as in several other bioscope shows owned by Thurston, Studt, and others, illustrations were given of the aviation week at Rheims, "the grand pageant in the air", "the invasion of England and its possibilities", etc.'[62]

The showmen certainly, had always met with enthusiasm when they applied the new techniques on the fairground at St Giles's. In 1855, for instance there was, 'a camera obscura, giving a living picture of the humours of the fair, a cosmoramic exhibition, of great merit, in the same ornamental structure at night'.[63] In 1861, 'an interesting variety of views admirably executed'[64] were 'very well patronized'. In 1906, 'La Morte', or the X-Rays (from Paris), in which, by an optical illusion, a woman was apparently transformed into a skeleton'[65] was the most advanced show of its kind. Illusion shows retained their hold on the fairground well into the twentieth century. There was always a profusion of peep-shows at St Giles's, often of a topical character. In his pamphlet on Otmoor, Bernard Reaney refers to the alarm excited by a peep-show of the 'late scenes

60. *J.O.J.*, 6 Sept. 1911.
61. *O.T.*, 9 Sept. 1909.
62. *Ibid.*, 11 Sept. 1909.
63. *J.O.J.*, 8 Sept. 1855.
64. *Ibid.*, 14 Sept. 1861.
65. *Ibid.*, 8 Sept. 1906.

in Paris' showing at St Giles's Fair, during the riot of 1830.[66] In 1854 'the Russian war' was one of their subjects,[67] in 1858 'the chief scenes of the . . . Indian mutiny', which were depicted as horrors and barbarities never dreamt of by the most audacious historian of the great revolt'.[68] The peep-show owned by Lord George Sanger's father in the 1830s 'had twenty-six glasses, so that twenty-six persons could see the views at the same time, the pictures being pulled up and down by strings. At night it was illuminated by a row of tallow candles set between the pictures and the observer, and requiring very regular snuffing.'[69] Tragedies were always successful, and he was particularly proud of the patter he provided, as a small boy, to accompany the story of Maria Marten, 'Murder in the Red Barn'. One of Mayhew's street performers described the types of peep shows in the country in the middle of the century:

> There are two kinds of peep-shows, which we call 'back-shows' and 'caravan-shows'. The caravan shows are much larger than the others, and are drawn by a horse or a donkey. They have a green-baize curtain at the back, which shuts out them as don't pay. The showman usually lives in these caravans with their family. . . . These caravans mostly go into the country, and very seldom are seen in town. They exhibit principally at fairs and feasts, or wakes, in country villages. . . . The scenes of them caravan shows is mostly upon recent battles and murders. Anything in that way, of late occurrence, suits them.[70]

The first projected moving pictures appeared in London in 1895, at the Regent Street Polytechnic, and they were later transferred to the old Empire Music Hall in Leicester Square where they ran for eighteen months. At their first showing in America where they had been advertised as 'Edison's machine showing Life', the audience had been so amazed at the sight of waves breaking on Dover Beach, that they had ducked to avoid the splashes.

Despite the excitement engendered by the new discovery, moving pictures found no permanent home for the first ten or fifteen years of their existence. Music halls used moving pictures as a sort of curtain-raiser between acts; shopkeepers converted the back part of their rooms into primitive viewing rooms while ordinary custom

66. Reaney, *op. cit.* part IV.
67. *J.O.J.*, 9 Sept. 1854.
68. *O.C.*, 11 Sept. 1858.
69. Sanger, *op. cit.*, pp. 48–9. There is a moving account of the performance of Maria Marten in a fairground booth in Joyce Cary's *Except the Lord*, London, 1953.
70. Henry Mayhew, *London Labour and the London Poor*, Dover edn, New York, 1968, Vol. III, p. 88.

continued in the front, but it was the showmen who pioneered the movie industry. On the fairground, films were shown continuously from ten o'clock in the morning until late at night. One visitor to St Giles's Fair in 1898 described being lured inside a tent to see an early bioscope show of 'Mr Gladstone's funeral procession'.[71]

Living Pictures, mechanized joy-rides, the coming of cheap mass travel, and the growing sophistication of the technological apparatus of the fair revolutionized St Giles's in the second half of the nineteenth century. But they did not extinguish its traditional elements. Swing-boats, coconut shies, boxing booths, dancing saloons, the freaks and other curiosities all survived the impact of industrialization. Even the old-fashioned forms of entertainment disappeared slowly, for their hold on the public was tenacious. For example 'Shippy' Buckland's pony roundabout maintained its position in front of the Martyrs' Memorial until the early years of the twentieth century.

Inevitably, the loss of once-popular entertainments provokes nostalgia. It seems sad that the primitive roundabouts described by Lord George Sanger should have been swept aside with the introduction of steam-power,

> The horses were enlarged examples of the rough penny toys that please the little ones even now. Their legs were simply stiff round sticks. Their bodies were lumps of deal rounded on one side. Their heads were roughly cut from half-inch boards, and inserted in a groove in the bodies, while the tails and manes were made of strips of rabbit skin. They were gaudy animals, however, their coats of paint being white, plentifully dotted with red and blue spots.[72]

It seems even sadder that live performers, strollers, acrobats and comedians should have been replaced by living pictures. But the nostalgia looks indulgent and misplaced when we realise the successors to the primitive roundabouts were the three-, and later, four-abreast gallopers,[73] and that the living pictures provided the same sorts of entertainments as the shows that they had replaced. The form of fairground entertainments changed; their basic content did not.

The content of the early peep shows and theatrical booths was drawn almost exclusively from notorious crimes, wars and their atrocities, 'potted' versions of Shakespeare and other well-known melodramatic tragedies. Representations of religious or traditional ritual were always popular. The first bioscopes, and other cinematographs, presented shows of very similar character. If the form of

71. *O.T.*, 10 September 1898
72. Sanger, *op. cit.*, p. 43.
73. The first set of steam-driven gallopers to appear at St Giles's was in 1886. Four-abreast, driven by electricity arrived ten years later.

presentation had altered, then the popular tastes had not. At St Giles's, in the 1840s, it was Nelson's funeral that drew the crowds at the peepshows; in the early 1900s, it was Mr Gladstone's which filled the bioscopes.

In 1849, the audience watching a dramatic representation of the tragedy of Stanfield Hall, a celebrated Norfolk murder, did not seem to mind that 'the perpetrator of these foul deeds, as well as the father and son who were the victims of his revenge, were attired in Spanish costume, sported their doublets, and their caps with plumes, while some of the scenes led the imagination to believe that the tragic events occurred nearer Turkey than that spot which was sullied by them.'[74]

This audience must have been much the same one that visited Thurston's living pictures, sixty years later, and – 'groaned and sighed when apparent tragedy was acted', and 'applauded gallant rescues and so on with as much feeling as if the thing were realistic. Many of them failed to see, the report continues, that 'an episode of Indians attacking a settler's caravan was a put-up piece of acting, probably carried out in some picturesque, though ultra-civilized part of France'.[75]

Thus the fairground showmen were able to extract from society its technical inventions to use them for their own independent ends. Mechanization, in the form of the steam-powered joy rides, and the electric bioscope, served positively to rejuvenate St Giles's Fair in the last years of the nineteenth century. It was not nineteenth century industrialization but the development of mass communications in the twentieth century which pushed St Giles's Fair from its unique place in the calendar of proletarian Oxfordshire. By the 1920s, living pictures had moved from the fair to the picture palace, rural buses had made the dancing saloons less exotic and the depopulation of the countryside had in turn reduced the significance of the fair as an annual assembly of rural labour. The Fair was in some sense becoming a relic: a relic not of some medieval past, but of the cultural universe of the Victorian Working Man.

74. *J.O.J.*, 8 Sept. 1849.
75. 'Some impressions of the Fair', *ibid.*, 11 Sept. 1909.

SELECT BIBLIOGRAPHY

Of all the chronological periods associated with urban history, the nineteenth century has been most prolific in terms of research and publication. No select bibliography could do this fertile subject of scholarship justice, and yet, to enable readers to pursue the topics, a number of key works are included below. For the most part these are thematic overviews. Studies of specific towns and cities are not reproduced except where they address wider issues or debates. Nor are general works of social history included, though many of these contain important dimensions of an urban character. For further references on themes and specific towns, consult *Urban History* (formerly *Urban History Yearbook* 1974–91) which annually contains some thousand or more bibliographical entries. The place of publication is London unless otherwise stated.

GENERAL

Abrams, P. 'Towns and economic growth: some theories and problems', in P. Abrams and E. A. Wrigley (eds), *Towns in Societies Essays in Economic History and Historical Sociology* (Cambridge 1978).

Alonso, W. 'A theory of the urban land market', *Papers and Proceedings of the Regional Science Association*, 6 (1960): 149–58.

Briggs, A. *Victorian Cities* (1963).

Cannadine, D.N. 'Urban development in England and America in the nineteenth century: some comparisons and contrasts', *Economic History Review*, 33 (1980): 309–25.

Carter, H. and **C.R. Lewis** *An Urban Geography of England and Wales in the Nineteenth Century* (1990).

Castells, M. *The Urban Question* (1977).

Checkland, S.G. 'The British industrial city as history', *Urban Studies*, **1** (1964): 34–54.

Corfield, P.J. *The Impact of English Towns* (1982).

Dennis, R.J. *English Industrial Cities of the Nineteenth Century: a Social Geography* (Cambridge 1984).

Dyos, H.J. and **M. Wolff** (eds) *The Victorian City: Images and Realities*, 2 vols (1973).

Foster, J. *Class Struggle and the Industrial Revolution: Early Industrial Capitalism in Three English Towns* (1974).

Fraser, D. (ed.) *A History of Modern Leeds* (Manchester 1980).

Fraser, D. and **A. Sutcliffe** (eds) *The Pursuit of Urban History* (1983).

Harvey, D. *Social Justice and the City* (1973).

Johnson, J.H. and **C.G. Pooley** (eds) *The Structure of Nineteenth-Century Cities* (1982).

Morris, R.J. 'Urbanization', in J. Langton and R.J. Morris (eds), *Atlas on Industrializing Britain 1780–1914* (1986).

Morris, R.J. 'Externalities, the market, power structures and the urban agenda', *Urban History Yearbook*, **17** (1990): 99–109.

Morris, R.J. 'Urbanization and Scotland' in W. Hamish Fraser and R.J. Morris (eds), *People and Society in Scotland, 1830–1914*, vol. 2 (Edinburgh 1990).

Offer, A. *Property and Politics 1870–1914: Landownership, Law, Ideology and Urban Development in England* (Cambridge 1981).

Robson, B.T. *Urban Growth: an Approach* (1973).

Shaw, G. and **A. Tipper**, *British Directories: a Bibliography and Guide to Directories published in England and Wales (1850–1950) and Scotland (1773–1950)*, (Leicester 1989).

Thompson, F.M.L. 'Town and city' in Thompson (ed.), *The Cambridge Social History of Britain: 1750–1950*, vol. 3 (Cambridge 1990.)

Waller, P.J. *Town, City and Nation: England, 1850–1914* (Oxford 1983).

Williams, R. *The Country and the City* (1973).

POPULATION AND MIGRATION

Dennis, R.J. 'Intercensal mobility in a Victorian city', *Transactions of the Institute of British Geographers*, **2** (1977): 349–63.

Grigg, D.B. 'E.G. Ravenstein and the laws of migration', *Journal of Historical Geography*, **3** (1977): 41–54.

Jackson, J.T. 'Long-distance migrant workers: St Helens', *Trans. Hist. Soc. Lancs. and Chesh.*, **131** (1982): 113–37.

Law, C.M. 'The growth of urban population in England and Wales 1801–1911', *Transactions of the Institute of British Geographers*, **41** (1967): 125–43.

Lawton, R. 'Population' in J.Langton and R.J. Morris (eds), *Atlas of Industrializing Britain* (1986).

Lawton, R. 'Population and society 1730–1900' in R.A. Dodgson and R.A. Butlin (eds), *Historical Geography of England and Wales* (1978).

Lees, L. and **J. Modell,** 'The Irish countryman urbanized', *Journal of Urban History*, **3** (1977): 391–408.

Pooley, C.G. 'Residential mobility in the Victorian city', *Transactions Institute of British Geographers*, **4** (1979): 258–77.

Richardson, C. 'Irish settlement in mid-nineteenth-century Bradford', *Yorkshire Bulletin*, **20** (1968): 40–57.

Swift, R. and **S. Gilley** (eds) *The Irish in Victorian Britain* (1989).

Weber, A. *The Growth of Cities in the Nineteenth Century* (repr., Cornell 1963).

WORK AND EMPLOYMENT

Alexander, D. *Retailing in England during the Industrial Revolution* (1970).

Engels, F. *The Condition of the Working Class in England* (Hobsbawm (ed.), 1969).

Green, D.R. 'Street trading in London: a case study of casual labour 1830–60' in J. Johnson and C.G. Pooley (eds), *The Structure of Nineteenth-Century Cities* (1982).

Hopkins, E. 'The decline of the family work unit in Black Country nailing', *International Review of Social History*, **22** (1977): 184–97.

Jones, G.S. *Outcast London: a Study in the Relationship between Classes in Victorian London* (Oxford 1971).

Jordan, E. 'Female unemployment 1851–1911', *Social History*, **13** (1988): 175–90.

Malcolmson, P.E. 'Getting a living in the slums of Victorian Kensington', *London Journal*, **I** (1975): 28–55.

Rodger, R. 'Concentration and fragmentation: capital, labor, and the structure of mid-Victorian Scottish industry', *Journal of Urban History*, **14** (1988): 178–213.

Samuel, R. 'Workshop of the world: steam power and hand technology in mid-Victorian Britain, *History Workshop*, **3** (1977): 6–72.

Shaw, G. 'Changes in consumer demand and food supply in nineteenth-century British cities', *Journal of Historical Geography*, **11** (1985): 280–96.

Treble, J.H. *Urban Poverty in Britain 1830–1914* (1979).

HOUSING, HEALTH AND THE BUILT ENVIRONMENT

Ashworth, W. *The Genesis of British Town Planning* (1954).

Aspinall, P.J. 'The internal structure of the house-building industry in nineteenth-century cities', in J.H. Johnson and C.G. Pooley (eds), *The Structure of Nineteenth-Century Cities* (1982) pp. 75–105.

Bannon, M.J. (ed.) *The Emergence of Irish Planning 1880–1920* (Dublin 1985), 131–88.

Beresford, M.W. *East End, West End. The Face of Leeds During Urbanisation, 1684–1842* (Leeds 1989).

Burnett, J. *A Social History of Housing 1815–1970* (Newton Abbot 1978).

Cannadine, D.N. *Lords and Landlords: the Aristocracy and the Towns 1774–1967* (Leicester 1980).

Chalklin, C.W. *The Provincial Towns of Georgian England: A Study of the Building Process 1740–1820* (1974).

Chapman, S.D. (ed.) *The History of Working-Class Housing: A Symposium* (Newton Abbot 1971). Studies by Wohl (London), Butt (Glasgow), Beresford (Leeds), Chapman (Nottingham), Treble (Liverpool), Chapman and Barlett (Birmingham), Smith (mainly Rochdale, Milnrow, Middleton, Ball (Ebbw Vale).

Cooney, E.W. 'The building industry', in R. Church (ed.), *The Dynamics of Victorian Business: Problems and Perspectives to the 1870s* (1980), pp. 142–60.

Daunton, M.J. *Coal Metropolis: Cardiff 1870–1914* (Leicester 1977).

Daunton, M.J. *House and Home in the Victorian City: Working-Class Housing 1850–1914* (1983).

Dennis, R. 'Hard to let in Edwardian London', *Urban Studies*, **26** (1989): 77–89.

Dennis, R. 'The geography of Victorian values: philanthropic housing in London, 1840–1900', *Journal of Historical Geography*, **15** (1989): 40–54.

Doughty, M. (ed.) *Building the Industrial City* (Leicester 1986).

Dyos, H.J. *Victorian Suburb: a Study of the Growth of Camberwell* (Leicester 1961).

Dyos, H.J. 'The slums of Victorian London', *Victorian Studies*, **11** (1967): 5–40.

Dyos, H.J. 'The speculative builders and developers of Victorian London', *Victorian Studies*, **11**, (1968): 641–90.

Dyos, H.J. and **Reeder, D.A.** 'Slums and suburbs' in H.J. Dyos and M. Wolff (eds), *The Victorian City: Images and Reality* (1973), pp. 359–86.

Elliott, B. and **D. McCrone** 'Urban development in Edinburgh: a contribution to the political economy of place', *Scottish Journal of Sociology*, **4** (1980): 1–26.

Englander, D. *Landlord and Tenant in Urban Britain 1838–1918* (Oxford 1983).

Foster, J. 'How imperial London preserved its slums', *International Journal of Urban and Regional Research*, **3** (1979): 93–114.

Gaskell, S.M. *Model Housing: from the Great Exhibition to the Festival of Britain* (1986).

Gaskell, S.M. (ed.) *Slums* (Leicester 1990).

Hamlin, C. 'Muddling in Bumbledon: on the enormity of large sanitary improvements in four British towns, 1855–1885', *Victorian Studies*, **32** (1988/9): 55–83.

Hardy, A. 'Diagnosis, death and diet: the case of London 1750–1909', *Journal of Interdisciplinary History*, **18** (1988): 387–401.

Hopkins, E. 'Working-class housing in the smaller industrial town in the nineteenth century: Stourbridge – a case study', *Midland History*, **3**, **4** (1978): 230–54.

Kellett, J.R. 'Property speculators and the building of Glasgow 1780–1830', *Scottish Journal of Political Economy*, **8** (1961): 211–32.

Lewis, J.P. *Building Cycles and Britain's Growth* (1965).

Luckin, W. 'Death and survival in the city', *Urban History Yearbook* (1980): 53–62.

Luckin, W. *Pollution and Control: a Social History of the Thames in the Nineteenth Century* (Bristol 1986).

Malchow, H.L. 'Public gardens and social action in late Victorian London', *Victorian Studies*, **29** (1985): 97–124.

Matossian, M.K. 'Death in London 1750–1909', *Journal of Interdisciplinary History*, **16** (1985): 183–97.

Melling, J. (ed.) *Housing, Social Policy and the State* (1980).

Melling, J. 'Employers, industrial housing and the evolution of company welfare policies in Britain's heavy industry: west Scotland 1870–1920', *International Review of Social History*, **26** (1981): 255–301.

Melling, J. *Rent Strikes: People's Struggle for Housing in West Scotland 1890–1916* (Edinburgh 1983).

Muthesius, S. *The English Terraced House* (New Haven, Connecticut 1982).

Olsen, D.J. *The Growth of Victorian London* (1976).

Pooley, C.G. 'Residential differentiation in Victorian cities: a reassessment', *Trans. of the Institute of British Geographers*, **9** (1984): 131–44.

Pooley, C.G. 'Housing for the poorest poor: slum clearance and rehousing in Liverpool 1890–1918', *Journal of Historical Geography*, **11** (1985): 70–88.

Powell, C.G. *An Economic History of the British Building Industry 1815–1979* (1980).

Pritchard, R.M. *Housing and the Spatial Structure of the City: Residential Mobility and the Housing Market in an English City since the Industrial Revolution* (Cambridge 1976).

Reeder, D.A. 'A theatre of suburbs: some patterns of development in west London 1801–1911' in H.J. Dyos (ed.), *The Study of Urban History* (1968), pp. 253–71.

Rodger, R.G. 'Speculative builders and the structure of the Scottish building industry 1860–1914', *Business History*, **21** (1979): 226–46.

Rodger, R.G. 'Political economy, ideology and the continuing problem of working-class housing in Britain, 1840–1914', *International Review of Social History*, **32** (1987): 109–43.

Rodger, R.G. *Housing in Urban Britain 1780–1914: Class, Capitalism and Construction* (1989).

Simpson, M.A. and **T.H. Lloyd** (eds) *Middle-Class Housing in Britain* (Newton Abbot 1977).

Steffel, R.V. 'The Boundary Street Estate: an example of urban redevelopment by the London County Council 1889–1914', *Town Planning Review*, **47** (1976): 161–73.

Sutcliffe, A. *Multi-Storey Living: the British Working-Class Experience* (1974).

Sutcliffe, A. *Towards the Planned City: Germany, Britain, the United States and France 1780–1914* (1981).

Swenarton, M. *Homes Fit For Heroes: The Politics and Architecture of Early State Housing in Britain* (1981).

Tarn, J.N. *Working-Class Housing in Nineteenth-Century Britain* (1971).

Tarn, J.N. *Five Per Cent Philanthropy: an Account of Housing in Urban Areas between 1840 and 1914* (Cambridge 1973).

Thompson, F.M.L. *Hampstead. Building a Borough 1650–1964* (1974).

Thompson, F.M.L. (ed.) *The Rise of Suburbia* (Leicester 1982).

Ward, D. 'The Victorian slum: an enduring myth', *Annals Association American Geographers*, **66** (1976): 323–36.

Ward, D. 'Environs and neighbours in the "Two Nations": residential differentiation in mid-nineteenth-century Leeds', *Journal of Historical Geography*, **6** (1980): 133–62.

Whitehand, J.W.R. *The Changing Face of Cities: A Study of Development Cycles and Urban Form* (Oxford 1987).

Williamson, J.G. 'Disamenities and death in nineteenth century towns', *Explorations in Economic History*, **19** (1982): 221–45.

Wohl, A.S. *The Eternal Slum: Housing and Social Policy in Victorian London* (1977).

Woods, R. 'Mortality and sanitation in the "Best governed city in the World" – Birmingham 1870–1910', *Journal of Historical Geography*, **4** (1978): 35–56.

Woods, R. and **P.R.A. Hinde** 'Mortality in Victorian England: models and patterns', *Journal of Interdisciplinary History*, **18** (1987): 27–54.

Woods, R. and **J. Woodward** (eds) *Urban Disease and Mortality in Nineteenth-Century England* (1984).

Yelling, J.A. *Slums and Slum Clearance in Victorian London* (1986).

TRANSPORT AND COMMUNICATIONS

Barber, B. 'The concept of a railway town and the growth of Darlington 1801–1911: a note' *Transport History*, **2** (1979): 283–92.

Barker, T.C. 'Urban transport' in M.J. Freeman and D.H. Aldcroft (eds), *Transport in Victorian Britain* (Manchester 1988).

Barker, T.C. and **M. Robbins** *A History of London Transport* (1963).

Dyos, H.J. 'Workmen's fares in south London 1860–1914', *Journal of Transport History*, **1** (1953): 3–19.

Dyos, H.J. 'Some social costs of railway building in London', *Journal of Transport History*, **3** (1957–58).

(Dyos's work on urban transport is reprinted in D. Cannadine and D. Reeder (eds), *Exploring the Urban Past: Essays in Urban History by H.J. Dyos* (Cambridge 1982).

Kellett, J.R. *The Impact of Railways on Victorian Cities* (1969).

Lee, C.E. 'The English street tramways of George Francis Train', *Journal of Transport History*, **1** (1953): 20–7, and 97–108.

Ochojna, A.D. 'The influence of local and national politics on the development of urban passenger transport in Britain 1850–1900', *Journal of Transport History*, **4** (1978): 125–46.

Pearson, R.E. 'Railways in relation to resort development in East Lincolnshire', *East Midland Geographer*, **4** (1968): 281–94.

Simmons, J. 'Suburban traffic at King's Cross 1852–1914', *Journal of Transport History*, **6** (1985): 71–8.

Simmons, J. *The Railway in Town and Country* (Newton Abbot 1986).

Ward, D. 'A comparative historical geography of streetcar suburbs in Boston, Massachusetts and Leeds, England: 1850–1920', *Annals of the Association of American Geographers*, **54** (1964): 477–89.

CLASS, COMMUNITY AND NEIGHBOURHOOD

Atkins, P.J. 'The spatial configuration of class solidarity in London's west end 1792–1939', *Urban History Yearbook*, **17** (1990): 36–65.

Crossick, G.J. *An Artisan Elite in Victorian Society: Kentish London, 1840–1880* (1978).

Davidoff, L. 'Mastered for life: servant and wife in Victorian and Edwardian England', *Journal of Social History*, **7** (1974): 406–28.

Davis, J. 'From "rookeries" to "communities": race, poverty and policing in London, 1850–1985', *History Workshop*, **27** (1989): 66–85.

Delheim, C. 'The creation of a company culture: Cadbury's, 1861–1931', *American Historical Review*, **92** (1987): 13–44.

Dennis, R.J. and **S. Daniels** '"Community" and the social geography of Victorian cities', *Urban History Yearbook* (1981): 7–23.

Donajgrodski, A.P. (ed.) *Social Control in Nineteenth-Century Britain* (1977).

Englander, D. 'Booth's Jews: Jews and Judaism in *Life and Labour in London*', *Victorian Studies*, **32** (1989): 551–71.

Foster, J. 'Nineteenth-century towns – a class dimension' in H.J. Dyos (ed.), *The Study of Urban History* (1968).

Feldman, D. and **G.S. Jones.** (eds) *Metropolis London: Histories and Representations since 1800* (1989).

Gray, R.Q. *The Labour Aristocracy in Victorian Edinburgh* (Oxford 1976).

Hall, C. 'Private persons versus public someones: class, gender and politics 1780–1850' in C. Steedman, et al., *Language, Gender and Childhood* (1985).

Henriques, U. 'The Jewish community of Cardiff 1813–1914', *Welsh Historical Review*, **14** (1988): 269–300.

Jones, G.S. *Outcast London: a Study in the Relationship Between Classes in Victorian Society* (1971).

Joyce, P. *Work, Society and Politics: the Culture of the Factory in Later Victorian England* (Brighton 1980).

Kidd, A.J. 'Charity organization and the unemployed in Manchester c. 1810–1914', *Social History* **9** (1984): 45–66.

Lees, L.H. *Exiles of Erin: the Irish in Victorian London* (Manchester 1979).

Lees, L.H. 'The study of social conflict in English industrial towns', *Urban History Yearbook* (1980): 34–43.

Morris, R.J. (ed.) *Class, Power and Social Structure in British Nineteenth-Century Towns* (Leicester 1986).

Morris, R.J. *Class, Sect and Party. The Making of the British Middle Class: Leeds, 1820–1850* (Manchester 1990.)

Rose, M.E. *The Poor and the City: the English Poor Law in its Urban Context 1834–1914* (Leicester 1985).

Rubinstein, W.D. 'The Victorian middle classes: wealth, occupation and geography', *Economic History Review*, **35** (1982): 602–23.

Smith, D. *Conflict and Compromise. Class Formation in English Society, 1830–1914: a Comparative Study of Birmingham and Sheffield* (1982).

Swift, R. and **S. Gilley** (eds) *The Irish in the Victorian City* (1985).

Swift, R. 'The outcast Irish in the British Victorian city: problems and perspectives', *Irish Historical Studies* **15** (1987): 264–76.

Sykes, R. 'Some aspects of working-class consciousness in Oldham, 1830–1842', *Historical Journal*, **23** (1980): 167–79.

Thompson, F.M.L. 'Social control in Victorian Britain', *Economic History Review*, **34** (1981): 189–208.

Trainor, R. 'Urban élites in Victorian Britain', *Urban History Yearbook* (1985): 1–17.

White, J. *Rothschild Buildings: Life in an East End Tenement Block* (1980).

Williams, B *The Making of the Manchester Jewry 1740–1875* (Manchester 1976, repr. 1985).

Wolff, J. and **J. Seed** (eds) *The Culture of Capital: Art, Power, and the Nineteenth-century Middle Class* (Manchester 1990).

THE MORAL ENVIRONMENT: EDUCATION, RELIGION AND CRIME

Bailey, V. (ed.), *Policing and Punishment in Nineteenth Century Britain* (1982).

Behagg, C. 'Custom, class and change: the trade societies of Birmingham', *Social History*, **4** (1979): 455–80.

Behagg, C. Myths of cohesion: capital and compromise in the historiography of nineteenth-century Birmingham, *Social History*, **11** (1986): 375–84.

Brown, C.G. 'Did urbanisation secularise Britain?', *Urban History Yearbook* (1988): 1–14.

Burstyn, J. *Victorian Education and the Ideal of Womanhood* (1980).

Cunningham, H. *The Volunteer Force* (1975).

Davis, J. 'A poor man's system of justice: the London police courts in the second half of the nineteenth century', *Historical Journal*, **27** (1984): 309–35.

Davis, J. 'The London garotting panic of 1862: a moral panic' in V.A.C. Gattrell, *et al.*, *Crime and Law: the Social History of Crime in Western Europe* (1982).

Digby, A. and **Searby P.** *Children, School and Society in Nineteenth-Century England* (1981).

Dunae, P. '"Penny dreadfuls": the late nineteenth-century boys' literature and crime', *Victorian Studies*, **22** (1979): 133–50.

Dyhouse, C. *Girls Growing up in Late Victorian and Edwardian England* (1981).

Emsley, C. *Policing and its Context 1750–1870* (1983).

Gilbert, A.D. *Religion and Society in Industrial England 1740–1914*, (1976).

Gillis, J.R. 'The evolution of juvenile delinquency in England 1890–1914', *Past and Present*, **67** (1975): 96–126.

Gomershall, M. 'The education of working-class girls 1800–70', *History of Education*, **17** (1988): 37–53.

Hillis, P. 'Presbyterianism and social class in mid-nineteenth-century Glasgow: a study of nine churches', *Journal of Ecclesiastical History*, **32** (1981).

Horn, P. 'The education and employment of working-class girls 1870–1914', *History of Education*, **17** (1988): 71–82.

Hurt, J. *Elementary Education and the Working Class 1850–1900* (1979).

Inglis, K.S. *Churches and the Working Class in Victorian England* (1963).

Inkster, I. and **J. Morrell** (eds), *Metropolis and Province: Science in British Culture, 1780–1850* (1983).

Johnson, R. 'Educational policy and social control in early Victorian England', *Past and Present*, **49** (1970): 96–119.

Kargon, R. *Science in Victorian Manchester* (Manchester 1977).

McLeod, H. 'Class, community and region: the religious geography of nineteenth-century England' in M. Hill (ed.), *Sociological Yearbook of Religion in Britain*, **6** (1973).

McLeod, H. *Religion and the Working Class in Nineteenth-Century Britain* (1984).

Morris, R.J. 'Clubs, societies and associations', in F.M.L. Thompson (ed.), *The Cambridge Social History of Britain, 1750–1950*, vol. 3 (Cambridge 1990).

Purvis, J. 'Separate spheres and inequality in the education of working-class women 1854–1900', *History of Education*, **10** (1981): 227–43.

Reeder, D. 'Predicaments of city children' in D. Reeder (ed.), *Urban Education in the Nineteenth Century*.

Reeder, D. (ed.) *Urban Education in the Nineteenth Century* (1977).

Rubinstein, D. *School Attendance in London 1870–1914: A Social History* (Hull 1976).

Sanderson, M. 'The National and British School Societies in Lancashire 1803–39: the roots of Anglican supremacy in English education', in T.G. Cook (ed.), *Local Studies in the History of Education* (1972).

Sanderson, M. 'Social change and elementary education in industrial Lancashire 1700–1840', *Northern History*, **3** (1968): 131–54.

Sindall, R. *Street Violence in the Nineteenth Century* (Leicester 1990).

Snell, K.D.M. *Church and Chapel in the North Midlands: Religious Observance in the Nineteenth Century* (Leicester 1991).

Steedman, C. *Policing the Victorian Community: The Formation of the English Police Force* (1984).

Stephens, W.B. 'Early Victorian Coventry: education in an industrial community 1830–1851', in A. Everitt (ed.), *Perspectives in English Urban History* (1973).

Storch, R.D. 'The plague of blue locusts: police reform and popular resistance in northern England 1840–1857', *International Review of Social History*, **20** (1975): 61–90.

Swift, R. 'Urban policing and social control in early Victorian England, 1835–86: a reappraisal', *History*, **73** (1988): 211–37.

Yeo, S. *Religion and Voluntary Organizations in Crisis* (1976).

POLITICS, GOVERNMENT AND MUNICIPAL ADMINISTRATION

Allan, C.M. 'The genesis of British urban redevelopment with special reference to Glasgow', *Economic History Review*, **17** (1965): 598–613.

Beattie, S. *A Revolution in London Housing: LCC Housing Architects and their Work 1893–1914* (1980).

Bellamy, C. *Administering Central–Local Relations 1871–1919: The Local Government Board in its Fiscal and Cultural Context* (Manchester 1988).

Briggs, A. 'The background to the English parliamentary reform movement in three English cities', *Cambridge Historical Journal*, **10** (1952).

Cannadine, D. (ed.) *Patricians, Power and Politics in Nineteenth-Century Towns* (Leicester 1982).

Falkus, M.E. 'The British gas industry before 1850', *Economic History Review*, **20** (1967): 494–508.

Falkus, M.E. 'The development of municipal trading in the nineteenth century', *Business History*, **19** (1977): 134–61.

Fraser, D. *Urban Politics in Victorian England: the Structure of Politics in Victorian Cities* (Leicester 1976).

Fraser, D. 'Politics and the Victorian city', *Urban History Yearbook* (1979): 32–45.

Fraser, D. *Power and Authority in the Victorian City* (Oxford 1979).

Fraser, D. (ed.) *Municipal Reform and the Industrial City* (Leicester 1982).

Garrard, J. *Leadership and Power in Victorian Industrial Towns 1830–80* (Manchester 1983).

Gaskell, S.M. *Building Control: National Legislation and the Introduction of Local Bye-Laws in Victorian England* (1983).

Hassan, J.A. 'The growth and impact of the British water industry in the nineteenth century', *Economic History Review*, **38** (1985): 531–47.

Hennock, E.P. 'Central/local government relationships in England: an outline 1800–1950', *Urban History Yearbook* (1982): 38–49.

Hennock, E.P. *Fit and Proper Persons: Ideal and Reality in Nineteenth-Century Urban Government* (1973).

Hollis, P. *Ladies Elect: Women in English Local Government 1865–1914* (Oxford 1987).

Kellett, J.R. 'Municipal socialism, enterprise and trading in the Victorian city', *Urban History Yearbook* (1978): 36–45.

Matthews, D. '"Laissez-faire" and the London gas industry in the nineteeth century' *Economic History Review*, **39** (1986): 572–87.

Owen, D. *The Government of Victorian London* (1982).

Roebuck, J. *Urban Development in Nineteenth Century London* (1979).

Tarn, J.N. 'Housing reform and the emergence of town planning in Britain before 1914' in A. Sutcliffe (ed.), *The Rise of Modern Urban Planning* (1980).

Waller, P.J. *Democracy and Sectarianism: a Political and Social History of Liverpool 1868–1939* (Liverpool 1981).

Young, K. and **P. Garside** *Metropolitan London: Politics and Urban Change 1837–1981* (1982).

LEISURE AND RECREATION

Bailey, P. *Leisure and Class in Victorian England* (1978).

Cannadine, D.N. *Lords and Landlords: the Aristocracy and the Towns 1774–1967* (Leicester 1980) (Section 3).

Gaskell, S.M. 'Gardens for the working class', *Victorian Studies*, **23** (1980): 479–501.

Korr, C.P. 'West Ham United', *Journal of Contemporary History*, **13** (1978): 211–32.

Lowerson, J. and **J. Myerscough** *Time to Spare in Victorian England* (Brighton 1977).

McKibbin, R. 'Working-class gambling in Britain, 1880–1939', *Past and Present*, **82** (1979): 147–78.

Mason, T. *Association Football and English Society* (Brighton 1981).

Meller, H.E. *Leisure and the Changing City 1870–1914* (1976).

Perkin, H.J. 'The "social tone" of Victorian seaside resorts in the north west', *Northern History*, 11 (1976): 180–94.

Storch, R.D. 'The problem of working-class leisure: roots of moral reform', in P. McCann (ed.) *Popular Education and Socialization in the Nineteenth Century* (1977).

Walton, J.K. *The English Seaside Resort: a Social History 1750–1914* (Leicester 1983).

Walton, J.K. 'Residential amenity, respectable morality and the rise of the entertainment industry: the case of Blackpool 1860–1914', *Literature and History*, **1** (1975).

INDEX

377

Index